Technological Change and
Co-Determination in Sweden

In the series
Labor and Social Change

edited by Paula Rayman and Carmen Sirianni

Technological Change and Co-Determination in Sweden

Åke Sandberg

Gunnar Broms, Arne Grip, Lars Sundström

Jesper Steen, Peter Ullmark

Foreword by Andrew Martin

Temple University Press

PHILADELPHIA

Temple University Press, Philadelphia 19122
Copyright © 1992 by Temple University. All rights reserved
Published 1992
Printed in the United States of America

The paper used in this publication meets the minimum
requirements of American National Standard for Information
Sciences—Permanence of Paper for Printed Library Materials,
ANSI Z39.48-1984 ⊚

Library of Congress Cataloging-in-Publication Data

Technological change and co-determination in Sweden/Åke Sandberg . . .
[et al.].
        p.   cm. — (Labor and social change)
    Includes bibliographical references (p.   ) and index.
    ISBN-0-87722-918-X
    1. Industrial management—Sweden—Employee participation—Case
studies.   2. Employees—Sweden—Effect of technological innovations
on—Case studies.   I. Sandberg, Åke, 1944–   .   II. Title:
Technological change and co-determination in Sweden.   III. Series.
HD5660.S9T43   1992   91-26917
331'.01'12— dc20   CIP

Contents

Tables and Figures

Foreword

by Andrew Martin

This book describes efforts to meet the strategic problems that labor unions in Sweden face in improving the quality of working life. As is so often the case, experience in that small country has intriguing implications for those concerned with similar issues elsewhere. To appreciate those implications, however, we must understand how that experience has been shaped by conditions specific to Sweden. Åke Sandberg and his co-authors tell us much of what we need to know to do that, but it may be helpful to provide a broad preliminary overview of the context in which the strategic problems the book addresses have arisen.

Improving the quality of work has become an important goal of the Swedish labor movement. The metalworkers' union (Metall), for example, organized its whole 1989 congress around a document outlining a "Solidaristic Policy for Good Work." The Swedish confederation of blue-collar unions (LO), to which the metalworkers are affiliated, followed up by focusing its 1991 quinquennial congress on a program on "Developmental Work"—work that enables people to develop, grow, and expand their capabilities. In these and other formulations, good work is defined partly by contrast with work that is bad in familiar terms: physically dangerous, highly controlled, monotonous, stressful, isolated, and the like. Good work is envisioned as safe while it provides scope for increasing responsibility, autonomy, variety, and social interaction. The democratization of decision making about work is deemed crucial, both for the process of replacing bad work with good and for the content of good work. Through national policy and local action, managements need to be induced

vii

and constrained to incorporate the requirements of good work into job design. The devolution of responsibility for production to autonomous groups of workers and their participation in the choice of technology and work organization are themselves among the key attributes of good work.

The importance Swedish unions attach to the quality of work conceived in this way is a relatively recent development. It marks a significant expansion in the scope of their concerns over the past twenty years or so. Earlier, they concentrated almost exclusively on bargaining over wages and closely related aspects of the terms on which their members worked, leaving it essentially up to management to determine how the work was done. Thus, they confined themselves to what Sandberg and his colleagues describe as "distribution issues," which they contrast with the "production issues" involved in the quality of work. This earlier focus on wages, and especially the specific approach to wage issues that was adopted, was partly a matter of choice and partly of necessity, reflecting both the exceptional power of the Swedish labor movement and its limitations.

Unions in Sweden organize a larger portion of the labor force than in any other country, increasing from around half to around 85 percent during the four decades ending in the mid-1980s. This membership is divided between unions affiliated with the LO, whose share of the labor force grew from two-fifths to half during this period, and white-collar unions belonging to separate confederations, the Central Organization of Salaried Employees (TCO) and The Swedish Confederation of Professional Associations (SACO-SR), whose share rose more rapidly, from under one-fifth to over one-third.

The unions' strength in the labor market has had important political consequences. This was especially true of the LO unions. From their origins, they have been organizationally and ideologically linked to the Social Democratic Party (SAP). The political resources they provided the party were decisive in enabling it to govern Sweden for fifty-three of the last fifty-nine years, longer than any other party subject to the repeated test of free elections. Although the white-collar unions are not linked to the SAP or any other party, a large minority of their members have tended to vote for the SAP. This, plus the existence of a small left party, has brought the SAP enough additional support to make the social democratic labor movement formed by the LO unions and SAP the dominant force in Swedish political life, at least until recently.

While the strength of the unions in the labor market and of the SAP in the political arena has enabled them to exercise a great deal of influence on the economy through collective bargaining and government policy, the dominant force in the economy remains the privately owned firms that conduct most of the production for the market in Sweden. Because the nonsocialist political opposition to the SAP has been divided among three main parties (referred to in Sweden as the "bourgeois" parties), private capital is not represented by a single party that can effectively challenge the SAP—the only alternative to a SAP government so far is a fragile coalition. However, most of the private-sector employers are organized in a strong, centralized association, The Swedish Employers' Confederation (SAF), that serves as an effective vehicle for collective action not only in the labor market but, increasingly in recent years, in the political arena as well.

For a long time, then, the distribution of power in Sweden could be characterized as essentially a balance of power between highly organized labor and capital. The "Swedish model" of a welfare state was defined by an implicit "historic compromise" struck between these two forces in the late 1930s. It has been interpreted as a mutual recognition by labor and capital that neither could displace the other from its positions of strength in the state and the economy, respectively. In effect, capital accommodated to the social democratic labor movement's newly attained political dominance, providing that the latter used its power in the political arena and labor market only to influence the macroeconomic environment of production and distribution of its output, leaving private ownership and control of the means of production undisturbed.

One element of the compromise was an explicit agreement between LO and SAF—the so-called Saltsjöbaden agreement of 1938—to govern the collective bargaining process jointly without government intervention. The result was a considerable centralization of the industrial relations system, with control over the weapons of industrial conflict—strikes and lockouts—concentrated in the two peak associations. It was also a system that excluded production issues from collective bargaining and narrowly confined it to distribution issues. SAF had insisted all along that the way work was done and who did it were the sole prerogative of management, going so far as to require (in paragraph 32 of its statutes) that all contracts with unions negotiated by its members include a clause reserving the "right of the employer to engage and dismiss workers at his own discretion" and "to direct and allot work." The historic compromise did not change this.

Although the unions recurrently tried to negotiate some limitations on managerial discretion in matters like dismissal, they had only marginal success. On the other hand, the unions did not press very hard for a voice in production issues so long as they did not feel the need to. Indeed, although ideas about worker participation and industrial democracy were part of the labor movement's ideological heritage, most union leaders were suspicious of them. They feared "double loyalty" if unions shared responsibility for production decisions and competing loyalties if worker participation in such decisions were organized through separate bodies. Hence, it was easy for them to acquiesce in SAF's adamant refusal to concede any voice on production issues to unions as part of the overall compromise.

While the unions had concentrated on distribution issues in the past, however, their concern was not limited to distributing whatever output the economy spontaneously yielded. It extended to the conditions for stable growth in that output, at a rate sufficient to maintain full employment. Thus, in the early postwar years, the LO unions adopted an approach to wage bargaining that made it part of a comprehensive strategy for sustaining full employment. The attainment of full employment was viewed as crucial. It was the most important means for reducing poverty and economic inequality, not only directly but also indirectly by bolstering the unions' bargaining power. But for unions encompassing so large a part of the labor force, particularly in the private sector where most production for the market occurs in Sweden, it was readily apparent that full employment could be jeopardized by the way that power was used. Thus, if all the unions individually pushed nominal wages up as far as they could, competing with each other to preserve or improve their relative positions, the result could be an inflationary wage spiral that would make full employment unsustainable, especially in the face of the dependence of Sweden's small open economy on international trade. To the unions, however, simply limiting wage claims across the board, as even the SAP government urged, was no solution. Such restraint, implying an abandonment of the unions' generic role as wage-bargaining organizations, was bound to fail and, in the process, undermine membership support. LO countered with a strategy conceived as more consistent with the unions' wage-bargaining function, and the government was eventually persuaded to implement the policies needed to make the strategy work.

The unions' part in the strategy was to pursue a common pattern of wage demands, agreed on within LO's governing body in advance of each round of wage negotiations, with LO coordinating its affiliates' wage bargaining in accordance with the agreed pattern. From the mid-1950s until 1983, central negotiations with SAF provided a mechanism through which LO carried out that coordination, but agreement among its affiliates was based on the traditional norm of equal pay for equal work, embodied in what was referred to as "solidaristic wage policy." Interpreted in practice as a general compression of differences in pay (mainly through wage increases in absolute rather than percentage amounts), this standard-rate wage policy was expected to feed into the overall strategy in two ways: by inhibiting inflationary interunion wage rivalry and by forcing firms unable to pay standard rates to become more efficient or shut down, thereby lowering inflation by lowering costs.

In other words, the LO unions relied on standard rates to force structural and technological change, encouraging rather than resisting it as some unions have done. At the same time, they were content to pressure management to increase productivity in these ways without trying to influence how it was done. However, their willingness to do so was contingent on government policies that assured alternative jobs to any workers whose jobs were eliminated in the process. The government was expected to provide this assurance by a combination of macroeconomic policies that kept demand for labor sufficiently (but not excessively) high and manpower, or labor market, policies that helped the affected workers move to new jobs by giving them training, job information, and financial support. The development of a universalistic welfare state that made health care, pensions, sick pay, and other benefits a right of citizenship rather than contingent on where one worked also increased the acceptability of labor mobility.

It was taken for granted that the social democratic labor movement's political power was a necessary condition for the implementation of this strategy for noninflationary full employment through structural change; only a SAP government could be counted on to implement the policy mix needed to make it work. The SAP amply met this expectation by maintaining full employment (even if it recurrently allowed excessive demand), and especially by allotting resources to labor market policies on a scale far greater than in any other country, as well as by implementing universalistic social policy.

At the same time, the strategy was largely acceptable to Sweden's organized employers. Although they resisted wage compression, they deemed it a small price to pay for avoiding interunion wage rivalry. This was especially true of the more efficient firms, which had no trouble paying the standard rates. Moreover, the strategy committed the government and unions to adapting the supply of labor to the composition of demand for labor, which was determined exclusively by management decisions about what should be produced and how. Precisely because it left such production issues up to management, the strategy conformed with the "Swedish model" in its classical form.

As the strategy was approximated in practice during the 1960s, however, some of its effects exposed both the SAP and the unions to growing attack from critics on the left and right and to loss of support in their own constituencies. The extension of the unions' agenda to production issues was a major component of their response to this challenge.

The heart of the problem with which the unions tried to cope through this strategic shift was the diminution in their role at the workplace level that accompanied the structural change strategy. As in the United States and Britain, and in contrast with many continental European countries, the Swedish labor movement had been built on the basis of a strong workplace presence, although employer resistance made it impossible for Swedish unions to anchor that presence in the degree of job control that Anglo–American unions established. On the other hand, Swedish unions gained a degree of power at the national level never attained by American or even British labor. A major factor enabling Swedish unions to do so was the capacity for unified collective action they achieved through the centralization of power within the labor movement. This included the shift of control over the strike weapon from the local to the national level and from individual national unions to all unions acting jointly through LO, as well as the shift of control over wage bargaining to the national level, marked by the elimination of membership ratification of wage agreements and eventually LO's coordination of the national unions' wage bargaining through its central negotiations with SAF. But the consequence was to leave less and less to be negotiated at the local level, even though local wage bargaining was not entirely eliminated.

While the scope for local union action on wage issues was accordingly diminished in the interests of solidaristic wage policy and the structural change strategy of which it was a part, there was virtually no scope for union action on the nonwage workplace issues over which employers prevented unions at all levels from having any voice. Yet those issues were being made increasingly important by the operation of the structural change strategy. It was imposing on workers a variety of costs that could not be fully compensated by labor market policy, despite its vast expansion. These included the cost not only to the displaced workers but also to the families and communities disrupted in the process—costs that had not really been anticipated. But many workers who were not displaced also felt the effects of intensified rationalization in the form of technological and organizational changes that diminished the quality of their work in various ways. There probably was also decreasing tolerance for working conditions that had not deteriorated, or may even have improved, among the younger, more educated workers without memories of mass unemployment. Thus, while dissatisfaction with work was growing, unions at the local level could do even less about such nonwage issues than about wage issues.

With respect to both kinds of issues, then, unions at the workplace level, where most workers had their only experience of the unions and where they had their only direct influence on them, seemed unable to represent their members' interests actively and visibly. This posed a serious threat to the unions, undermining their claims to member support and eroding the authority of union leaders.

The fact that some employers were apparently more responsive to quality of work issues only exacerbated the threat. Faced with increasing turnover, absenteeism, difficulty in attracting younger workers, and wildcat strikes, SAF as well as some individual firms initiated a variety of efforts to develop more participative forms of work organization designed to increase satisfaction and commitment. Thus, Swedish employers were already in the early stages of what has since become a widespread search for new forms of work organization. Unions were drawn into these efforts, and in some firms such as Volvo and SKF (the multinational bearings manufacturer), their role far transcended the limits set by paragraph 32 of the SAF statutes. Typically, however, they could only participate in a consultative capacity on terms defined by the employers. As a rule, then, management was responding to work dissatisfaction while preventing the unions from demonstrating any independent capacity to respond to it.

As a result of these developments, the unions' earlier reluctance to demand a voice in production issues was being replaced by the conviction that it was essential for them to acquire such a voice. The advocates of this view had been making headway, but what tipped the balance in their favor was a massive wave of wildcat strikes in the winter of 1969–1970, demonstrating dramatically the extent to which the unions' authority had eroded. To reestablish that authority, the unions' ability to contest managerial power in the workplace had to be enlarged. One way to do it, which had been repeatedly urged by opponents of centralization, was to give back to local unions the authority to formulate and press wage claims, along with control over the strike weapon, which had been transferred to national and confederal levels. But this would sacrifice the LO unions' capacity for concerted action, particularly in implementing the solidaristic wage policy, so this option was rejected. The other way to do it was to enlarge the local unions' power to press nonwage issues. That, however, could not be done without somehow overcoming SAF's insistence that such issues were managerial prerogatives in which unions could have no voice.

SAF was no more willing to abandon this principle than it had been in the past, agreeing only to marginal concessions such as short advance notice of dismissals and various forms of joint consultation. Unable to overcome the employers' resistance through negotiation, the unions turned instead to legislation. What made this alternative available was of course the SAP's power in the political arena; this political alternative proved to be a more effective one.

The ban on collective bargaining over production issues embodied in SAF's paragraph 32 was effectively nullified by the 1976 Co-Determination Act, referred to in Sweden as MBL (for Medbestämmandelagen). Like much Swedish law, MBL laid down the general principle and set minimum standards, leaving the details to be filled in through other processes. Thus, unions were given the right to negotiate agreements specifying procedures for a union voice in all matters concerning hiring and firing, work organization, and management of the enterprise generally. Included in the minimum standards was a requirement that management initiate negotiations before undertaking major changes in company organization, production processes, or an individual's tasks and working conditions, and a requirement to enter into negotiations initiated by unions over any other changes. This fell short of joint–decision making in the sense that management retained ultimate authority over decisions except to the extent that collective agreements provided for the delegation of that authority to joint union–management procedures. Thus, it was left to future collective bargaining to define the union voice in production issues, but employers could no longer refuse to engage in collective bargaining over those issues on the ground that they were managerial prerogatives.

MBL was the culmination of a burst of labor laws enacted over the preceding half decade. This change in the legal framework, described in more detail by Sandberg, put local unions in a substantially better position to bargain over production issues at the workplace. It began with a revision of the work environment law, expanding its scope beyond the narrow health and safety areas traditionally covered, extending it to virtually all employment, and strengthening the position of union safety stewards and union members of obligatory safety committees. Among other things, it gave safety stewards guarantees of job security and paid time to carry out their duties, guarantees that were extended to all union officials in another law. Management's authority to hire and fire was more broadly circumscribed in yet another law that placed on management the burden of proof that dismissals are "reasonable" and required that notice of layoffs be given from one to six months in advance, depending on the affected employees' age. A further law provided for tripartite union, management, and local employment office planning to minimize the scale and effects of layoffs. Laws entitling unions to put two employee representatives on company boards strengthened union access to information on firms' strategic planning, though board membership was not aimed at giving unions a voice in decision making through co-determination along German lines; Swedish unions preferred to gain such a voice by expanding the scope of collective bargaining, which MBL accomplished.

The SAP's control of the government and the LO's ties to the party might not have sufficed to produce legislation that went so far in meeting the unions' demands if TCO, the larger of the two white-collar confederations, had not joined with LO to press them. As more of an interest group that did not engage in wage bargaining, TCO had its own need to secure the support of its affiliates and their members; championing the empowerment of unions to press nonwage production issues at the workplace seemed an especially promising way to fulfill that need. For the SAP, embracing a cause common to TCO and LO offered a way to stake its claim for support of all wage earners, white collar as well as blue collar. But two of the bourgeois parties, the "middle parties," also competed for TCO voters, so they supported most of the legislation, with the result that the SAP failed to define a cleavage line between itself and the opposition by taking up the issue of "industrial democracy." Whatever the parties' tactical motives, the essential point is that the political context was highly favorable to the unions' drive to expand their power at the workplace.

The point is underlined by the changed political context between 1976 and 1982 when the government was controlled by a bourgeois party coalition for the first time since 1932. Now that the 1991 election has brought a bourgeois party coalition back into power, the point is likely to be underscored again. The unions had expected MBL's enactment to open the way to a national agreement with SAF spelling out their new rights. But after the 1976 change in government, SAF could negotiate in the knowledge that, for the time being at least, the political alternative was no longer available to the unions. It used the resulting improvement in its bargaining position to resist the demands jointly formulated by LO and the bargaining organization of private-sector, white-collar unions. From SAF's perspective, both the extension of collective bargaining to production issues and the fact that it was imposed through government intervention marked significant departures from the terms of the historic compromise. It consequently welcomed the change in government, which it saw as making possible a more aggressive stance in wage bargaining—reflected in a strike and lockout in 1980 that was the largest in Sweden in seventy years—as well as in negotiations over MBL implementation. While national agreements were rapidly reached in the several public and cooperative sector bargaining areas, negotiations with SAF dragged on until 1982. By then, SAF had perhaps concluded that it had circumscribed the expansion of union workplace power as much as it could and that it was best to incorporate its successes into a settlement before another election restored the political alternative by returning the SAP to office— which is what happened later that year.

While the private sector co-determination agreement fell short of the unions' initial hopes, its conclusion nevertheless reflected the fact that a major obstacle to a union voice in production issues had been overcome, opening up possibilities that had previously been closed off. As unions on all levels sought to realize those possibilities, however, they encountered a whole range of other problems, with which they were ill-equipped to cope.

This book offers an analysis of those problems and a description of some efforts to find solutions to them. Its empirical core is an account of several action research projects in which Sandberg and his colleagues collaborated with workplace unions to bring about changes in job design and work organization. The book draws on experience from these and similar efforts to determine the ingredients of a comprehensive union strategy for improving the quality of work. Many of these concern the new practices unions need to develop to press work quality issues at the workplace effectively. But the experience also points to ways in which effectiveness at the workplace level depends on what happens at other levels. This includes the support that national unions provide to workplace efforts and also the capacity of the labor movement as a whole to secure government policies on which the efforts crucially depend, including not only the provision of a favorable legal framework but also policies encouraging the development of technologies that enlarge the possibilities for improving work quality as well as economic policies capable of maintaining full employment. Hence, Sandberg argues, unions need a "multilevel strategy" to make a significant impact on the quality of work.

He rests this argument on his analysis of the new problems facing unions as they try to move beyond the wage issues to which they had been confined to nonwage workplace issues. One source of these problems was that unions were not equipped to deal with the latter by their experience with the former. The unions' organization, practices, and expertise had been built up primarily around wage and related issues concerning the terms of employment. Such issues primarily concern incremental changes in existing wage patterns and levels. In Sweden, as we saw, wage changes came to be defined broadly in central negotiations, specified more fully at industry level, and translated into individual earnings at the company and workplace levels, all in terms of the familiar quantitative common denominator of money. While the complex formulas for distributing increases in accordance with solidaristic wage policy and the diversity in firms' pay systems complicated the process, unions at all levels had accumulated the expertise to handle it. Union practices for formulating wage demands and negotiating and administering wage settlements were well developed and understood by the members.

However, neither the expertise nor the practices through which unions dealt with wage issues lent themselves readily to the new issues. At its core, improving the quality of work involves change in the design of jobs that are specific to particular workplaces, and addresses the specific shortcomings and possibilities for change in existing jobs. Demands for change in those jobs, unlike wage demands, cannot be formulated through the simple application of national or industry standards, along a single quantitative dimension, at discrete, periodic points in time. To be sure, high-level agreements can set norms that can be invoked in local negotiations, but these are most likely to be procedural, such as the right to be informed in advance of proposed changes, establish joint committees, or bring in outside consultants. Substantive goals cannot easily go beyond generalities like job enrichment, participation, or, as SAF insisted, efficiency. What they mean concretely for any workplace can only be hammered out there. Moreover, the process necessarily has to be sustained over extended periods.

Dissatisfaction with existing jobs is not easily translatable into demands for specific changes in their design. Apart from things like eliminating obviously hazardous conditions or alleviating boredom by rotation, which leave the jobs themselves unchanged, the ways in which they could be significantly improved are not likely to be readily apparent. Their design is integrally linked to the whole production process—the characteristics of products, the technology by which they are produced, and the organization of tasks involved in utilizing the technology. Signficant changes in those tasks are not likely to be possible unless changes in other aspects of the production process are made. To formulate demands for alternatives to existing jobs or to changes in them proposed by management, then, union workplace organizations must address a wide range of factors entering into the design of jobs, investigating the possibilities for change, identifying their potential effects, and forging a consensus over the kinds of change to be sought.

To engage in this kind of process, workplace union organizations need to devise new methods bearing little resemblance to those relied on in collective bargaining over wages. Thus, they have to develop the capacity to take part in planning and introducing changes in technology and work organization, which is likely to involve participation by local union officials and members in joint labor–management project groups. But this is complicated by the need to avoid co-optation and preserve the independence required to press their members' interests, including the formulation of proposals for change that can command wide support rather than benefit only some members at the expense of others.

As local unions attempt to deal with these problems, they are confronted by a further problem rooted in the virtual monopoly of the engineering and other technical expertise for designing the production process that managers enjoy. This is, of course, built into the fundamental structure of institutions for organizing production in industrial societies generally. Ownership, whether public or private, confers not only authority over decisions about all aspects of the production process but also control over the technical resources on which to base the decisions. In all but the smallest units, this authority is delegated to the owners' agents, the managers, who characteristically exercise it through bureaucratic hierarchies that put technical expertise at their disposal. When unions win a voice in job design, as they did in Sweden, the managers' authority over job design decisions is somewhat curtailed. However, since the managers' command of the technical resources on which to base the decisions is left intact, their effective power to shape jobs is undiminished, for the technical resources available to the unions are minuscule. Thus, while union officials and members may participate in joint project groups, they cannot do so on anything like an equal basis. Dependent almost entirely on management staff for technical support, their capacity for independent evaluation of management initiatives, not to speak of formulating alternatives of their own, is severely limited.

To have an effective voice in job design, unions at the workplace level accordingly need independent access to technical knowledge. Some can be provided by unions at the national level, which need to build up their capacity to do so. But they can hardly provide staff support that even begins to approach the technical resources at management's disposal. To close the gap further, outside expertise has to be tapped; for example, by incorporating consultants responsible to the unions into project groups or linking academic researchers to development projects. To make effective use of such outside expertise, both unions and experts must learn how to work together in ways which neither had been accustomed to in the past. Efforts to do so run up against yet another problem, however.

While workplace unions' access to technical knowledge can be increased with the support of national unions and the help of outside experts, the body of available knowledge itself is geared to the needs of management rather than those of unions. Aside from procurement by governments, particularly of military technology, it is primarily the managers of firms who shape the demand for engineers and technology, for they hire the engineers and purchase the technology. The directions in which engineering knowledge and the technology in which it is embodied develop are powerfully influenced by this demand, reflecting management's definitions of the problems to be solved and criteria for successful solutions. Thus, even when unions gain a voice in choosing new technology at an early stage, when options are still most fully open, the range of available alternatives from which to choose is likely to limit the possibilities for change in job design and work organization simply because none of the alternatives was designed to make such change possible. To be sure, there is scope for some choice in the ways most technologies are used, permitting variations in the content of work that can make a genuine difference to its quality. Available technologies may nevertheless pose serious obstacles to job redesign. For example, technologies designed on the assumption that product mix, material flows, and work pace are all controlled by management staff in offices away from the shop floor may preclude the devolution of real control over production to autonomous work groups. To expand the availability of technologies that make such changes in job design possible, the path of technological development must be changed in directions that make the quality of work as much a part of the way in which the problems addressed by engineering research and practice are defined as the specifications formulated by management.

Unions cannot have much impact on the direction of technological development on their own—while any influence they can exert on management's technology choices can have some effect on the demand for technology, the effect is limited by management's need to choose from whatever is available or nearly so. To have a more significant impact, unions need to act on the political level to influence government policies that affect the allocation of resources to technical research and development. Since government procurement is an important component of demand for technology, it can serve as an instrument of technology policy. The problem for unions is to win acceptance of work quality as an objective of procurement policy, along with such traditional functional goals as defense, communications, and health. Unions face the same problem with respect to the instruments of more general technology policy that supply funds to scientific and engineering education and research and to industrial R&D. To increase the availability of technologies that permit work quality to be improved, even more than to affect choices among available technologies, unions need support for R&D projects that they initiate and administer, and in which their members are actively involved, like those Sandberg describes. Such projects are essential to enable unions to discover, try out, and demonstrate possibilities for meeting job design requirements that they specify, independent of the employers with whom they negotiate. To generate new knowledge and genuine alternatives, such projects require the technical resources that academic researchers or commercial suppliers of technology can provide. But their participation, as well as facilities and equipment, obviously have to be financed somehow. The only significant potential source of funds is the government programs that finance other technological R&D. However, the bureaucracies that administer those programs (and in practice shape policy), for example, the National Board for Technical Development, are attuned to the interests and values of their traditional academic and business constituencies and not unions. They are unaccustomed, and ill-equipped, to incorporate work quality into the criteria for their funding decisions, and are resistant to supporting R&D addressed to problems identified by unions, particularly if the projects are to be run by unions alone rather than jointly with employers (enabling employers to block R&D addressed to goals they do not share). But the technology policy bureaucracies' understanding of their mission simply reflects the government's failure to define it otherwise. Technology policy will only become a source of support for the kind of R&D unions need in order to effectively press for improved work quality insofar as the government explicitly redefines the policy's goals to include work quality. Accordingly, action at the national political level to elicit that change in technology policy needs to be part of the unions' strategy for improving the quality of work.

The political prospects of such a shift in technology policy priorities were favorable as long as the SAP was in power, given the LO unions' close links to the party and the party's stake in securing TCO's support. A concerted drive for policies designed to change the direction of technological development by the two national confederations could thus be expected to achieve results, as it did in bringing about the legislation that strengthened the legal basis for union action at the workplace level in the 1970s. A further strengthening of that legal basis has turned out to be necessary, as Sandberg shows, and the chances for this were also reasonably good as long as the SAP controlled the government. But any prospects that a multilevel union strategy for improving work quality could succeed at the national policy level were drastically reduced by the 1991 election, which occurred after this book was completed. That election gave the SAP its worst defeat since 1928 and brought into power an even more splintered but more clearly antiunion bourgeois coalition government than those following the 1976 election. In this new political context, the prospects for union success at the industry and local negotiation levels are also diminished, probably to an even greater extent than when the unions were deprived of the political alternative between 1976 and 1982.

This is not to imply that management is uniformly resistant to redesigning jobs along lines urged by the unions, or to union participation in the process of redesigning jobs, or that legislation or the threat of it is the only way that management resistance can be overcome. On the contrary, as Sandberg indicates, employers display an intensified interest in redesigning jobs so as to increase flexibility and assure product quality and to elicit the commitment and growth in skills among employees needed to achieve those goals. Moreover, union officials and members are often not just informed about impending change in job design but are incorporated into the project groups engaged in planning and implementing the change. Significant improvement in the quality of work can be the result. But from a union perspective, the prevailing trends in management perspectives on work raise far-reaching issues of power and distributive justice.

As Sandberg describes them, those perspectives reflect the importance employers attach to preserving their power in the workplace. This leads them to seek technologies, forms of work organization, and associated payment systems that help them retain control over the performance of work, limit their dependence on workers' discretion and knowledge, and generally curtail the unions' influence in the workplace. Examples include computerized systems that facilitate monitoring of workers, jobs that can be done primarily with plant-specific rather than more general marketable skills, and pay systems that gear wages to individual performance rather than collectively bargained rates. In various ways, such job design options threaten to impair workers' bargaining power as well as limit the scope for improving work quality.

By fostering inequalities in autonomy, training, and pay, such job design choices simultaneously bring employers into conflict with unions over issues of distributive justice. Ultimately, those issues concern the social distribution of good work. While there is no doubt that managerial approaches to redesigning jobs are improving the quality of many of them, they have not improved others, including some whose quality has been diminished. The cumulative effect is likely to be increasing inequality in working life; it may mean a growing polarization between a core of workers with polyvalent skills, a large degree of autonomy, job security, and high pay, on the one hand, and a majority of workers with limited skills, subject to tight supervision, vulnerable to recurrent unemployment, and receiving low wages, on the other. Ultimately, then, the production issues that the unions have taken on are fundamentally distribution issues.

Whatever the shape of the potential stratifying effects of management approaches to job redesign—whether it takes the form of a sharp dualism or the widening of a more even dispersion—it would reverse the growth of social equality to which the social democratic labor movement's efforts have been historically dedicated and at the same time undermine the movement's capacity to pursue those efforts. Both in the labor market and in the political arena, the movement's strategy has been to maximize the scope and cohesion of its constituency by implementing universalistic policies—policies that extend common norms and rights across the widest possible range of particular groups. Thus, LO's solidaristic wage policy of standard rates and compression of differences between the rates served as the basis for agreement on wage demands among the unions organizing workers in different industries affiliated to LO. In the process, it reinforced the LO union members' identification with a single movement of which all the unions were part while it counteracted the potential for particularistic interunion wage rivalry. Similarly, the SAP's universalistic social policy, conferring on all citizens (or, more precisely, residents) rights to transfer payments and access to services according to common norms, served to define a common stake in the welfare state and secure a willingness to finance it through taxation across a wide portion of the electorate that extended well beyond the party's core constituency of LO union members, while avoiding the fragmentation of support for social policy that results from its division into separate programs targeted to different groups on different terms, as in the United States. But increasing inequalities in work, including inequalities in pay and fringe benefits as well as the quality of work, generate divisions within the movement's constituencies, making it more difficult to sustain agreement among unions through solidaristic wage policy and eroding the common stake in solidaristic social policies, thereby undermining the cohesion and power of the social democratic labor movement in both the labor market and the political arena.

Earlier, it was argued that the Swedish unions expanded their agenda to include production as well as distribution issues in an effort to regain the support they were losing as a result of the attenuation in their workplace role that accompanied implementation of their structural change strategy. When this shift in union strategy occurred two decades ago, changes management was making in the content and organization of work, which improved the quality of work for some while diminishing it for others, were already a source of challenge to the unions. Today they are a larger challenge than ever. Accordingly, the unions' need for an effective strategy for implementing what the unions refer to as a solidaristic work policy— which enlarges the possibilities for increasing skill, responsibility, and earnings for those gaining the most from management approaches to job redesign as well as those losing the most—has become greater than ever. Only through the pursuit of such a solidaristic work policy, as stressed in the LO document cited at the outset, can the unions hope to retain the support of all they claim to represent.

This book, then, offers ideas about how the Swedish unions can meet their need for a strategy through which to implement a solidaristic work policy. The 1991 election did make the political conditions for doing so less favorable, particularly at the national policy level of the multilevel strategy that the book outlines. But this does not necessarily mean that unions cannot expect to accomplish anything in the policy arena as long as the Social Democrats remain out of power. There are some elements within the current governing coalition with a commitment to industrial democracy as well as a political stake in attracting the support of union members, especially in TCO unions. To the extent that TCO and LO unions can again forge a common program for improving the quality of work as they did in the 1970s, they could conceivably make some further legislative gains, or at least prevent legislative setbacks. It is by no means a foregone conclusion that agreement on a common program can be reached, given the scope for jurisdictional conflict among unions inherent in the redesign of jobs to which Sandberg refers. Even if such conflict precludes effective action in the policy arena, however, Swedish unions remain so deeply embedded in the production structure that they can hope to make a significant difference in the way in which jobs are redesigned in workplaces all across the country, provided they can build on the kinds of experience Sandberg describes.

But what relevance does that experience have for unions in most other countries where they are weaker, particularly in the United States where they have suffered decades of decline? Given all the difficulties Swedish unions have been encountering in their efforts to improve the quality of work even under the most favorable conditions, how can unions be expected to have any impact at all under the extremely unfavorable conditions prevailing in the United States? The answer may be that a drive to improve the quality of work, both in workplaces that are still unionized and those that are not, offers the American labor movement its best chance to reverse its decline. It is up to American readers sympathetic to the labor movement, and we hope, within the labor movement itself, to decide whether this is so. If they agree that it is, the experience of Swedish unions described in this book can still provide some valuable lessons despite the immensely greater obstacles facing American unions.

Preface

The transformation of technology, work, and management—these will be the questions of the future at our workplaces. This book presents a broad discussion of new forms of job design and innovative trade union approaches to such changes based on examples and analyses of experiences in Sweden. A linchpin in this context is independent local union activity, such as knowledge development and broad studies among the members, supported by central union investigations and policy. We concentrate on issues of this kind, as delimited from problems relating to labor market and employment, although a close relation exists: Secure employment as well as a prounion labor law seem to facilitate constructive and proactive union approaches to production and work issues. There are several books on what has been called the "Swedish model"—although we prefer to talk about the Swedish or Scandinavian experience. But in contrast to most of them we concentrate our attention on experiences of innovative co-determination to create good workplaces. The "good work" has been lacking both as a goal and as an instrument in the macro-oriented and labor market–oriented Swedish model. We discuss the *Swedish model at work:* Extensive case material is presented and analyzed to fill this gap.

This book is based on many years of research into workplace changes at the Swedish Center for Working Life and other institutes and universities. The results of several research projects, essentially parts of one common research tradition or program at the Center, have been incorporated. Part of the book is based on the so-called Front project, and its collaboration with similar projects in four other

European countries, coordinated at Ruskin College, Oxford (Levie and Moore 1984b). One purpose of the project was to find interesting examples of union attempts to influence changes in technology and the work organization at local workplaces. Case studies were performed in four different sectors. In Sweden we studied the Postgiro, a dairy, an engineering workshop, and a sugar mill.

Although our cases illustrate both early and advanced employee involvement in processes of technological and organizational change, the general picture in Sweden is one with a lower union profile especially in the early stages of workplace change. The case studies show, however, that advanced and innovative union roles are possible. We discuss the preconditions for this in Sweden, taking into consideration industrial relations, management and labor strategies in relation to technological change, and the legislative framework. Many decades of cooperation between trade unions and Social Democratic governments form an important part of the background in Sweden, with a labor market policy directed toward full employment and labor law ensuring a strong position for unions and employees as key elements. Thus, some of the basic preconditions are sensitive to political changes.

We also offer a comparative perspective, bringing in the results from the other European projects, and reflections on the situation in North America. The book thus widens into a general discussion of technological change, job design, employee influence, and the future role of unions in working life. In this wider context results from several research projects at the Swedish Center for Working Life are introduced, such as the Demos project (action research with four local unions trying to influence job design), the Method project (on approaches in interactive research trying to combine support for local changes with theoretical work), and the Utopia project (the development of specifications for alternative technology in the printing industry, with cooperation between unions and researchers and with such goals as quality of work and product). Pelle Ehn was project leader of the Utopia project and an important member of the stimulating research milieu at the Center during those years; Kristen Nygaard, computer science professor in Oslo, inspired our research. There are also some reflections on trade union demarcation problems based on a recently finished project at the Center. The concluding chapter of the book is based on the considerations of ongoing research on post-Taylorist managerial strategies and their consequences for work and the unions. It turns out that these recent developments put the issues of this book even more into focus.

The bulk of our empirical material comes from the years 1975 to 1985. During the first half of this period the unions were on the offensive in workplace and co-determination issues. But during the 1980s conservative winds blew, the unions were weakened, and the employers' offensive emphasizing the individual dominated the ideological scene. Instead of collective co-determination based on independent union activity to reach the common goals of members (the "collective resources approach"), individual self-fulfillment within a framework of cooperation, joint consultation, and "new management" became the catchwords. The employers tried to replace industrial relations with individual employee relations. The "new industrial relations" do not, however, seem to be so new. Recent workplace development projects are, in this respect, very similar to those of the 1960s, that is, individual employee involvement in the company and little independent role for the unions. We know that this approach in the 1960s created problems with legitimacy and lack of real, lasting changes allowing for substantial employee control of their work; accusations of manipulative management were heard. We saw wildcat strikes and growing conflicts in workplaces around 1970.

There is now a clear possibility in the 1990s that we may experience similar reactions to those that followed in the 1970s. To avoid such reactions we must first avoid the "back-to-the-future" strategy that dreams of the good old 1950s and 1960s with the patriarchal family as a model for worklife organization. The labor movement had accepted, in a "historical compromise," capital's rationalization strategies and power in the sphere of production in return for possibilities for a social redistribution and welfare policy.

On the surface the 1980s was a glittering decade symbolized by success stories: managers as heroes; big profits in the finance and real estate sectors; yuppies, young men in splendid suits, driving Porsches (this car was reported to be more common in Stockholm than in any other city in the world) and drinking champagne at the Royal Opera Café Friday afternoons, called "finansvalpar" ("finance puppies") by Stig Malm, the chairman of the union confederation, LO. But below the surface, the ideas of the 1970s about democratization in work life have continued to live, and have reemerged in the 1990s. Employees today demand control of their work, to be *citizens at work*, not only outside the factory or office. This book builds on, and develops, the experiences of the 1970s and shows their fruitfulness in face of worklife transformation in the 1990s, with its emphasis on "the good work." The ideas of the 1970s thus come back under new circumstances, but they are now influenced by ecological thoughts, women's movements, the demands of young people for development and freedom at work, as well as the increased requirements of industry's international competitiveness. They come back in the form of demands not only for industrial democracy but also "good work" and employee competence as preconditions for productivity and for industrial transformation. Demands for formal democracy in working life have been supplemented with substantial demands for quality, competence, control, and efficiency. If the slogan of the 1970s was: "Democracy should not stop at the factory gates," the slogan of the 1990s is also, "The worker should not have to leave his or her head at the factory gate or office door." And, it is argued, allowing the worker to use his or her head within the factory is not only humane but also productive, creating competitive advantages for the Swedish production system (Metallarbetareförbundet 1989; LO 1990).

Acknowledgments

More than a decade of worklife transformation and accompanying research is the background to this effort to take stock. My task has been to function as the main author of this book, bringing sections from the original Swedish Front project summary report into a broad national background of industrial relations and workplace changes. I am solely responsible for Chapters 1 through 4 and 8 through 10, except for Chapter 1, section 5 (subsection on three union perspectives) and section 6 (subsection on systemization of different companies' strategies), which have been written by Peter Ullmark, and Chapter 8, section 1, subsection on twenty European case studies, which is based on parts of a manuscript written with Hugo Levie. Chapters 5 through 7 are the joint responsibility of the Swedish Front project group, and we have all worked through each other's sections; this is also true for parts of Chapter 4, including parts of section 2, the introduction to section 4, and the subsection on building blocks for strategies and section 5 on conclusions. The persons mainly responsible for the first version of individual sections in Chapters 5 through 7 are: Gunnar Broms (Chapter 6, sections 1–7), Jesper Steen and Peter Ullmark (Chapter 5, sections 1–6, and Chapter 6, sections 8–14), and Arne Grip and Lars Sundström (Chapter 5, sections 7–10), Peter Ullmark (Chapter 7, sections 2–4), and myself (Chapter 7, sections 1 and 5). Karin Gehlin took part in the case study on which Chapter 6, sections 1–7 are based. There are also longer separate reports on the respective cases.

Parts of this book are based on articles that were published as the different projects were completed. I want to thank the publishers for allowing use of the material in this book. Earlier, shorter versions of Chapter 2, section 1, Chapter 3, section 1, and Chapter 4 of this book were presented at Friedrich Ebert Stiftung's "Fachgespräch über betriebliche Formen von Arbeitnehmerbeteiligung." Werner Fricke and Wilgart Schuchard (Bonn) and Gerhard Strohmeir (Vienna) gave useful comments. The article was published in German, in *Beteiligung als Element gewerkschaftlicher Arbeitspolitik* (Bonn: 1984). A revised version in Swedish was published in the Norwegian journal *Sosiologi i dag*, no. 1 (1984); the editor, Trygve Gulbrandsen, made useful suggestions for its revision. The discussion of the "Demos project" in Chapter 1, section 6 and Chapter 4, section 2 is based on Pelle Ehn and Åke Sandberg, "Local Union Influence on Technology and Work Organization," in *Systems Design for, with, and by the Users*, ed. U. Briefs et al. (Amsterdam: North Holland, 1983) and Åke Sandberg: "Trade Union-Oriented Research for Democratization of Planning in Working Life," *Journal of Occupational Behavior* 4 (1983): 59–71; I thank Max Elden for editorial comments. Chapter 1, section 7, on our research approach, is based on my article "Socio-Technical Design, Trade Union Strategies and Action Research," in *Research Methods in Information Systems*, ed. E. Mumford et al. (Amsterdam: North Holland, 1985); Enid Mumford (conference organizer and book editor) gave suggestions that improved the text. My main work on this book manuscript was finished in 1987; in 1990 the empirical material was updated on some points, mainly on Volvo's new Uddevalla factory and on the recent trade union "policy of good work."

After this manuscript was completed, one paper based on Chapters 2 and 3 was presented at an ISA Conference in Hyderabad (published as "Participation and Democratization in Working Life— Some Swedish Experiences," in *Workers' Participation and Industrial Democracy—Global Perspectives*, ed. C. Lakshmanna et al. [Delhi, India: Ajanta Books, 1990]) and at a Spanish–Swedish seminar in Madrid (published as "Cambio tecnológico y democratizacion de la vida laboral—algunas experiencias suecas," in *Sistema: revista de ciencias sociales* 94–95 (1990).

Many people contributed to the research projects on which this book is based. And over the years many have commented upon articles and drafts of different chapters. The list is long, and it is a pleasure to thank so many colleagues and friends for fruitful cooperation. The Front project had a reference group with representatives from both the blue-collar (LO) and the white-collar (TCO) unions involved in the four case studies. Other projects discussed in this book often had similar reference groups. The members of this active union group were Åke Borg, Ingemar Göransson, Björn Jansson, Knut Jansson, Birgitta Olsson, and Leif Wisén. They have contributed valuable suggestions on the chapters based on the Front project. In the early Demos project Anders Wetterberg and Birgitta Frejhagen (LO) were among our union dialogue partners.

Our special thanks for comments on earlier versions of different chapters go to Hugo Levie (Amsterdam) and Anders Hingel (Brussels) and to the members of the other European teams; Matteo Rollier and Mino Vassoler (Italy); Horst Dachwitz, Birgitta Nentzel, and Matthias Knuth (Germany); Anton van Asch, Marten van Klaveren, Jack Christis, and Hein Hendricks (Holland); Roy Moore, Stephen Gourlay, and the late Erik Batstone (UK); and to our colleagues from Stockholm: Bengt Abrahamsson, Annika Baude, Peter Docherty, Pelle Ehn, Lars Ekdahl, Peter Enstöm, Bjørn Gustavsen, Rut Hammarström, Inge Janérus, Klas Levinsson, Rudolf Meidner, Casten von Otter, and Anders Wiberg; while working on the Appendix on laws and agreements, we were greatly assisted by Sten Edlund, and on the section on Volvo's Uddevalla plant by plant manager Leif Karlberg and representatives from the personnel department, and local unions, who enlightened us during a study visit, and by P.-O. Bergström and Ingemar Göransson of the National Metalworkers' Union who commented upon a draft version of this section. Over the years several sections have been presented at different conferences, especially within the International Sociological Association and its Research Committee No. 10 (RC10) on Participation and Self Management. György Széll (Osnabrück) and Cornelis Lammers (Leiden) and others gave valuable comments.

While making the final revisions of the manuscript I received critical and useful comments from, among others, Katharina Rehermann and Walter Müller Jentsch (Paderborn), Russel Lansbury (Sidney), Andy Martin (Boston), Thomas Sandberg (Uppsala), and, not least, from Mike Ames and others of the Temple University Press.

The research reported in this volume was largely based at and financed by the Arbetslivscentrum (Swedish Center for Working Life) in Stockholm except the first year of the Demos project, which was based at the Department of Computer Science at the Royal Institute of Technology in Stockholm. The Center in its turn is financed mainly via the Swedish Work Environment Fund (Amfo), which also directly contributed to financing the Demos and Utopia projects. The first part of the Demos project was also financed by the Bank of Sweden Tercentenary Fund, and the Utopia project also by STU (Swedish Board for Technical Development). I here want to thank these institutions. I want to express my special thanks to the Arbetslivscentrum for providing the means for carrying out this research. The Center also provided the intellectual environment for this type of relatively large-scale, change-oriented research project.

The library of the Center is a unique resource and its personnel are always competent and supportive of our research. Birger Viklund has helped with international contacts and with communicating research results to a wider audience. Cecilia Runnström, our book editor, and Christer Lindroth, conference organizer, have been most helpful. Many parts of the book were translated from Swedish by Keith Bradfield, Stockholm; for the rest, Keith checked and polished our English. The cooperation with Keith, with all his skills and intensity, was stimulating and demanding. While the manuscript was developing, it was typed by his secretary and by several assistants at the Swedish Center for Working Life; AnnBritt Bolin and Madeleine Richter were secretaries in the final stages. The original manuscript was typed; for the final work we used our computers for word processing. The office service staff of the Center over the years has given professional and enthusiastic support with anything from the fast copying of texts for seminars to repairing tape recorders and Arbetslivscentrum's "company bikes" for quick, nonpolluting transport to seminars or field sites. To all concerned, I wish to record my thanks.

Åke Sandberg

Abbreviations and Acronyms

ABL   Aktiebolagslagen
Limited Companies Act

AD   Arbetsdomstolen
Labor Court

ALC   Arbetslivscentrum
Swedish Center for Working Life

Amfo   Arbetsmiljöfonden (formerly Arbetarskyddsfonden)
Swedish Work Environment Fund

AML   Arbetsmiljölagen
The Working Environment Act

CF   Civilingenjörsförbundet
Association of Graduate Engineers

CNC   Computerized Numerical Control (computer-guided
machine tools that can be programmed at the machine
itself)

DEFF   Delegationen för förvaltningsdemokrati
Delegation for Democracy in the Public Sector

Fabriks   Svenska fabriksarbetareförbundet
Swedish Factory Workers' Union

FF   Försäkringsanställdas förbund
            Union of Insurance Employees

ISA   International Sociological Association

ISA–KLAR   Informationssystem för arbete–Klassificerade
            arbetsdataregister
            Information System for Work–Classified Work Data
            Register

KTK   Kommunaltjänstemannakartellen
            Federation of Salaried Local Government Employees

Livs   Svenska Livsmedelsarbetareförbundet
            Swedish Food Workers' Union

LO   Landsorganisationen i Sverige
            Swedish Trade Union Confederation

LSA   Lagen om styrelserepresentation för anställdaa
            Act Concerning Labor Representatives on Company
            Boards

MBA-S   Medbestämmandeavtal för den statliga sektorn
            Co-Determination Agreement for the Central
            Government Labor Sector

MBL   Medbestämmandelagen
            The Co-Determination Act of 1976

MDA   Människa, dator, arbetsliv
            People and Information Technology in Working Life

Metall   Svenska metallindustriarbetareförbundet
            Swedish Metalworkers' Union

OECD   Organization for Economic Cooperation and
            Development

PTK   Privattjänstemannakartellen
            Federation of Salaried Employees in Industry and
            Services

SACO   Sveriges Akademikers Centralorganisation
            Swedish Confederation of Professional Associations

SAF   Svenska arbetsgivareföreningen
           The Swedish Employers' Confederation

SALF   Sveriges arbetsledareförbund
           Swedish Foremen's and Supervisors' Union

SIF   Svenska industritjänstemannaförbundet
           Swedish Union of Clerical and Technical Employees in
           Industry

SJ   Statens Järnvägar
           Swedish State Rail

SOU   Statens offentliga utredningar
           Swedish Government Official Reports (Investigations).
           (In citations, SOU 1989:25 means report No. 25 of
           1989.)

ST   Statsjänstemannaförbundet
           Union of Civil Servants

STU   Styrelsen för teknisk utveckling
           Swedish Board for Technical Development

TCO   Tjänstemännens centralorganisation
           Central Organization of Salaried Employees

TCO–OF   TCOs förhandlingsråd för offentliganställda
           TCO Negotiation Council for Public Employees
           (TCO–OF is a merger between TCO–S and KTK)

TCO–S   TCOs statsttjänstemannasektion
           TCO Section for State Employees

URAF   Utvecklingsrådets arbetsgrupp för forskning
           Working Group for Research of the Development
           Council for Cooperation Issues

VF   Sveriges verkstadsförening
           Swedish Engineering Employers' Association

Technological Change and
Co-Determination in Sweden

1

Introduction

1. The Problem

New technology and computers, rationalization, new forms of work organization, management efforts to involve workers in the strivings of the company—these are dominating tendencies today at our workplaces and in our society. New products are being created following new demands and marketing efforts; decision making is being decentralized; workers are developing new skills, using new computerized "tools," which may in turn create a basis for a growing individual and collective influence on working life. "Good jobs" and productivity go hand-in-hand. This is the common picture painted in "pop" management and business journals and books.

But the business interests of the individual firm and the play of the "free market" can also have negative effects on working people and on our environment. What will post-Tayloristic management and employee involvement finally mean for the employees' work and unions? Will the new jobs also be good jobs? Will the new products also be useful ones? Or will involvement and development be transformed into profit-oriented burnout of humans and nature? The other face of these developments is deskilling, stress, and unemployment; sophisticated control using new economic and ideological instruments; bad quality products; the destruction of nature and the rest. This is why the employees and trade unions are beginning to raise their voices in many countries, demanding influence not only on wages but also on work organization and decision making in working life and in the economy as a whole. Issues of work and

1

production become equally important as issues of wages and distribution. A policy of the "good work for all" may even become, as we shall see, the basis for a long-term solidaristic policy of wages. The slogan Good Work *for All* hints at the importance of labor market preconditions for developing the quality of work. (Rudolf Meidner, one of the originators of the solidaristic wage policy, now emphasizes this relationship; oral communication with Sandberg.)

Today's structural changes in working life have two faces. Employees and their unions appreciate those occasions when management strivings toward profitable business coincide with the demands of working people for good jobs. These possibilities may in fact be partially due to pressure from the employees and unions. But this relative harmony may not be an eternal state of affairs. In our kind of society, capital and management have dominant structural power. Although today's managers say that "the personnel is our greatest resource," the trade union movement stands out in this book as the main force capable of pursuing in an uncompromising and persistent way the long-term interests of the employees. Such a democratically anchored voice of collective, long-term interests is essential in a situation of broad, deep transformation, where one face or the other of the change may become dominant, and where capital interest is secured by means of advanced forms of managerial control on the company level. An independent trade union perspective may be founded in such basic social values as solidarity going beyond the company, and as the quality of work, product, and the environment in which we live and work.

The development of technology and work is not a deterministic process but a matter of social choice, power, and negotiation. This means both that technological development is influenced by social processes and that a given technology does not determine the social organization in which it is used (cf. Noble 1978). It is sometimes assumed that the only alternative to "latching on" to technical and economic development in the major industrialized countries is to "lag behind." We believe there are other alternatives, which start from the quality of work and the quality of the product (cf. Odhnoff and von Otter 1987; Ehn 1988).

The dominating principle for organization and control of work in industrial production has for decades been Scientific Management or Taylorism after the American engineer who formulated its principles during the first decade of this century. Work is studied and divided into small tasks. The tasks are divided among specialized employees whose work is controlled in detail. Planning is thus separated from execution. Fordism is the application of these principles to mass production of products for mass consumption, with the Ford model T and the production line as its symbols. Harry Braverman (1974) renewed the studies of the labor process and specifically analyzed the spread of Tayloristic principles of organization and its negative consequences for labor. His work has vitalized labor process studies and started a wide debate over the character of work and tendencies toward change.

As is now the common standpoint in the post-Braverman debate, we do not see Taylorism as the only adequate form of organization of production under capitalism: There are alternatives. Nor do we see capital as a sole actor, whose intentions are unproblematically realized: The employees and their unions also act, and the work organization is the result of a social process of both cooperation and conflict. The unions not only offer resistance to changes but sometimes have alternative proposals of their own to make, and not only on the use of technology at the workplaces (the work organization) but also in advanced cases of the long-term development of technology itself. The possibility of such independent employee and union influence and perspectives has to do with the basic power structure of a society. With its strong labor movement, the Swedish experience may offer some empirical examples of possibilities of this kind, as well as of the new kind of problems they create for the trade unions. How might an independent and articulated "voice of the employees" be developed? Specifically, what could be said and how? The old demands put forward in straight negotiations on the "bread-and-butter issues" do not provide a complete model for trade union work on issues like technological and organizational change.

Questions relating to production, technology, and organization are naturally not entirely new issues for the employees and their unions. They are, however, new in the sense that they are now acquiring a greater scale and significance in the work of many unions, both locally and nationally.

To simplify matters somewhat, we can say that wage negotiations stand out as the primary trade union activity. The work of the unions is directed toward influencing the distribution of the results of production. *Distribution issues* concern securing an acceptable wage as well as general conditions of employment like decent working hours, and—more generally—acceptable consequences of the fact that production is taking place. If questions concerning the work organization were pushed, this was usually in the form of demands regarding wage systems and wages. The fact that work was performed under detailed and Tayloristic managerial control may have contributed to this union emphasis on distribution issues.

These issues have been fundamental and decisive, and they will continue to be so. But to a growing extent they will parallel issues relating to production itself: What is produced and how is it produced? Concern for technology and job design, the product and its quality, and the effects on the environment is essential for the quality of work in a wide sense. We call these issues *production issues*.

How could trade unions and their members approach this new kind of issue? The present book concerns trade union efforts to influence the choice of technological solutions, and the use of technology at the workplace, to the end of achieving a good work organization. Innovative developments in internal trade union work and new ways of relating to the local employer are discussed. We also discuss questions relating to the actual development of new technology. A key aspect is the interplay between levels. We find examples of multilevel strategies of two supplementary kinds: first, on the workplace level an interplay between changes of work organizations and individual and group influence in the daily work and representative influence on management through the local union; second, an interplay between trade union strategies at the local and national levels. We find examples of a renewal of *both* the procedures and content of trade union work. Renewal implies that traditional negotiation procedures are not enough when trying to influence work and production. Negotiation procedures interplay with participation in managerial decision making, all based on independent trade union preparations and investigations to create a platform anchored among the membership and its experience of working life.

These are the tendencies toward a transformation within unions that we find in Scandinavia. More specifically, we have studied advanced employee and union attempts in Sweden to influence the choice of technology, the working environment, and job design and training in the context of technical changes at workplaces. We have studied the most advanced cases, so the general picture of Swedish working life and unions is less innovative than the cases, taken by themselves, may indicate. The Swedish experience, as we have said, is interesting due to the country's strong trade union movement: Not only is it well organized and strong at the national level, it also has active and strong workplace union organizations with locally elected officials. It is part of a labor movement in political power for decades, with an active labor market policy that takes full employment as its primary goal. The degree of organization is extremely high, above 80 percent, not only among blue-collar workers, but also among the growing number of white-collar workers (compare with just over 40 percent in the United Kingdom and just over 10 in France). Production in Sweden is technologically advanced. An aspect of special importance for our present purpose is the comparatively advanced labor law on co-determination, right to information, and conditions for trade union work, and also the state support extended to such union activities as training and research.

These preconditions and new rights and possibilities have put the unions in a position to try out new and advanced forms of co-determination. A growing body of experience is helping to clarify both the possibilities and also the problems of extending democracy in working life. This book tries to give a concrete overview of these developments, drawing on both empirical and theoretical research and focusing on the workplace level.

Co-determination and production issues are growing in importance at the workplace for several reasons: the higher level of education and raised demands from workers regarding the quality of their working hours; worker and union demands for the democratization of working life; and changes in the product markets, creating needs for flexible production processes, which leads in its turn to a greater dependence on the skills and involvement of workers.

2. Involvement in Production

The established means of defending employee interests in working life have been the trade unions and collective bargaining. Today, however, it is a common notion that industrial relations are falling into decline. There are many reasons for this: prolonged slumps, high unemployment, conservative and employer political offensives against the trade unions, a shift from industrial work, new types of workers and jobs in computer and service sectors without a strong trade union tradition, and new types of management trying to create more individual relations between workers and companies, replacing "industrial relations" with "employee relations" (cf. Berta 1986:3ff).

The basis of the growing trade union movement, in its search for collective solutions, was made up of workers in classical mass production. In several types of production, management is now trying to utilize the new capacities, skills, and planning abilities of a growing number of employees, as well as their motivation to "do their best when needed"—rather than acting counter to essential parts of their personal potential. This is nothing new. It has happened earlier, in the craft occupations. Today, we encounter it in various expanding branches of the economy. Examples include the process industry, where disruptions of its continuous flow can demand fast, responsible, and skilled action to prevent destruction on a large economic scale. Another example is the service sector, where the employee has to "sell" the company and its product in every encounter with the customer. But also in many other sectors, even in that traditional ideal type of Taylorism, the automotive industry, customer orientation and flexibility are growing in importance.

We may wonder whether the "new," skilled workers who identify themselves with their job will have their need of belonging and collectiveness fulfilled by more or less benevolent managements, through the trade union movement, or both. To be able to play a role, the trade unions have to develop their culture and working procedures. They must create a relation between their members' involvement in their work and their involvement in a collective movement that can promote "Good Jobs for All," with the whole worker involved but without the worker being exploited or manipulated.

The trade unions can be regarded as the collective organization defending the interests of the commodity "labor power." The changes in production and managerial philosophies mentioned above imply that capital is interested in utilizing more of the skills, enthusiasm, involvement, and planning capacity of the worker. To defend the basic interests of its members the trade union movement has to expand its activities into these "new" areas.

The key development, however, is the fact that trade unions are entering the sphere of production and are finding a new role for themselves—regardless of whether management is marked by detailed, Tayloristic control or decentralization and involvement. The fact that management today wants to involve the employees in their companies emphasizes even more strongly the importance of transformation within the trade unions. This fact makes the experiences and reflections of this book even more important. The new challenges and possibilities created for the trade unions by "new management" are discussed specifically in Chapter 10.

3. Production—Future Issues for the Trade Unions

In this book we describe and discuss various efforts made by the unions and their members to advance in what is partly a new field. We believe that these efforts have produced results and provided interesting experiences. The unions have a new role to play in production issues, with a broad activism at the local level, and a new interplay between the local and national levels: national union support to local union activity and local union support to the development of the members' job content and influence. This fundamental view shapes our subsequent treatment of the subject, for example, our discussion of union action in different cases. This is not to imply that distribution issues are without interest; it is simply that we are concentrating here on the production issues. The new trade union role, however, cannot be developed overnight. New procedures and strategies are required. We point to certain possibilities and successes, but also to constraints and problems. In the face of these constraints, it may be tempting to revert to trade union work mainly with the traditional, fundamental issues of distribution. A further development of the trade union work with production issues, however, is a precondition for shaping the forms of co-determination, and filling them with a content that will render such future issues as work content, choice of products, and quality of product major trade union issues.

Part of this development will be to emphasize the close connection between distribution issues and production issues. New forms of pay (for example, pay by results) and other benefits (for example, profit sharing) are being used by the employers to control production. Also, distinctions in material terms (levels of pay, terms of employment) between workers and salaried staff are creating boundaries both within the work organizations and among unions. Distribution issues thus affect the production issues.

Conversely, today's decisions and negotiations on technology and the work organization will have their effect on future wage issues. This takes place in two phases. The solutions found for the production issues have distributive consequences in that they affect the distribution of qualifications, development opportunities, and other qualitative aspects of the work among different jobs and individuals. (In this sense one could also say that production issues are also distribution issues, but of a new type.) This, in the subsequent phase, creates the terms for changes in the pay picture. The solution accorded to the production issues affects the distribution issues. (This aspect has been raised by some Swedish unions; see, e.g., Metallarbetareförbundet 1985; LO-tidningen 1986.)

When we speak of production issues as issues of the future, it is thus not at the expense of distribution issues. The case, rather, is that a trade union involvement in production lends a new context to the distribution issues and offers new opportunities to pursue them. Such a connection with the traditional issues also means that the production issues can be pursued with greater force.

4. Union Perspectives on Technological Change

Trade union perspectives on technology and work are changing. To regard technological change as a political issue (this section), and to regard not only wages and hours but also the work organization and even the quality of the product as essential questions for the trade unions (section 5), has fundamental consequences affecting both the form and content of trade union work.

One can distinguish analytically among four ways of regarding technological change, which are based on an analysis by Lindkvist (1981). Our summary of the four approaches is a modification of Lindkvist's discussion. With an *optimistic* approach to technology, technological development is seen as both necessary and desirable. Nothing should be allowed to prevent it, and our task is to promote it and give it as much free play as possible. A *radical* approach involves a critical view of technological development. Such development is not good as it stands, but it is possible to get it on to other, alternative tracks. The *conservative* approach has no faith in technological development, and assumes it to have negative consequences. The only possibility of hindering this development is to revert to previous stages of development or to maintain the status quo. A *pessimistic* attitude regards technological development as necessary; nothing can prevent it, and it has more or less negative consequences.

If we can now allow ourselves to use these concepts to characterize the attitude (not, of course, an unambiguous one) of the Swedish trade union movement to technological development over the past decades, we can perhaps venture on the following description. The dominant view until the mid 1960s was an optimistic one, which found concrete expression in a strategy for cooperation between the social partners with a view to a technological development and structural transformation that would lead to ever-greater material resources to distribute.

In the middle of the decade, Robert Blauner's criticism, for example, of working conditions at the medium level of mechanization was introduced (1964), thus giving union ideology an element of technological radicalism: Technology is not good as it stands, and the object is to get it onto other, alternative tracks. Even so, this attitude could probably still be described as technologically optimistic, in that continued technological development toward an ongoing automation would lead to improved working conditions.

Around the mid 1970s, a technologically radical view broke through in a number of contexts, owing to the negative effects of technological change. Harry Braverman's (1974) thesis concerning the degradation of many people's work and a polarization of the structure of qualifications began to emerge in the union literature. Technological development had to be influenced and technology used in a different way, if the previous negative consequences were not to become entirely dominant. This was to be promoted by increased union influence and co-determination. Union programs with radical demands for a changed course of development were formulated. Today we find once again, side-by-side with a strong radical approach, a tendency to technological optimism, which views technological development as a way of securing jobs, and also good jobs.

On the employer side, technological optimism seems to have dominated on the whole throughout the period.

If we try to abstract the view of technology one encounters in certain sociological research and in statements and publications by the unions, it is possible to supplement and further develop the concepts put forward in the fourfold analysis of attitudes toward technological change, so as to arrive at outline sketches of more coherent technological ideologies. A brief attempt at such an abstraction follows.

In the technologically conservative ideology, the ideal is traditional craft work. The problem is that the old trades are disappearing, and old workers are falling by the wayside. Changes in qualifications are measured by the type of qualifications possessed by the old craftworkers.

In the technologically radical ideology, the problems can perhaps be summed up by the union slogan, Computers—but on our Terms. One can distinguish a couple of variations on this theme. In the first, the ideal is "a new craftsmanship," in which the computer becomes a tool for highly skilled workers, who can do the new job well or better than they could the old job with the old technology. The qualifications required are partly the old, technology-independent professional skills, partly specific skills for the new working tool.

In the second version of the radical ideology, the ideal is a qualified job in a highly automated production process. The problem of "computers on our terms" relates here to the possibility of developing a collective, intellectual control over a scientifically based production process. The qualifications are, to a large degree, new scientific, engineering, and economic qualifications, combined with involvement and an ability to work together in critical situations in production.

In some current versions of the technologically optimistic ideology, one ideal appears to be a job without stress or pressure. The problems relate to the possibilities of securing, by using the new technology, industrial competitiveness, employment, and wage-paying capacity. There is no need to worry particularly about the consequences as regards work content, as everyone can learn fairly easily how to handle the various controls. In another version, ongoing automation is seen as leading to the disappearance of unskilled jobs and to increasing numbers of workers finding skilled work.

If the technologically conservative ideology that we have outlined says that most things are getting worse and that the object is to
stop technological development and try to return to the old crafts,
the optimistic ideology says that we just have to wait and see, most
things get better, provided that technolgical development is not hindered. Both versions of the radical ideology emphasize the conflicts
between different ways of developing and using technology, and
contradictions between tendencies to an impoverishment of work
and potentials for the development of new skills and competence.

5. The Changed Union Approach to Work

Views on technology and technological ideologies are connected with views on work and working conditions. If work is seen
as a productive activity in which there is an interest in the quality of
products and professional skill, then there is perhaps a greater prob-
ability of adopting a technologically radical attitude than if work is
seen as something from which to wrest a safe and secure livelihood.
In the latter case, actual production, and the work involved, will
perhaps be less central than competitiveness and the survival of the
company. A version of the technologically optimistic view may then
lie closer to hand. The essential thing is not the work itself but what
one gets out of it in the way of wages and conditions of employment. Such a union attitude is compatible with an instrumental view
of work. This may be termed the return or distribution perspective
on work, or the traditional wage-laborer perspective.

Another basic union perspective can be called the producer
perspective. Central to this perspective are the opportunities for employees to assume responsibility for the products and their quality
and the opportunities for people employed in production to exploit
and develop their special qualifications.

A third perspective, that of future union potentialities, emphasizes the role of the actual organization of production in making the
employees a unanimous and capable collective (Ullmark, Steen, and
Holmgren 1986).

The Three Union Perspectives

The return or distribution perspective relates to the situation of
the individual. It stresses the role of the union as the guardian of
people's entitlement to a reasonable life. It therefore has to consider
the possibilities of a positive return and the risks of a negative return. The positive return consists primarily of security, a fair wage,

personal contacts with fellow workers, a good physical environment, freedom of movement, an overview, and a rich and varied job. The unions have traditionally concentrated on the first two factors, security and a fair wage. The negative return comprises accidents, health hazards, responsibilities that the worker is incapable of carrying, demands for performance and an attentiveness that cannot be achieved, and working hours that disrupt the rhythm of sleep and prevent a normal social life. Traditionally, the unions have concentrated on accidents, health hazards, and working hours.

The producer perspective focuses attention on both the products and the production system. The attitude of the employees to the products is characterized by their own experience as consumers and as users of various types of technical equipment at work. It is also characterized, however, by occupational traditions that create certain conditions and norms regarding the properties and quality of the products or services in question.

The perspective of future union potentialities concerns the opportunities of employees to develop a conscious, efficient, long-term program of collective action. It thus relates to the conditions for solidarity and collaboration among employees at the workplace and their opportunities to influence future changes in a democratic manner. These conditions are created partly in the production process itself, partly in the activities of the union.

In production, the differences among groups as to their level of know-how and self-assertiveness must not be too great. Production must be so designed as to avoid competition and conflicts among individuals and groups. The necessary coordination of different groups and units should be handled by those directly concerned, and not by any special bodies, so that their daily work becomes a training in democracy.

However, if the resulting sense of solidarity is to lead to any well-underpinned union demands, there must be the time and opportunity for joint discussion. People with different occupational backgrounds and from different sectors of production must be able to exchange experiences and develop ideas together. It must also be possible to collate these ideas into programs of action. Demands, therefore, must also relate to improvements in the conditions for union work. In Table 1 later in the chapter, these three perspectives on work may be related to managerial strategies of rationalization. To get a grip on the strategies designed best to use existing resources, the return perspective is dominant. When it comes to handling the strategies relating to which new technological solutions will be exploited, and how the new technology is to be developed, the other two perspectives are essential.

Employees demand of the production system that it develop and exploit their professional skills, so that the properties and quality of their products can be continuously improved. The technical equipment should function as a good tool, which inspires the development of new methods of work. A desirable goal is cooperation to render the handling of day-to-day problems simpler and more effective. From the standpoint of management, whether of a private company or a public activity, the professional skills and creativity of personnel are not exclusively an asset. Management is in danger of becoming increasingly dependent and losing control over the work process. This can have economic consequences and also, in the long run, consequences in terms of power. Therefore, management attempts to exercise control over the employees, but it then runs the risk of restricting also such creativity that would be in management's interest. This, in many cases, reduces flexibility in production and the ability to adjust to major changes in the company's or organization's environment. In Chapter 10, we discuss post-Taylorist methods meant to combine managerial control with employee creativity and competence.

The union role from the return perspective can best be described as a monitoring of the "traditional" union aspects, while the union role from the producer perspective means a greater involvement in issues affecting the company's entire operation, the area traditionally reserved for management. This approach means less passive monitoring and more in the way of offensive proposals. This is treated in depth in Chapter 4, sections 2 to 4 on union strategies. We discuss there the distinction between distribution issues and production issues. The perspective of future union potentialities, which also implies a greater involvement in technological and organizational development, is treated in connection with the production issues.

The Dual Character of Work

The distinction between the producer perspective and the return or wage-labor perspective can be related to the Marxist concept of the dual character of the capitalist production process, as a labor process for producing use value and at the same time as a valorization process, that is, the creation of surplus value. More specifically, it can be related to the dual character of labor, that is, labor as an existential activity and labor as a commodity.

West German industrial sociologists Horst Kern and Michael Schumann (1984) develop the concept of the dual character of work itself as the basis for what they term the workers' dual relationship to work: the perspective of the wage laborer and the perspective of the subject/producer. The assumption is that workers have the opportunity to find an identity in their work and that this is fundamental to their concept of work. The two perspectives exist simultaneously, and the relation between them and the degree to which they are manifest depends on the historical and actual situation. This can change over time, both in long waves and at short intervals.

The preliminary results of their recent empirical investigations led Kern and Schumann to conclude that although the workers' life span outside work has increased considerably, as have their material means for filling their leisure time with activities, work is not turning into a marginal activity. No pure wage-laborer, or instrumental, perspective is developing. How can this be explained?

Kern and Schumann find a tendency for capital to utilize labor power in a new way, which includes not only physical strength and subordination, but also workers' skills and intellectual and motivational capabilities (cf. also PAQ 1983; Haug 1985). In the present developmental phase of production, Kern and Schumann see this trend as limited to some of the core sectors of modern industrial production. More peripheral work forces, and those unemployed, will not be affected.

Within the new type of automated work, "efficiency is supposed to be achieved through the workers' productive capacity and not against major elements of their personal potential" (Kern and Schumann 1984, 61). In this way, workers may become more involved in all aspects of the production process.

If the labor process changes in such a way that trade union members become more involved in the actual productive activity, this raises a challenge for the trade unions themselves. Should they become involved at all in this new area? If so, how could a union-oriented practice and producer perspective be developed—a perspective that allows for individual and collective worker involvement in the production process—as part of a democratization of working life—that is, a socially useful product with production methods that enhance worker capabilities?

The desirability and possibility of such developments must be seen against the background of managerial efforts to utilize worker potentials in management's own interest by means of different types of control systems and ideologies that try to integrate the workers as individuals into the corporate culture.

Some Illustrations

Illustrations of some of these approaches to technology and work can be seen in various unions' program declarations on the field of technology and work organization. (These illustrations from the mid 1980s are not necessarily fully representative of the organization in question.)

The Printing and Allied Workers' Union (Grafiska Fackförbundets Kongress (1982) stresses the necessity of an offensive for qualified professional training and considers that printing workers in the future, in addition to, for example, a good knowledge of layout and form, will need an in-depth knowledge of programming and data technology. The Civil Servants' Union (Statstjänstemannaförbundet 1982a and b; Wisén 1983) places a certain emphasis on the producer perspective by indicating as a quality of work the development of new products and better service to the general public. The Swedish Food Workers' Union (Livsmedelsarbetareförbundets Kongress, 1981; LO-tidningen 1986) is the only union of the few that we have looked at that has a clearly expressed producer perspective. It maintains that a good job involves, among other things, opportunities to take professional responsibility for product quality and production efficiency; the usefulness of the products and the interest of consumers are central factors. It also strongly emphasizes the necessity of having a policy on technology and research, for the development of a technology that promotes professional skill, and for a union influence on industrial research and development (R&D), especially in the national production of machinery.

These three unions can be said to take a technologically radical view, while publications from the Metalworkers' Union and LO (Swedish Trade Union Confederation) also contain traces of a more technologically optimistic view. LO (e.g., 1981, 106) emphasizes with particular force that industrial policy and technological development are fundamental to the possibilities of achieving various union objectives. The Metalworkers' Union (Metall) (Metallarbetareförbundet 1981) emphasizes that it has always, even during the unemployment of the 1930s, taken a positive view of rationalization and new technology. It asserts that they are necessary, but that union regulation of their content is essential, too. Recently, Metall and LO have placed a stronger emphasis on trade union influence in creating a socially acceptable development and use of the new technology. Aspects of this more technologically radical philosophy are demands for training as a part of every job and state support for the development of Swedish production technology, on the basis of trade union demands for tools for skilled workers cooperating in groups. The title of the report is *The Good Work* (Metallarbetareförbundet 1985). In Chapter 10 we return to union responses in the late 1980s to the "new management" ideas of the last decade.

An example from the local level is the Union of Clerical and Technical Employees in industry (SIF) at the Ericsson telephone company factory in Stockholm. The union questions whether its members can be forced to construct telephone systems that facilitate bugging and control on a large scale "for a country with a dubious government." "Can one say that this is a product in which the employees can take professional pride?" the local union asks rhetorically. And to the national Congress they proposed that "all types of control and registers be subject to negotiation. The design and sales of such computer technology should also be kept under supervision. When software that can be used in this way is produced, some form of built-in blocking device should be introduced in the program" (*Dagens Nyheter*, Nov. 13, 1984).

I make no attempt to explain all the different union views held on technology and work; nonetheless, I should like to reflect a little on them. (I return to these questions when commenting on our four case studies in a later chapter.) Conditions that seem to contribute to a technologically radical ideology are state or cooperative ownership and a market with restricted national and international competition. Craft unions seem to be more critical (conservative or radical) of technical change than the large industrial unions (cf. Bamber 1986; Holm et al. 1986). The printers' craft unions, in a sector which faces only limited international competition, have been critical toward technological change in most countries. There are however interesting national differences. While printers in the United States and the United Kingdom, and this is in line with the industrial relations traditional in those countries, seem to have been bargaining "after the event," and attempting to say "no" to new technology, Scandinavian printers have to a large extent said "yes—but on our terms," and they have also taken part and negotiated throughout the whole process of change. The Swedish metalworkers' big industrial union on the other hand, which represents labor employed by privately owned companies subject to fierce international competition, has traditionally taken an optimistic view of technology. Members of a craft union like the printers' union are experiencing drastic changes. The metalworkers have been experiencing changes, too, but less drastic ones, and only for smaller parts of its membership at a time. They thus see solving problems as they arise as feasible. With today's intensified competition, market orientation, automation, and changes in the work organization and leadership throughout the entire manufacturing industry, the Metalworkers' Union as a whole is experiencing a drastic challenge to the future of skilled work for its members. At the same time the union envisages a possibility of raised competence, by an alternative use of the new technology. This may explain the recent development of a more technologically radical view.

The unions in general still lag far behind the employers in the field of technology and work organization. But the case studies we present in Chapters 5 and 6 show that there exist today concrete examples of proactive local trade union activities, within the framework of a national offensive for the training of members and the development of trade union action programs.

6. Managerial Strategies of Rationalization

So far we have discussed trade union perspectives on technological change. What follows is a brief, analytical presentation of managerial strategies of rationalization. These are discussed here under the headings of work productivity and intensification; direct control and responsible autonomy; sociotechnical systems design; the systematization of different companies' strategies; and finally, the "frontiers of rationalization." These strategies are here seen mainly as deriving from capital's interest in profit and control; however, the issue of the influence of worker and union resistance and demands is raised, especially in the first two subsections.

Work Productivity and Intensification

The openings for trade union action and influence depend on the type of technological change or type of rationalization. A newspaper and a repair shop clearly illustrate this point. (These examples are taken from the Demos project; see Chapter 4; see also, Ehn and Sandberg 1983; Sandberg 1983.) The introduction of computers at the newspaper is symptomatic of a worldwide technological revolution in the printing industry, which makes possible enormous increases in productivity. Highly technical knowledge is needed to understand and influence this new technology. The skills and experiences of the workers alone are not enough. Even an extremely strong local union mobilization cannot control significantly the development of the technology.

In contrast, at a Swedish State Railways repair shop the proposed new technology involved a computer-based production planning and control system called ISA-KLAR. This system did not require any changes in the technology for production but could have been used for more detailed control of the work and possibly as the basis of a speedup. The benefits of the new system were probably not as important as management initially thought, but the drawbacks for the workers could be enormous: the deskilling and routinization of work, lower wages, and the like. In this case, the knowledge needed to formulate union demands could be based largely on the workers' own experiences and knowledge of the existing organization and planning system. The possibilities were very good for a broad union activity around basic demands (e.g., "we oppose detailed control") and for the development of local union alternative proposals regarding the work organization. The system was not introduced.

Maximum intensity in the use of labor power (the locomotive repair shop) and the introduction of new technology, which increase the productivity of the work force (as at the newspaper), are two central components in the efforts of company managements to rationalize.

Direct Control and Responsible Autonomy

A further discussion of the struggle around the ISA-KLAR system at the repair shop also gives us two examples of rationalization strategies aimed at the intensification of work. ISA-KLAR is a modern example of the direct control of work in accordance with the principles of scientific management. By feeding general method–time–measurement (MTM) data and work studies data from the plant into a computer system, the basis for detailed control of the repair workers could be created.

Examples of operations stored in the ISA-KLAR system are:

1. Fetch tools x and y
2. Go to bogie
3. Crawl into position
4. Remove split pin
5. Remove bolt and washer
6. Repeat operations 3 through 5 for remaining 5 bolts
7. Transport out
   Estimated time required for this job: x minutes.

The full introduction of such a system would have entailed the replacement of a skilled occupation by unskilled labor executing operations prescribed for them in detail on a computer printout. The workers in the repair shop agreed with management that planning and work were badly organized. They, however, wanted to find a solution aimed in quite another direction: to develop the partial group self-management that existed at the time into a more advanced system of self-planning by the work group. They also wanted to improve overall production planning in the shop; they wanted to improve the supply of parts, material, and tools; and they wanted these decisions to be subject to union co-determination.

This case illustrates, on the one hand, how the union's proposal to develop further a group-based work organization that was already in existence could improve the work situation. On the other hand, this union alternative might also function as an example of another way for management to raise the intensity of the work. This managerial control strategy, which Andrew L. Friedman (1977) calls responsible autonomy, is also illustrated in the Swedish Employers' Confederation's (SAF) concept of "co-ordinated independence" in its "new factories" project. Friedman sees responsible autonomy as a strategy in relation to key groups of workers, especially under favorable labor market conditions.

In this context, it is also interesting to speculate whether the prevention of the installation of the ISA-KLAR system depended on union strength and activity or to what extent it was due purely to the knowledge developed during the process: a knowledge that perhaps showed management that the union alternative was, given the complicated nature of repair work, an alternative that allowed for more efficient rationalization and an even higher intensity of work than the direct control that would result from the new computer-based system.

Today, more than a decade after our project at the repair shop, Swedish State Railways, in close cooperation with unions, are developing new forms of organization, including raised competence and a high degree of group self-management. This, however, takes place within budget frames and goals set by higher levels, also using new forms of managerial control not known within the State Railways in the 1970s.

Tayloristic detailed control can mean a polarization of the structure of qualifications, with a degradation of work for a large section of the workers as the result. This can lead to the development of a strong and conscious collective, but also to passivity—with perhaps different effects in different types of questions. Responsible autonomy can lead to a splitting up of the worker collective into smaller groups (with a fairly rich work content) competing with each other, but coupled to the firm's profit motive by means of a decentralized system of economic incentives and control (e.g., profit centers). It can, on the other hand, lay the foundation for a local development of competence and cooperation among workers in their daily work and within the trade union. The problems and potentials for both capital and labor, when we compare direct control and responsible autonomy, is an expression of the contradictions in capitalist society. It is the contradiction at the ideological level between the "systems' need for qualification, education in different types of knowledge and experience, and of subjection" (Therborn 1976, 23; Therborn 1980). This contradiction seems to be growing in strength, and is probably of fundamental importance when we try to develop an understanding of the new managerial philosophies that are discussed in Chapter 10.

Sociotechnical Systems Design

Group work and "responsible autonomy" have a background in the sociotechnical tradition. The sociotechnical tradition emphasizes the interrelationship between the technical system and the social system and the necessity for working with both when designing a new production system. The approach is influenced by projects at the Tavistock Institute of Human Relations in London. The institute was established in 1946 by a group of social scientists, many of whom had been working at the Tavistock Clinic, a therapeutic establishment staffed by psychologists concerned with mental health and individual development, and using among other things small group therapy (Mumford 1987.) During the war, founding members, all clinical psychologists, of the institute had acquired experiences of man–machine interaction (Eric Trist) and leaderless groups (Wilfred R. Bion). The early and well-known field project in British coal mining was a major contribution to sociotechnical theory, especially the concepts of an "autonomous group" and of joint optimization of social and technical systems.

> The early hand-got method of mining had enabled the miners to work in small, tightly knit, self-regulating social groups. Mechanization removed these groups and substituted an impersonal system of mining in which forty or fifty men would be strung out along a coal face, each man responsible for a single task only. The new system required a cycle of work in which different operations were carried out in each shift. If one shift failed to complete its work, men on subsequent shifts would experience serious difficulties. The new system therefore created a situation which bred interpersonal and intergroup conflict. . . . The team began to recognize that if the technical system is optimized at the expense of the human system, the results obtained will be suboptimal. The goal must therefore be joint optimization of the technical and social systems. . . . [Through a visit to a] pit in South Yorkshire the notion of autonomous groups brought itself to the attention of the researchers. The men there had chosen to work this way, even

though their colliery was mechanized, because they were working faces that were short in length. By reverting to the small group form of work organization that had been associated with hand-got methods they secured the advantages of a socially close, cooperative environment while working on a mechanized face. (Mumford 1987, 58)

On the basis of these and later experiences, the group at Tavistock developed principles for sociotechnical analysis and design. With this approach, a production system is analyzed in terms of inputs, transformation, and outputs. A key concept in the analysis of the production system is variance, which is to say deviations from some standard or norm that affects the system performance or output. An essential question when analyzing the technical system is, "What are the key variances and how are they controlled?" Social systems analysis focuses upon how different individuals and groups accomplish their tasks and how they perceive their work. The social system is analyzed by means of interviews and questionnaires that ask employees to describe their attitudes to their work situation and also by means of such indicators as turnover, absenteeism, and the role of the trade unions. (For an overview, see, e.g., Bostrom and Heinen 1977.) The traditional sociotechnical group theory was supplemented with open systems theory and an emphasis on values that can give direction in "turbulent fields."

By the beginning of the 1960s the Tavistock Institute had arrived at "(1) the concept of a socio-technical system, (2) a view of the organization as an open system, (3) the principle of organizational choice—the need to match social and technical systems together in the most appropriate way, (4) a recognition of the importance of autonomous groups, and (5) better understanding of the problems of work alienation" (Mumford 1987).

The above techniques are usually used either in managerially controlled projects of change or in projects where the employees directly affected and, sometimes, their union representatives also participate. The sociotechnical expert performs the technical systems analysis, conducts the interviews in the social systems analysis, and proposes an optimal sociotechnical solution. After analysis comes the design phase. A key design principle here is the breaking down of big systems into small, coordinated subsystems that have a certain degree of autonomy and, also, a learning capacity that enables them to cope with local variances.

Steering by actual orders from customers presupposes control of the system as a whole, so that one knows what product will come out when, and at what level of quality. The total flow has to be organized so as to ensure high stability. Some types of group organization may contribute to the solution of this problem by reducing the need for detailed control and giving the management more resources for overall control and its relations to the environment. At the same time, group organization can solve certain personnel problems by leaving more to the discretion of the individuals concerned and also by ameliorating the physical work environment and providing opportunities for social contacts. Against this background, we can understand the initial interest of SAF's (Swedish Employers' Confederation) Technical Department in the sociotechnical principles of work organization.

Sociotechnical ideas first become known in Sweden through the Norwegian program for industrial democracy. Its scope was much wider than that of the more micro-oriented sociotechnical design presented above. The context was a debate on industrial democracy that covered both board representation and the work organization.

Theoretically, the Norwegian program was based on the Tavistock Institute's coal-mining and textile-mill studies, with their emphasis on group work. In Norway, psychological job requirements and the principles of job design were further developed. The framework for the Norwegian experiments was provided by Australian psychologist Fred Emery's and also Eric Trist's development of sociotechnical thinking (Emery and Trist 1973). Emery stresses the *critical importance of democracy*, that is, for the necessary commitment to common values, people must be enabled to participate in developing those values. This theory was not only a diagnosis but also a prescription for action: "By starting a concrete change process on the shop floor it would be possible to change the relationships of production and create a force that would eventually roll back the traditional enterprise organization and replace it with a new one. The emergence of a new type of enterprise organization would in turn ensure new types of participation and policies on the level of society" (Gustavsen 1985; 463). In developing strategic thinking, Norwegian psychologist Einar Thorsrud made important contributions (Emery and Thorsrud 1976). Successful experiments were conducted at several Norwegian workplaces, but the expected diffusion did not take place. Reasons that have been suggested for this are, among others, that managements on the experimental sites were not prepared to understand the consequences for the enterprise as a whole, as changes went beyond the shop-floor level; new sites were not able to start changes without the close support of researchers; the support from top-level labor market organizations did not grow concurrently with the developments, consequently, financial backing was lacking. (See Gustavsen 1985 also for further references.)

A Systematization of Different Company Strategies

How, then, can these and other company strategies be systematized, so that we are able to distinguish their effects on working conditions? For the majority of companies in our economic system, the overriding goal is a good return on the capital invested. The most important concern then becomes cutting costs and increasing receipts. (For a basis for this systematization, see Björkman and Lundqvist 1981; Ehn and Sandberg 1983; Ullmark, Steen, and Holmgren 1986.)

In all productive activity, people through their labor, and with the aid of instruments of labor (tools and machines, for example, a typesetting machine), shape a work object (raw materials or semimanufactures; semimanufactures are made from raw materials, but require further processing). As will be illustrated, rationalization can be directed toward the *actual labor*, against the *instruments of labor*, or against the *object of labor*. What is of importance to our present discussion is that regardless of the focus of rationalization it has consequences for both the organization and content of work. The following discussion of management rationalization strategies is also presented in tabular form (see Table 1).

Reduced costs can be achieved, first of all, by an increased exploitation of labor. Given a specific technique, and specific raw materials and products, that is, by the better utilization of existing resources, there are in principle three ways of going about this. The working day can be prolonged, at an unchanged wage. This strategy has been successfully combated by union organizations. Recently, however, it has entered the picture once more in the form of working hours that are adjusted to current business levels. The price of labor can also be reduced by a further division of labor and lowering of the qualifications required. The intensity of work can be raised by, for example, greater supervision, pay by performance, and group work (direct control or responsible autonomy, see above).

Second, costs can be reduced by increased exploitation of the existing instruments of labor: the machinery and the premises. Here, again, we find several means that greatly influence actual working conditions. Operating hours can be prolonged by shift work. More workers can learn different working duties, so that they can be continuously reassigned according to the availability of machinery. New routine procedures can be developed for supplying the plant with raw materials and semimanufactures as well as for the exchange and repair of tools.

Third, costs can be cut by reducing the capital tied up in the objects of labor during the manufacturing process as well as those kept in stock. Examples of means affecting the employees include an increased rate of throughput in production by a more controlled tempo of work, a work organization in groups along the flow of production, new routine procedures for the ordering of raw materials and input goods, and production planning that is directly regulated by orders from customers, which avoids unnecessary stockpiling. Another possible means is a continuous reallocation of labor to avoid unnecessary bottlenecks.

Fourth, costs can be cut by preventing disruptions. The means available for this to some extent offset those used to cut other costs, and they are in some cases to the advantage of employees. For example, staffing greater than that for the normal operating situation can be essential if faults are to be located and rapidly corrected. This can sometimes lead to a postponement of some parts of the process of automation. Also, more comprehensive training and more daily collaboration between the people working in sensitive parts of the production process can facilitate action in crisis situations, so that production is rapidly resumed. Usually, however, these inputs are concentrated in a small group of employees.

In the somewhat longer term, costs can also be reduced by investing in new equipment or in modifying the premises. In the really long term, entirely new technologies can be developed and utilized. These can relate to raw materials and components, and to the instruments of labor, the machinery, and the premises. Unions' opportunities to handle these more long-term strategies are very different from those related to day-to-day strategies. To influence the development of new technologies, for example, a central, long-term union policy is generally required, whereas the use of existing technologies can to a large extent be influenced locally.

Given new technical equipment, labor costs can be reduced by production with lower levels of staffing, especially at night. Also, sensors and other equipment for measurement and control can replace human judgment, which reduces training requirements and thus wage costs. The intensity of work can also be increased by more continuous production processes, in which the tempo of work is controlled by machines. A new technology can also be used to aid supervisors in their control of the workplace.

New technical equipment can also cut the capital costs for products in process. By a complementation of the technical system, narrow sectors can be eliminated so as to increase the speed of

Table 1

Methods for Reducing Costs, Increasing Receipts, and Increasing Control over Development

A. Reducing Costs through:

Increased Use of the Work Force			Increased Use of the Instruments of Labor		Less Capital Tied Up in the Objects of Labor		Prevention of Disruptions	
Better use of existing resources								
Longer working hours: Economy-adjusted working hours	Reduced price for labor: Lower qualifications; Division of labor	Increased intensity of work: Stronger supervision; Pay by performance; Competition among production groups	Increased use of machinery: Extended operating periods with shifts; Reduced stand-still time by constant reassignments	Increased use of premises: Reallocation of production lines and machines	Increased rate of product throughput: time schedules and coordination of all flows	Reduced stocks: New routines for orders and deliveries	Increased staffing and better standby system: Retention of certain manual phases; Training in collaboration; Training of key personnel	Preventive maintenance: Drafting of a maintenance program
Investment in new equipment or premises								
Limited staffing during certain periods: Night shift with limited staffing	More skilled tasks assigned to machines: Increased use of technical measurement and control systems	Increased control over pace of work: Continuous transport and production systems; Computer systems for orders and reports	Minimization of bottlenecks and standstills: Simplified readjustments for different products; Simplified maintenance	Direct adaptation of premises to production flow: Conversion or extension	Control systems based on product values: Computer systems for simulation, orders, and reports	Supply of components steered by customer orders	Parallel production flows: Computer systems for rapid transfer of production data	Simplified maintenance: Fewer movable parts; Simple repairs by exchange of parts
Development of new technology								
Employees freed for repairs and maintenance	Know-how concentrated in a few employees	All operations predetermined by machinery	Simpler processes and long series, through modern and standard-	Premises and machinery an integrated whole	Integrated order, planning, and control systems	New and cheaper raw materials and components	Self-correcting processes	Sensitive phases eliminated by use of modified products and components

B. Increasing Receipts through Production Measures:

Increased Marketing		Adaption to New Markets		Maximization of Available Capital
Ensure new variants of products for special customers	Ensure rapid modification of appearance and packaging	Ensure rapid increase of production	Eliminate obstacles to a broadening of the market: limited product lifetimes	Create flexibility for new products	Use subsuppliers; rent machinery and premises

C. Increasing Control over Development through Personnel Measures:

Reduced Dependency on Employees		Upper Hand in Knowledge and Information over Employees		Favorably Structured Procedures for Cooperation with Employees
Make the majority of employees easily exchangeable and favor the key people: An increased division of labor	Create further alternative production possibilities: More production units; Readiness to use subsuppliers	Secure the superiority of management: Build up own, effective information system; Separate different sections of production, so as to hinder an overview	Take over the employees' ideas: Keen-eared supervisors; Quality-circles without union participation	Limit co-determination to the employees' day-to-day conditions	Maintain freedom of action in planning and decision making

Source: Based on Ullmark et al. 1986, 67–79.

throughput, especially for expensive products. A new technology can accelerate exchanges of tools, adjustments for different versions of the product, running maintenance, and repairs. Computer systems can facilitate the entire production planning process, monitoring and directing, for instance, the supply of raw materials and input goods.

Increased receipts can be achieved primarily by improved marketing. This sometimes demands the capacity to change certain properties of the product rapidly, for example, its appearance and packaging. As a result, investments in equipment to facilitate work may be withheld. Management can maintain that it does not pay off to invest that much, since one never knows how long a product will survive on the market. On the other hand, real flexibility in production, to be able to produce substantially different variants of a product for varied and varying customer demands, *may* necessitate investment in new technology that enhances the skills, creativity, and responsibility of the employees.

Receipts can also be increased by the exploitation of new markets. Here, too, the potential for making rapid changes in the product can be important. The requirements of customers on these markets may be different. An ability to increase production rapidly is also essential. The effect of this on the employees' working conditions will differ, however, from one situation to another.

Finally, revenues can be raised by an increase in the available capital and an improved yield on it by various types of speculation. This may lead, for example, to machinery and premises being rented rather than purchased, and employees will then have greater difficulty in asserting their interests.

A company, however, cannot concentrate all its energies on measures immediately translatable into economic terms. Such a policy would focus excessively on the short term. The third group of strategies is thus aimed at giving management *increased control* over the future free play for action vis-à-vis various interested parties, both internal and external. The most important internal parties involved are the employees and various groups of owners, the external parties, the suppliers, special customers, competitors, and government bodies.

In the case of the employees, control can be increased by the company reducing its dependence on the specific professional know-how of major groups. To secure its operations, the company can then put the emphasis on a smaller group of well-trained persons who will receive a higher wage and other benefits. It can also reduce its dependence on the employees by acquiring further alternative means of production in the same or other plants. In addition, management can ensure that it continues to have the upper hand as regards know-how and information. Management will also try to exploit the initiative of different individuals. Finally, it is possible to create well-considered procedures for cooperation. Co-determination, for example, can be concentrated at such low levels within the organization as to hinder any coherent union action.

The "Frontiers of Rationalization"

What are the frontiers of rationalization today? It is difficult to give any general answer to such a question, but let us try to outline some tendencies. We will start with strategies for the utilization of the work force and the capital bound up in machinery and products. We follow here the conceptual framework developed by Björkman and Lundqvist (1981), and Berggren and Kjellström (1981, 88ff.), who distinguish between "traditional" (1950s and 1960s) and "new" (1970s and beyond) modes of rationalization in the engineering sector, both in large series and mixed production. The "new" strategies were breaking through toward the end of the 1980s.

Three strategies are aimed directly at the workers. *The lengthening of the working day* declined in importance from and including scientific management. Today, however, there is a growing interest in shift work with a view to the better utilization of expensive machinery and a demand for a brake on the numerous enactments of the 1970s establishing parental leave and leave for studies and other purposes; the inability to compete at the international level is cited as the reason for the employers' reluctance.

Lowering the price of labor by the division of labor is a basic strategy, but in a number of sectors today we notice instead a return to a reduced division of labor. Employers, however, are seeking to increase the spread of wages, since the unions have succeeded to a high degree in leveling out wage differences.

An increase in labor intensity used to be a central strategy, with MTM studies, control, and moving belts and the rest. It is still important both per se and as an aspect of other changes. For example, breaking up an assembly line into shorter parallel belts can increase the intensity of work in that it is easier to "keep everyone going" at top speed when so deployed; the same may be true for group work.

Other strategies are directed at the means of production, at the instruments of labor, and at the objects of labor. *An increased use of machinery* was a central strategy both in mass production by moving belt (line systems) and mixed production (long series by a functional organization with similar machines grouped together, as in a lathe department). Such organization still persists in sectors of production, in which the price of the details is not crucial. Flow grouping, on the other hand, reduces machinery utilization. Production with limited staff raises machinery utilization above the eight-hour "normal" working day. In mass production, parallel belts often mean a lower utilization of machinery.

Reduced costs for stocks of material and in-process inventories (goods in process) have acquired a great and growing importance. In mass production, attempts are made to achieve a faster total throughput by breaking up long lines with buffers or by a parallel grouping, which makes the overall system easier to control and less sensitive to disruptions. In mixed production, flow groups and single-product workshops are being developed.

The strategies described above relate to the *use* of labor, material, and machinery. The following strategies relate to the *development* of new technology (material and machinery) and new products. The development of new technology and new products can at the same time set one of the previous strategies in motion. In different subsectors and at different points of time, the emphasis may fall on either "use" or "development." In the current situation, with tough international competition and the breakthrough of electronics in many products and production processes, the development of new technology is of major importance. And the new technology is developed not only, or even primarily, at individual workplaces but in special research and development units, often with the manufacturers of machinery, that is, in a different sector from the people who will actually use the technology. This affects the opportunities of employees to participate in change.

One further group of strategies should be commented upon. These are strategies for the *protection of the production process from disruptions* at the work organization level, the disruptions in question being both those caused by personnel and those related to weaknesses in the technology and production planning. The traditional posture, of course, is Taylorism's MTM-based control over details. The detailed planning of individual work operations was not linked to a corresponding control over the entire production process, which became vulnerable to disruptions. In the new strategy, attempts are made to prevent disturbances and build up the organization in such a way that it is able, thanks to its decentralized form, to adjust to disruptions and variations, both internal and external (the market). Large processes are divided up into smaller ones; long lines are divided up by buffers or laid out in parallel; the functional organization is replaced by flow groups and product shops, particularly for expensive details and products.

The above, of course, is only a brief outline of tendencies taken from a special type of production. But if we may assume, even so, that it tells us something about more general changes, it becomes interesting to ask why these changes have come about. We content outselves with some suggestions. One explanation of the new forms of work organization, such as flow groups and product shops, may involve the internal efficiency of the company; the traditional type of rationalization leads to problems with both production and personnel (Chapter 3, section 2).

Another explanation may lie in external efficiency—with changing market demands for various high-quality products. Sharper international competition from low-wage countries, particularly in standardized mass production, is forcing countries like Sweden to concentrate on more sophisticated products in shorter series and offer several versions adapted to the requirements of customers; rapid adjustment and short throughput times then become crucial. The Front project case study from the machine tool industry, Pullmax AB Ursviken, is one example of this (see Chapter 6, section 1).

If it is true that we are seeing a shift in emphasis in capital's efforts at rationalization, from measures directed at labor to measures directed at the instruments and objects of work (capital rationalization), what consequences will this have for the content of work and for the opportunities for union organizations to exercise influence? This question cannot be answered here. One thing is certain, however, and that is that the "new" efforts at rationalization involve changes in the content of work, autonomy, and professional skills, changes which workers must study carefully and quickly in order to obtain a basis for their own demands. One generalization can be made: The capital rationalization of the 1980s does not entail per se any general rise in qualifications. That would require such rationalization to be combined with the abolition of the radical division of labor involved in the previous rationalization directed at labor (Björkman and Lundqvist 1981, 360).

A new organization of production emphasizing flexibility, customer orientation, and the flow of production can be combined with very different levels of division of labor and ways of organizing work. The intensity of work may become very high for both manual and clerical employees. Customer-oriented production with small buffers and lean inventories leads to a very disjointed production with "rush orders" interfoliated with waiting times. Groups of production workers, with a certain amount of autonomy in day-to-day decisions, have to take a common responsibility for a certain output determined in the overall planning. Clerical and technical employees are moved from office buildings to special areas behind glass windows in the factory building, and intense pressure is put on them to solve all kinds of problems related to personnel, materials handling, and customers. Replanning and stress in the relationships between planners and production workers, and in relationships with suppliers and customers, are common. The strain between manual workers and technical and clerical employees organized within the LO and TCO unions respectively can also create tensions in the relationships between unions. Central planning may be reduced and become less detailed, which has many desirable effects, but planning and information exchange in the new factory office or on the shop floor nonetheless still require time, resources, and knowledge (*SIF-tidningen* 1987).

While it may be true that rationalization efforts today are being directed toward capital (material and machines) rather than toward employees, the latter are not being left entirely alone. There is a tendency to combine decentralization, task integration, product shops, and group organization with various kinds of "symbolic management" and profit responsibility, to get individuals and groups to identify with the company and work harder toward company goals. This can be seen as a way not only of protecting the production process at the work organization level, but also of further developing the overall control and securing the legitimacy of the given decision-making structure in the company, and in society at large. We return to this type of "new management" in Chapter 10.

7. From Action Research to Praxis Research

Research related to change, in one way or another, is the dominating model in social science and in natural science. Research in such fields as mathematically based systems design, architecture, and medicine is to a high extent experimental and interacts with efforts to develop new solutions, new systems design, new ways of building houses, or new cures for illnesses. This kind of research is thus not only oriented toward change and experiments but also toward clearly pronounced, extrascientific goals.

The same is true also for a large part of social science research, which is very often oriented toward problems and goals formulated by decision makers in companies, in political bodies, or in the public arena. Here the research problem is relatively easily stated and the researcher makes a study and writes a report, which is delivered to the decision maker for his or her later use. When the actor is not a strong decision maker but, for example, a local trade union or a group of workers, there is a need for much more dialogue and interaction in the formulation of the research problem and the use and spreading of the results of research process. There may also be a need for interaction and dialogue during the research process itself; there is thus a difference between applied social research related to strong decision makers and research related to actors who are less powerful. This difference helps explain why the problems of the relation between theoretical work, on the one hand, and change and dialogue, on the other hand, are coming up in a very pronounced way in the latter type of research. (For an overview of change-oriented research approaches within the International Sociological Association [ISA] Research Committee 30, see Himmelstrand 1982, and for RC10, see Széll 1988, with further references.)

There is a kind of change-oriented research related to local actors, which seems to be well accepted, that is a research approach often used within business administration. Business leaders, however, have more resources than local union people and workers do, so the problem of interaction may be less pronounced in that instance. But, still, the interaction seems to be quite close and the problem of independent theoretical development therefore quite great. The fact that this is not seen as a big problem, and is not often discussed, may be explained by the fact that business interests seem to be more legitimate when it comes to guiding social research than trade union and worker interests. One explanation may be that in common theories of the firm, management is often seen as a neutral broker between group interests represented by capital owners and unions.

The similarities between research related toward actors at the central level and the less powerful actors at the local level is emphasized by Edmund Dahlström (1982), using the terms macroaction research and microaction research or established and local action research. This is a very important distinction. Basically most research is "action research" in the sense that it interplays with change and action. But when research activities interplay with powerful actors and with changes in nature or technology it is usually called simply research. And that is perhaps the term we should use also in change-oriented social research. There may, however, be a need for a special term, as so many social scientists still argue that good social research must be clearly decoupled from social change—although in their practice they often interact with powerful decision makers. We argue that the term action research should not be used to characterize processes of change with researcher participation without being part of a long-term research endeavor.

During the first half of the 1970s, an intense and critical discussion was waged within social research. The criticism concerned theories, methods, perspectives, the choice of problems, and the areas of application. Research was criticized for having concentrated on serving established and powerful interests, rather than the interests of the majority, when studying, say, democratization and social change. (For the debate see, for example, Schmid 1973, Sandberg 1976, pt. 1.) This criticism of the dominant approach to research was supplemented by efforts to develop alternatives. The action research developed in Scandinavia, and in Norway in particular, can be seen as an effort to find a procedure for research in cooperation with, and in support of, the weaker groups in society. This research was aimed at developing knowledge and assisting action. The ideas put forward in this section are based mainly on experiences with re-search projects in cooperation with local trade unions. Our own con-clusion, to which we will return, is that the activity called "action research" should be seen as an action and local-change aspect of a larger research effort, which we call "praxis research or interactive research." Only in this context is it reasonable to talk about "action *research.*" (This section is based on Sandberg 1985. See also articles in the Swedish sociological journal, *Sociologisk Forskning*, 1982.)

It is usually said that action research is characterized by a close interaction between action and research, between practice and the-ory, in a process of change. Such an interaction can be of a more or less intimate kind:

- The researcher evaluates the process of change and subse-quently feeds the results back to those concerned.
- The researcher's evaluation is fed back continuously to those concerned, during the process.
- The researcher participates in the process of change by supply-ing knowledge that will promote an understanding of the situ-ation among those concerned, for example, concepts, theories, methods for the clarification of problems, intentions, and the conditions for action will be discussed. The methods used in-clude those for investigation, planning and change, and for the articulation of "everyday knowledge."
- The researcher participates with his or her knowledge in inves-tigating and developing alternatives for action.
- The researcher participates directly in actions with those con-cerned.

Action research as defined above can interact with different types of actors. Organizational or systems development for, and with, management could be one example, but the Scandinavian tra-dition of action research has developed in close cooperation with the weaker, underprivileged groups and their efforts to control their own situation, their own conditions. It is associated, above all, with efforts toward democratization in working life.

The values underlying this type of action research are that people should be treated as subjects in a research process (not as the objects of research), and that such an approach is in accordance with strivings toward participatory democracy. Action research is assumed to contribute to our finding means for the development and use of knowledge by the people concerned. One scientific motive for action research is that dialogue and participation in change processes are good ways of obtaining certain types of data, and of developing our knowledge regarding processes of change. From both perspectives, the procedures and working approaches of action research are central. In the dialogue between researchers and practitioners in the action and local change phase, different kinds of knowledge are used and developed. Both the researchers and practitioners contribute to, and both get something out of, their dialogue. The setting up of forums for dialogue, working groups or study circles (with workers, trade unionists, and researchers), is a common method within the action research approach (especially in cooperation with the unions). Action research also uses knowledge that has been produced with different kinds of methods: survey research, interviews, participant observations, field experiments, historical studies, and/or the development of concepts.

The problem in many action research projects is to develop a functioning interplay between action practice (for example, that of the trade unions) and scientific practice. This is a very important issue (Schmid 1973). A strong emphasis on the difference between an action practice and a scientific practice brings to light the weaknesses in the type of action research, which, in too unproblematical a way, tries to combine the two types of activity. This is therefore a challenge, encouraging a further development of the theory and methods of action research.

Research can be regarded as a social practice characterized by the fact that the researcher must be able to use his or her professional qualifications and in order to do this he or she must (individually and via the research community) demand control over the research process, a long-term perspective, access to information, and the opportunity for open publication. In this way the researcher can develop new knowledge and show the research community that he or she can produce results and have them criticized. Trade union practice, on the other hand, is directed at the creation of conditions favorable for promoting the interests of members; only sometimes can this, in a nonproblematic way, be conjoined with conditions for the scientific search for knowledge. Differences in the objectives of the trade unions and of research are: a short-term perspective versus a long-term perspective; solutions and clear guidelines versus a study of the problems and a widening of perspective; the articulation of views and demands through the organizational hierarchy versus through the research process; locally useful knowledge versus theories and generalizations. This common, dualistic picture may be somewhat blurred. Union movements can have a long-term interest in gaining knowledge, once they develop their general perspectives, ideologies, and goals.

The efforts of action research to bring together these two practices seem to lead to one's being subordinated to the other; with scientific practice being subordinated to the action practice of either management or the unions. Alternatively, the "combination" leads to problems of the kind just noted. These problems, however, are not necessarily an expression of incompatibility. They may also be a sign of, and a driving force toward, the development of a joint practice. (They may also be a reflection of unfavorable external conditions.)

If the two courses of action and research must be kept apart and largely developed according to their different conditions, does this not mean a return to the traditional division between investigatory work subordinated to the specific demands of an organization, and scientific research in academic environments completely separated from "action"? Does this mean that action research is an impossibility? In answer to the last question we want to say "both yes and no." Yes, because action research that is characterized only by an interplay between action and theory cannot on its own constitute a scientific practice. No, in the sense that we see the possibility of development from action research to *praxis research*, by which we mean a research process that is characterized by participation, dialogue, and interaction with the people who are otherwise "objects of research." This research has an action component that is partially subordinated to an action practice, and a conceptual or reflective component that is subordinated to a scientific practice. The two components are clearly separate activities because they imply different relations to the practice in working life and because they are carried out in different parts of a research organization or over different periods of time.

While the action component and the conceptualization and reflection component are both parts of a larger research process, there is, of course, an interaction between the two. This interplay is not an immediate combination or mixture but rather an exchange. Previously developed scientific knowledge will be used in the action, and experiences from the action will be used to develop the ongoing research process. This is an interplay over a long period of time. The action phase or aspect is framed by theoretical and methodological reflection. Knowledge is used in the action, and knowledge is produced there, and in the subsequent analysis and conceptualization. *Praxis research* is characterized by a conscious and planned interaction between an action phase of research and a phase characterized by a more remote conceptualization and reflection. In so-called action research, the latter is often lacking. Even if there is a declaration in principle of the necessity for a cumulative development of knowledge and theoretical reflection, the tendency, as we have seen, is to neglect these necessary parts of the research process in favor of the action aspect. This interaction distinguishes praxis research from consultation, and from development and change projects in general. We may also call this research approach *interactive research*.

The two components of praxis research must be carefully developed to make this interplay possible. The problems that are handled in the action part must be selected so that the experiences and results obtained will be of value in scientific work by providing relevant data and stimulating new concepts. The researchers must document the processes of change in a way that renders the data of value to future scientific work. The researchers participating in an action phase therefore need a degree of professional autonomy. Scientific reflection, on the other hand, must be so oriented as to contribute in the long run to a better understanding of the possibilities and limits of action for change. An essential question becomes: What theories and methods are appropriate for such a task? Procedures and methods in the action phase will need to be documented, developed, and perhaps standardized, so that the researchers can avoid unnecessary mistakes, clarify sources of errors, and enable others to interpret and test their results without difficulty. This is true, for example, of the well-tried method of organizing working groups or study circles with researcher support. It also relates to an understanding of how various other research methods (for example, interviews and observation) can be introduced in a way that is compatible with researcher participation and dialogue in the action phase.

The *dialogue* between researchers and practitioners takes place not only in the action phase, where researchers support change and also get practical field experiences. Dialogue also takes place afterward, on a more general level. *Practitioners* use their experiences from the action phase, together with other knowledge, as a basis for their studies and reflection to further develop their worldview, ideology, and goals. *Researchers* use their experiences from the action phase to guide and illustrate their theoretical work. A *second-level dialogue* between researchers and practitioners takes place during and after these respective reflective exercises, but it is a dialogue concerning worldviews, explanations, and interpretations, rather than concrete action possibilities. We may thus talk about a *short-cycle* interaction in the action phase as well as a *long-cycle* interaction concerning worldviews and concepts. Both research and action practices have both time perspectives.

If praxis or interactive research is seen as possible and necessary, then the researcher is faced with a need for large scale and long-term efforts that contain both practice and theory, the interplay between the two, and the development of both.

This desire for further development within action research is based on a need among those who work within the tradition to develop their experiences theoretically and methodologically. It is also a reaction to criticism from those engaged in "traditional research." Such criticism is necessary and often fruitful, but it would be more valuable if other kinds of applied and change-oriented research were critically analyzed as well. It is difficult to discuss research strategies when the "problematic action research" is compared with an idealized picture of other research strategies.

Problems often mentioned in connection with action research, such as the close relationship between researchers and events, also arise with traditional, applied, commissioned research with powerful actors. A specific problem in locally oriented praxis research is a need to see development projects and dialogue phases as consciously chosen methods to gain an understanding of problems and to acquire empirical knowledge in contexts where the actors are less articulate and have fewer resources. These methods are used as supplements to traditional empirical research methods such as interviews, participant observation, or questionnaires. In some kinds of so-called action research, the action phase, often in the form of local development projects, has come to dominate the entire project. Such projects are of course legitimate and may be very useful from a practical point of view, but they have little to do with research as we define it here. Using the name of research for such development activities has hindered the establishment of praxis research or interactive research as a scientific activity.

The result may be that research with phases of action and dialogue as well as phases of theoretical–empirical work and reflection is discredited as a scientific endeavor and is replaced by pure change projects supplemented by traditional academic research at a distance, and without any relation to change. The alternative is theoretical work within the change-oriented tradition itself, that is, praxis research.

Praxis research implies that there is a continuing dialogue between the practitioners and researchers in the action part of a study and a more selective dialogue during and after the reflection phase. Under what conditions is this a suitable research strategy? We suggested earlier that studies of action opportunities in particular situations, and of conflicts of interest among the actors, may be an essential background to the action phase of a research effort. This may help us to answer such questions as: Is it possible to succeed with these actions? Will the experience of limits to these actions lead to a fruitful type of reflection? An answer to the question on the usefulness of praxis research requires that it be compared with other types of research.

The forms of knowledge seen as essential for interacting with change will depend upon one's own view of society and social change. To simplify a complex question, there are three viewpoints. If social change is viewed as essentially the result of uniquely created local factors, then the conclusion will be drawn that relevant knowledge is created directly in the local dialogue, and "action research" will become a central research strategy. If, however, social change is viewed as a conscious change of structures and conditions, then a general knowledge of causes and structural contradictions and possibilities becomes of central importance. This type of knowledge may be developed and used as an "expert strategy" for a centrally controlled change. But there can also be participative situations in which social change takes place through an interplay between planned structural change and local activism and problem solving. Parts of the research may then take the form of "praxis research," with action and reflection phases.

Praxis research, or interactive research, is a fruitful approach in a field where the democratization of working life is of essential value. Praxis research allows for direct worker participation in development and design work, at the same time as these local efforts are seen and analyzed in the wider context of societal structure and change.

2

Industrial Relations
and Co-Determination

1. Industrial Relations

Sweden had a late industrial development. In Britain, for example, the agricultural population was outnumbered by that in industry and the crafts as early as the first years of the nineteenth century, while in Sweden this did not occur until more than a century later. (This section is based on Korpi 1978;55ff; Abrahamsson 1980; and Hammarström 1987. For an analysis of modern Swedish welfare capitalism, see Korpi 1978; Himmelstrand et al. 1981; and Therborn 1987.) Sweden is a small country with an advanced industry in certain niches such as cars, paper, ball bearings, steel, and household appliances. This industry is highly dependent on export markets with their fluctuating demand. The niche strategy must thus be combined with flexibility of production and an ability to restructure industry. Flexibility can be facilitated if the employees have a high level of competence, influence, and involvement in production. Restructuring can be facilitated by an active industrial and labor market policy, supporting profitable industries, and training for the employees they need.

The "Swedish model," furthered by a strong union movement and labor government in cooperation, has most of these characteristics. Other pertinent characteristics of the Swedish economy are a high level of employment, a high labor-market-participation rate among women, a narrow wage spread, and a large public sector. The goals of the "Swedish model" in the labor market, often called the Rehn-Meidner model, may be summarized as follows: (almost)

38

full employment, equality (equal pay for equal work), and solidarity (limited wage gaps). The way to reach this goal is inflation-free growth, which is in turn realized by means of a restrictive, general economic policy; a selective labor market policy; and central framework agreements for wage determination.

The emergence of trade unions in Sweden was relatively rapid, and unionization achieved a high level even in the first decade of the twentieth century. LO, the Swedish Trade Union Confederation, was established in 1898. When the Swedish Social Democratic Party was founded in 1889, fifty local unions were among the seventy sponsoring organizations. Since then, close links have existed between the Social Democratic Party and unions within LO.

The level of unionization is high. Most salaried employees are members of unions within TCO (Central Organization of Salaried Employees, established in 1944), while smaller numbers are members of unions within SACO (the Confederation of Professional Associations, established in 1947). Eighty-three percent of the labor force in Sweden is unionized, as compared with 22 percent in the United States, 42 percent in West Germany, and 55 percent in the United Kingdom (according to a U.S. Department of Labor report quoted by Deutsch [1986b,35]). According to the 1981 standard-of-living survey in Sweden, 85 percent of blue-collar workers (80 percent of women and 88 percent of the men) were organized. For white-collar employees the figures were 86 percent, 87 percent, and 86 percent respectively (Kjellberg 1983). The 1988 union density was 85 percent (OECD 1990).

Significant in Swedish trade union development is the early dominance of industrial unionism over craft unionism. In 1908 no less than twenty-five out of the thirty-eight unions in LO were craft unions, but they comprised only about one-quarter of the membership. In 1912, the LO Congress decided on industrial unionism as the principle by which member unions should be organized. In 1975, only 5 percent of all LO members were members of craft unions, 10 percent were members of mixed unions (in transport and commerce; similar to industrial unions), and 86 percent were members of industrial unions (Korpi 1978:64f.). The affiliated unions of LO today have a total membership of around two million.

Because TCO, unlike LO, does not take part in wage negotiations, three distinctive negotiating bodies have been formed in the white-collar area. Within the private sector, seven unions affiliated with TCO and fourteen affiliated with SACO negotiate jointly with the employers through the Federation of Salaried Employees in Industry and Services (PTK). There are also negotiating bodies within TCO for the local (KTK) and national (TCO–S) government sectors;

KTK and TCO–S have recently been merged into TCO–OF. There is a similar system within SACO.

In the salaried employees sector, most TCO members (roughly 75 percent of the million members) are organized in industrial unions covering industry, commerce, banking, insurance, and national and local government. Categories represented by craft-type unions include nurses, teachers, journalists, and officers of the armed forces (TCO 1988, 6). In contrast to this mainly industrial and vertical unionization, SACO continues to organize horizontally (craft or occupation). Boundary disputes occur between the SACO and TCO unions, and there are no demarcation agreements. Between the TCO and LO unions there are a number of demarcation agreements. Territorial disputes, however, can acquire renewed importance in times of fundamental technological and organizational change; tendencies toward vertical integration between mental and manual labor may blur the boundaries between LO and TCO unions that are so basic in the Swedish trade union structure.

The relative strength of the national level in the trade union and bargaining system, together with the principle of industrial unionism, has probably contributed to the stability of Swedish labor relations. The Swedish Employers' Confederation (SAF), founded in 1902, is a highly centralized organization. The centralization of collective bargaining and of decisions on strikes and lockouts is an important background to the fact that industrial relations are regulated with little intervention by the state and that the level of industrial disputes has been low since the mid 1930s. Until the early 1930s, the level of disputes was high and state intervention was common.

In 1906 a compromise agreement was reached between LO and SAF. Workers were accorded the right of association, while employers were accorded the right to decide on hiring and firing in the labor force. This is expressed in section 23, subsequently section 32, of the Association's Statutes: The employer has "the right to manage and assign work, freely to hire and fire workers, and to use workers regardless of whether or not they are organized." This section came to symbolize the right of the employer to exercise control over his company. When it was called into question intensively in the early 1970s, the great slogan was "Abolish Section 32." In 1906, legislation had been passed that also provided for mediation in labor disputes, and the instrument of mediation was established. This meant a certain recognition of the right of association on the part of the state. Legislation providing for collective agreements and a labor court was ratified in 1928.

In 1932, the Social Democrats came into political power, and this was a precondition for what Walter Korpi has called "the historical compromise," the symbol of which is the Saltsjöbaden agreement between LO and SAF in 1938 (Korpi 1978, 1981; Meidner 1986; Johansson 1989). Labor and capital were to cooperate to support economic growth. The labor movement was to permit capital and management to exercise their power in the companies. In return, the labor movement could use its political power to build a full-employment welfare society. A strong trade union movement in cooperation with a political system of social democracy may thus be in a position to enter broad negotiations with industry, with potentially favorable results. This "historical compromise," based on cooperation for technological change and economic growth, is the common ground for rationalization (management's prerogative) as well as employment and higher and equal levels of living (the task of the state via labor-market policy). Technological change leads to growth that is distributed by means of negotiations. Technological change may also lead to problems with work organization, which are handled as "cooperation issues" between the labor-market parties. This is another way of summarizing the "Swedish model."

The Saltsjöbaden agreement itself is basically a regulation of negotiations, stipulating that negotiations must go to the highest level in attempting to resolve conflicts; only then are the parties allowed to take strike or lockout action. This necessitated a centralization within LO of the right to call strikes. This centralized system reduces the number of local conflicts and puts pressure on the parties to prevent national conflicts that might have severe economic consequences for "third parties." Industrial action is allowed only when contracts have either expired or been properly terminated. Collective agreements between management and labor organizations thus occupy a central role in the Swedish negotiating system. These agreements also apply to employees who are not union members, but who work in the sector covered by the agreement. During the term of the agreement, industrial peace is maintained. Disputes regarding interpretation of an agreement or legal norm, so-called dispute negotiations, are settled, ultimately, by the Labor Court. Disputes over issues not covered by an agreement are settled by collective-bargaining negotiations, sometimes underpinned by such industrial actions as lockouts or strikes.

Another factor contributing to the centralization of certain decisions within the trade unions was the fact that the Social Democratic government after World War II wanted trade union support in its effort to stop inflation. During the 1960s the efforts to implement a "solidaristic" wage policy (with equal pay for equal work regardless of the profits of the individual company) contributed to the same effort (Schiller 1983).

The high degree of organization in the Swedish union movement can be ascribed to structural factors, such as the concentration of ownership and the size of workplaces, and to historical factors, such as the degree of unity among the members of the working class. The interplay between political and union resources of power is emphasized (Korpi and Shalev 1979). In an attempt to explain the building up of the unions during the initial decades of this century, the vital factors that emerge include the degree of homogeneity and concentration in the working class and the economic strength and composition of capital. Both are determined by the timing and character of the industrialization process, and by ethnic and religious factors. In Sweden, where the process of industrialization was both late and rapid, differences in professional skill are not of decisive importance and industrial unions and socialist ideas are accepted. Socialist ideas are accepted because the labor movement's union branch and its political branch emerged almost simultaneously. More recent development of union strength can be traced to the historically defined nature of the labor movement (including the degree of unanimity and the relations between the unions and the Social Democratic party) and to the relative strengths of labor and capital (on the labor market and in terms of political ideology) (Kjellberg 1983, chap. 8).

LO's solidaristic wage policy meant equal pay for equal work and also trying to narrow wage gaps. This was a welfare goal that in itself furthered equality. It was also a key element in national union cooperation and solidarity. Later on, it became an instrument for an active labor market policy, furthering industrial renewal and high employment. Declining industries and inefficient companies that could not afford "equal pay" were forced to rationalize or close down, and the policy called for supporting the establishment of new companies in advanced branches of industry, with retraining for employees and, if necessary, support for workers moving to more prosperous regions.

Starting in 1969, a series of both large-scale and small unofficial strikes swept over Sweden. The negative effects of the historical compromise had become visible in the form of deteriorated jobs and a forced movement of people from north to south. The trade unions, now with a high level of organization and coordination, turned to government to obtain state legislative intervention to change the power structure prevailing in working life. The employers, strengthened by higher levels of unemployment and a nonsocialist government in 1976, broke with their traditional role as a neutral organization on the labor market and turned into an active right-wing political force. A state of confrontation and a politicization of the relations between the social partners developed during the 1970s (Korpi 1978; Leion 1985; Edlund 1986).

As to wage determination, a system of central, branch, and local negotiations has been operative, with the upper level providing "frame agreements" for the lower levels (Table 2). In recent years, however, centralized negotiations have been criticized especially by employers, who maintain that the system has become too rigid and too fixated on maintaining the pay level that a particular group has already achieved in relation to other employee groups. In negotiating the agreements for 1984, the Engineering Employers' Association (VF), the largest employers' group within SAF, refused to accept central negotiations between SAF and LO and negotiated on its own, signing separate agreements with the Metalworkers' Union. (In this short overview we use the LO–SAF area as an example.) For the other sectors, there were separate negotiations and agreements among them. Then the government intervened with economic policy measures because it feared too large wage increases, and it brought together the labor-market parties for deliberations. Since then the government has taken the intitiative more often than it did during the 1970s and earlier. Government intervention probably contributed to the fact that LO–SAF framework agreements were concluded for the years 1985 and 1986–1987. The LO–SAF agreements before 1984 had been dependent upon acceptance by both the different national unions and the employer associations, but once they were accepted they were binding in detail. The new framework agreements were recommendations rather, and much remained to be agreed upon on the sector level, where the right to strike and conflict remained, whereas earlier, after the LO–SAF central agreement had been signed, there was a general embargo on strikes and lockouts. In 1988 there was, as in 1984, no LO–SAF agreement, but one was concluded for 1989–1990. In summary, during the second half of the 1980s agreements have been less binding on the national LO–SAF level.

A new employer philosophy of wage determination evolved from the SAF congress in 1987. Local management would have control over wage increases, which then could be based on the employer's appraisal of the individual employee. This way of handling wage increases may be seen as a part of a general development of new management philosophies (see Chapter 10).

SAF, however, wants to see central agreements that provide a framework for local wage determination. One reason for favoring central agreements is that they may be able to keep wage increases within the limits that economic growth allows. Another is that, after a central agreement has been concluded, no strikes are allowed, and

Table 2

Bargaining Organizations for the Main Economic Sectors

Sector	Employees	Employers
National Government	TCO-OF (Negotiation Council for Public Employees) State Employees' Union SACO (Swedish Confederation of Professional Associations)	SAV (Swedish National Agency for Government Employees)
Local Government	TCO-OF (Negotiation Council for Public Employees) Swedish Municipal Workers' Union SACO (Swedish Confederation of Professional Associations)	Swedish Association of Local Authorities Federations of the Swedish County Councils
Private	PTK (Federation of Salaried Employees in Industry and Services) or its affiliates LO (Swedish Trade Union Confederation) or its affiliates	SAF (Swedish Employers' Confederation) or its affiliates SFO (Organization for State-Owned Industries)

Source: Based on TCO 1988.

thus the distribution of wage drift (or wage increases unforeseen in the central agreements) could be determined by the employers, with the local unions having only limited countermovements available to them.

To sum up, the situation seems to be that the employer associations are striving toward a decentralization of wage determination to the company level without any real local union influence. In the public debate today, employers tend to dominate and define the agenda. They argue for decentralization of negotiations to the company level, but at the same time they tend to keep, in practice, strong central control of local wage agreements, fining local employers who exceed the level of wage increases decided upon by SAF centrally. In this new situation, the trade unions have not managed to coordinate themselves very well. What they, at least the LO unions, seem to be aiming at now is general, central, collective agreements based on a national wage policy that will provide a framework for local wage determination and also real possibilities for local union influence. This would mean a combination of central and local negotiations—but with a changed balance and a wider scope for local influence. It is too early to say what the consequences will be for the power relations between employers and labor. Much depends on trade unions' abilities to adapt their structures to the growing importance of the local and the European levels, and to involve their members locally in production and work organization issues.

We have emphasized these new tendencies in industrial relations since they are at the same time crucial to the development of the "Swedish model," and are related to new management philosophies focusing on the individual employee. A departure from the idea of "equal pay for equal work" across employers will influence such issues as industrial renewal, employment, equality, and power relations in working life and the economy at large.

With others, we have stressed the centralized character of the Swedish trade unions, especially the LO. A study of power relations on the labor market in twelve countries, however, shows that the Swedish trade unions are both centralized and decentralized. Anders Kjellberg (1983, 243ff.) concludes that in most countries having both central and workplace collective bargaining and union organizations on the shop floor is not the rule. Instead, employees have been represented by more or less nonunion bodies at the workplace, work councils, for example, and employees have thus been less motivated to become union members. Countries with this type of dual employee representation tend to have a low level of union organization. In the Scandinavian countries we find not only central negotiations but also frequent local negotiations—as distinct from most European countries, but similar to the United States and the United Kingdom.

Local negotiations in Sweden are quite informal, as they are in the United Kingdom. The local union boards are elected directly by the membership and are independent in relation to the wider union, although close contacts exist. In the United Kingdom, and also in Scandinavia, the unions established themselves locally at workplaces as early as the end of the nineteenth century. Unions do not appear as superfluous actors in Swedish working life because they, for the most part, have decided on wages and conditions without interference from any income policy by associated governments (as in some European countries) and because they typically provide unemployment benefits. One of the weaknesses of the Swedish unions is that, at least until the mid 1970s, they confined themselves almost exclusively to wage issues. Another is that local unions, during periods when a national collective agreement is in force, have no means of bringing pressure to bear on the employer because of their obligation, as laid down in the central agreements, to preserve the industrial peace (Kjellberg 1983, 77ff.).

What we see today, due in large part to the development of co-determination, is a revitalization of the local trade union level, both unions covering a small geographical area (called local branches of national unions) and workplace or workshop "trade union clubs" that organize each national union's members at a given workplace.

As an illustration of the industrial relations aspect of technological changes at workplaces, we can take the Front project case study of a state-owned factory in the machine tool industry (Chapter 6). There are three different "workshop clubs" in the factory. The Metalworkers' Union (Metall) organizes the workers, SALF (the Swedish Foremen's and Supervisors' Union) organizes the supervisors, and SIF (the Union of Clerical and Technical Employees in Industry) organizes the salaried employees.

According to the Co-Determination Act of 1976 and underlined in the Co-Determination Agreement of 1979 for the state-owned companies, workshop clubs have a key role in the development of workers' and employee influence on work organization and, to a lesser extent in this agreement, technological change. The means are local co-determination agreements, which develop various forms of information, participation, and negotiation. The co-determination agreement emphasizes the importance of collaboration between LO and TCO unions, and it is noted that there is an agreement between these unions on the trade union coordination of co-determination issues, which proposes the creation of joint local Co-Determination

Councils. At the machine tool factory studied by the Front project there are some informal contacts among the three workshop clubs, but very few formal ones. There is not yet any local co-determination agreement, but there is a national agreement at the branch level. No Co-Determination Council has been set up.

In the case studied, the workshop club for the metalworkers is the main actor on the union side. Its growing salience does not seem to be directly based on rights accorded by the Co-Determination Act, but it probably can be attributed to union education that raised interest in and consciousness of, among members and representatives, such "co-determination issues" as technology, work, and production.

2. The Legal Background

With particular emphasis on the right of union organizations to information, and their right to negotiate, this section describes the Co-Determination Act, discusses certain problems connected with it, and outlines certain central agreements on co-determination. More details and an overview of other parts of labor law appear in the Appendix.

The Co-Determination Act

The Co-Determination Act of 1976 (MBL) is, above all, a reform of negotiating procedures. It is based on the established negotiating traditions of the labor market, which have already resulted in employees and their organizations gaining influence on other matters besides pay and other material working conditions.

The underlying principle of the act is that the employer still remains the one who, ultimately, determines the activities of the company or public authority, both in general matters and in the management and assignment of work at the individual workplace. Employers' real decision-making powers, however, have been reduced in various ways as a result of the employees having become entitled to participate in the decision-making procedure through their organizations. Employees are entitled to negotiate on practically all issues that concern them. Employers are required to take the initiative in holding negotiations before a decision is made. Employers must inform employees about company affairs. Similarly, unions have acquired extensive priority rights of interpretation in disputes concerning the implications of agreements, and they have also acquired a veto in certain circumstances. In order to develop a more dynamic picture of the development of labor law we present some problems arising from and criticisms of the Co-Determination Act.

Employers have frequently expressed their appreciation of the fact that good information at an early stage of events is a prerequisite for meaningful co-determination. At the same time, they have indicated that any wider obligation to inform incurred by employers should be accompanied by a reduction in the primary obligation to negotiate.

The main criticism from the employers' side is that the primary obligation to negotiate covers too wide a field. It is further claimed that the employer has to make preparations over a certain period before any meaningful negotiations can take place and that union criticism of the law and practice on this point is therefore unjustified.

Criticism from the unions relates primarily to shortcomings in information, to its being incomplete and, above all, provided too late. Some has come so late that the value of primary negotiations has been negated; therefore the right of requesting negotiations prior to a decision (section 12) is often worthless in practice.

The fact that the legislation has put negotiation in the foreground and linked the employer's obligations to the making of decisions has the disadvantage, in the eyes of union critics, that employers contact the union later than they might otherwise. One solution might be a "primary obligation to provide information," as a cornerstone of co-determination, an obligation, in other words, to provide information in the very first stages of a decision-making process, before the obligation to negotiate arises and before the union asks for negotiations (cf. Victorin 1982). Such a primary obligation to provide information at the stage when guidelines are formulated for future investigations and planning was demanded by local unions at the 1986 national congress of the Swedish Paper Industry Workers' Union.

Experience from workplaces where MBL is functioning well suggests that adequate information at an early stage is a crucial factor (cf. also Hammarström et al. 1982, 174ff.). In Jonas Leffler's research project on trade union information systems (1963), he concludes that although unions have the right to continuous information on the development of the company, in practice this right is very restricted. Unions have the right to "sort out" the information they want from the employers' books and systems, but if trade unions want to process the information in any substantial way—and even more if they want to collect and process new information—the law lends them very little support in terms of necessary resources.

They are usually only secondary users of the management's own information systems. In Leffler's project, an alternative information system was developed with a local union that wanted to analyze the situation at one particular workplace (geographically), rather than functionally, according to what product was produced but not where. In another trade union information system, it was possible to show that management's idea that the staffing level was too high was based on miscalculations; more fundamentally, it was also possible to show that personnel costs were a very small part of total production costs and that openings for rationalization would have to be sought elsewhere. The development of alternative information systems like these demands a strengthened trade union right to use company resources for information analysis and processing.

The unions have also been concerned to see an expansion of the area in which primary negotiations will take place, that is, of what is meant by a "major change." They would like the wording of the law amended in order to bring it into agreement with legal practice, as regards, for example, the obligation to negotiate on management-level appointments and decisions on budgets. They also want the obligation to negotiate extended to cover certain questions that by current legal practice are exempted from this obligation; this applies, among other things, to decisions on management's setting up investigations of possible changes in production and work.

Many of the above experiences and criticisms are summarized in a report of the state official investigation (SOU, Statens offentliga utredningar) set up to follow the introduction and application of the Co-Determination Act "MBL i utveckling" (Co-Determination in Development) (reported in SOU 1982 No. 60; cf. also TCO 1983a). When labor and management in most of the private sector finally reached an agreement on co-determination (spring 1982), this commission found itself in a different situation and concluded that it should wait for more reports on the new agreement before any amendments to the legislation were considered. In its summary, however, the commission considers certain possible developments of the act, or corresponding developments in the agreements. Within the commission (on which labor and management were both represented), agreement appears to have prevailed concerning the importance of providing early and thorough information to employees. This could be achieved by a right to primary information, as mentioned above, or by viewing the obligation to provide information as part of a more radical primary obligation to negotiate.

One widely discussed problem concerns the relationship between co-determination and the Companies Act and other legislation that imposes limits on co-determination. The conflicts of practice occurring hitherto have been more or less coped with through minor statutory amendments and decisions by the Labor Court. The State Commission felt prevented by the directives of the government from giving closer consideration to this extensive and formidable complex of problems. Sooner or later, however, the Companies Act in particular will probably need to undergo a thorough review if impediments to the achievement of advanced co-determination through collective agreements are to be effectively eliminated. The Companies Act requires the executive board of the company to act in accordance with decisions taken at its Annual General Meeting, the AGM. The AGM is not permitted to delegate decisions concerning, for example, fixed capital, rules for the appointment of executive directors, and the responsibility for financial statements. One possibility, however, appears to be the delegation to wage-earner dominated bodies of a specified right of decision, combined with a veto on the part of the legal principals (the company management, ultimately the AGM) (Arbetsmarknadsdepartementet 1977; Broström 1982, chap. 4).

Central Agreements on Co-Determination

The Co-Determination Act is "framework legislation," which is to say that it presupposes its supplementation by collective agreements in different sectors of the labor market, covering such fields as rationalization or personnel policy within the organization. Collective co-determination agreements (MBAs) of this kind have now been reached at a national level in all sectors of the labor market. In addition, local agreements have been reached in certain organizations.

The Co-Determination Act (Section 32) states that agreements, if the labor side so requests, "should be reached" on matters relating to "the management and assignment of working duties, and the conduct of the operation at large." (The well-known article 32 of the Swedish Employers' Confederation [SAF's] Statutes required its members to retain the right-of-decision to hire, fire, and organize production when entering collective agreements.) If collective co-determination agreements have been reached on matters covered by article 32, the labor side enjoys, as mentioned above, priority of interpretation until the dispute has been settled. (The normal progression moves from local negotiations to central negotiations and, finally, for questions that could set a precedent, to the Labor Court.) This priority of interpretation can function, among other things, as a "postponement rule."

In the state and cooperative sectors, co-determination agreements were reached fairly soon after the act had come into force. In the private sector, however, it took until the spring of 1982. One can speculate how much this was due to the low priority this question had for labor and management, and how much was due to limitations in the sanctions permitted by the act for pushing forward an agreement, the "remaining right to conflict." This right means that, if, for example, labor requests negotiations on a co-determination agreement, both labor and management are entitled to take industrial action, even if collective agreements involving an obligation to maintain the industrial peace have been concluded in the wage sector. A necessary condition, however, is that the requests for negotiations concerning a co-determination agreement on certain specific issues have been made in the context of wage negotiations (MBL, section 44).

The "remaining right of conflict" has been linked to wage negotiations in a way that perhaps makes it less interesting from the union standpoint. Also, it may be particularly difficult to apply when business levels are down. At any rate, it has never been used. The fact that the employers have been fairly reluctant to conclude any far-reaching co-determination agreements can also be seen against the background of the unions' relatively strong position— thanks to their priority of interpretation—once an agreement exists.

If we look at the content of the co-determination agreements, it is possible to obtain some idea of the direction in which co-determination is developing. To a greater extent than the Co-Determination Act, the agreements so far emphasize flexible, locally adapted forms of co-determination. This is especially true of the most recent central agreement, the Development Agreement, which covers the private sector. The content of the agreements is summarized in the Appendix.

The report of the commission comments on the status of agreements of this type: Agreements, as compared with legislation, are considered to have the advantage that they can be adapted to the local circumstances.

> The corresponding disadvantage, of course, is . . . that one does not in central frame agreements of this kind achieve solutions that are so directly and legally imperative as a fully implemented legislation would be. . . . The agreement approach is based more in a common understanding, and a joint concern to achieve something that works in practice. It is not always that clear answers are given to the sort of issues that could be a subject of dispute, should it prove that the common under-

standing and mutual concern are insufficient. (SOU 1982, 250ff.)

A hint as to the legal value of the general provisions contained in the co-determination agreements can be obtained from a verdict of the Labor Court (AD 1982, No. 107, cf. also Hydén 1984, 152). This relates to the agreement for state authorities (MBA-S), which states that the employer, in the context of rationalization, shall try to avoid dismissing personnel. The verdict states that this provision is a "direction of will," which is not so concretely worded that it can be directly used as a basis for the award of damages. However, the provision can have significance for the interpretation of other, more concrete rules contained in the agreement.

For the most part, the co-determination agreements concentrate on the actual forms and procedures of co-determination. They do not normally go beyond the minimal level prescribed in the Co-Determination Act, which is to say negotiations before the employer makes a decision. The Development Agreement emphasizes delegation to the individuals concerned; it also focuses on union influence by participation in the company's line organization and in special bipartite bodies. There is a tendency toward a higher degree of integration of co-determination into the company's decision-making structure. To the extent that substantial questions like kinds of work organization are treated in the agreements, the language is often vague and imprecise. The difficulty in making general, substantial agreements is for many unions a main argument for changing the procedure rules in the Co-Determination Act to give the union a stronger position in the decision-making processes. Demands have been raised, for example, for union self-determination in certain questions (more important questions than those covered by MBA-S): a union right of veto and an obligation for the union and the employer to reach an agreement before the employer makes a decision (see Grenninger 1983).

The Development Agreement includes these procedural kinds of provisions: trade union information on paid working hours; trade union meetings among all unions in different companies within a group of companies; descriptions of the consequences of technological change both economically, and as it affects the work environment and employment; opportunities to take part in designing and changing individual job situations; and as early training as possible for new jobs. (As is evident, we have here a sliding scale between directly binding rules and fairly vague ambitions.)

The form of co-determination that is to the greatest degree integrated in the company's ordinary organization is *line negotiation*. In its commentary on the Development Agreement, LO observes that such a form presupposes a good union basis:

> Before we choose line negotiations, we should discuss and answer the following questions:
>
> - Is this a very important area for us?
> - Do we know a lot about it?
> - Do we know what we want? Have we worked out any procedure program [that is] relevant to our intentions?
> - Are many people active in the union?
> - Is the company's union organization well coordinated? [Are there] good contacts between the committee and shop-floor representatives and others?
> - Do members have great confidence in the union's elected officials?
> - Do we have elected officials with adequate union experience, and of personal forcefulness?
>
> If we can answer yes to the majority of these questions, then we are perfectly safe in choosing line negotiations.
>
> If the answer is no, or we are doubtful, we should for the present choose a different form. Line negotiations, on the other hand, can be a long-term objective for us—but they do need extensive and well-considered preparation. (1938b, 175)

In its commentary on the Development Agreement, PTK compares the rights enjoyed under MBL with the alternative forms proposed in the Development Agreement:

> In practice, the employer's primary obligation to provide information and negotiate is negated when the parties agree that co-determination should be practised in other forms than those indicated by MBL. The union organization, however, is still entitled to lift out a particular issue for regular MBL negotiation. But the right to MBL negotiation has to be exploited before a decision has been made. From the union standpoint, it is thus a question of reacting in time, if we expect the employer to produce proposals that we cannot accept. (1984, 71)

Both LO (1983b) and PTK (1984) have published ambitious commentaries and handbooks on the use of the Development Agreement. The main theme seems to be cooperation with the employer to develop efficiency and the work organization and to secure future employment. This is seen as a long-term development, with the central agreement first adapted to different branches, and then, gradually, local agreements at different workplaces in different areas. LO believes that even if the effects of the new labor laws introduced around 1975 were greatly disappointing, there has in fact been a positive development. Trade unions are treated with a new respect by employers, thanks to their rights of information and negotiation. And the unions and their members have learned a lot about companies and the way they work: The Co-Determination Act was supplemented by massive education and studies both of general subjects and of how employees could investigate their own company, its economy, and production. The unions and employers received special resources for "co-determination education" from the Work Environment Fund. This was important when trying to establish, for example, the work organization as a central theme for union activity.

In a commentary on the Development Agreement, the Metalworkers' Union (Metall 1984) strongly emphasizes the necessity of a long-term, local trade union strategy for co-determination issues. It also suggests that the local unions should not accept employers' ambitions to "debureaucratize" co-determination, for example, by introducing line negotiations before such issues as a more decentralized and democratic work organization have been resolved. It suggests that procedural questions should not be regulated until substantial changes have taken place in the work organization.

Management has not published any corresponding material to advance local development agreements. The director of the Employers' Confederation (SAF), however, has delivered a speech entitled "Cooperation for Efficiency, Profitability, and Growth" (Ljunggren 1983). The positive view of new technology in the Development Agreement is referred to, and technological renewal is seen as necessary for competitiveness. Training is needed: "It is essential that everybody in a company should possess a knowledge of the company's economic conditions and the demands of the market." "Real co-determination" is seen essentially as a question of decentralization, within both the company and the union organization: The "responsibility for profit" must also be decentralized.

There exist today branch-level agreements—with only minor modifications, as compared with the central agreement—covering most sectors within both the manual worker (LO) and salaried employee (PTK) areas. Local agreements are also appearing.

Earlier Proposals for Co-Determination

To give a short historical background to today's Co-Determination Agreement in the private sector, let us take a look at earlier proposals from LO–PTK and SAF. The trade unions' (LO–PTK) first proposal in 1977 was far-reaching and covered six areas. The demand regarding the work organization was that the unions should have a right of veto over decisions involving important changes affecting the work organization, for example, the technology. The union should decide on the size and composition of work groups and their working conditions; within such limits, the groups themselves should make decisions about tasks and planning. The company should draw up a development plan for the work organization, and the union should determine the goals and content of the plan. The union should also set salary forms and working shifts.

In the case of systems development and computers, the union, by the terms of the LO–PTK proposal, should have a right of veto over the introduction of new systems as well as changes in existing systems.

Also in 1977, SAF presented its proposal, the most important section of which concerned the forms of co-determination. The employers wanted to replace negotiations under MBL with various kinds of joint consultation. They wanted co-determination to be related, as far as possible, to the "normal decision-making process of the company and not the newly created bodies." It was proposed that special workplace representatives, appointed by the union, should receive information from management, either by participating in the managerial body or by obtaining information from senior executives, and that information on management issues be imparted to a company council with a maximum of two representatives of each union organization. Management would then have fulfilled its obligation to provide information. The employers also wished to restrict the right to pass on information to other union members.

These two early proposals make clear the chief original differences between the two parties. In 1978 SAF presented a new proposal for an agreement, which was still based on the idea of replacing the employers' obligation to negotiate and provide information. All negotiations would have to start with a trade union initiative. This idea was modified slightly in a later version of the SAF proposal, but providing information to the workplace representatives was still seen as the normal procedure. An agreement seems to have been quite close at this time, but there were still differences and disagreements over the settlement of disputes arising from the agreement (the unions wanted the Labor Court to decide, not a spe-

cial board of arbitrators), and over the unions' prior right of interpretation, which the employers wished to modify. No agreement
was reached until the spring of 1982 during a time of economic crisis
and when the labor movement was less on the offensive. As compared with the original union demands, the 1982 agreement moved
quite a bit in the direction of the employers' proposal.

The LO, PTK, and Metalworkers' commentaries on the Development Agreement indicate that the emphasis on flexible and integrated co-determination does not mean that there is now no role for
formal negotiations. These comments emphasize the necessity of
formal, substantial agreements on changes in the work organization
as a precondition for "debureaucratized co-determination." They
also emphasize the necessity of independent trade union investigation and study as a precondition for participation in management
decision making. The actual agreements are, as we have seen, much
weaker than the original proposals from LO and PTK. And the emphasis on formal procedures is not so strong as it was around 1976
when the Co-Determination Act was introduced. But the "de-regula-
tion" is in no way total.

The Co-Determination Act was partially a reaction to the insuf-
ficiency of informal cooperation and bipartite bodies during the
1960s. The act emphasized formal agreements and the role of an
independent trade union party. The later co-determination agreements in turn emphasized informal cooperation. Today we may be
approaching a new stage, namely a synthesis of the last ten years'
experiences of two different types of co-determination: independent
trade union work, formal negotiations in key issues, and participation in ongoing change projects; and the other, a revised work organization with direct influence on the part of the employees. The
case studies in Chapters 5 and 6 provide several examples of these
types of development.

3

Innovations in Production and Work Organization

Historically, the union organizations in Sweden have given businesses a free hand in rationalization and structural transformation. At the beginning of the century employers pushed through a right to "manage and allocate work" (as it was put in Statutes of the Swedish Employers' Confederation), and on this basis they could make decisions on, for example, new technology and a new work organization, often on a Taylorist ground. The emphasis in the efforts of the unions lay on the distribution of the actual results of production. Their foundation was a "wage policy of solidarity," which would give all employees the same wages for the same work, regardless of the firm in which they were employed. As a complement to this there was an active state labor-market policy, designed to lend structural transformation, as a consequence of companies being "knocked out" in the competition. New companies were supported in crisis-struck areas, and employees were given training. In line with the Saltsjöbaden agreement of 1938 (Chapter 2), wage issues were regarded as "issues of interest," that is, issues where there was a conflict of interest. Issues of productivity and rationalization were called "issues of cooperation," which were characterized by consensus (Janérus 1983).

From the beginning of the century until the 1950s, little expansion can be seen in employee influence on the companies. A state commission under Social Democratic chairmanship (Ernst Wigfors) in the 1920s discussed and investigated industrial democracy as a logical step after political democracy, but the commission's proposals did not lead to any new legislation. It was not until the 1960s and 1970s that significant new laws were enacted, notably the Co-Determination Act of 1976 (Hadenius 1983). In the meantime, however, employers' right to exercise command at the workplaces did not remain unrestricted. The main central agreement of 1938 stated that the employer was to inform, and on request consult with, the employees' representatives on certain questions relating to dismissal. The supplementary collaboration agreements providing, for example, for works councils (1946; joint production committees) and work studies (1948) entailed further modifications in the employers' right to exercise command. The co-influence on which the parties agreed was limited: The collaborating bodies were consultative, and they were not to deal with questions relating to company policy at large. The unions accepted this restriction, since many feared that if the workers took on any responsibility for company policy, it could prove an obstacle to union goals and growth. So despite the constraints introduced, the employer's right to "manage and assign work" still held at the end of the 1960s.

1. The Past Twenty Years

Strivings toward change in Sweden's working life have varied in thrust and form over the past twenty years. The emphasis on productivity as compared with "humanization" has shifted, as has the emphasis, on the one hand, on collaboration and participation, and, on the other, the social partners' internal buildup of resources and negotiations between them. (For this section and for further references, see Dahlström 1978; Sandberg 1979, 1982; T. Sandberg 1982; Janérus 1983; see also Elden 1979.) The shifting emphasis on participation and negotiation applies to the policy of the central union and employer organizations, respectively. At the local level, the fluctuations may have been less turbulent. The condensed view here takes up some of the events already mentioned in the preceding chapters and gives an overview of some of the changes that are developed in subsequent chapters.

In the 1960s an optimistic view of technological development prevailed. Robert Blauner's vision of a requalification of workers with the advent of automation was accepted and also influenced union ideologies (1964). The late 1960s however gradually revealed a succession of negative consequences of the radical technological and structural change in production. The employers encountered personnel problems (turnover, absenteeism, etc.). There were also production problems because the Taylorist principle of organization did not always prove effective in complicated production processes;

planning and quality problems of different kinds became evident. There were protests at the workplaces against the degradation of work; there were some unofficial strikes. About half of these stoppages were over issues concerning work environment and control at the workplace (Korpi 1978). Gradually, union demands emerged for a modified work organization and for democratization at the workplaces. This was a shift in union policy, which was formerly relatively hostile to workshop participation due to fears of a loss of independence. All this should be viewed against the background of the prevailing favorable economic situation, with growth and full employment; a higher educational level for many young workers; and a radical political climate.

The problems just mentioned were investigated from the mid-1960s on by SAF's technical department. This gave the employers a superior know-how and an edge over LO and TCO when, toward the end of the 1960s, a number of projects were initiated that were to contribute both to the humanization of working conditions (as measured by job satisfaction) and to increased productivity. The so-called Development Council for Cooperative Issues (established in 1966 by SAF, LO, and TCO) had set up a special group for research (URAF), which started ten projects anchored in development groups at the company level. The central aspect of these efforts toward industrial democracy was an amended work organization, in accordance with sociotechnical principles. Job enlargement and "autonomous groups" were common methods.

The sociotechnical approach was, especially in the state-owned enterprises, supplemented with various forms of democratic institutions, for example, a departmental committee consisting of three workers and the supervisor, and a departmental meeting of all employees. In the state administration, one method tried was the participation of employee representatives in various decision-making bodies. Initially, several of these experiments developed in a promising manner. In the phase, however, at which the proposed changes were to be implemented, conflicts arose. This is understandable, in part, in the light of the disparate strategic aims of the respective parties: productivity and solutions to personnel problems, on the one hand, and, on the other, an ongoing process of democratization. In the private sector, cooperative efforts fell off. In the sector of state enterprises, open conflicts broke out, in some cases between the researchers and unions on one side and management on the other.

During this time, private employers had pursued their own development work in cooperation with various companies, and this was intensified when the bipartite work in due course broke down.

The SAF's "new factories" program, with models for new production technology and a new work organization, took shape with "coordinated independence" as its slogan. Partially independent subsystems in production would permit a direct, if limited, influence on the part of employees over their daily work, all, however, under the coordination of management.

Like the employers, the union organizations applied their experience of these attempts at industrial democracy in their unipartite work on co-determination in working life. The union organizations (notably LO in 1971) formulated radical demands for indirect, representational, and democratic influence at workplaces, plus radical general demands for a democratic work organization. These demands for power for the workers at all levels of the company were met by management resistance to the extension of employee participation beyond direct participation at the office or on the shop floor. This resulted in another shift in union policy. The unions mobilized political support and demanded legislation. These efforts resulted in 1976 in the appearance of the Co-Determination Act, which together with other legislation introduced at roughly the same time is customarily described as the labor legislation offensive. This was followed by an educational offensive within the unions, covering subjects such as new laws, computerization, and work organization. The forms deployed included both "specialist courses" and broad study circles at the workplaces. In this way the unions began to "politicize" the former cooperation issues, and make these, too, "issues of interest," where the interests of the parties may differ (Janérus 1983).

During the mid-1970s, a union movement for the democratization of working life by means of laws and agreements developed: "From Consultation to Co-Determination" was the slogan and the title given to LO's training material. At the same time, employers were further developing a sort of sociotechnical approach, with a production-technical thrust. The latter half of the 1970s was a period in which both sides built up their knowledge and strategies and consolidated their positions. Unions were dissatisfied with the employers' response to their criticism. Memberships were mobilized. Ideas of industrial and economic democracy were discussed within the Social Democratic Party. Wage-earner funds were proposed. Harry Braverman's (1974) thesis of the degradation of work was a dominant theme both in critical research and in many union discussions. The workers and the unions often had negative experiences with the introduction of the new technology and computer systems. Old skills were destroyed, and the 1970s generation of computers were often bad tools—or no tools at all—for the workers. They were often perceived as alien forces rather than as useful tools.

The Co-Determination Act, it was envisaged, would soon be followed by central, and subsequently local, co-determination agreements. In the central negotiations, LO and PTK, for example, demanded a union right of veto and self-determination with regard to computers and the organization of work. The employers wanted to "integrate" co-determination in the normal decision making of the company. They chose to use the term "co-influence" rather than "co-determination." The gap between the parties' proposals was very large, and it was a long time before agreements were reached, particularly in the private sector. No change in the labor law had been made that could pave the way for co-determination agreements in the way many unionists had expected. The line pursued by the central organizations (LO and PTK) then became that where no agreements existed, the act's various rules on information and regular negotiations should be strictly applied.

Central co-determination agreements covering, among other things, technological change and rationalization were, however, gradually concluded in the various sectors of the labor market. The most recent of these, concluded in the spring of 1982 in the privately owned sector, is called the Development Agreement. It strongly emphasizes new technology, productivity, and cooperation. The central agreements are supplemented with branch-level and local agreements. Issues such as power and influence have been played down. "From co-determination to development" is a phrase that may serve to summarize something of the change in union language used between 1976 and 1982.

The dominant strivings toward change in Sweden's economic life during the first half of the 1980s can be characterized as increased productivity through a powerful effort in the field of production technology. On this point, labor and management were in agreement. With varying degrees of force, the argument was that successful productivity development will presuppose the utilization and development of the employees' knowledge and a development of the work organization in a democratic direction. The economic crisis in Sweden was the motivating force behind this argument. High costs, low-capacity utilization, and relatively high unemployment were dominant features of the economic situation that was causing the labor movement to put its weight behind "a future for Sweden." Politically conservative winds were blowing, with a nonsocialist government between 1976 and 1982, and the employer side emerged as a rallying force in politics and the molding of public opinion. A supplementary factor may have been that union organizations experienced the strategy of the 1970s—with its emphasis on the legal and formal aspects (rather than the content, the production issues) and on the relationships between the parties and formal ne-

gotiations (rather than the creative development of new solutions)—
as insufficient in the 1980s. To proceed beyond the formulation of
general objectives and demands, concrete activity to promote change
and development is needed in the workplaces. This presupposes
well-developed local union work on these issues and well-developed
procedures for contacts with employers. Employers may have understood that to succeed in spreading ideas like the "new factories"
to numerous workplaces, they require some form of legitimation.
This they perhaps hoped to achieve by involving the union movement in future development efforts.

   In the field of change and research into working life, this has
meant a strong emphasis on bipartite development projects for the
introduction and exploitation of new technology to increase the
competitiveness of Swedish industry and at the same time develop
the work organization in a direction that utilizes the employees' resources. The integration of tasks at the level of the individual and
the group is a way in which companies can meet the fluctuating
demands of a market that is becoming steadily tougher. These new
potentials with employee competence as a precondition for productivity are part of the new situation that is helping to promote cooperation between management and unions. This does not mean a return to the situation of the 1960s, because, in the meanwhile,
experience of and training in co-determination have raised the level
of knowledge and consciousness among the unions and their memberships.

   The renewed experience of both positive and negative results
from bipartite development projects in the early 1980s, Sweden's
economic recovery with extremely low rates of unemployment, and
the stronger position of Social Democracy all contributed to a new
situation in the second half of the 1980s. Attention is once again
being accorded to the independent role of unions, a clear policy as a
basis for participation, and a multilevel strategy. One of the setbacks
in the recent development of new work organizations is that, while
they may create rich jobs, they may also produce a very high intensity of work with its resulting stress for many employees. Employers
on their side are emphasizing business aspects and the profit orientation of groups and individuals—"everyone a businessman."

   All in all, the situation at the end of the 1980s was both open
and contradictory. Some people are saying that now, finally, below
the glittering surface of the 1980s, some of the progressive ideas of
the 1970s regarding competence and self-determination for individuals and groups at work are actually becoming a reality. At the same
time, the ideas of the 1960s, which envisaged an unproblematic situation with common interests, remain strong, but today's supposed

common interest is at a "higher level" than in the 1960s. In the early 1960s, strivings for productivity were supplemented with strivings for a good physical work environment and, around 1970, also with job satisfaction. In the 1980s, competent and responsible employees were seen as a precondition for productivity and competitiveness.

Many people, these past years, have been concerned to put parentheses around those visions of the 1970s that relate to the democratization of working life and a stronger collective influence for the employees and the unions. There are signs, however, that these visions were also alive beneath, and sometimes even above, the glittering surface of the 1980s. The Metalworkers' Union began a critical analysis of new forms of work organization and management and how they are perceived by their members. The foundation for a new, independent strategy has been laid and further developed (Metallarbetareförbundet 1989) within LO's investigation of democracy and influence. The Social Democratic government has set up a commission to investigate the "worst jobs" and strategies to change them. There is also a stronger trade union stress on the content of development; the unions' experiences have enabled them to begin formulating more concrete and substantial goals and demands for "good jobs." "From Development to Policy on the Good Work" is a phrase that can serve to summarize the essence of this union tendency. "From Development to Business" may be seen as the corresponding slogan on the employer side. Comparing the 1970s with the late 1980s one may summarize the shift of union policy: from "Democracy must not stop at the factory gate" to "Workers should be allowed to bring their heads inside the factory gate."

2. Problems with Taylorism and the "New Factories"

As we have seen, problems with the traditional Tayloristic type of work organization became apparent in the 1960s. The manifest ones were personnel problems (such as turnover and absenteeism) and production problems (due to difficulties in optimizing and coordinating in detail a large and complicated production system). The result was a bad production economy. Several types of production economy losses are discernible. It was difficult to subdivide tasks so that everyone along a conveyor belt was working all the time (that is, difficulties in balancing the line). Owing to the short time allowed for some jobs, the workers may have had to leave an unfinished product, which led to low quality and a need for subsequent control and adjustment (system loss). Short job cycles mean longer periods for moving details and tools. In aggregate, these different types of production-economy losses in line production can amount to 40 to 50 percent (Sandberg, 1980; 75ff; 98ff., Berggren and Kjellström 1981).

New types of work organization that break with Tayloristic direct control can reduce the different types of loss. By breaking up the line with buffers in between parts or by using several shorter, parallel lines, line balancing and systems losses can be reduced. Longer job cycles lead to reduced times for the handling of details and tools.

The social losses due to personnel problems are perhaps smaller, in business economic terms, than the production-economy losses. New types of work organization sometimes lead to job enlargement and often to a better physical work environment. This may help to reduce the social losses. The changes from this perspective have in most cases been relatively marginal; they will be stable and further developed due essentially to the production-economy advantages they afford and perhaps also due to an ideological function as expressing a company's "humanistic policy." But in several recent cases, like Volvo's new Uddevalla plant, the changes in work organization are fundamental (below).

From the business-economics point of view, production problems rather than personnel problems would probably emerge as the main reason underlying many cases of employers' search for new forms of work organization and technology. In reports from the Employers' Confederation, however, such efforts are explained as much in terms of solving personnel problems as production problems. In any case, both kinds of problems seem to demand similar types of solutions: Social considerations, it is now argued, are a precondition for a good production economy. As we will discuss below, a low unemployment level contributes to a high importance of social aspects for work reform.

The planning problems in large systems with an extreme division of labor lead, among other things, to an inefficient flow of material and high costs for stocks of goods in process. In a famous speech in the early 1970s Curt Nicolin (at that time chair of the Swedish Employers' Confederation) gave an example from an industry in which the capital costs for in-process inventories were almost twice as large as the capital costs for machinery and buildings. The solution that Nicolin proposed was a very high degree of automation, with workers present in the factory only during the day. This solution is not applicable everywhere. It presupposes a far-reaching standardization of products. It also, in some cases, runs counter to another problem with the older large production systems. This problem relates not to the "inner" efficiency of production, that which we have been discussing so far, but rather to the "outer" efficiency, which has to do with market and sales. Highly automated systems, as well as conventional line production, can render difficult a production steered by customer orders, with numerous variants on the product. The social problem with this type of automation strategy, if it is pursued to any great extent, is that although the remaining jobs will be mainly daytime jobs, many workers will be rationalized out of the market (cf. Björkman and Lundqvist 1981). Technological development during the 1980s, however, points to new possibilities of combining automation and Tayloristic jobs with a high degree of flexibility. Japanese style "lean production" may serve as an example of that style.

SAF's "New Factories"

Another type of solution, however, was also being sought by the Technical Department of SAF and by the joint research group of the Development Council for Cooperation Issues (URAF), established by SAF, LO, and TCO in 1969. Initially, there were close relations between the programs of these two institutions. Gradually, however, SAF became critical, mainly because of what they considered to be too little emphasis on production technology and the slow pace of the Development Council's research program. (The rest of this section is based on primary material from the Employers' Confederation, such as SAF 1974 and Agurén and Edgren 1980, secondary material such as T. Sandberg's dissertation, which gives a good overview of autonomous work groups in Scandinavia in the 1970s; 1982, a report from Arbetarskydddsfonden [Work Environment Fund], edited by Göransson [1978], in particular the contribution by Jan Kronlund; and Hallinder et al. 1985.)

During the 1970s, the SAF Technical Department formulated a concept for mixed production in the engineering industry. While keeping the workers in the factories, they wanted to develop an efficient production flow by means of better technical solutions, material administration (logistics), and group organization. An overall control of the flow of material and "goods in process" is combined with the workers' working in groups and taking care of the detailed planning. This, in its turn, is encouraged by means of a wage system offering a bonus to the group of workers as a unit.

Abolishing the individual piece-rate system was, in fact, a very important motive for the employers' interest in group organization, in addition to the reasons given above. The individual piece-rate system gave rise to a development of wages at different workplaces that was beyond the control of the central wage negotiation agreements. SAF took a strategic decision to support small-group activities on the shop floor. When its Technical Department was established in 1966, all the people hired were industrial engineers, most of them from the steel firm of Fagersta. They had conducted experiments with group organization and group wages in the early 1960s. The competence of this group gave the Technical Department its key role of collecting, developing, and distributing, through publications and training programs, concrete experiences of new kinds of work organization and production technology. The group also took an interest in sociotechnical systems design.

From May 1969, SAF's Technical Department took part in a large number of development projects at Swedish companies. The department tried to include a "model company" with a good reputation in every key branch of production. Apart from its more extensive involvement in certain specific companies, the Technical Department refers in its publications (e.g., SAF 1974) to contacts with hundreds of local development projects. These projects grew out of concrete problems in production and were often connected to important, ongoing changes in production technology or layout. The local employer, through its production engineers, was the actual motive force of the project, and efforts were made to develop cooperation with the local trade unions.

The basic ideas in SAF's 1974 book were that production should no longer be organized in departments with different types of machines, but rather that production groups should be organized along the flow of the product and that whole departments could be organized as "complete factories" with different types of machines or processes. This proposal meant a fundamental shift from a process-oriented, functional organization to a product-oriented or flow-oriented organization, which would simplify planning and promote throughput.

Two examples of SAF's experiments, both from the car industry, are well summarized by Thomas Sandberg:

> The solutions worked out in the SAF experiments were at least as varied as the problems the experiments were intended to be attacking. The Saab-Scania gasoline engine assembly is one of many examples of a combination of a new design of the technical system with an organizational change. This can involve either a modification of an individual-based organization or, as in the engine operation, a shift to a group organization. The new element in the technical system both at Saab-Scania and at Volvo's Kalmar plant was the replacement of a fixed-pace assembly line by a non-paced trolley for each engine or car. The dependency relations between activities were thus loosened

and conditions were created that made possible the further measures needed in struggling with the sensitivity to disturbances, and the meaningless jobs, that are characteristic of a conventional assembly operation. At Södertälje, assembly took place in seven parallel assembly loops placed alongside a materials handling loop, which also contained a buffer of engines that were waiting to be assembled or that had been assembled. At Kalmar, all the assembly trolleys, bearing autobodies, followed the same path through the plant. Assembly took place in different departments, each of which was given responsibility for assembling one system in the car. Buffers of cars were placed between the departments.

The most obvious limitation at Saab-Scania and Volvo, especially the latter, concerned the vertical division of work. Operators could influence working methods and the division of labor, but very little else. At Saab-Scania's Södertälje plant, development groups were launched on a large scale. In these groups, the supervisor, the industrial engineer and some of the operators from a section took part. The emphasis, in their discussions, was on the work environment and production issues. At Kalmar, one of the work teams within a section established a consultation group with a similar make-up. (1982, 192f.)

SAF's Technical Department has published several reports summarizing its experiences with actual cases. From a research point of view, some of these reports seem somewhat public relations–oriented and difficult to assess. Outside researchers have not been allowed into the plants to produce any supplementary evaluations of these experiments (Dahlström 1980, 117, 158). In the first such summary report (SAF 1974), job enlargement is held up as part of the solution. The concept of the "group" is also a key issue. The "production group" is the name given to permanent groups working in direct production along the flow of production, producing a component or a whole product; another type of group is the so-called development group. These permanent groups meet "outside" actual production, once a week, say, to analyze and discuss production problems, the development of methods, and so forth. These groups can be seen as forerunners of today's interest in Japanese-style "quality circles."

As noted above, the Technical Department was influenced, initially, by the sociotechnical tradition. In its evaluation, however, of some of these Swedish experiences, SAF (1974, 49) couples autonomous groups to what it regards as political—and unrealistic—ideas regarding a democratic renewal of working life as a whole. Characterizing the development projects that failed to develop in an entirely satisfactory way, SAF (1974, 22ff.) mentions that they were often described as "industrial democracy" or "sociotechnics," and that they were often organized by an outsider who had been given a "playground" in a laboratory situation within a delimited part of the company. Among other characteristics of what SAF regards as unsuccessful projects, we find the following: experiments that started with ambitious, written programs; models that were developed in a laboratory situation and then directed in the works by outsiders; and projects in which cooperation took the form of a system lateral to the line organization.

According to SAF's evaluation, the successful projects displayed quite different characteristics: They started with modest and concrete ambitions, with actual problems at the workplace, rather than any general program for change; the actual work organization was developed, and one could see the concrete changes; and the main actors were the line organization, with its engineers, supervisors, and workers.

The above ideas were further tested, developed, and formulated in SAF's "new factories" project, which published a series of reports in 1977 that were subsequently edited and summarized in a publication in Swedish in 1979 (in English, Agurén and Edgren 1980). The new factories are said to have basically two goals: more effective operations and better jobs for individuals. It is further argued that these goals can be developed in harmony with each other. Some of the basic solutions in the factories from the standpoint of technical organization are summarized here, following the report by Agurén and Edgren (1980, chap. 4; see also Figure 1): The functional organization is replaced by flow groups and product shops. In the functionally oriented shop, machines of the same type, for example, lathes, are grouped together, and different products pass through. The product shop is designed in such a way that a given product is manufactured from start to finish within the shop, and each shop can function as an independent profit center. With product shops, planning and follow-up are simplified because the shop can be regarded as a planning point. Throughput time is shortened and less capital is tied up in in-process inventories. The possibilities of group work are greater. It is easy to obtain an overall view of what is going on within the shop and to promote employee identification with the product and the company.

Product shops are set up at the finished product level. Flow groups have a similar purpose, but are set up at the machine group level and are a way of organizing component manufacturing. A group of different machines is set up for the complete manufacture

Figure 1
Functionally Oriented Shops and Product Shops

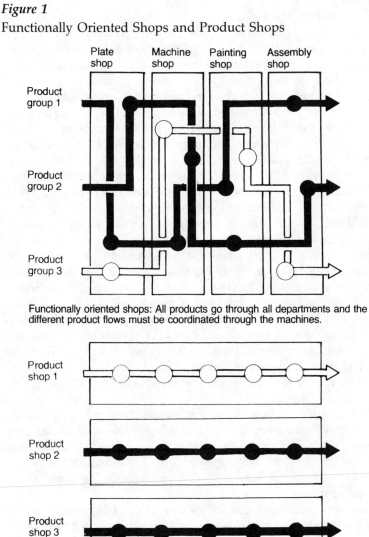

Functionally oriented shops: All products go through all departments and the different product flows must be coordinated through the machines.

Product shops: Each shop is designed so that a certain product is manufactured from start to finish within the shop. Each shop can function as an independent profit center.

Source: Agurén and Edgren 1980, 52.

of a family of components that are similar from the standpoint of machining.

The product shop and flow group principles can complement each other: A product shop can be built up gradually, by creating flow groups, for example, for a single product part at a time. However, there is no necessary relationship. A product shop can be organized entirely without flow groups, and vice versa.

The conventional assembly line can be broken up and replaced by parallel groups. As discussed at the beginning of this chapter, the assembly line is an inflexible system that involves problems with the balancing of different workstations, and also with narrow limits on jobs. With parallel grouping, the line is divided into several parallel groups, each with far fewer workstations than the original line. This means that the task cycle per station becomes much longer, which together with the possibility of group work enhances the content of the job. From the production standpoint, parallel grouping means less vulnerability to disturbances (both technical disruptions and absenteeism) and greater flexibility when changing production volume. The problems to be solved relate to materials handling and the supply of components. The assembly of gasoline engines in Södertälje described above is an example of parallel grouping.

Another alternative to the assembly line is a line divided into several sections, with a production group responsible for each section. If this is planned and designed in advance with regard for materials handling, each group can form its own part of the factory, with its own entrance, personnel facilities, and so forth, as in the Volvo Kalmar plant.

These kinds of new solutions may in turn facilitate further automation. Flexible manufacturing systems (FMS) with numerically controlled (NC) and computer numerically controlled (CNC) machines and robots is in a way "group work," with different machines as the most common "members" of the group and with production in limited spaces.

The new factories reports thus develop certain general principles. We can take the two fundamental principles of the new factories to be "coordinated independence in small systems" and "stability of production." Two other criteria are "attractive working duties" and "a good production environment." In somewhat more detail Edgren (1977) claims that: "Coordinated independence in small systems" is to be achieved by dividing up the big, cumbersome production system into subsystems manufacturing complete products or parts (p. 3f.). These partly independent production units are coordinated by an overriding general planning. "An important part of this overriding co-ordination will be to design systems of economic control that emphasize responsibility for results within the different production units" (p. 8). "Stability of production" is sought through a simple flow layout and an insulation from disruptions as the production groups work fairly independently of each other (pp. 10–14).

Experiences

Any empirically based treatment of the new factories has to consider how far changes of the sort described above really contribute not only to more efficient production but also to "attractive jobs," and to changes in the work organization in line with union demands for self-determination and qualifications (i.e., not only subjective satisfaction). In a discussion based on studies of the motor industry in Sweden, Berggren concludes that many new factories are simply forms of modified line production. "It is true that the jobs (in several Volvo and Saab cases studied) are somewhat less bound and repetitive, but on the other hand the intensity of work is higher (the short, frequent waiting times along a 'traditional' line have more or less disappeared)" Berggren 1982, 12). Examples are also noted in which promising job designs involving group work and the development of competence have deteriorated. Without any clear collective agreements, there is a tendency for job cycles and buffers to be diminished and educational programs postponed. As a supplement to worker participation in the creation of new solutions, there is thus a fundamental role for classical bargaining to establish agreements concerning such quantitative limits as the "least acceptable job cycle" and minimum buffer levels. And all this, Berggren concludes, presupposes a strong and active trade union (1982).

It is now possible to look back at the experience acquired both at Volvo's Kalmar factory and Saab-Scania's engine factory. The Kalmar factory has been evaluated by a labor–management committee. Certain indications are given of the development of job content and the attractiveness of the jobs to the workers. Although work at the Volvo plant in Kalmar is regarded as more attractive than traditional assembly-line work (54 out of 67 workers regard group work as "good" or "fairly good"), 16 out of 32 assembly workers in Kalmar consider that they have no opportunity to use their education and skills in their work, and a further 16 workers consider the opportunities "fairly small." Thirty out of 39 assembly workers say that they have fairly small or no possibilities of training for other tasks at the Kalmar plant, and 32 of them think they have no or fairly small opportunities of learning anything new in their work (Agurén et al. 1984).

During the past years, an intense rationalization process has been under way at the Kalmar factory, which around 1985 had the lowest assembly costs of all Volvo factories. Thanks to new methods and a time-measurements system, production management has better control over the flow. The assembly time of one car has been cut by 1.5 hours, and the supervisor with a profit responsibility for subordinates sees to it that staffing is kept down. The control and adjustment of errors can be more easily achieved in a decentralized way, thanks to the long job cycles and the flexible transport system with carriers. The intensity of work is higher than at a conventional assembly line like that at Volvo Torslanda in Gothenburg. Despite the ergonomic advantages of the Kalmar factory (such as the possibility of tilting carriers, which enables workers to do their job in better positions), and despite a certain job rotation within the groups, injuries from excessive loads are common (Berggren and Holmgren 1985).

Christian Berggren and Anna Holmgren studied the Kalmar facility and reported their findings in a 1985 article. When the factory was started, it incorporated a number of innovations that made the assembly work different from that at most factories. These original ideas are still more advanced than those at most other assembly factories, for which they provide a source of inspiration. The innovations have, however, to some extent been gradually eliminated. One new idea was that the group should be able to work harder for a time to build up a buffer that would allow for a longer break. Because the groups are coupled to each other in a sequence, this did not work in practice. If all the groups work hard at the same time, for example, it is impossible to fill a buffer. The buffers are used today only to compensate for technical disruptions.

Originally there was a possibility of dock assembly. The carrier was moved to one side of the track, and the whole group could work together to finish their job while the car stood still, instead of its being divided up over four or five stations. Taking the carrier aside created a lack of order in the sequence of cars, which the planning system could not handle. With a growing variety of car models, this problem became still more pronounced.

"The straight assembly work in Kalmar thus entails *line jobs* almost as bound and controlled as in the Gothenburg Torslanda factory, although the wage system has no supplement for tightly controlled work. The difference is that the intensity of work is higher on average and the job content greater. The assembly workers often follow the carrier through the area of the group, . . . for up to 25 minutes" (1985, 199). This greater job content is important to and appreciated by the workers. It also shows that assembly work, if it is to be efficient, must not be broken up into intervals of a few seconds.

The idea of group work was an important one when the Kalmar factory was designed, and the physical layout of the factory emphasizes that. The workers seem to identify with the group, and this fact is used by the company to create a common feeling of responsibility for the quantity and quality of production. "This responsibility does not, however, have its counterpart in any real authority and discretion at the group level" (1985, 202). To sum up, with Berggren and Holmgren, some of the main experiences of the Kalmar line:

- As we have noted, the buffers afford no independence as between groups.
- The hierarchical line organization has been strengthened, with an emphasis on supervisors with a profit responsibility; the group is not a level of decision-making so far as, say, production planning is concerned.
- There are no common tasks for the group except to keep the area in order. The workers do their jobs individually or in pairs. Due to changes in the products, it has proved impossible to stick to the idea that each group should assemble a complete function of the car, such as the electrical system.

Berggren and Holmgren report that:

"Group work" has a positive connotation. The Kalmar factory has undoubtedly involved essential changes as compared to a conventional line. But one has to ask what is really meant by "group work," if the "groups" lack both technical and administrative autonomy in common tasks, as well as any discretion for decision-making of their own.

In relation to the goal of creating essentially better working conditions, the Kalmar factory has been only a small step forward. Volvo CEO Pehr G. Gyllenhammar said: "There is a lot still to do as regards job design. I can imagine a much greater freedom and autonomy in work" (*Ny teknik* 1984, 26).

What actually is meant by "autonomy" and "group work" has also been an issue in discussions regarding changes on the Saab–Scania engine assembly line in Södertälje (Enqvist 1983; Berggren and Bergman 1984; Simonsen 1986). Between 1972 and 1983 the engines were assembled in seven small parallel loops, instead of one long line. On each loop, four (women) workers could choose whether they wanted to assemble one part of all engines or one whole engine each. In practice each one came to assemble a complete engine, which equals a job cycle of 30 to 40 minutes. Each loop could run at its own speed, provided it kept to the daily production target. But within any given loop, the women had to work at the same speed, because they had to move the engines at the same time. The work was individual but the interdependence of the four women was high.

The system afforded high productivity, with few errors. The pace of work within the loops was pushed up, and each day's work was finished so early that it was possible to take an hour or two's rest before leaving the factory. A group of U.S. auto workers visited the Saab–Scania plant, and tried working there. They found it superior in ergonomics and environmental conditions to plants in the United States, but noted that the women worked harder than anyone in Detroit (Goldmann 1976). Many women at Saab–Scania could not stand the pace or the stress. They sustained problems with their necks and backs. The levels of sick leave and turnover were high. Production management, given the technical and organizational preconditions, was unable to lower the pace of work.

The solution has been a new production system, in which each assembly worker works individually. After a brief preassembly process, robots perform some monotonous short-cycle jobs (tightening of nuts) and one heavy job (assembly of a flywheel). (The job cycle is thus shorter than in the old system.) The engines (on advanced assembly carriers) are then ready to be "called in" by the individual operators, who then work individually at their own speed, at ergonomically well-designed workstations. As their tasks are completed, the workers send away finished engines and order up new engine carriers according to their individual work pace. It is hoped that this system will eliminate the problems of stress and excessive physical work loads.

The old system, now replaced by individual work, was called by the company "group work" or "autonomous groups." This terminology was criticized by Christian Berggren and Paavo Bergman (1984): The old shop was not an example of autonomous groups because the women could not actually *work* together, and the groups could not make decisions on the planning of production, staffing, or short leaves. In fact, the four women were dependent on each other in a negative way. They had, however, quite a long job cycle, they were close to each other, and they could chat and joke during the work. The company chose to solve the problems by eliminating all types of interdependency and closeness. "To avoid stress, the management introduces social isolation. This is perhaps better from a medical point of view, but at the same time adds a new sort of load in the work as a whole. An alternative approach would have been to develop positive dependencies and higher qualifications in the assembly work, as a basis for a supportive social spirit of community" (Berggren and Bergman 1984, 32).

We have dwelt at length on the development of two well-known examples of the "new factories," because they illustrate the complexity of these developments and that the renewal of working life is an ongoing process, in which the solutions and models presented at any given time are seldom the final solutions and in which new problems will always turn up. Those problems often seem to relate to an employee perspective: job intensity, influence, competence, cooperation, and similar issues.

3. Trade Union Perspectives

How do the unions regard work organization and technology? Decisions by union congresses during the 1960s and 1970s reflect a growing criticism of Taylorism. The unions later criticized the employers' "new factories" group organization.

Multilevel Strategies

Until the beginning of the 1960s, there was little discussion within the trade union movement (or on the employer side) about possible alternatives to a Tayloristic work organization. Detailed division of labor and monotonous work were in fact seen as "an integral part of the technological structure of modern society" (from LO's journal *Fackföreningsrörelsen* 1961:371, quoted in T. Sandberg 1982, 134).

At the LO Congress of 1966, both the congress reports and background reports from researchers criticized conventional work organization, with its repetitive tasks. The 1971 LO Congress put forward demands for new kinds of work organization, above all, group organization. As regards the form of influence, the congress demanded new laws that would give the unions co-determination by means of a statutory right to negotiate both on questions affecting the individual in his or her daily work and on managerial issues (LO 1971).

This multilevel strategy for changes in work organization, and in the companies, was in contrast to SAF's policy, which was formulated during the same period. SAF's policy was to secure the existing power structure in the companies and in society at large, while allowing for changes in the day-to-day job situation of the individual.

During the second half of the 1960s, LO was well informed concerning the Norwegian experiments with the sociotechnical work organization, but hesitated—owing to the strategic differences between the trade unions and the employers—to involve itself in the experiments of SAF's Technical Department. Another reason was that LO was dubious about the group-bonus wage system that was part of SAF's experiments; it was afraid that this might entail competition and strain within and among groups. LO was in favor of a fixed monthly salary.

LO wanted new experiments in the private sector of the same sort as those already started in state-owned companies, which is to say multilevel experiments that would include sociotechnical changes in the work organization as well as changes in the representative system. The idea was that such model experiments could provide a basis for new laws regulating co-determination in working life.

When experiments in the various sectors stagnated or came to an end, LO concentrated its efforts entirely on proposing new forms of influence via new laws conveying a right to negotiate. As we have seen, the employers continued to develop concrete ideas and examples for organization and technology, that is, for the content of future factories. The union organizations thus fell behind the employers in building-up competence in this area. (For an overview of this development, see T. Sandberg 1982; see also Hallinder et al. 1985.)

At the level of general demands and programs, however, the trade unions continued to develop their ideas on the future work organization (and to a lesser extent on future production technology). TCO formulated a multilevel strategy for co-determination. A report to its 1976 congress states that co-determination is a necessary supplement to the employees' influence within groups on questions about design of the work organization and overall planning (TCO 1975, 30ff.).

At the LO congress of 1976, industrial democracy was seen as a continuous process of development. A congress report (LO 1977) and a background report on work organization (LO 1975) contain numerous references to work research and to the multilevel experiments then under way in state companies. LO posited that, although the emphasis was for the moment on questions relating to work organization, influence in managerial issues, at the expense of the influence of capital, must also be developed. Self-determination in the daily work situation (often group work) and co-determination for such managerial questions as planning were seen as two interacting parts in the process of democratization (LO 1977,50ff. 59ff.). LO consequently criticized SAF's Technical Department: "In its development projects, SAF stressed the individual, in a form which complicated collective solutions and the openings available to the trade union movement" (1977, 66ff.).

Trade Unions and the "New Factories"

When SAF's Technical Department published its series of reports in 1977 with ideas and examples of "new factories," it encountered trade union criticism based on decisions made at the LO Congress of 1976. In May 1978, the Work Environment Fund (Amfo) arranged a conference in Uppsala with participants from the trade unions, the employers, and research institutes. The background material comprised reports from the unions and employers, but most of the discussion centered around the "new factories" publications. The formal addresses and the debate at the conference have been edited by Göransson (1978).

The preconditions for the conference have, I think, been well summarized by Bertil Gardell (Göransson 1978, 115). He observes that we have, on the one hand, the employers' side, which despite certain deficiencies can point to interesting experiences and concrete alternatives, but which appears to be refusing to put these efforts toward a renewed production technology in the context of developing a democratic work organization. On the other hand, we have the trade unions, which have been working to develop laws that will give them the instruments to influence the work organization, but which have no concrete demands to make regarding the new technology and lack experience of the connections between employee influence at different levels.

Participants at the conference pointed to good and interesting technical solutions and alternative technical possibilities presented in the "new factories" material. The more dominant theme in the discussion, however, was trade union criticism of the "new factories," with the assistance of criticism from work researchers. Criticism was forthcoming of the undemocratic organization of the "new factories" program itself and of the limitation of the program to the level of the individual.

The vice chairman of LO, Lars Westerberg, criticized the fact that LO had not had any real opportunity to influence either the goals of the "new factories" program or work on the series of reports from the program (Göransson 1978, 20). This criticism was in line with early LO demands (1970) for negotiations that would ensure some control over SAF's local experiments:

> According to information we have received, experiments are taking place in a number of companies spontaneously, some-

times with the label of "autonomous groups" (but without there being any justification for the use of this term), and sometimes with the application of large parts of the solution to work organization problems developed in the Norwegian experiments, but without any thought of accomplishing the same objectives.

In the opinion of LO, this trend is potentially troublesome with respect to the future of research and development work in this area. Many fundamental problems remain to be solved, and much of the experience gained needs to be further evaluated, before we can recommend any broad diffusion and application of autonomous groups. It is most urgent that these serious, carefully prepared experiments not be compromised by errors resulting from attempts to conduct experiments in companies where the necessary conditions are lacking or in the absence of guidance from competent advisors. (LO 1970, translated in T. Sandberg 1972, 164)

Thomas Sandberg notes in his study:

This commentary contains a number of symptomatic references. The experiments were taking place locally, where the central trade union confederations had little contact, and where the local unions seldom had access to resources of money and knowledge similar to those which the employers had at their disposal. The employers were using autonomous groups, not to increase the influence of the employees, as had been done in Norway, but to make production more efficient. (T. Sandberg 1982, 165)

As to the content of the "new factories" ideas, the basic criticism made by both LO (Westerberg, Andersson, and Wetterberg, in Göransson 1978, 20ff., 50ff., and 74ff.) and TCO (Isaksson-Perez, in Göransson 1978; 98ff.) was the limitation of the "new factories" design to the level of the work group and the individual, and the neglect of questions of co-determination at higher levels, such as planning:

SAF talks about a co-ordinated independence for small systems. This independence is subject to such limits, rules and economic control systems that the independence is illusory. The control exercised by the higher decision-making bodies is clear, and is spread out in appropriate doses, through the departments, further down to the small groups. This is in clear contradiction to LO's and PTK's demands, which emphasize above all the importance of co-determination over the planning of the activities of groups. (Westerberg, in Göransson 1976, 20)

SAF's view on this question is illustrated by the following quotation, where the criterion is the individual's subjective experience of independence:

> Purely objectively, one can naturally point to the circumstance that from the standpoint of individual behavior within the "sub-group" the restrictions can be as great as at a long moving belt. But in solving the problem of "restrictions," we have to start from the criterion "experience." Most people do not experience the working team, which works towards common goals, and where there is a natural sense of working community, as a dependency that is forced upon them, with strong and mutual constraining ties. (SAF 1977, 40)

In addition to the basic criticism of the remaining vertical division of labor between conception and execution, between planning and actual work, Isaksson-Perez raised the problem of solidarity: "The groups are isolated from each other, and people are deprived of contacts with workmates outside their own group. The opportunity to develop solidarity is thus diminished. . . . There is also a risk of rejection within the group for those unable to contribute as much as others to its joint production" (in Göransson 1978, 100).

What has been said so far can mean that the opportunities for decentralization underlined by SAF (Agurén and Edgren 1980, 72) are offset by a centralized production control that presents the group with the stress-inducing task of handling variations and disruptions in production (Björkman and Lundqvist 1981, 358). A further criticism is that the material "does not discuss at all the way in which the new technology is developed; or, rather, it presupposes that technology is developed in the traditional way, by experts, and then introduced over the heads of the employees" (Isaksson, in Göransson 1978, 98).

The meeting in Uppsala took place in 1978, during the months in which the negotiations for a co-determination agreement, based on far-reaching demands from LO and PTK, were at a critical stage (see Chapter 2, section 2). The Development Agreement of 1982 emphasizes new technology and a changed work organization. Local development projects can be started within the framework of the agreement. It is still too early to say how far they will lead to the development of concrete alternatives for technology and work organization that overcome the limitations and risks pointed to by the trade unions at the Uppsala meeting. A bipartite program of researcher-supported local development projects run by the Work Environment Fund was concluded in 1990, but the analysis of the results is not yet available.

4. The "Development Program"

By the mid 1980s, however, some progress had taken place regarding more substantial union ideas on work organization. The Swedish Metalworkers' Union (1985), for example, has published a report on "the good work," part of which is available in English (Arbetsmiljöfonden 1987a). We return to the recent trade union initiatives and ideas in the concluding chapter. Also, since the 1978 meeting in Uppsala efforts had been made by the Work Environment Fund and by SAF's Technical Department to start a new joint labor–management program for the development of models of new work organization. In 1982, the same year as the Development Agreement for private industry was concluded, the so-called Development Program (Utvecklingsprogrammet, UP) was launched. (It ran from 1982 to 1987.) What follows are our preliminary comments on UP.

The idea of the Development Program, agreed upon by labor and management on the board of the Work Environment Fund, was to support projects of technological and organizational change that were under way or just started in industry and in the public administration (Arbetsmiljöfonden 1987b, 1988a). The goals of the program were that projects should have strategic importance for the organization, they should involve "new technology," they should have significance for the work organization and skills, and they should be well anchored in the local line organization and supported by senior management and unions. The Development Program provided support (money, consultants, a network) to ensure that the potential to develop further competence and skills was really tested out. The program also documented the experiences in order to make them available for others. It was emphasized that this was not a research program; researchers were employed but as process consultants, not as researchers. Briefly, we can say that the goal of the Development Program seems to have been part of an effort to put the issues of technology, productivity, and work on the national agenda as a common effort by the unions and management.

Some two hundred companies were visited in search of good examples; forty projects were supported, and about fifteen were regarded as so successful that they were presented in separate case reports. The UP emphasized, however, that one could also learn from the less successful cases. A comparatively high proportion of the successful cases came from the public sector. This is an outcome similar to the one in the Front project, and some possible explanations for this are discussed in Chapter 8. Some of the key experiences acquired in the Development Program are summarized here (Arbetsmiljöfonden 1988a, summary report written by the union–employer joint program management). The starting point was an analysis of the business idea: The new technology is important, but the efficient use of it depends on organizational creativity; the emphasis has changed from the need to introduce new technology quickly (which can always be bought or copied by competitors) to the priority of human and organizational development as the main factor in developing competitiveness. "Without a thorough development of competence new technology is often a 'dead' resource" (p. 8).

One very interesting example is an SKF factory in Gothenburg where flexible manufacturing systems (FMS) were to be introduced. The background for SKF's cooperation with the Development Program was its problem with product quality and delivery stemming from a high turnover of personnel and difficulties in recruiting young, well-trained workers; given three or four years of secondary school technical training, young people are not likely to accept a job that they can learn in two weeks. The local unions agreed to take part in a creative project, leaving today's demarcations between jobs and trade unions behind, provided that management also accepted changes and new ideas and agreed not to pick out parts of the new ideas and solutions and introduce them in other parts of the company where the preconditions and the influence secured by the unions within the Development Program did not exist. (Compare this to many North American unions' resistance to new forms of work organization that may endanger the traditional forms of influence; see Chapter 8.)

The project led, with trade union and employee participation, to changes in the work organization, to competence development, and to massive training that was decentralized to the factory level where theory and practice could interact. The result was greater job satisfaction, a better work environment, and increased productivity. The new technology, however, was in several cases a disappointment. As a result, one factory unit maintained its old technology, but with a new work organization with fewer hierarchical levels and better qualified workers with more integrated jobs. This unit has a very high productivity. (The SKF case study is reported in Arbetsmiljöfonden 1988b; see also Björkman and Sandberg 1988. The examples are also commented upon by LO representatives in the program, Frejhagen 1987 and Pettersson 1987.)

The example of the FMS installations at SKF is interesting in a historical perspective. One important discovery made in the early coal-mining projects undertaken by the Tavistock Institute was that, given the new mechanized technology, it was possible to revert to the type of group work associated with the old methods. The sociotechnical principle of organizational choice was thus formulated. The SKF case also shows the possibility of organizational choice; here, however, automation, which had been thought of as a precondition for designing "good jobs," turned out instead to be a spark that helped people to see the possibility of "good jobs" even with the old technology, which had been associated with Tayloristic principles of job design. So other explanations than the technological must, in this case, be sought to explain the Tayloristic organization of decades of industrial work.

The achievement of high quality depends essentially on the commitment of the individual (Arbetsmiljöfonden 1988a). Management and the unions together must create the security and confidence that support the individual's involvement. In Sweden the interaction between the social partners is an advantage when it comes to achieving such goals as competitiveness and welfare.

The Development Program summary report concludes that a "learning organization" is desirable: Advanced technology is seen as contributing to good jobs and to competitiveness, and thus to the ability to secure jobs. It is assumed that people have the ability and the desire to take responsibility and learn at all levels of the organization; competence development is the key to both effectiveness and human development. On the other hand, it is emphasized that there has been a tendency to look at learning and organizational change in too shortsighted and price-conscious a way: The involvement of all concerned presupposes that competence development is seen as a long-term investment. We still have a long way to go: There are still monotonous jobs, shortcomings in training, disparate conditions for men and women, and injuries from physical wear and excessive work loads, which later cost society around SEK 25 billion (U.S. $4.3 billion) a year. An LO representative states: "The trade union movement has a great responsibility to push through a personal development for all employees and a just distribution of the education resources in the companies" (Pettersson 1987).

In line with current trends emphasizing "co-determination" as a resource in business development, the UP summary report says that the unions have been able to create the "security that the individual needs to be able to participate on an equal footing in the projects." Swedish unions have traditionally been very positive toward renewal and technological development. "What has made it possible for unions to hold this Swedish line is that one has been able to take part and to influence the changes" (p. 24). The report also states, however: "For the trade unions there is a difference as compared with the demands of the 1970s for union participation and competence development to be able to participate and represent the members in development work. The emphasis is now on the right of the individual to an active participation in development work and the individual's need for knowledge and competence development" (p. 19).

The summary and quotations above reflect one line of thought within union–employer cooperation in Sweden in the mid 1980s. As we have seen, the picture of the work organization is quite clear: We are in a post-Taylorist era; we have to see to it that all workers become involved in the necessary competence development. But the picture of the role of the trade unions is unclear and ambivalent. On the one hand, the important factor is the development of the influence of the individual. On the other hand, strong unions with a real influence are, according to the report, a basic precondition for "constructive participation rather than delay and resistance" (p. 24). The report bears some traces of a compromise.

The Development Program can be regarded as an expression of an effort to further the spirit of cooperation between labor and management after the 1970s, with their conflicts and demands for democratization. This was emphasized by the employers at one of the final program conferences. The program was said to have created a common faith in development and cooperation, the "bible" of which could be the summary report on the program. At the same conference, union leaders from both LO and TCO underlined the need for competence and training for *all* employees: One and a half million employees get practically no in-company training whatsoever. The increased dependence of companies on their employees' competence was also seen as giving a new dimension to the concept of democratization in working life.

It may be of interest to compare the Development Program to the earlier SAF new factories program. While the new factories were to be introduced in a few steps, the Development Program accords a great importance to gradual learning. While the new factories tried to find ways of creating work roles that would satisfy individuals, given the introduction of the new technology, the Development Program seems to ascribe greater importance to finding technological solutions supporting a flexible work organization. The Development

Program stresses, very much in line with "modern management," the importance of corporate cultures and, specifically, the business idea within the organization as a whole, and in all its parts.

The unanimous and strong union criticism of SAF's new factories program at the 1978 conference can be summarized under three points:

1. The trade union movement had little possibility of influencing the projects.
2. Although interesting technical and organizational solutions were developed, they were all limited to the level of the individual and the small group, while co-determination over the planning and coordination of the "independent small systems" was neglected.
3. The actual development of technology was not discussed.

Based upon the summary report from the Development Program, it seems reasonable to offer the following preliminary comments. The program is clearly confined to the use of new technology and not to its development. (The new MDA program discussed in Chapter 9 relates to the development of technology.) On the first point it is clear that the unions have been well represented on the board and the program management group. This is in clear contrast to the one-sided employer-controlled new factories program. But the role of the unions in the various individual projects seems unclear. It would appear that there was no discussion of special resources to support an independent union development of competence or of networks among the local and central unions involved as a basis for their participation on terms comparable to those of management (see the discussion of "formally equal treatment" in the conclusions of earlier development projects summarized at the end of this chapter).

Early informal union discussions of the results of the program point out the value of participation as a way of furthering the competence of the union and its members; such participation is seen as a supplement to independent union investigatory work. The possibility of a union involvement that is less reactive is also discussed. Attention is also drawn to the need for a further renewal of the union organization and for the involvement of competent members.

On the second point above, namely union co-determination at the company planning level, the summary report is vague. Its emphasis is rather on the role of management in formulating and "conveying the long term goals and giving the individual the support and possibility to participate actively" (p. 24). A role of the unions is to "make the goals clear and to communicate the goals so that everyone becomes involved. This is a necessary complement to the engagement of individual employees in development projects" (p. 16). Apart from this, little is said about co-determination (there is a tendency to talk rather in terms of "influence"). In the union comments on the "new factories," at issue was whether or not they could be part of a process of democratization, in the same way as the sociotechnical small-group experiments performed in Norway were seen as the start of a process of societal change; this does not seem to be an issue in the Development Program.

5. The New Volvo Uddevalla Plant

The new Volvo assembly plant in Uddevalla is expected, for the first time, basically to break with line production, Taylorism, and Fordism in mass car production. How was the plant design developed? How does this human-centered design—based on the skilled craftsperson and autonomous groups producing "whole cars" during several hours—compare with the Japanese team concept and "lean production" still based on divided work and job cycles of a few minutes and seconds? Will Uddevalla succeed? That depends on technological and job design matters as well as on labor markets in competing countries.

In Section 2 above we concluded that the renewal of working life is a process full of contradictions, in which each new step forward reveals new problems. This is well illustrated by this new plant in Uddevalla on the west coast of Sweden. Production tests started in spring 1988, and gradually capacity will be built up to produce Volvo model 740 cars in a new factory in a former shipyard area. As the Uddevalla plant embodies a new concept of car assembly, the "breaking-in" and training period is long. What is presented below is the process of development of the new assembly concept. In 1985 the Swedish government presented its "Uddevalla package" to solve the industrial crisis that arose there as a result of closing the state-owned shipyard. The most important part of the package was the SEK 200,000 (approx. U.S. $34,000) in subsidy Volvo would receive for every person employed, although that was not more than 15 percent of the real investment cost. The rest of the money came from Volvo's tax-exempt investment funds, in total SEK 1.2 billion (U.S. $0.2 billion). Volvo was also able to buy the land and buildings at a low price, and the Swedish government agreed to extend the highway from Gothenburg all the way to Uddevalla, the so-called Scan-link. This facilitated Volvo's just-in-time (JIT) transports and was also an important investment in the region and in future road transportation. Environmentalists and others protested.

The normal picture of the worker in a car factory is a healthy young man below the age of thirty. Volvo will not be able to find many such workers in Uddevalla, so the ambition is to adapt the factory and the tools to accommodate women workers and workers over the age of forty-five years; the target is that in each group at least 40 percent should be women and about 25 percent over the age of forty-five. For example, new tools are being developed with smaller grips to suit women's hands; it turned out that no standard measures existed for women's hands, so at first two hundred women's hands had to be measured! This adjustment means a better work environment and better ergonomics for all workers (*Arbetsmiljö* 1987).

Volvo long kept the planning process of the new Uddevalla plant secret. However, half a year before production tests were to start, *Metallarbetaren*, the journal of the Metalworkers' Union, published an article presenting the main stages of the process and the production-organization ideas incorporated in the plant. (The following is based mainly on an article by Tommy Öberg in *Metallarbetaren* 1987b, and also on *Arbetsmiljö* 1987 and the employers' *SAF-tidningen* 1988. The text has also been updated with information received during a factory visit in June 1989 and from two reports based on a study by researchers who had the opportunity to follow the Uddevalla project. See Ellegård 1989 and Ellegård et al. 1989.)

The project group for the Uddevalla plant met for the first time in February 1985 in Gothenburg. The project had a steering group with representatives from management and the different unions. The unions had full-time local officials working in the project group and its subgroups. The Metalworkers' Union (Metall) had its own reference group made up of its representatives in the project, supported by national union officials. Involved in different ways in the Metall's work were representatives from the national union, the Volvo Gothenburg union, and the Metall local in Uddevalla. These officials have supported the creation of a new local Metalworkers' union "club" at the Uddevalla factory. Also at an early stage metalworkers from ten different Volvo factories took part. Union coordination and mutual support allowed an active multilevel union role from the first stages of planning, although Uddevalla was a new site.

Originally Volvo planned a complete car factory with body plant, painting plant, and assembly plant. Volvo waited for concessions from the authorities for environmental protection. Because Volvo had not received concessions for the body and painting plants in January 1986, they decided to discontinue planning. This event delayed the whole planning process but at the same time allowed time for creativity and rethinking in planning the assembly plant.

The metalworkers' union representatives presented their ideas about the "good work," that is, development of the work content for all workers. Ideas and solutions were suggested in three areas: group work without detailed supervision, training as part of the job, and wage systems that support development of competence on both the individual and group level. (On the role of the unions I focus upon Metall because there is a research report describing its role: Ellegård 1989.)

The first phase of the project was dominated by the production engineers, who proposed a Japanese-inspired *line assembly* layout with all assembly workers contributing to the production of each car. This would mean—and all the problems were known at the time—a continued detailed division of labor, with a job-cycle time as short as two minutes. It was planned to solve the problem of suboptimal use of capacity as less work-intensive car models passed along the line, by making the line more flexible: The sequence could be broken, and one car pass another. But both the unions, Metalworkers' and the Clerical and Technical Employees in Industry (SIF), and Volvo group management rejected this solution. The union representatives regarded twenty minutes as the minimum acceptable job content/cycle time. More radical demands were not formulated in the first phases; the impact of Tayloristic thinking was still strong.

The trade unions took the initiative more in the second phase of the project, and the metalworkers put forward such basic, proactive demands as: assembly of stationary cars (dock assembly); workers' control of pace; a rich and varied work content; and a buffer capacity between workstations. Some of the representatives of management wanted an alternative to the line production. They proposed a solution with eight workshops in series, one after the other, and with each car passing all eight, each workshop with parallel stations. One-eighth of a car was to be assembled in a station in each workshop.

This solution turned out to be very costly, however, so another alternative was proposed. It was to consist of six independent, parallel small plants, so-called product workshops, for the assembly of cars. Each product workshop, with about eighty employees, would build a whole car. Each workshop was divided into four group areas (with two groups each) linked in a series. One would thus have six parallel flows instead of one line. Each group area was to build one-fourth of a car. This meant that each worker would take part in building a fourth of a car, and would thus need the training to assemble at least that quarter of a car. The job would be performed in a dock assembly similar to the original concepts underlying the Volvo Kalmar factory. The carrier with the car would stop in the group's area, so that the group members together could perform their work on the car. Even some unionists wondered whether such a factory could produce efficiently enough to ensure competitiveness. A fair amount of doubt, however, was felt in the project group itself; again and again the group returned—on the basis of technical and economic arguments—to more traditional solutions. But Volvo group management reacted positively to the new ideas.

A training workshop started in spring 1986; activities there provided the testing needed to determine changes and new solutions for the production layout. The training workshop was thus built before the plant; this gives an indication of the importance given to competence, and especially competence and ideas developed out of experience in a craftlike way.

The vision of an alternative was promoted by SIF and Metall trade unionists and by some of the company's bolder production technicians, one of whom had long been working on the concept of "whole-car-assembly" of buses and trucks. They asked: Why move the car around so many times within the workshop? Why not build the whole car at one and the same place within a group area? Although each worker would handle no more than in the above proposal, he or she would be able to see "his or her cars" being finished. This would facilitate learning. This vision of car production without the use of a sequence of workstations linked to each other was put on paper in the third phase of the project. Both the steering group for the project and the top management of Volvo's passenger cars division were skeptical. One important event, however, helped to put the ball in play again. A researcher and consultant at the Chalmers Institute of Technology in Gothenburg took a Volvo apart, down to the last piece, and then constructed a theoretical model for assembling it in a "functional way," that is to say, organizing the assembly work so that all the components that belong together are assembled together. (This is in contrast to the conventional grouping of tasks in assembly work, where the essential aim is to get the line balanced.) An assembly worker was then asked to assemble a whole car by following the new instructions. This proved to be perfectly possible! "Functional assembly work" drastically reduces the time needed to learn the job, as parts are assembled in a logical way, building upon and enhancing the worker's understanding of the car. Around that time, Volvo Group Chief Executive Officer Pehr G. Gyllenhammar is reported to have said that "only the best is good enough for Volvo's workers."

So the vision was further developed. A single group area totaling twenty workers was to assemble the whole car, in the functional mode. In each of the six parallel product shops there were four parallel group areas; there would thus be twenty-four parallel flows. Each worker should still have the competence to build one-quarter of a car. The content of the assembly workers' work would be very rich, as compared to the traditional situation. And ergonomically the work would be better done, thanks largely to the capacity for tilting the car in different ways. This solution has been the basis for the continued work on designing the plant at Uddevalla.

How rich will the job of the individual assembly worker be in this last model? How long will the job cycle be? The model is very flexible, so many alternatives are possible. Each group area is divided into four workstations (or docks). With one finished car leaving the group area every hour, the car could, for example, move from station one to station four and stay one hour at each with one-fourth of a whole car built at each workstation. The car could also stop fewer times within the group area and thus lengthen the job cycle. With this same production layout, the car could also be moved around among not only the four workstations in a group area, but also the four group areas within a shop; this would result in a job cycle of fifteen minutes, which brings us back to the second phase above.

The plant was opened for public visits in June 1989. The six product workshops are divided into two buildings at each end of the materials workshop. This plant receives material from both Swedish and foreign suppliers. Automatic carriers transport parts to the workshops; the plant has a powerful computer system. Much of the sorting of material is now performed manually, but may eventually be automated. The automatic carriers glide between the very high racks and shelves until they are loaded with the components for one step of the assembly work. The carriers park until they are called for from the terminal of a work group. The organization of the product workshops has been further developed from the plans above. Since January 1988, the idea has been to let each group (two in each group area) build a whole car. There are eight groups per workshop with ten workers in each group, so there will be a total of forty-eight parallel flows. Each group has two workstations, and the car is moved only once instead of twice as it was before. This arrangement also requires less space. The first three product workshops were working on this system until summer 1989.

Each product workshop has a shop manager; there are no supervisors, but each group has an "ombudsman" (or woman), a representative who has special training, and who must be accepted by both the group and the shop manager. At least two representatives rotate in that function in each group. The representative takes care of the daily administrative tasks of the group as well as some planning tasks. The goal of forty percent women in each group has been reached.

Within the groups, members are now encouraged to take training in different special tasks in addition to their assembly work. Such tasks are normally done either on a full-time basis by specially trained workers or they are part of the staff departments of the company. The idea is to keep the central staffs small and to create a wide range of development possibilities for all workers; workers with a broader competence are able to meet the variations in production. The wage system gives extra pay to workers who have training for extra competences: in serving as group ombudsman or -woman, in being able to build more than one-fourth of a car, in quality control, production technology, personnel issues, economy measures, maintenance, and in teaching or instructing.

Whatever the detailed layout and division of labor will be in Uddevalla in the future, it will be a car factory that differs from all others and that has a job content far greater than that found in other large-scale car assembly plants. The atmosphere of learning and acceptance of uncertainty has allowed this drastic change from an initial plan for a factory with seven hundred workers assembling a car to a factory where a group of ten workers assembles a whole car.

Many factors contributed to this development: both Volvo's top management and the unions wanted a fundamental transformation of car-building; the enthusiasm of project group members, both experts and company and union representatives; the presence of union representatives working full time on the project and unconventional production technology experts; the utilization of important experience from the training workshop; the climate of learning and openness to new ideas and rethinking; and the time to develop in practice the concept of functional assembly of whole cars (Ellegård et al. 1989). Other factors were the tight labor market in Sweden and state economic support for the Volvo establishment in Uddevalla.

One main technical characteristic of this factory is its flexibility. The work organization and division of labor can be varied, with a job content in assembly work ranging from fifteen minutes to four hours. It would be possible to run different shops with differing divisions of labor, depending on the labor market situation, training levels, and the type of production (simple standard models or complex models with numerous customer-determined variants). In April 1990, the job cycle in three workshops was around ninety minutes, and in the other three around two hours. This flexibility also explains why it is not possible, at this stage, to give an account of the way the Uddevalla factory will be running in the future. The factory has still to prove its economic efficiency, moreover, its productivity is for the moment lower than that of conventional factories, but it is increasing steadily.

A second strategic characteristic from the production-management perspective is the possibility of separating those parts of production that can be automated or mechanized from those that cannot (with the existing technology)—the manual jobs. The rationalization of direct assembly work, typical manual work, aims at raising job intensity—and this management is trying to do with post-Tayloristic methods. Another important job at an assembly plant is the handling and transportation of material and parts; this job will be separate, more routine work, which may be automated later on.

A third strategic aspect of this kind of assembly work, with its relatively rich job content, is that the company may be able to evoke greater responsibility from and motivation among the employees and thus higher quality and efficiency. Part of the efficiency may result from the higher intensity of work.

A fourth strategic aspect is the magnitude of the investment in training of assembly workers. Work in the training workshop has gone on simultaneously with the work in the project and has influenced many of the new ideas. Among other things, the training workshop showed that job cycles much longer than twenty minutes are possible provided that "functional assembly" is used. The initial training course is sixteen weeks long, which allows the worker to assemble a quarter of a car; this is followed by further training periods. This large training investment means that work and pay must be such that the company is able to retain the workers. We have already mentioned new tools. But ergonomic thinking with people in the center affects the whole plant. The assembly workers can do their work in a standing position—hydraulic lifts that tilt the car make this possible. In traditional layouts, about 20 percent of the work can be done in a standing position; the goal is to raise this to 80 percent. The plant will be relatively silent—all suppliers of equipment were given a noise limit of 70 decibels. Their first reaction was that this specification was impossible to maintain, but finally all suppliers succeeded in meeting it.

From a strategic employee and trade union point of view, these characteristics mean, according to the Metalworkers' Union, that detailed control is reduced in the direct assembly work and that the metalworkers will enjoy greater freedom and self-determination at work; they will be more qualified and better trained. Their value to the company, as individuals and as a group, will grow, and they will be less easily interchangeable. Assembly work becomes more skilled. At the same time, new types of managerial control are being developed that try to combine control with motivation. With a high level of union organization, and with rights to co-determination and low unemployment, the Scandinavian unions have a basis on which to develop their influence in this new strategic situation. (At the Uddevalla plant only one metalworker is not a union member.) The situation is perhaps more problematic for U.S. unions which base their influence more on detailed job control. (See Chapter 8 on comparative perspectives.)

According to the Metalworkers' Union, the key remaining problem in Uddevalla, just before production tests were to start, was the *work organization*. Although the production organization was continuously changed, these comments may point at some characteristics that are always important from an employee perspective (Göransson 1987 is the source of the comments below). The rich job content is the result of a mainly horizontal integration of tasks at the level of the individual and the group. As yet, however, little had been decided regarding the vertical division of labor. The union's analysis was as follows: In manual work, of which assembly work is an extreme form, rationalization is directed toward raising the intensity of work. All working time should be used to direct work in actual production; the shortest micropause or task outside this central direct work is regarded as a "loss" in the system.

The Uddevalla plant may, according to Metall, mean that almost all micropauses and "losses" in the system will disappear (see section 2). The intensity of work in the direct assembly work may thus become very high. This may create the risks of injury due to excessive physical loads, and rejection from the labor market. It is not, however, a solution to revert to the old style of line production, with its obvious problems of production economy, ergonomics, and job content. Metall's solution is to find ways of reducing the intensity of work at the same time as job content is further enriched. Every worker should be entitled to more than straightforward assembly work; indirect and administrative work should also be justly distributed within the organization. These indirect tasks include, for example, the handling of material, quality control and the correction of faults, service and maintenance. Other indirect, administrative tasks, including work at computer terminals, are ordering of materials, decisions on work schedules, and the planning of vacation and time off. In the future Metall is proposing that workers become involved in customer contact and other tasks that are traditionally handled by white-collar employees. On some of these points resistance may be encountered not only from management but also from the white-collar unions, as boundary problems between the unions arise. (Interviews at the research project on Uddevalla show, according to Ellegård et al. [1989, 34f.], that the high expectations of work in the new plant were met for most workers, but many white-collar employees were less satisfied with their jobs.)

The integration of indirect and planning tasks with the direct assembly work may reduce the intensity of work. As we have seen, several indirect tasks will be handled by the group itself, and it thus seems as if several Metall demands may be met. A crucial issue, however, is the planning of staffing levels that will create the conditions for a decent intensity of work as well as room and time for training, communication, and cooperation in the group; new resources must be allocated to the teams so that they can fulfill some of the functions by means of competence development and cooperation in the group itself. This is a key issue for union co-determination. Responsibility without power often means stress and pressure, rather than freedom in work. Workers interviewed in a trade union journal (LO-*tidningen* 1990, 13–16) commented on the dependence among the group members and the group pressure not to take sick leave or parental leave, because the group gets no replacement if a member is absent for such reasons.

A further problem from the job content and union perspectives has to do with the management strategy of separating out materials and parts handling from the straightforward assembly work. One important element in materials handling will be putting together all the many small and varied parts for each car, especially considering the large number of variants that are produced. The separation of this process from the assembly work may thus create a new, low-qualified, short-cycle job, perhaps for women workers, organized in such a standardized way that it can be automated later on. This possible polarization between skilled assembly workers and those who put together the parts is another strategic problem for the unions. It may be part of the other side of the coin to the impressive development of assembly work now taking place in Uddevalla. And a problem to be solved in the ongoing dialectic between new solutions and new problems in worklife change.

Although there are still problems the Uddevalla factory, it marks a major step forward in the development of "good jobs" in car production by finally breaking with Fordist line production. And being such a fundamental break with the Tayloristic principles developed and refined over half a century, the new Uddevalla whole-car production design will need years to prove its possibilities and perhaps decades to achieve sophistication.

Like the "Swedish model" in working life in general, the Uddevalla whole-car concept has been declared dead several times. The Swedish model is treated elsewhere. The Uddevalla factory is still running but has problems with reaching production goals, mainly because of logistic problems due to the autonomous decisions taken by the productions groups. Management and unions work with these problems and continuous progress is being made in cutting costs and raising productivity. Solving these logistical problems may also help solve the problems on the human side of high job intensity and stress.

As compared with the Japanese team concept, also introduced in their "transplants" in the United States, stress, pressure, and factory regimen seem to be much less military and more humane in the Swedish group work. It is essential to make this distinction between the Japanese team concept and the Scandinavian group work (cf. Bergström 1990), for the team concept is basically still a Taylorist one, with a detailed division of labor, assembly-line production, some horizontal but little vertical job integration, strong roles for forepersons and discipline, a small role for unions, little autonomy for group decisions, and few buffers. All this results in very great pressure on the workers. Workers are encouraged to develop their suggestions for rationalizing production—without being given control over their work or changing their work in the direction of integration of tasks horizontally and vertically. Job rotation or becoming a teamleader/foreperson are more or less the only ways to develop in their work.

Swedish group work, on the other hand, is characterized by sociotechnical principles of design and union ideas about "good work," which may also be productive. Job cycles are long and horizontal integration is supplemented by some degree of vertical integration, which gives a certain autonomy. Buffers along the production process is one method that reduces pressure on workers to work with high intensity but that may also hide problems in work and logistics. Incitements to solve problems and innovate must be created in other ways. The role of group leader rotates, and all group members may get continuous training for the role of leader and for broadening their production and administration tasks—but of course there are limits to such widening of tasks and demands. And the necessity of productivity and competitiveness may bring forward other mechanisms to raise job intensity. This is a key issue in industrial relations in this type of group-based production, and Swedish unions now argue for what they call "negotiated management by objectives," that is, negotiating production goals, resources, and the like to secure an acceptable job intensity with room for cooperation, communication, and breaks. One recent tendency within

Swedish management's group work ideas is to focus on the production process as a whole and to achieve rationalization and productivity by saving costs and time in the planning and office work preceding and following direct production. The focus of rationalization is on the whole production system, rather than raising the job intensity of the individual worker in direct production. An example of this type of global or "systemic" rationalization strategy is ABB, the new "multidomestic company" resulting from a merger of Swedish Asea and Swiss Brown-Boveri. ABB produces, among other things, locomotives, turbines, atomic plants, and robots for industry. Their "T-50" time-based management project has a goal of reducing all production times by 50 percent. The key figure is the total time from a customer's order to final delivery. Decentralization and competence development are instruments.

As we discuss in Chapter 8, the Swedish industrial relations system, with its strong local and central unions and its co-determination system, is probably one of the preconditions for union and employee acceptance and even positive attitudes toward this renewal of work organization. In contrast, U.S. union reluctance stems from its reliance on job control based on the division of labor and seniority rules.

Another basic precondition is Sweden's long-time low unemployment figures, partially as a result of its "active labor market policy," which has contributed to workers' and unions' positive attitudes toward technological change. Low unemployment and well-trained workers contribute to union strength and demands for "good jobs." Workers leave the Tayloristic jobs, and unions demand job redesign, so both the "exit" and "voice" mechanisms are in operation (Hirschman 1974).

Toward the end of the 1980s, unemployment started to grow in Sweden; the need for competitiveness of industry in face of European integration gained in strength in public debate. The role of the unemployment level seems to be crucial to understanding workplace reform. With growing unemployment, Volvo has reduced its program for redesign of its Gothenburg Torslanda factory, which still basically uses line production. After 50 percent of the Saab automobile company was acquired by General Motors, its new Malmö factory was closed; like Uddevalla, it had group-based production, but with a job cycle of around twenty minutes. Events before the final closedown were a bit tragicomic. The new U.S. management decided to buy back the old Saab conveyor belt at an auction and reinstall it, in modified form, in the Malmö factory. Before this return to Fordism, the decision was made to close the plant. In its other plant in Trolhättan, Saab applies parts of the Japanese "lean production" concept. (This concept is also applied in Japanese transplant installations in the United States. Preconditions seem to be a weak labor market, weak unions, and later paying much higher wages than the surrounding labor market.) At the same time, ABB in Sweden carries through its program of post-Taylorist work organization. ABB does not pursue such changes with the same intensity in some other countries. This may perhaps be understood as an effect of still higher unemployment and weaker union and employee demands in those countries.

So far, looking at the Swedish scene, full employment seems to be a main factor explaining the humanization of industrial work, at least in the short term. But would full employment in Sweden be enough? Is "the good work" possible in one country? The fact is that Volvo tends to reduce production volume in Sweden, while keeping and raising volume in its plant in Gent. In Belgium, production is conventional as compared to Uddevalla. In Belgium, too, unemployment levels are much higher than those in Sweden, job security is lower for workers with frequent absence due to sickness, and pay is higher than for other industrial jobs. These factors contribute to the workers' accepting jobs with detailed control and a low skill level. We conclude that the future of the Uddevalla factory and of "good work" in Swedish car production and probably working life in general depends on similar worker and union demands in other countries, and these in turn seem to be drastically influenced by the level of unemployment combined with worker education and training levels in those countries. Recently we hear signals from Japan of difficulties in recruiting workers for "lean production" in the car plants. Such tendencies may hint at possibilities for a future for "good work" and international union cooperation.

6. A Final Comment

Again and again we find that the employers, in their policy statements and development projects, focus on the level of the individual and the group, giving little attention to vertical division of labor and power issues. But behind, and guiding these local processes, there are central powers both nationally within SAF and within each company's management nationally or transnationally.

The interest of SAF's Technical Department in sociotechnical solutions was of a limited, technical nature as compared with the Norwegian program and Emery's ideas. The sociotechnical solutions were seen as tools by which to solve the specific production and personnel problems of the employers, whereas the Norwegian experiments were part of a strategy toward democratization at all levels of working life (Gustavsen 1976). The Swedish employers' development projects were "confined to influence on the immediate job. . . . The development in Sweden has seen 'shopfloor issues' being elevated to exclusive importance, rather than as stepping stones to other changes. There has also been a clear shift away from human and social considerations toward such goals as improved productivity and reduced turnover and absenteeism" (Gardell 1983, 357). Issues of collective influence and power are neglected (see T. Sandberg 1982, 139). SAF's interest in the sociotechnical tradition can be seen against the background of discussions concerning employee representatives on company boards. SAF (1971) made the policy decision not to cooperate in the development of solutions that took the right to decide, and the responsibility, from management and transferred it to labor. The ownership of capital was seen as something that should convey the right to control its disposition in the future. The superiority of the market economy was to be demonstrated by showing that profitable companies could be organized in such a way that the jobs of the individual employees were attractive.

Union-oriented research and development projects in Sweden during the second half of the 1970s were, on the other hand, of a multilevel character. They were, as we will be considering again in Chapter 4, related to a trade union offensive for democratization at various levels, including co-determination at the workplace.

We have thus encountered again the antithesis between the employers' delimitation to individual and group level change and the trade unions' multilevel strategy of democratization. We also meet here the problem of how to secure structural and institutional support for ongoing development processes. The relation of development projects to either labor or management has the advantage of support from an existing national structure and strategy; on the other hand, the legitimacy of such research and development can be continually called into question and obstacles raised. To relate projects to a specially constructed bipartite structure may have the advantage of ensuring legitimacy on both sides, but the drawback sometimes seems to be the lack of any common and substantial strategy regarding the long-term goals and the generalized application of the results. There can be an overemphasis on procedures and processes, the goals of which are very unclear. With a view to finding a common denominator, controversial issues may be declared "taboo"; these may include power inequalities among the parties. Such a situation, of course, is particularly unsatisfactory for an actor who sees a need for fundamental change and for the democratization of working life.

The tendencies of the 1980s were in line with the comment that Thomas Sandberg (1982) made on several occasions in his study of the history of autonomous groups in Sweden during the 1960s and 1970s: Employers are gradually, and in different phases of development, building up their theoretical and practical competence as regards technology and work organization; trade unions are sometimes offered the opportunity to join in, but they repeatedly decline, the reason apparently being that they are lagging behind and do not have the knowledge and resources necessary to take part on an equal footing. Thus, what is needed is an independent trade union development of knowledge in this field as a basis for participation in joint projects. In the 1980s there were once again, as we have seen, examples of trade union involvement in broad programs, and also in single projects like Volvo's Uddevalla factory. This may be understood as a consequence of the weaker union position due to the recession around 1980, or as an expression of union self-confidence due to the knowledge built up in production issues over the past ten years. Union experiences of these last joint programs seem to emphasize once more the need for independent development of knowledge about production and "good jobs."

We conclude with some reflections based on experiences of action-oriented research into working life during the last twenty years. These conclusions are of course also applicable to organizational changes in work that are part of any special research or development program:

1. Not only individuals and small groups but entire departments, companies, and even networks of companies, should be included in the changes. The vertical division of labor and the relationship between planning and execution may require modification.

2. For local experiments to become part of a larger developmental process, it is essential to establish whole networks of coherent workplaces in specific branches or regions that can support and inspire each other in promoting development. This is emphasized within the LOM-program (Management, Organization, Co-determination) just finished that was supported by the Work Environment Fund. (The Work Environment Fund is a key resource in the development of knowledge about working life. Under a board dominated by the parties on the labor market, it finances research, development, and education in working life. The Swedish Center for Working Life is financed mainly from this fund.)

3. There should be a strong local union organization. The direct influence that individuals and groups exercise over their work should be developed in a way that interacts with a develop-

ment of the collective union influence over the terms of such influence, that is, over planning and decision making at higher levels, for example, concerning production goals and staffing levels.

A further reflection is that the fundamental question may not be the actual forms for relationships between the employers and the unions. We have seen fluctuations between joint work and negotiations. More fundamental, perhaps, is the internal work of the unions and the partly new content of this work in terms of technology and the work organization. The union organizations that in the 1970s concentrated on the formal procedures for co-determination and on a broad build-up of knowledge among their members today must catch up with the employers' lead in the field of production technology and work organization. They must use this "know-how" to enhance professional skills and ensure union independence.

4. The union needs special resources and special support in development projects if it is to be able to participate on an equal footing with management. (Formally equal treatment in a project can mean unequal treatment in practice; the party that already has the resources is in a better position to exploit the new opportunities afforded by a development project.) Such support can take various forms. It can be extended to the union at specific workplaces or it can support the development of a union network. The latter type can consist of support to a network between local union participants in different projects; support for the work of central union organizations in coordination and developing joint ideas and approaches; special research resources to support, follow, and reflect upon the work of union participants; and special research projects to develop alternative technical solutions. (Employers already have such networks, for example, those that developed in the "new factories" program and subsequent activities.)

5. When, in the course of local development projects, one encounters limits to, say, the design of good workplaces and jobs, these may be to some extent related to currently available technology. Local development projects may therefore need to be supplemented with central projects for the development of alternative technical and organizational solutions, from the standpoint of quality of work. The Utopia project at the Swedish Center for Working Life was an attempt to develop such alternatives for text and image processing in the production of newspapers (Utopia 1985; see also Chapter 9, section 4).

4

Local Unions and Technological Change

This chapter contains an overview of local trade union strategies in relation to technological and organizational changes in working life. It is based on experiences of various action-oriented research projects with trade unions in Scandinavia over the past ten to fifteen years. We explore traditional strategies and look at examples of new directions in development.

This chapter focuses on the *forms* of union influence, rather than on the *content* of their demands. This mirrors the trade union concentration on the actual forms of co-determination. Only in the past few years have we seen incipient efforts, within unions and in work research, to develop a more specific knowledge of and criteria for technology and work organization: the policy for the "good work."

1. Union-Oriented Research

Strikes, demands for democratization at the workplace, and an expansive economy are some of the factors that we must assume to have contributed to union demands for a more radical co-determination in working life during the first half of the 1970s. The unions adopted, as we saw in Chapter 3, a policy of building up their own resources, formulating action programs, and negotiating with the employer. In the context of these union efforts toward democratization, a collaboration developed with work researchers, for example, in action-oriented projects relating to technological changes. Trade union efforts and projects have been based on a radical perspective on technology, and several of the unions had to some extent a producer perspective on work, which emphasizes the quality of both the work and the product. In this chapter we illustrate the problems that local unions meet when trying to work with qualitative production issues on the basis of old procedures like the wage-negotiation model. We examine the unions' experiences of trying out alternative models. Finally, we offer a systematic discussion on "analytically" constructed alternative models.

The following discussion of three local union strategies is based on several such projects, including the pioneering Norwegian "Iron and Metalworkers Project," headed by computer scientist Kristen Nygaard, the Danish Due project, and the Swedish Demos project. (For summaries of the ideas underlying these projects, see articles by Nygaard and others in Sandberg 1979, 1983; and Ehn and Sandberg 1983.) These three projects are part of what might be called a Scandinavian School in the study of computers, work, and democracy. A common theme has been the stress on "collective resources" of the employees. (See Ehn 1988.) Other action-oriented projects in this area are summarized in the anthology *Forskning för förändring* [Research for Change] (Sandberg 1981), which includes a report on the Work Environment Group at the Royal Institute of Technology in Stockholm. Here we refer mainly to projects that we ourselves have been more or less involved in, such as Demos and Front (this chapter), Utopia (Chapter 9), and Lake (Chapter 10).

As compared with most systems and organizational development projects, these projects took into consideration societal preconditions and the trade unions as actors. The value orientation was democratization and quality of work. The methodology was a further development of action research, emphasizing also theoretical reflection; we have called it "praxis research" (Chapter 1, section 7).

Many earlier projects relating to organizational redesign and systems development had been influenced by sociotechnical thinking. These have been criticized on several counts. The organic view of organizations conceals existing conflicts of interest. The sociotechnical design of organizations is technocratic, with an expert analyzing and optimizing a system. We find a concentration on the individual and small-group level; collective resources and power aspects are neglected. Individuals are seen as objects for interviews, instead of their being allowed, as subjects, in groups and in their trade unions, to create their own work organization—with the support, perhaps, of research (cf. Sandberg 1985; Mumford 1987).

One common application of sociotechnical thinking seems to be subject to this kind of criticism; such a use by management consultants is perhaps, in practice, the most common and most influential approach. At the same time, we find examples of sociotechnical ideas put into a context of democratization, even at the societal level.

As mentioned in Chapter 1, sociotechnical studies were a part of the Norwegian experiments in industrial democracy. These and others have shown that the scope of sociotechnical analysis can be widened to include not only organizational choice once the technology is given but also choice among existing technical solutions and even the development of new technological solutions (Herbst 1971; Rosenbrock 1982; Mumford 1983). The belief that sociotechnical analysis will result in an expert, optimal solution has given way to a recognition that all the interested parties can take part in a process of reconciliation and negotiation (Mumford 1983). Sociotechnical systems analysis can also be used—and has been used—in projects involving workers and their trade unions, and not management, for example, in the Norwegian priting industry (Ødegaard 1981).

Researchers within the sociotechnical tradition have emphasized the risk of their clients being caught in a hostage situation when participating in systems design. They have emphasized the need for real communication between the experts and their clients in design groups. This presupposes changes in values and reward systems (Hedberg and Mumford 1975, 57f.). The next step is to emphasize the need for "changes in the distribution of power . . . to give voice to human needs and desires" (Hedberg 1978, 8).

If we take the question of user power seriously, we must not restrict ourselves to direct, individual user participation in managerial projects and activities related to technological change. This may be sufficient if we are concerned only with changing the day-to-day work situation, but if we are concerned with questions about the development of new technology and planning and control in companies (e.g., the coordination of "autonomous groups"), we are then dealing with collective issues in which employees' interests are identified and monitored by the trade unions. This is why we must examine the trade union strategies seriously and find ways to further their collective competence in the field of technological change. The Demos project illustrates our efforts to create a concrete researcher–union cooperation. (The plans for this project are presented in Carlsson et al. 1978; some results are documented in Ehn and Sandberg 1983 and Sandberg 1983.)

The Demos project was to cooperate with the local unions in an effort to influence technological and organizational changes as well as theoretical thinking on the strategies and conditions for change. After visits to about twenty-five workplaces and discussions with the respective local union leaders, the researchers selected four workplaces as "field sites": a newspaper, a repair shop, a metal factory, and a department store. This selection was based on criteria that were formulated during the research process in collaboration with trade union representatives. These were as follows:

> There had to be an acute problem that the local union wanted to solve. The problem should have general scientific interest within the fields of competence of the researchers.
> The local union itself should be committed to developing both independent union knowledge and the broad mobilization and education of its members.
> The concrete problem should be one that could be generalized into an analysis of strategic questions concerning the limits of and possibilities for democratization.

With these criteria being met, local "investigative groups" were established jointly with the local union committee at the four workplaces. These groups included both experienced union people and workers with little union experience. The groups studied their own enterprises (using the researchers as "resource persons") and formulated action plans to support both local and central negotiations in issues such as computerization and planning. In addition, these local participatory research projects became a way for the local trade union to engage more of its members.

The work of these groups has provided important data on new possible working approaches for the local unions and has clarified to some extent what sorts of issues can be influenced on the local level. The work of two of these groups has already been referred to in Chapter 1, section 6.

In the Swedish State Railways repair shop in Örebro, the investigative group studied production-planning technology. Management was planning to introduce a new computer-based work measurement system (ISA–KLAR), which could have entirely changed the way in which production was planned and controlled. This system would have allowed detailed and direct control of the repair work. The investigative group in the department store intended to study staff policy and administration. They foresaw dangers in the development of a new computer-based system for the registration of working hours, sales, and personnel data. At *Svenska Dagbladet*, the conservative newspaper in Stockholm, the typographers faced the introduction of a new, computer-based technology. The local trade union group wanted to investigate such problems as staffing levels, work organization, and planning with the aim of solving key problems at the design stage before the new technology was introduced.

Finally, the group at the rolling mill at a big steel plant in Oxelö-sund was responding to management attempts to develop more advanced systems of production planning and control. The trade union felt that the new system would diminish the content of jobs and that the jobs themselves would become more isolated.

Research strategy of this kind focuses on the trade unions as a strategic actor concerned with creating "good work" and democratic decision making in working life. The relationship between union and management is a key dimension in this process, as is the internal work of the trade union: investigations, study circles, and mobilization among the membership.

Certain aspects of internal trade union activities are not, however, treated at any great length in most of the projects. The inability to address these aspects shows up some of the limitations of our research tradition and points to possible and important criticism. One neglected area is demarcation problems and even struggles among the unions as the technology and the jobs change; this question is now being studied in a new project at the Swedish Center for Working Life (the New Front project). We have seen this problem, for example, in relations between journalists and graphic workers in the Demos and Utopia projects reported in this book. A second limitation is that most projects point up the development of knowledge and competence among the union and its members; we believe this to be a fundamental aspect of the development of trade union activities today, but these new elements could perhaps be better related to traditional trade union activities vis-à–vis the employer: strikes, resistance, a broad mobilization behind basic demands, and so forth. And also to the traditional area of wage negotiations; this is to some extent done in the new union policy for "good work" (Chapter 10). A third limitation, and a very important one in our research tradition oriented as it is toward competence development, is that most action-oriented projects have been organized with strong and active local and central unions, and with skilled workers on whom the companies are dependent. This may give a false picture of the influence of the trade unions and of the possibility of designing jobs and technology in such a way that employees obtain "good work" with opportunities to develop competence, social interaction, and so on. Our research says little about the less skilled or low-status workers (like women in the printing industry, in repetitive assembly work in the electronics industry, in retail trade, or in the packing departments of many factories, e.g., the Front project's sugar refinery case) or about the role of the weaker unions. (This third limitation has been commented upon by Williams 1987.)

These limitations exist, and we comment on them in the course of presenting our research, but the focus naturally is on what skilled workers in strong unions may be able to do under favorable conditions. We also explore whether these conditions can be developed in other areas. With these reservations, however, our results are of general interest and illustrate creative developments at the workplaces and within the unions.

2. Three Strategies for Local Unions

The analysis made of practices within the Demos project distinguishes among three union strategies for achieving influence over changes at the workplace. One starting point in researcher–union cooperation was criticism of a union strategy in relation to technological change that could be described as participation in the company's investigative groups. As an alternative, a strategy based on independent union investigations followed by negotiations with management was tested.

Three ideal strategies are presented below, starting with a traditional trade union wage-negotiation model, that is, trade union mobilization and negotiation. The participation strategy is the second, but it was regarded as too easy a solution to the problems encountered when applying the traditional model in new areas. The third focuses on independent union development of knowledge, which is designed to get beyond the "undialectical pendulum" between the wage-negotiation model and pure participation.

Union mobilization and negotiation can be regarded as the traditional institution for negotiations at the local level. The union works independently of the company, clear demands are formulated in discussions among members, and negotiations with the employer are then entered upon. Typical issues are pay and working hours.

Sverre Lysgaard's (1961) theory of the workers' collective, and his ideas on the formulation of "mandates" from the workers to their representatives, can give us some help in understanding the problems encountered by unions in trying to apply this traditional strategy to issues like technological change (see also Hoel and Hvinden 1979). Of course, unions did not always use this strategy before, and it is also true that challenges like technological change are not entirely new to the unions. What is new, however, is the importance and the quantity of these questions in local union work. That is why union strategy and role are brought up today, in both theory and practice, as very basic questions.

Subordinate employees, according to the theory of the workers' collective, build up a sort of opposition system to management and to the technoeconomic system with its immoderate demands. They construct a collective "dug-out," a buffer that enables them to maintain a distance from management. A basic norm is equal treatment among members of the collective. A negotiating institution regulates relations with management. A spokesperson or representative is chosen who is authorized to negotiate on behalf of the collective. The spokesperson then reports back to the membership. The spokesperson is able to withdraw from negotiations, and the workers can also withdraw their mandate from him or her. For the guarding of member interests to function in such "simple" matters as pay and working hours a limited debate within the union is often adequate: These representatives are familiar with opinion and traditional procedures, and they can easily be redirected. (For similar views, see Hart 1984, 60.)

Traditional union issues, such as pay, working hours, and terms of employment can be called *distribution issues* (see Chapter 1). In such issues, there are, as a rule, relatively well-developed and established union objectives; clearly formulated demands, often also quantified and measurable (e.g., in monetary terms); demands based on the workers' own day-to-day experiences; and clearly delimited, short wage-negotiating sessions annually.

It is with this prospect of such clear negotiating situations, and with well-developed objectives and demands, that mobilization occurs and management can be subjected to pressure during the negotiating period. This is a well-tried and tested approach. The negotiating sessions are relatively well structured and demands can usually be formulated quantitatively, within a trade union return perspective (Chapter 1, section 5). But what does the union do

- when there are no clearly formulated union objectives?
- when the demands are difficult to formulate in a simple way and to quantify or measure?
- when the employees' practical on-the-job experience must be supplemented with a more abstract/scientific knowledge of the technology and organization, in order to be able to formulate detailed demands and alternative models?
- when the decision-making process is drawn out over time, and when it is difficult to distinguish any clearly defined negotiations, and when the real situation and the knowledge required change over time?

These issues are different from distribution issues, and may be characterized as the "new" co-determination issues. These include issues in regard to work organization, production and products, and other problems that we have called *production issues*. The situations involved are often "unstructured," and the issues are qualitative ones, which should be understood within a trade union producer perspective. Several of the conditions relevant to the institution of the wage negotiation are not present. Problems of internal union democracy become crucial as demands are not so simple to express as they are not familiar ones.

Moreover, in co-determination negotiations, the trade unions as a rule lack the kind of sanctions they are in a position to use in traditional negotiations, which lead to a collective agreement. Co-determination negotiations, unlike wage negotiations, do not always lead to agreement, and if there is no agreement, the employer makes the final decision (Hart 1984, 30ff.).

What, then, are the unions to do when faced with difficulties in their traditional approach? They have several alternatives. They can try to formulate simply expressed demands and push them in *traditional negotiations,* perhaps actually "translating" qualitative issues into quantitative measures. Questions regarding new work organization can be translated into the number of people at different qualificative or wage levels; an example is job grading in Britain. Alternatively, one can try to distinguish the quantitative aspects and arrive at collective agreements on, for example, the number of hours people may spend per day at a computer display terminal or the length of work cycles or breaks at a conveyor belt. An example from the German IG Metall is a proposal for agreements on work cycles and breaks (see WSI Information 1982).

In the United States, the issues of work organization, for example, appear to be handled from the standpoint of the members' immediate needs and demands, in much the same way as the monitoring and negotiation of wage issues, and often in close association with these. In Chapter 8 we compare our results to European and North American experiences. A Swedish example is the painters union's total boycott of dangerous solvent-based paints in favor of water-based paints. To put pressure on the authorities, the union, with a strongly mobilized membership, formulated this simple demand without the support of experts. They encountered broad understanding in the media and among the public. According to an interview with the union chairman (LO-tidningen 1987a), the boycott strengthened the union as a militant organization and bolstered the self-confidence of its members.

These pure negotiation strategies appear, however, to be less common in Sweden. Perhaps this is a result of the centralization of wage negotiations. It might also be explained by the fact that local unions have been able to develop other strategies.

A prerequisite for the pure negotiation strategy is that management must have the resources, competence, and will to carry out the investigations that the agreements imply. There is, of course, the risk that the union, as it relies upon management for knowledge, will not have the detailed knowledge sometimes needed to control and evaluate management's investigations and proposals.

Whether one tries to translate the qualitative issues into quantitative ones or uses the quantitative aspects only, the result may be that one is grasping only part of the whole problem. (Of course, at times, this may be a reasonable level of ambition!) In quantitative terms, it may be possible to formulate restrictions on a future work organization (for example, the speed of an assembly line and the number of persons with different wages). This does not, however, automatically lead to a work organization that employs people with skills according to the grade-levels that were negotiated. Constructive problem solving and design of new models for work seem to require more in-depth consideration of qualitative aspects than may easily be fitted in an unchanged negotiation model. Nevertheless, given limited union resources the classical negotiation model may still be viable, especially as a *key element* within a renewed strategy.

The second traditional model allows union *participation in management's activities*. Unions can participate in managerial activities both in permanent bodies and in ad hoc groups. Our interest focused on the type of major changes where management usually sets up some sort of project organization, with project management and one or several project groups working on the change. Management usually appoints all the participants, often including someone from the staff affected. (The trade union strategy in this case consists essentially of trying to influence the choice of employees for the group. The Co-Determination Act gives some possibilities for negotiating project organization.)

This may appear an easy solution, especially when the wage-negotiation model fails to work. The union becomes involved close to the decision-making process and often at an early stage. A constructive climate for problem solving may be created, with the trade union contributing expert knowledge from the shop floor and insights into possible reactions from the workers, and also perhaps legitimizing the final decision. The gain for the trade union is that it may influence the decisions made, in the long run, by introducing trade union ideas into the process. Such an influence demands competence on the part of the trade union representatives, it presupposes that union ideologies be articulated, and it may mean that action programs must be formulated (see Hart 1984; see also section 4 below on internal trade union work). It also presupposes that employers can adjust to union viewpoints without endangering their own interests. Because the union representatives lack any instruments of power, they may easily, unless they have a very clear and well-anchored program, become "integrated" in the employer's decision-making process and way of thinking. The producer perspective—if formulated—will appear as the equivalent more or less, of a managerial perspective.

To move beyond the pure wage-negotiation model and the pure participation model a strategy of *independent trade union investigation and negotiations* has been developed. A union following this strategy will, when major changes are envisaged at the company, start an independent investigation. The result of this investigation provides the basis for negotiations with the employer. Unions with a producer perspective may tend to try this strategy. Also, on distribution issues, the union naturally prepares itself by producing a basis for negotiation, but the need for studies and investigations of its own is drastically reinforced in the context of radical changes in the technology and the organization of work.

What was tried out in research projects like the Demos project, in collaboration with union organizations, was a long-term buildup of a relatively in-depth expertise on the part of the union. This would make it possible to clarify the experiences and demands of employees and relate these to a real knowledge of management's plans, the new technology and its opportunities and limitations, and, on this basis, to formulate new, well-grounded, and detailed demands and ideas, which are well-anchored among union members.

A "negotiation model" for independent trade union investigatory work, negotiations and participation in management's project groups was developed within the Demos project (Figure 2).

> The main purpose of the negotiation model is to serve as a form within which the union may develop knowledge and realize its demands in a democratic, efficient manner; a second objective is to facilitate what in planning theory are seen as preconditions for "quality in investigations"—for example, critical analysis, alternatives, openness. Also from this point of view it is desirable for the union to make its own investigations and prepare its own alternatives. (Ehn and Sandberg, in Sandberg 1979)

One shortcoming of the model is its inability to deal with conflicts of interest and perspective within the work groups themselves. Within some of the investigatory groups, for example, conflicts developed between certain of the more experienced, active trade unionists and those with limited union experience. Those with less

Figure 2

A Model for Union Investigation, Negotiation, and Participation

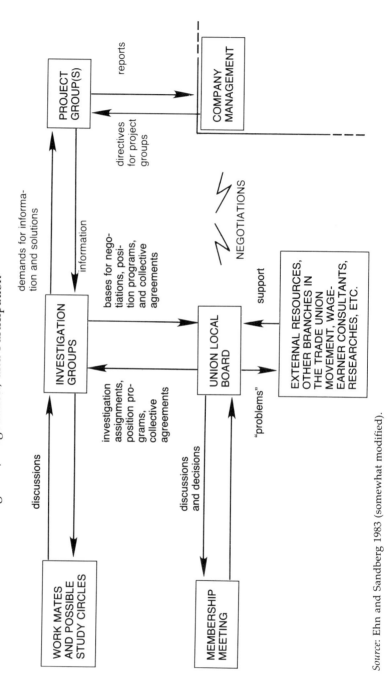

Source: Ehn and Sandberg 1983 (somewhat modified).

union experience tended to appreciate the chance to discuss day-to-day experiences and problems with their fellow workers, whereas more experienced unionists wanted to speed up the discussions and go directly to in-depth investigations of the technological and organizational future of the workplace. If the research design does not handle this problem, there is a risk that the more active and seasoned unionists will dominate. Instead of including and motivating as many people as possible, this approach might then result in widening the gaps of knowledge among workers, thereby undermining solidarity. To counter such a possible tendency among workers, it may be necessary to begin union invesitgative work on two levels, that is, to have one small investigatory group with experienced and active union members and a broad-based study group or study circle for less-experienced members. The study group would try to understand the general issues and formulate demands as well as serve as a general support and discussion partner for the investigatory group. Of course, even with this two-level design, there is still the possibility of contributing to a division between long-time union activists and others. If, however, the two activities are developed in a single context, they could become part of a long-term development of knowledge and activation of many members of the union, thus helping to reduce potential schisms within the worker collective.

The study circle has historical roots in the Swedish and Scandinavian labor movements. Among the characteristics of the studies developed within the movements are the following:

- The leader of the group was primarily an organizer and administrator with no special theoretical qualifications.
- To supplement their own studies, circle members attended lectures or meetings.
- Members learned to discuss, to argue, to show consideration for others, to accept defeat, and to share responsibility.
- The participants experienced a sense of solidarity and community.
- The knowledge the members acquired bore a direct relation to the practicalities of their everyday lives.
- The circle members began study at their own level, and their studies were directed by their own needs. (Brevskolan 1980)

A characteristic of the pedagogics of the study circle is the collective nature of learning. In a dialogue with others, the participants are constantly appraising their knowledge, comparing notes, and helping each other to achieve new insight and arrive at new knowledge.

Everybody must play an active part and make an active contribution to the common endeavor of the study circle. Each one must feel that he or she is the equal of all the other members of the circle (including the leader). The knowledge and experience that the participants bring to the circle must be supplemented with information that the participants acquire by ascertaining facts, reading study material, going on field trips, consulting outside specialists, and so on (Brevskolan 1980).

Tools and techniques used in the union investigatory work have to be adopted to special preconditions, such as limited resources; specific union goals; inexperience in abstract work, writing reports, and planning; and, finally, often only a "tacit knowledge" of the labor process on the part of the workers. The tools used must be concrete and reflect the experience of the workers; most of them are used in group discussions and study circles. These tools can help, for example, in building up a comprehensive knowledge of the pros and cons of the current situation at the workplace regarding technology and work organization. Another area is the understanding of management planning of technological change. Visits to other companies and trade shows and cooperation with researchers and technicians are useful. Tools and techniques are also needed by which to formulate concrete demands on future work and technology (Ehn and Kyng 1987).

It is safe to say that some of the Scandinavian projects have achieved some success. Among the Front project cases, for example, this is best illustrated by the Postgiro and the dairy. It proved possible to formulate well-anchored and well-grounded demands and to push them through. But there are basic obstacles to such a "know-how strategy" on the part of the unions. For example, the union organization has very limited resources compared to management's. Figure 2 shows the problem in practical terms. In the original figure, management was represented as one small box beside all the different trade union activities, rather than the big, open "box" it would be in actual practice. In our society, the union is seldom in a position to acquire the knowledge and plans that can measure up to those of management in quantity and quality—even if it sometimes has the advantage of being better able to use the involvement of employees and their experiences. And even if management is not always the rational and well-informed protagonist it is sometimes assumed to be.

The problem of the union's relatively small resources is exacerbated by the fact that the union's resources must be used not only for a sort of miniature "parallel management activity" but also, and primarily, for work in the traditional areas monitored by the unions, and for contacts with the membership, broad studies, and the like. (One empirical study showed that trade unionists spend as much as 60 percent of their "trade union time" together with the employer [Hart 1984, 39].)

A common and decisive problem in union strategies thus appears to be the limited resources of the unions in relation to the scale and type of change. We have seen how major technological changes are both new and very difficult issues for the unions. In a situation of more limited change, perhaps a modification of the work organization rather than a whole new technology (Chapter 1, section 6), or perhaps a change in personnel policy or terms of employment, the chances are surely better that both union mobilization and a build-up of union know-how will pay a dividend in the form of concrete progress. (The risk, however, is that the simplicity and the application of a "traditional union model" will have been won at the price of overlooking the larger context of which the change is part.) Other circumstances favoring union influence occur when the union itself can take the initiative and when the union tries to influence an issue that is not central for management. In basic technological change, a realistic union approach might be to desist from trying to develop a "parallel management knowledge" and to concentrate instead on aspects of specific interest to the membership, in which there seem to be possibilities for some discretion and free play for action and success.

But it is also important, when limits to influence are encountered, that these limits first be analyzed and also an effort be made to overcome them. External support activities from the central union level may be possible and necessary. Limits may depend on existing technology, laws and agreements, or lack of knowledge about alternatives. Raised consciousness is a first step toward more basic change. We have discussed action research in support of the development of local union work. This may be one way to develop innovative models for union work, but it is not, of course, a part of normal union activity. Another type of such support to unions, and one that may be more continuous and wider in scope, is that provided by wage-earner consultants, who are experts working for the unions. Because in-depth development of knowledge regarding new technology and the work organization is necessary if the unions are to have a role in future production issues, this type of support may be crucial, at least in a period when the unions are searching for new ways of working. We treat the role of wage-earner consultants next and then return to our main theme: the importance of an internal union development of competence, with a key role for the mutual support of different levels within the union movement.

3. Wage-Earner Consultants

In the context of large-scale changes, it can be difficult for the union to know what is most relevant amid all the information available, to know what to look for by way of further information, to process and interpret the information, and finally, to use it to formulate its own positions and demands. (This section is based in part on Kjellén 1980 and 1983; Dilschmann 1981; Hammarström 1983; and on the various co-determination agreements.)

Background

One possibility open to the union is to draw on the help of an expert, a consultant who can guide it in obtaining and processing the information required. The co-determination agreements for various sectors regulate the union's opportunities to use "wage-earner consultants," as they are termed. A wage-earner or employee consultant can be briefly described as a person who works on a defined task at the request of a local union organization and is paid by the employer or from special funds. The experiences of wage-earner consultation are of interest to us because they give indications of the general preconditions for efforts by the trade unions to acquire and use information in an advanced way.

Wage-earner consultants work in different ways. Some are attached to a union organization on a long-term basis, others undertake shorter commissions. Some work exclusively with union commissions, others do not specialize. There are a few firms that work exclusively as wage-earner consultants. Arbetstagarkonsult AB is the oldest and largest of these. Arbetstagarkonsult had been commissioned for a task in the Postgiro, which is reported in one of our case studies (Chapter 5). The union organizations have no consultancy firms of their own, as they do in the field of labor law, although staff members employed at some central unions' research departments not infrequently work part-time as wage-earner consultants. Some indication of the scale is given by the fact that LO has some fifty or more consultants in its network of contacts; roughly half of these seem to specialize in work as wage-earner consultants. A survey shows that one out of five local unions has used consultants since 1977. The proportion is the same for 1978 and 1980. Very few unions report resistance or obstacles when they have wanted to use a consultant (Hart and Hörte 1982, 71).

The functions of the consultant include knowing what information to ask for, making that information available to the union, and interpreting it. This, naturally, involves not simply passing on management's picture of reality, but also demonstrating, for example, the sometimes ideological nature of management's use of calculating methods and other means of communication, and even formulating alternative, union "counterpictures." Support for the development of trade union alternatives, action programs, and organization is possible within the long-term commissions. Short-term commissions for unions usually involve as an essential component the expert investigation of a fairly well-defined problem within the company.

Agreements

The terms on which wage-earner consultants operate are regulated by co-determination agreements that cover the entire labor market. The only exception is the municipal sector, where the agreement does not cover this feature. There is however, as in other sectors, a bipartite fund (Trygghetsfonden) with the goal of preventing unemployment and supporting training for those who are unemployed. Money from this fund may sometimes be used for wage-earner consultation.

At central government authorities, the local union organization is able at certain times, for example, during changes in the organization or technology, to request consultative support from its own central organization. The central union organizations in the sector then decide what consultative inputs should be made within the framework of an annual grant from the state, at present SEK 8 million (U.S. $1.4 million). This sum is established annually in negotiations among the central parties. In the distribution of this grant among individual commissions, the central unions concerned have to be in agreement. After due notice has been given to the authority, the consultant has the right to the information needed for this task.

At state enterprises and consumer-cooperative enterprises, the local union organizations are required to start negotiations with the employer on a plan covering the scale of work, its cost, content, and other conditions before a consultant is appointed. If agreement is not reached, the plan is established, in state enterprises, by the local unions. In cooperative enterprises, the employer can request central negotiations, and if agreement is not reached in these, the right to appoint a consultant and establish a plan passes to the central unions. The consultant receives information in accordance with the Co-Determination Act and Agreement. Agreements in the fields of banking and insurance are roughly similar to the agreements for the state and cooperative enterprises.

In the case of private companies, wage-earner consultation is regulated by Section 12 of the Development Agreement. It is stated by way of introduction that co-determination is based primarily on the development of the union representatives' own competence. In special cases, which are important for the company's economy and for employment, the union is entitled to wage-earner consultants. A consultant can be appointed in other cases if the parties so agree; should agreement not be reached, either party can refer the matter to the Council for Development Issues, a joint body, the judgment of which, however, is not legally binding. After central negotiations, the case may be brought before the special Arbitration Board for a final decision. Meanwhile, the local union has the priority of interpretation, that is, if the parties do not agree on the interpretation, the union's holds until the board has ruled.

A special note in the Development Agreement states: "In cases where the trade union organizations participate in project work or in some other way as referred to in Section 8, it is assumed that the experts employed by the company will make available information for an all-around illumination of the matters relating to what was put forward by all those involved in the project work."

This agreement also contains provisions concerning the competency of the consultants in the economic field (they must be certified accountants or be judged by the union organizations to possess corresponding competency) and concerning confidentiality.

Information and Compromise

By the terms of the acts and agreements, the consultant has the right to ask for necessary information. One obstacle here is that the consultant, like the union in general, often comes into the decision-making process late, at a closing stage when the alternatives have been investigated and a proposal may have already been drafted. (On the basis of fairly long experience, today some unions sometimes manage to get into the process at an early stage.) Another restriction arises from the self-evident circumstance that access to information is strongly influenced in practice by relations to the company management. If relations are poor it takes a long time to obtain the information, and the consultant receives only precisely what he or she had asked for.

Now the co-determination agreements say that if agreement on a consultative input is not reached in negotiations, then the union itself can decide, and, within the central government administration, the central union organizations can make an independent decision. In the private sector, however, the special Arbitration Board decides. That a successful employee-consultation input depends as a rule on management's benevolent attitude toward the provision of information—and of course on its making a decision favorable from the standpoint of its employees—means that the sovereignty of the union as laid down in the Agreements is in practice limited. Attempts are often made to reach a compromise with the employer at the local level. A compromise that makes the employer see the usefulness of a consultant creates a good climate for the consultant's work.

The compromises, however, can be of various kinds. And this brings us from the tactics of acquisition of information to the basic question of the role of the wage-earner consultant in relation to management and the local union. The first kind of compromise occurs where the union tries to interest management in seeing a certain "obvious" problem (often relating to the actual survival of the firm) and tries to find a solution with the help of a consultative input of its own. In the second kind of compromise, management and the union may formulate a common problem that the consultant then treats in an "all-round" way, including specific aspects of interest to the trade union. A third form of compromise may come about when management and the union agree on the necessity of a technological change, but the wage-earner consultant, given that starting point, investigates those problems, aspects, and alternatives that are of primary interest to the employees. The kind of compromise arrived at can depend on the nature of the problem as well as on the strategy and strength of the union.

The Consultants' Relation to the Parties

The development of wage-earner consultants' commissions will depend directly on the development of the forms of co-determination in terms of both internal union work and relations with management.

In the state sector, wage-earner consultation has been taking place for more than ten years, since the Co-Determination Agreement (MBA–S). The spectrum of studies is quite wide, but a primary focus has been on major reorganizations and technological–organizational changes and rationalization. Such "change" commissions are often long-term, and in many cases contain large elements of support for the buildup of the local union's basis of knowledge, action programs, and alternatives. This is true, for example, of the Union of Civil Servants (ST), where the interaction between local commissions and the central union's development of a long-range policy in the organizational and technological fields seems to be quite close. The central union seems to be aware of local developments and is often able to support local unions at an early stage of the decision-making process.

This type of clearly "party-oriented" wage-earner consultation in the state sector is facilitated by the fact that the unions themselves have state funds at their disposal for the purpose, by the strategic awareness of the unions, and also by the principle of public access to documents held by public authorities, which makes the consultant less dependent on management for access to information. These cases are often an example of the third kind of compromise (to use the terminology introduced above). The Postgiro case study in the Front project may serve as an illustration of part of this discussion (for another case study, see Dilschmann 1981).

A basic precondition for this union strategy was local co-determination agreements on concrete change processes, stating, for example, goals like reduced division of labor and union resources for its own investigations. As managements in the public sector gradually discovered that the Co-Determination Act gave unions little power to secure local agreements, "party-oriented" consultation has diminished in importance. Toward the end of the 1980s, most consultancy projects in the state sector were long-term and bipartite. Such projects have also developed in the municipal sector.

In 1975 an agreement was reached covering economy committees and wage-earner consultants in the private sector (SAF and LO–PTK). This agreement was linked to the Agreement on Joint Consultative Committees that was terminated by the employees in 1977, when the Co-Determination Act came into force. Commissions in this sector have tended to be rather short-term inputs for companies in some kind of economic crisis. They have been dependent on the good will—and the financing—of the employer. The consultants have often made expert investigations of a problem area characterized by a "common interest": the short-term survival of the company, that is, an example of the first kind of compromise.

The Development Agreement of 1982 states that local unions are entitled to use wage-earner consultants in questions that are "of major significance to the company's financial/economic position and the jobs of its employees." How is one to decide in advance what questions are of major significance? What does the restriction to the financial–economic position and the jobs of its employees involve? LO's (1983b) commentary maintains that, for example, investments in new production techniques or new machinery come under this heading. The PTK commentary emphasizes that a local union, on the basis of information about the company, may come to the conclusion that change is necessary. "The union then does not have to wait for initiatives from the employer, but may demand that a consultant be appointed" (1984, 80).

The Metalworkers' Union has had the provisions of the Development Agreement tried before the Board of Arbitration. The board has established that if the union has good grounds to expect that a change can take place that will essentially affect the economy of the company or employment there, it has the right to use a wage-earner consultant. The necessary condition is that such fears are based on concrete, newly apparent factors. This and other cases that the board distinguishes can be taken as a specification of the right to use wage-earner consultants that is in line with the views of the unions (Söderholm 1987).

Integrated co-determination was discussed in the state-sector agreement, MBA–S, but, as we have seen above, wage-earner consultation there has been party oriented. Following the Development Agreement's general emphasis on the integration of co-determination into the company's line organization and into bipartite bodies of various kinds, there is an ongoing discussion about the role of wage-earner consultants *if* the tendency toward an integration of co-determination becomes very strong (see Hallerby 1983; Sundström 1983). The role of "party" would thus to some extent be erased for the union, and, consequently, for the consultant. At the same time, it is stressed that this would in any case be a question of long-term changes, and that meanwhile the union would need the traditional type of party-oriented support by consultants. It is also suggested that if the trend toward union participation in management organs becomes dominant, the forms applied in commissioning wage-earner consultants will be affected—whether they are "all-round" or "party-oriented" in content. Instead of clearly delimited tasks, a more continuous and recurrent support within "framework agreements" will probably become common.

One sign that the "party" role of consultants in the private sector can be minimized in the future is apparent in the Development Agreement. The agreement states that when the union participates in, for example, project groups or other management bodies, it "is assumed that the experts employed by the company will make available the information for an all-round illumination of the issues" (Development Agreement 1982, 25). The future will show what this means. Does it mean that management's "ordinary" experts will be required to broaden their investigations to cover questions that may be of interest mainly to union representatives in a group? (In its commentary on the agreement, LO [1983b, 170] highlights this point.) Does it mean that special wage-earner consultants will as a rule be considered superfluous? Or will the "party-oriented" wage-earner consultation be able to continue as a support for the unions' participation in various bodies. To date, wage-earner consultation in the private sector is still mostly short-term, union-oriented projects in crisis situations.

The fact that co-determination in the private sector may become integrated to a greater extent does not, of course, necessarily

mean that there will be no independent trade union work and increase in knowledge. Such independent union work is an important
basis for participation in managerial bodies. Thus, there may still be
a need for wage-earner consultants working in cooperation with local unions.

4. Relations to the Employer and Internal Union Work

The three local union strategies discussed in section 2 were developed and used as empirically based ideal types in union–researcher cooperation in action research projects. To develop these
concepts further, we distinguish analytically between their two dimensions: relations to the employer and internal union work. We
place various activities in these two dimensions, and then combine
them to abstract six union strategies from the three mentioned
above. It should be emphasized from the start that these strategies
are abstractions, designed to facilitate an understanding of concrete
activities, which are often multiple sorts, or combinations. Indeed,
we can say that it is the combinations that constitute the strategies,
and that the six alternatives are rather the elements of which strategies can be comprised. Given a union activity relating to changes in
new fields, we think it is important to have concepts that make it
possible to reflect on the union's own approaches and possible alternatives. In Chapter 7, section 5, we test these concepts in our four
case studies.

Internal union work in regard to technological change may be
weak; its strengthening may require building up a new competence
in this field or mobilization of the membership around basic union
demands. The *relationship with the employer* can assume the character of participation in the employer's project groups or decision-
making bodies or negotiation. Before further discussion, it is worth
noting that we are here considering influence through the union organization. In an interplay between the union executive level and its
membership, a union policy is devised that is pushed in negotiations or through representatives on company management bodies.
But it is also possible, of course, for employees, to a greater or a
lesser extent, to take part "directly" in the day-to-day decision making. Such participation can be promoted precisely by union influence over changes in the organization and supervision of work (Gardell 1983).

In Chapter 1, we noted a new direction of the thinking in managerial circles, the purpose of which was to involve the employees in
the problems of production and in their solutions in day-to-day

work. Management's increased dependence on the involvement of employees increases its propensity to link employees to the company's objectives. It also, however, opens up new opportunities for influence on the part of employees. For the union organizations, it has become urgent for them to find ways to combine the involvement of their members in their own work with an involvement in the union to continue their efforts to alter and democratize the workplace and working life in general (see Samko/TCO 1984).

Such an effort presupposes a development of the relationship between the union executives, and the membership. This could have been set off as a third dimension for study, over and above internal union work and relations with the employer, but we have considered it as a part of work within the union and thus perhaps have not accorded it the importance it deserves.

Relations to the Employer

Participation means that trade union representatives take part in an organized way in management's decision-making bodies and in project groups of different kinds. On the basis of several research projects (Hammarström et al. 1980; the Demos project and others in Sandberg 1981) and on the trade union's own evaluations (e.g., LO 1983b), one can summarize some of the advantages and drawbacks of this type of relation to the employer:

Advantages: Access to the real decision-making center and to information in the early stages of the decision-making process is facilitated. A constructive and creative milieu in which to solve problems of common interest may be created.

Disadvantages: The worker representatives have no means of exerting real power. Deep involvement may lead to an "integration" with the employer through acceptance of that perspective and the responsibility felt for decisions taken by the group. This integration may be an obstacle to contacts with union members and to the development of trade union competence and alternatives. The return for giving management access to "shop-floor information" is unclear; trade union participation can in fact be part of a managerial strategy to make it easier to implement the changes planned.

Negotiations mean formal negotiations in accordance with the traditional institution for employer–union relations, and, also, that information from the employer be conveyed to the union at formal, informative meetings.

Advantages: A clear separation between the two parties is facilitated, which makes it easier to maintain different perspectives. This diminishes the risk of the union taking responsibility for decisions that it does not support; it also facilitates the development of trade union proposals and alternatives. Negotiation is also a well-established institution.

Disadvantages: The atmosphere of negotiation may be hostile, which means that the employer will not be willing to give any early and in-depth access to information and decision making. The negotiation procedure may become a formalistic ritual that falls outside the real decision-making process and does not, on the employer side, involve the experts in various fields. Constructive problem solving may prove difficult.

A Brief Digression on Negotiation and Participation

How frequently is negotiation used in relation to integrated co-determination? How common the different kinds of relationships between union and management and the different procedures for co-determination are in private and public workplaces was studied by Hart and Hörte. A questionnaire survey performed in 1978 and 1980 provides some data on frequency from the responses (Hart and Hörte 1982). These surveys were followed in 1985 by a similar study based on a different sample. The study sample of 1978 and 1980 was made up of workplaces with at least one hundred employees, in both the private and public sector (the building industry was excluded). The sample covered some five hundred workplaces out of a total population of around three thousand. The questionnaire was sent both to the employer and to the local unions. The figures reported below are a rough average of the data supplied by both parties.

In 1978, union participation in project groups took place at 80 percent of the workplaces; in 1980, the proportion had dropped to 75 percent (Hart and Hörte 1982, 52). In 1985, it had risen again to 87 percent (Hart and Hörte 1989, 33; this is a follow-up study, but based on a different sample; subsequent page references are to Hart and Hörte 1982 or 1989). The number of managerial bodies (e.g., the board, local management) was tending to decrease, but the number of bodies in which the unions participated remained essentially unchanged. The proportion of managerial bodies with union participation thus increased from about 45 percent to 65 percent (1982, 100).

Information in accordance with the Co-Determination Act of 1976 (MBL) is provided in several different ways. Easily the most common solution was special information meetings, which were held in 90 percent of all workplaces surveyed. In some 50 percent, information was provided to representatives in joint groups; the proportion, 40 to 45 percent, applied for representatives on managerial bodies (1982, 133). The figure for information meetings remained stable over the years, whereas information in managerial bodies declined to below 50 percent in 1982 and increased to 65 percent in 1985. Information in joint groups increased in 1980, but decreased again in 1985 to 40 percent (1989, 95).

The average number of negotiations doubled between 1978 and 1980 from 11 to 22 and was down somewhat to 19 in 1985 (1982, 148ff.; 1989, 104). The most common method for co-determination negotiations was separate negotiations meetings comprising around 60 percent in 1980 and 1982, but only 45 percent in 1985. Negotiations through representatives on managerial bodies comprised around 50 percent in 1978 and 1985, with a low of 34 percent in 1980, whereas joint groups increased from 34 percent in 1978 to 41 percent in 1980 and 1985. A pattern is thus a decrease in separate negotiations and an increase in negotiations through management bodies between 1980 and 1985 (1982, 160; 1989, 115).

The negotiating organization fell into three categories, each accounting in both 1980 and 1982 for roughly one-third of the sample: only the relevant bodies (managerial or joint); both bodies and negotiations; and separate negotiations only (1982, 191). By combining the forms existing for the purposes of information and negotiation, it is possible to obtain an overall picture of how co-determination is organized (1982, 191f.). The completely integrated type of co-determination (both information and negotiations within existing bodies) occurred in 6 percent of the sample; the entirely separated model (outside existing bodies) was reported in 20 percent. The clearly mixed model was noted in approximately one-third.

If the mixed model tending toward the integrated or separated model were transferred to these categories, we find integrated, mixed, and separative models each accounting for one-third of the study firms in both 1980 and 1982. In 1985, the mixed model still accounts for one-third whereas the separated one has decreased to just above 25 percent and the integrated model has increased to almost 45 percent. As we saw above, this is mainly explained by the growth of integrated forms of negotiations. The tendency is thus that the weak growth of separated models just after the introduction of MBL has changed into a relatively clear increase in the use of integrated models during the first half of the 1980s (1989, 132–33).

The questionnaire material was specially processed to illustrate contacts between employers and unions in different circumstances (Hörte 1980). The results revealed, for example, that companies, and even more economic associations, were dominated by the integrative model, while public authorities tended more toward negotiation. This held true regardless of the kind of operation. The kind of ownership was also a major factor. Central and local government operations were dominated by the negotiative model, while privately owned operations displayed a more even distribution over integrative, mixed, and negotiative models, with a slight dominance by integration. Taking into account the type of operation, we find the most integration-oriented not only among private manufacturing and trading companies but also among central government manufacturing companies. The highest proportion of integrative models are found in state-owned companies.

Internal Trade Union Work

A weak trade union activity naturally entails such disadvantages as dependence on the employer and integration into the employer's decision-making process. The **formulation of basic, simply expressed trade union demands** offers an alternative to involvement in managerial issues. Instead, the trade union formulates basic demands on management; these demands may function as restrictions to management activities and as criteria for their evaluation. In combination with broad membership activity and mobilization in the formulation of the demands, this is the traditional trade union strategy for quantitative questions.

Advantages: Mobilization around basic demands is a well-established trade union strategy. The demands are clear and based in the workers' actual experiences, which facilitates contacts with members and internal union democracy. It also facilitates a clear line of demarcation between union and management.

Disadvantages: As we have seen, the formulation of demands in relation to fundamental technological change may prove a difficult matter. There is also a risk of losing the initiative to management, since the basic demands may be too general to influence concrete decision making. Because the union is "leaving it to management to manage," dependence on management competence will be high.

A **union development of competence** means that the trade union will try to develop its own resources including: know-how, detailed and complex demands regarding both the technology and work organization, and new procedures. The combination of technical, expert knowledge, trade union goals, and member/worker experiences is crucial. The unions may sometimes have special investiga-tory groups; these may in turn sometimes obtain support from wage-earner consultants. Typically, the development of competence covers the whole area of managerial activities and problems, but there may also be a focus on certain specific aspects. The union's in-depth investigations may or may not be combined with the corre-sponding education of members.

Advantages: The trade union is in a position to put forward in a proactive way, detailed and complex demands and proposals at strategic phases of the decision-making process. The union is not dependent exclusively on the competence and goodwill of man-agement in investigating problems of importance to the union members.

Disadvantages: With its emphasis on a relatively sophisticated technical and organizational competence, there is a risk that trade union investigatory groups will become integrated into managerial thinking and ways of working, and thus isolated from the rest of their members. The demanding activity of investigation may reduce the resources available for broad studies and contacts with the mem-bers and thus weaken the internal democracy. Trade union work on traditional distribution issues may also be affected.

How common is the union development of competence? A sur-vey on union influence in strategic decision making in companies with more than fifty employees shows that this varies greatly with size. In companies with fifty to two hundred employees, slightly less than 50 percent of the unions develop their own competence in strategic issues, using study circles, wage-earner consultants, or conferences with other unions within the same branch of produc-tion. In companies with more than five hundred employees more than 90 percent of the unions develop their own information. Asked about the source of data used in a concrete strategic change, 38 per-cent of the unions say they developed their own information (Levin-son and Holzhausen 1987).

Building Blocks for Strategies

The two dimensions can be combined into a matrix, giving us six ideal trade union strategies, or the building blocks for more com-posite strategies. They are characterized by both trade union rela-tions to the employer and the nature of internal trade union work. The six strategies are applied to union work in direct relation to proj-ects involving change. In addition, sometimes in the background,

Figure 3

Local Trade Union Strategies in Project Work

		Internal trade union work		
		Development of simply ex-pressed basic union demands and mobilization	Development of in-depth competence	Weak
Relation to the employer	Participation	A	B	C
	Negotiations	D	E	F

Source: Sandberg et al. 1984, 115.

there are other methods of union struggle such as strikes or working strictly to rule, by which to apply pressure on the employer. Such a conflict can relate, for example, to the very existence or actual thrust of a major innovative project. The union can also, as in the Postgiro case, seek support from outside, not only from consultants, full-time union staff, and researchers, but also via the mass media and public opinion. These are a couple of additions to our matrix, over and above those discussed initially in section 1 above.

Implicit to our horizontal dimension in Figure 3 are assumptions regarding the relationship between members and representatives. The typical relationship in the first column (basic demands) is discussion of the problems and demands during work as well as in big union meetings to mobilize members. In the second column, where more in-depth knowledge is developed, representatives and members will typically meet in union investigatory groups or broad study circles, working regularly at several meetings over a longer time period on the development of information and more complex demands and proposals.

In the matrix we can locate the three trade union strategies developed in section 2 in boxes D, C, and E respectively. In this section, we make a few supplementary remarks, illustrate the possibilities of combinations, and discuss some of the preconditions favoring one or the other strategy. (For a background on strategies, see Sandberg 1976, pt. 3.) It is, however, important to remember that in practice local unions, in different situations, use strategies that are combinations of those that we have so clearly demarcated in separate boxes. The union, as the weaker party, has to use all possible modes of influencing the employer in inventive ways.

Union participation in decision making, without any basis in independent trade union work (C), may conceal trade union inability to exert any influence, may legitimize management's decisions, as well as contribute ideas from the workers' own experiences. Negotiations that have no basis in internal trade union work with the subject matter concerned (F) may be reduced to formalistic discussions that take place outside the real decision-making process. (This tendency may also exist when negotiations have a better foundation.) The functions may be the same, to some extent, as in the preceding case. Both these strategies can be regarded as seemingly easy solutions to the basic trade union problem of finding a strategy for new, qualitative questions, which will complement the traditional strategy (D). In this traditional wage-negotiation strategy the trade union is fairly independent both of managerial procedures and of the content of managerial knowledge and ideology. Clear demands facilitate contact with membership and foster internal union democracy. As we have seen, however, it is difficult to formulate demands over production issues. The union fails to develop any alternatives on its own and simply reacts to the proposals of management.

In modifying this traditional strategy, the union can move in two directions. When it replaces negotiation with participation (A), the union is still formulating demands. But in a relationship of cooperation, it tends to rely on managerial competence in production issues; compromises may be found, and, also, the existing decision-making structure may be legitimized (Skärvad and Lundahl 1979, 101f.) It may, in practice, be difficult to combine participation with a broad mobilization of member support.

If, instead, the trade union continues to negotiate but tries to develop its own in-depth competence (E), the subject matter of such trade union work could contribute to an integration into managerial thinking; or the negotiating relationship to the employer could facilitate independent work that might lead to an alternative content.

The risk of integration, of course, is even greater if we move to the strategy of development of competence, combined with participation (B) (Skärvad and Lundahl 1979, 103f.). On specific questions where the union and management have common interests, this strategy might afford good conditions for early access to information and for constructive problem solving.

If there are conflicts of interest, a successful trade union strategy of this kind would demand great competence and high legitimacy on the part of the union representatives, probably based on a broad activation among the membership (D). Otherwise, the main function could well be a contribution of in-depth knowledge and worked-out alternatives to managerial decision making, as well as legitimizing it. This may be a hindrance to contacts with members and the development of trade union alternatives.

Local Strategies under Different Conditions

Different conditions influence local union strategies. Some of these conditions are treated very briefly, as they have already been extensively discussed.

Type of issue and perspective: The traditional form of negotiations (D) was developed for handling quantitative, distribution issues within a return perspective (see Chapter 1, section 5). The growing importance of qualitative production questions, often seen from a producer perspective, is determining the trend toward a reorientation of trade union strategies, complementing the traditional negotiation model with participation and negotiation based on independent trade union investigation and studies (B, E).

Management's competence and strategy: Negotiation or participation based on trade union demands (D, A) presupposes a management that has the resources and the competence to meet these demands and develop alternatives. A further factor that can influence union strategy is management's strategy of change (Brytningstid 1983, 119f.). In rational and global planning, the entire problem is handled from the beginning, and a detailed final solution is presented. This will tend perhaps to lead the union, in the absence of any possibility of making its own thorough investigation, to decide on a mobilization around basic demands, followed by negotiation on the final solution. If instead, management first presents rough sketches and vague alternative plans and introduces the various components of the system gradually, it may be inviting the union to participate continuously in its decision-making processes or making a gradual buildup of union know-how seem feasible. That the former situation is difficult for the union organizations to handle is clear from both research reports and union programs. The latter situation, which is customarily said to offer an opportunity to "learn" or be "democratic," also has its definite disadvantages from the union standpoint: Employees are often forced into detailed technical and economic discussions on stage-by-stage introductions of machinery in a long, drawn-out process (C), without having any opportunity to raise basic union demands and overall alternatives with their starting point in the organization of work (D and E). (The gradual, informal type of decision making is also an obstacle to articulated trade union influence when participating in different types of decision-making bodies; Hart 1984, 54.)

Trade union resources and level of ambition: With limited resources (of time, people, or knowledge), the trade union's ambitions to develop its own solutions within a producer perspective may have to be reduced. It takes fewer resources to formulate basic demands regarding the social consequences of new technology (e.g., employment, working hours) and to check the consequences after the event (A, D). Another alternative is to give up the possibility of any substantial trade union demands, and "just participate" (C) or "just negotiate" (F). There seems to be a tendency to enter into an unfruitful oscillation between, on the one hand, the traditional wage-negotiation strategy and "pure participation" on the other. To get beyond this stalemate, the necessary union resources must be developed.

Structure of jobs and the trade unions: An important factor is the boundaries prevailing between existing jobs and union organizations and how they relate to the jobs and work organization that would be possible with a "new technology." The development of a trade union producer perspective and of creative alternatives (B, E) may be facilitated if most employees are organized in the same union, or if is good interunion cooperation.

In the case of strong demarcation conflicts between the unions (or among factions within a union), the dominant strategy may tend to be the monitoring, within a return perspective, of such traditional aspects as employment and wages (A, D) (see Dilschmann 1983, 93 ff.). If a knowledge-based strategy is nonetheless developed, this may tend to be done by the (male) skilled workers, with little effort devoted to the larger, less qualified groups (see Gunnarsson and Lodin 1984).

Conflict or harmony of interests: Discussion in this chapter has been based on the assumption that there are important conflicts of interest between management and labor in questions about work organization and technology: a trade union producer perspective would not be identical with a managerial perspective. An essential task of the trade union would thus be to organize an independent buildup of competence as a basis for its influence through negotiations (E) or participation (B), combined with negotiations on basic issues (D). If there is no such conflict of interest, there is no basic need for any development of in-depth competence within the trade unions. It would be enough to formulate demands in such a way that changes assume a socially acceptable character, and to strengthen the management's competence, for example, by passing on the knowledge and ideas of workers to management. This latter task could perhaps best be organized by management itself, directly in the line organization or in "quality circles." Under certain conditions, however, independent union work may give the union the useful role of "devil's advocate" in management's decision-making process.

Co-determination and line organization: If trade union efforts are successful, the workers will acquire better working conditions and a better work content, including better opportunities to influence their own work situation individually and in groups. The trade union may also try to influence the decision-making procedures at higher levels (including, for example, planning) in a democratic direction. It is in order to achieve changes like these that the unions deploy the various strategies that we have discussed above (von Otter 1980 strongly emphasizes this aspect of co-determination).

On issues and in parts of the organization where the trade union has been successful, the need for any detailed, day-to-day trade union involvement will decrease, and the union's role will be more evaluating development and foreseeing the need for changes in the future. The fact, however, that employers, in a country like Sweden, have the fundamental power of decision making in managerial questions will give the union more than enough to do.

5. Conclusions

The conclusion drawn from the above discussion, and from many research projects in this field, is that the more fundamental dimension is the one relating to internal union work. Independent union work, both in preparation and as a follow-up, is necessary in the context of both negotiation and participation. (See, for example, on the Demos project above, Mohlin 1982; Docherty and Loman 1983, 106ff.; see also Chapter 9, section 1 on long-term perspectives, where relations to the employer seem to be a more important dimension and negotiations an important form.)

Given that the combination of participation and mobilization behind basic union demands is probably problematic, the following discussion concentrates on three strategies: the two strategies based on a buildup of competence (B, E) and one on mobilization and negotiation (D). Knowing that the latter strategy is inadequate by itself in production questions and knowing that a union development of competence claims considerable resources, it seems natural to seek a solution in some combination of strategies.

On the basis of a broad mobilization around fundamental demands, the union negotiates with management on the formulation of problems for the project work, on the conditions and forms for project work and participation, and on basic demands and solutions in principle (D). The union also builds up its in-depth competence, which makes it possible to formulate more detailed demands and solutions and allows it to develop visions of and models for future work. In an interplay with this independent union activity, labor participates on a relatively even footing in the dialogue with management over projects that are judged important and with which labor can cope (B). Participation is supplemented by union follow-up and negotiations at decisive points (E and D). The Civil Servants' Union has a well-developed idea relating to formal union influence by stage-by-stage negotiations in connection with any major technological changes; this involves agreeing, in an initial negotiation, on the conditions for saying yes to subsequent stages in the process of investigation as well as agreeing to a final solution. These conditions relate to job security, the work organization, a reduced division of labor, improved service, and the procedures employed in investigations. This idea has been tried out in several cases. (One example is the Swedish Postgiro; see the case study in Chapter 5.)

We tend to see the three strategies discussed in these last paragraphs—combined in different ways, depending on actual conditions—as a possible strategic whole for unions seeking a way in which to handle qualitative production issues. We emphasize internal trade union work as the fundamental dimension and we see the development of in-depth trade union competence as a necessary supplement to the development of basic demands.

In sum, we have argued that the traditional union model for wage negotiation is inadequate for production issues and we have given examples of alternative models. One solution builds more in-depth union know-how and specifies constructive union demands and solutions as a basis for negotiations. Another has union representatives and individual employees participating in different bodies and directly in the line. Participation, as we have seen, has sometimes been adopted as a "simple" solution: Simple in the sense that people have "simply participated" in the employer's decision-making processes, without any independent union know-how, indeed hardly any internal union work on the issue.

One sometimes gets the impression that this is what is meant by "integrated co-determination" or "direct influence." One must distinguish, however, as we have done above, between two dimensions: relations with the employer and internal union work. The former can be integrated in the sense that co-determination is exercised by participation and consultation rather than actual negotiations.

Integration, however, presupposes that at least two things are integrated. In this instance, the two would be the union's know-how and demands and the employer's know-how and demands. These emerge in the course of independent preparations. The union's preparations for "integration"/participation are as important as its preparations for actual negotiations. Indeed, successful participation makes particular requirements regarding purposiveness, know-how, and anchorage among the membership. This is bound up with the fact that participation often relates to complicated production issues with a close and long-drawn-out relationship with the other party. Finally: *A basis for participation is as necessary as a basis for negotiation!*

5

Case Studies
The Dairy and the Postgiro

As part of the European cooperation on research mentioned in Chapter 1, case studies have been made of four Swedish workplaces. These studies were to trace major technical changes at workplaces where local union organizations had made interesting attempts to influence development. It is naturally impossible, on the basis of four case studies, to give an overall or representative picture of conditions in a whole country. Nor was this the intention: We were looking, simply, for "good examples." We therefore do not offer any exhaustive motivation for the choice of cases but content ourselves with certain comments.

Ideas regarding possible cases were obtained from the researchers, from central union representatives of the unions concerned, and subsequently from members of the trade union reference group for the research project. Two of the cases quickly emerged as more or less self-evident examples of unions that were trying out new paths.

According to the plans drawn up for the European project, a brewery was to be included among the case studies. We failed, however, to find any current, interesting technical changes at a Swedish brewery. On the other hand, a research project had played a role in union work on the planning of the new Southwestern Dairy (Sydvästmejeriet) in Malmö. At a very early stage, the local union developed its own base of knowledge and a program of action affording an overall view of the new facility and of the work performed there. With the support of the legislation and agreements, it also negotiated a project organization. As a result, it could enter on a comparatively equal footing into cooperation with the company's technical division.

The Postgiro, the postal check account system, also soon emerged as an interesting case, although it is not at the core of the banking/insurance sector as its counterparts in the European project were. The union consistently tried to apply and exploit the Co-Determination Act and co-determination agreements and the Working Environment Act (AML). From the standpoint of the project, this seemed to contribute to a concrete evaluation of an apparatus of laws and agreements that in the European perspective stands out as radical. At the Postgiro, the union consistently tried to draft an agreement covering both organization of the process of change and demands regarding the content of any acceptable solution. This agreement raises a good working environment, the organization of work, and good service to the customers to the level of measures by which to judge, among other things, the selection and use of production technology. The local union was supported by wage-earner consultants and full-time central union staff.

Both the Postgiro and the dairy are striking examples of local unions trying to involve themselves and influence early stages of the decision-making and planning process. They are exceptions to the general picture described in a national survey by Christian Berggren (1986): Unions have little role in the formulation of problems and the taking of initiative in the first phase. Their most common role in the phase of investigations and developing alternatives is to ask for more information. Only in about 30 percent of the companies did the unions—according to the managing directors interviewed—play a more active role, such as proposing alternatives or setting constraints. Our cases thus do not give a representative picture. But they show what it is *possible* for active unions to do in Sweden today. In Chapter 6, two more "everyday" cases are described.

At each of the four workplaces, researchers interviewed representatives of the union and management and the participants in project groups in connection with the changes. The documents available on the process of change were also studied. Those interviewed were given an opportunity to comment on the preliminary versions of the report. (The full-length case descriptions have been published in English: Steen and Ullmark 1985a [the Dairy]; Grip and Sundström 1985 [the Postgiro]; Broms and Gehlin 1985 [the Machine Tool Factory]; and Steen and Ullmark 1985b [the Sugar Mill].)

1. The Dairy

The Malmö dairy is a member of Skånemejerier (Scanian Dairies), a company that covers most of the Skåne, or Scania, Sweden's southernmost province. The company also has a monopoly on sales of the dominant products within its area. The price of these products is set by the government, within the framework of the agricultural negotiations (see section 5).

The special feature in the planning of the new Malmö dairy was that the employees prepared themselves by union group work at a very early stage. Group work was dominated by members of Livs (the Food Workers' Union), but members of SIF (the Union of Clerical and Technical Employees in Industry) and SALF (the Swedish Foremen's and Supervisors' Union) also took part. This group work resulted in an independent program that not only covered the traditional union issues but also presented an overall approach to the new plant and to work performed there. It was called "A Program for the New South-Western Dairy and for the Future."

This group work was facilitated by a research program in which the central union organizations were involved. Its purpose was to give employees in different sectors access to a planning basis of their own when faced by major technological and organizational changes. The Malmö project was one of three cases covering the dairy industry.

A further special feature is that the union program greatly influenced the development of the new plant. The engineers at Skånemejerier and the consultants who were called in took the demands and ideas of the employees seriously. The project organization was also so structured that the employees' representatives acquired valuable insights into the work and were able to question and discuss all decisions. Most important of all was participation in the project management group. Both parties consider cooperation to have been very good. This well-developed collaboration was also something new in Skånemejerier. Previously, and even to some extent subsequently, cooperation has been characterized more by formal procedures under the Co-Determination Act. In many situations, the union has criticized both the company's way of providing information and its deafness to union views. This union influence, however, does not mean that the new dairy is in all respects different from other new dairies. The differences at the technical level, for example, as compared with recently built dairies in Linköping and Stockholm, are limited.

2. Union Group Work

There were several reasons for setting up union working groups prior to the building of the new dairy. One important reason was the change of generation that had just occurred in the executive committee of the workshop club. This meant that the issues of tech-

nology and organization at the workplace were attracting increased
interest, parallel with the traditional union issues of wages and
workers' protection. A corresponding rejuvenation of the leadership, and a shift of interest toward new questions, had taken place
in the central Food Workers' (Livs) Union. One important result of
this reorientation was the above-mentioned research project. (For a
summary of this process of change, see the chronology in section 6.)

The research project also played a decisive role, in that it established the possibility of group work during paid working hours. The
companies concerned were originally hostile to this idea and to the
research project as such. After central negotiations, however, the
union organizations succeeded in convincing them that union group
work setups would be of benefit to future projects.

Agreement between the unions at the central level also made it
natural to collaborate locally. How well this collaboration worked
varied among the three dairy companies concerned. In Malmö collaboration between Livs and SALF was good, despite differences of
opinion regarding the organization and supervision of work. SIF,
which was affected only regarding the central operations and order
offices, was not as deeply involved. However, agreement prevailed
within the group concerning the content of the program.

Conditions for the group work in Malmö were also special in
that the company's planning of the new dairy failed to start at the
time originally envisaged. It was postponed in favor of a new cheese
dairy in Kristianstad. The reason for this was the rising consumption
of cheese, due in its turn to the system of food subsidies. The effect
of this investment in rationalization was also much greater. The new
Malmö dairy involved no structural rationalization, nor did it offer
openings for any great savings in personnel. It was seen essentially,
as a reinvestment. This delay was not in itself desired by the union,
as the old Malmö dairy was very run-down, and working conditions
were in many respects substandard. It did, however, provide a
breathing space that was used to develop union demands. Once
again, the research project played an important role in ensuring that
this happened.

The working group met some twenty times in the course of
two years. It was sometimes necessary to cancel meetings due to a
shortage of personnel in production. One particular problem was
that all employees were incorporated in a work schedule with off-
duty weeks. Therefore, not everyone could attend all the meetings,
which led to a certain amount of repetition. The group also made a
study visit to the dairy in Lunnarp, Skånemejerier's most recently
built plant. The researchers took part in a couple of meetings and
between times maintained contact with the leader of the group by
telephone.

On the whole, work followed the pattern suggested by the research project, which involved six phases. The researchers devised special printed matter and made it available to the working group. The phases were:

1. What would be the results of a new construction project? A run-through of conditions at new dairies.
2. What is the present situation? A run-through of current conditions in the different departments.
3. What are the union's objectives? A discussion of desirable conditions over the long term.
4. What does development look like? A run-through of technological development, the motivating forces underlying it, and current technical solutions for different sections of production.
5. What demands shall we make? A discussion of concrete, "realistic" demands, and their compilation into a program.
6. How is the discussion to be disseminated and demands anchored in the membership; and how are these demands to be pushed through? A discussion around anchorage and the project organization.

To get a grip on the complicated relationships involved, and produce demands that were actually compatible with each other, work proceeded in a number of rounds. Toward the end, the researchers also helped by testing the compatibility of demands. This they did with the aid of a number of different sketches of the future plant. In the course of work, views and ideas also came in from the other groups set up. This exchange was possible because the leaders of group work at the three dairies were also members of the research project's "editing committee." The Malmö group was led by the chairman of the Livs workshop "club."

3. The Program

The program devised for the new dairy consists of three parts: the dairy in society, the dairy, and the dairy's departments. The programs drafted by the other groups are similarly structured. The first part is common to all three programs. It was worked out by the editing committee, and subsequently approved by the three groups. It contains objectives for the development of the dairy industry from the union standpoint and a program of action designed to bring about changes in, for example, agricultural policy. The other two parts are specific to the group's particular program. They contain long-term objectives and demands adapted to an assessment of what it should be possible to achieve. The second part, the dairy, raises general principles relating to working hours, training, the work organization, influence over day-to-day operations, and the design of premises.

The most important demands relate to the work organization and day-to-day influence. According to the program, the work organization should be built up of self-governing teams of six to twelve persons in each department. These teams should be able to rotate in their entirety between different working duties, so that a team might be employed in packaging one week and in storage the next week.

The daily production of each department would be planned by representatives of these teams at brief morning meetings. The work of the department over the long term would be planned at departmental meetings in which all employees take part and are entitled to vote. The frameworks for the respective departments would be determined after negotiations between the company management and the union organizations. The third part, the dairy's departments, describes the six departments. These do not follow the organization of the old dairy. The most important changes are that milk processing is merged with the laboratory and packaging is merged with the cold storage. The purpose in both cases was to give the independent teams a greater range of working duties around which to rotate.

The program for each department starts with a brief formulation of objectives. These are followed by demands, which raise, initially, the issues of work organization and the control of production in relation to the technical equipment. The subsequent demands relate to the capacity of the technical equipment, the design of the technical system and premises, and the individual machines. Certain demands directly indicate a desirable solution, while others are more generally worded. The majority of the later and more concrete demands have been formulated directly in the course of the group's work. All three groups found it more difficult to formulate their more complex and general demands. The researchers helped with this and also provided illustrations for a whole number of demands; they were also responsible for the graphic design of the programs.

The programs for the three dairies were completed at different times. The Malmö group's was the last to be finished because the project had been postponed. It was printed and distributed to all employees. The Livs union adopted it as a program of action at a meeting held in the summer of 1981. The SALF and SIF workshop union clubs have not made any formal decision of this kind. During the course of work on the project, however, their representatives took it as a starting point in discussions and negotiations.

How well were the program's demands anchored among the employees? It can be noted, quite generally, that the number of employees is limited. They know each other fairly well, and there was a good sense of solidarity at the old dairy. The centrally located dining room played a key role in contacts. It is also clear that many members of the group carried the discussion out to their workmates as work proceeded. It is difficult to say whether this meant that the majority of workers favored the demands put forward. At any rate, there was no opposition. At one of the most labor-intensive departments, packaging, a special meeting was held so that the union representatives in the project could be certain of support for their views.

It has also been difficult to establish how widely the program was read once it had been distributed. Experience shows that many people find the thicker sorts of publications too much for them. Probably only a few people read more than the sections affecting their own department.

4. Union Influence

What, then, influenced the work of the union? The clearest differences vis-à-vis other dairies relate to the layout of plant, the communications system, and the design of the premises. Great effort was devoted to creating a closeness between and natural points of contact for various groups. The central location of the dining room affords a clear example of an acceptance of union demands in this respect. Another important effort was to achieve natural daylight lighting in all working premises. This has been best achieved in the packaging department, where many people work.

However, there are also other important differences. These relate chiefly to process control, and they are due to a different approach to workers' role in relation to computer systems. These systems are less centralized, and the sequences controlled automatically are not as comprehensive. Certain functions that are normally automated at modern dairies are also manual here. The fat content of the milk is regulated manually with the help of what is known as the "cream screw." Here the professional skill of the dairy workers is put to use—and the control maintained over the fat content is at least as good as that at more automated dairies. Much the same is true of the machine that homogenizes the fat particles in the milk. This gives the apparatus operators responsible for milk processing a great leeway in which to use their traditional occupational know-how.

Nor have there been any cuts in staffing. In fact there has been an increase in workers in the cold storage, an increase that is considerably greater than originally reckoned on, because orders are now put together in the cold-storage room, and not in the distribution trucks as before. This has improved the work situation of the drivers. In the long term, however, it is likely to reduce the need for distribution trucks and drivers. After the breaking-in period, certain jobs may also prove superfluous. The union, however, calculates that the end result will be at least the same number of jobs.

Even if the union has thus had considerable influence, not all the problems have been solved. Some problem solving had been postponed until the plant was broken in. Operations started in April 1984. The union and management agreed not to introduce any major changes in the work organization until they knew how the technology worked. This, however, is not the only explanation. The reason quite a lot of important problems remain is that it was proved impossible to arrive at solutions acceptable to both parties. This applied to two problems in particular. The first was the principle of work supervision. The union program demands extensive independence for groups and departments. The company had been unwilling to depart from a traditional setup with supervisors. It was agreed, however, that a decentralization of planning and decision making was desirable. Renewed discussions on this will be started as soon as the breaking-in period is over. So far, the organization and supervision of work follows the principles applied at the old dairy.

The other problem was the cold storage. The union demanded that work in temperatures of less than $+ 16°$ C be eliminated. This demand was supported by the Livs Congress. In the course of planning, a sharpening of the regulations governing work in cold conditions was also discussed by the National Institute of Occupational Safety and Health. However, no new instructions were issued before planning of the project was complete.

The engineers at Skånemejerier were open to the idea of solving this problem. They could not, however, immediately arrive at any solution that was sufficiently reliable in operation. Also, the costs were judged to be high, around MSEK 15 (U.S. $2.5 million). Management, in the framework for a general paring of costs on the project, then decided to postpone these measures. For the present, the handling of goods in cold storage was to be done in the traditional way, that is, working in $+2°$ to $+4°$ C.

The union accepted this solution, provided it was seen as temporary. It also demanded that the company participate in a newly undertaken research project aimed at new technical solutions. The company accepted this in an MBL negotiation (negotiation under the

Co-determination Act). It is still unclear, however, what will happen and when. However, the increased staffing in the cold storage may accelerate the process, provided the result is more automated handling in the cold storage.

How did the union's program acquire such an important influence on the work of planning? Again, there are several answers. One important factor was that *the company's own planning work* for the new Malmö dairy was not seriously under way when the union program was presented in the spring of 1981. (See the chronology in section 6.)

The decision to set in motion the postponed planning operation was taken by the Board of Skånemejerier in the spring of 1980. For the rest of 1980, certain investigatory work took place that resulted in what was termed a "project planning basis." This contained data on products and packaging, production volumes, and preliminary data on the dimensions of the technical equipment and premises. Technical data were also provided on the site, which had been purchased in 1975. This basis was used, with the approval of the union in an MBL negotiation, for a competition (by invitation) for ideas on the design of the new dairy. Those invited were the technical department of SMR (the National Association of Swedish Dairies), Alfa-Laval, and the consultant who had been mainly responsible for the new Kristianstad cheese dairy. A Danish company supplying turnkey dairies also submitted a proposal on its own initiative.

The four proposals were received and discussed during the autumn of 1980 at meetings of the company management and the plant unions. Union work had already reached a stage that made it possible to participate actively in critical scrutiny of the proposals. Outline proposals from the research project were also available as a starting point. The company's technical management and the unions drew the common conclusion that none of the proposals, without major changes, could provide a basis for subsequent planning and project work.

Preliminary project planning started early in 1981. The spring was devoted mainly to setting up the work and calling in consultants. The primary consultant was the person who had worked with the company in connection with the Kristianstad cheese dairy. The union approved this choice. No real work on the actual design had been started by the time the union program was complete. It was presented to the technical management and the consultant by the group and the researchers in the summer of 1981.

Both the company's "production program" and the union's "working environment program" existed before the planning proper commenced. This meant that various demands could be taken into account at the same time that the new plant was being designed. Demands regarding the working environment thus did not enter the picture as adjustments to an already designed facility. As a result, they did not give rise to any of the demonstrable cost increases and delays that managements often use as a reason to reject union demands.

Another important reason for the union's success was the project organization. Such an organization had been set up for the choice of site before the project was put on hold. Before the preliminary project planning, however, the union took the initiative and negotiated a change in this organization. From having been only a participant in a reference group, it now had representation in the actual project management group. Also, it had representatives in the working groups formed for the various sections of production.

This the union negotiated with the technical manager. Somewhat later, however, the managing director learned how corresponding project work was taking place in Arla, the biggest milk-producing company in Sweden. The union there had had to content itself with a reference and negotiating group. The managing director then requested renewed negotiations on the project organization. The union opposed any changes in its representation in the project management group, and no changes were made. Management, however, reinforced its grip on the project by setting up a special control group for the economic follow-up.

Parallel, however, with work on the formal project organization, an intensive informal collaboration took place between the technical manager, the consultants, and the Livs club's working committee, especially the chairperson. The basis of this collaboration was a mutual respect for each others' know-how and intentions. Because the unions not only went to great lengths to accumulate data on the old installation but also acquired knowledge and familiarity with new technical solutions, development trends, and other factors, their level of skills in the qualitative sense of the term was more on a par with that of the technicians. The union's program, which was studied very carefully by the engineers, played a major role in building up this mutual confidence. They could see that the employees' demands stemmed not from a greater concern with their own comfort and convenience but from a desire to assume responsibility for production. The availability of the active support of researchers during the course of the project work and the fact that the technicians treated the discussions seriously, was obviously important for the self-confidence of the union representatives and for the elaboration of their strategy as time went by. Regardless of the character and the leverage that the unions could have exerted by virtue of their strength, it would have proved very difficult to generate an atmosphere of understanding for union demands and ensure that they found expression in concrete reality if the technicians had displayed a different attitude toward the discussions.

This mutual understanding was reinforced by a joint rejection of a proposal from a member of the Board of Skånemejerier to assign the entire project to a firm of contractors on a turnkey basis. The control exercised by the company would then have been restricted to what could have been formulated in a program attached to a contract. The influence of both the technical management and the union would then have been drastically reduced. Together they succeeded in convincing management and the rest of the board that this would mean poor utilization of the competence built up within the technical department. Instead, a special consultant was employed for the follow-up on costs and time schedules.

A third reason for the union's success was the company's financial ability to invest in the new plant. With the renewal of the Malmö dairy, the company would acquire a plant of rare modernity in the dairy industry. No further major investments in the plant would be required for the next decade. The pressure as regards costs was thus not as great as it usually is when planning new facilities. That some pressure still existed is demonstrated by the cutback that took place in the final stage of the project, hitting those employed in the cold storage. However, this on-the-whole favorable situation had been achieved by sacrifices over a number of years on the part of the employees, the farmers, and the owners in the form of lower adjusted prices.

Returning to the dairy in 1990, half a decade after our case study was finished, we find that the two "remaining problems," that is, work in the cold storage and the traditional work organization, have not been solved. In spite of agreements, the research project to develop a new cold storage system has not been realized so far. And decentralization and autonomy in the work organization have not yet been achieved. How can these negative experiences be understood? There are explanations on several levels. As we have seen, individuals were important in the positive developments. Soon after the start of the operation of the new plant, the leader of the local union got another job in the trade union movement, and the director of the production department retired. A new, strong and economy-oriented managing director came, and he emphasized cost reduction as a main goal to raise profitability. And the pressure for this was high from the owners after a long period of heavy investments in new technology and new plants. This economic pressure contributed to the unions' return to more traditional and reactive strategies.

5. Basic Facts

The Company

Skånemejerier is an economic association owned by 2,800 farmers. It is obliged to handle all the milk its owners produce. It has no competition in its area in the sale of dairy products.

The price of dairy products is determined by the government after negotiations between the farmers' organization (the LRF) and the Board of Agriculture's "consumer delegation." The object is to compensate the farmers for increased costs and ensure them an income development comparable to that of other workers. To guarantee the farmers the same price for unprocessed milk regardless of its end use, the dairy organization operates a system of charges and subsidies for different products. These are determined on the basis of a theoretically calculated normal cost for the production of each product. This means that a dairy association that can keep its cost below this level can pay its owners more for their milk. An element of competition thus exists, despite the sales monopoly.

Skånemejerier was formed in 1964 by the fusion of a number of smaller dairy associations. It is Sweden's second-largest dairy enterprise. However, the largest association, Arla, accounts for 58 percent of all unprocessed milk.

In 1981 the company had a turnover of MSEK 800 (U.S. $136 million). Its paid-up capital and reserves were 25 percent of the total, which is roughly normal for the food industry. Its subscribed capital is MSEK 57 (U.S. $9.7 million), of which MSEK 26 (U.S. $4.4 million) had been paid in by 1981. Amortization is by the month. There is no direct yield on this capital. The owners enjoy a share of profits by receiving a higher price for their milk. In 1981, the annual surplus used for consolidation amounted to MSEK 2.5 (U.S. $420,000).

The Skånemejerier board consists of eleven farmers, the managing director, and two union appointees. The managing director and two board members constitute a working committee. All major decisions are made by the board. Sometimes, however, they are simply confirmed after the event. Under the managing director are two assistants: One is responsible for marketing and finance, and the other for production and handling the day-to-day managerial function. The Head Office is divided into departments for personnel, technology, and so forth. The local managers at the places of operation have limited responsibility and authority. They have no budget of their own and are responsible only for daily operations. They do, however, handle the hiring of collectively employed labor and the planning of vacations.

In 1981, the company had 550 employees, of whom 470 worked at the places of operation and 80 at the Head Office. Only a few people at the Head Office are concerned with the development of products and production. When major investments are envisaged, consultants are called in: The technical department has a well-developed network of contacts and is itself responsible for control and coordination. Investment planning is for one year at a time. Requirements are collated by the technical manager in order to produce an investment forecast. By calling it a "forecast" rather than a plan, the management tries to avoid negotiations under the Co-Determination Act.

There are four places of operation within the company. The Eslöv plant produces mainly yoghurt, the Kristianstad plant produces cheese, and the Lunnarp and Malmö plants produce mainly consumer milk. The number of employees at the old Malmö dairy was around 150.

Relationships between the Social Partners

All those collectively employed, including the drivers and the workshop and maintenance personnel, belong to the National Food Workers' Union (Livs). Local plants' branches, or "clubs," exist at the various places of operation. The Livs club at the Malmö dairy has four meetings of its membership a year, in accordance with its statutes. These take place at the dairy, at the end of the working day. Some thirty to thirty-five members normally attend.

The club executive board, elected at the annual general meeting, consists of five persons. It meets about seven times a year. Within the executive group there is a working committee that meets daily at the club office. No negotiations take place without at least the working committee having discussed the question. For some years now the club chairperson has also been the chief safety and health delegate. This particular solution has been chosen because of the current planning situation. He works full-time on union issues. The others on the working committee spend at most 25 percent of their working hours on union business. The club chairperson also serves on the regional executive board and is an alternate on the national union executive group.

The supervisors in production, and the laboratory and local managers, fifteen people in all, belong to the Foremen's and Supervisors' Association (SALF). They constitute a workplace club belonging to the Scanian Dairymen's Association, which in turn belongs to the Swedish Dairymen's Association. The entire club holds informal meetings during working hours once a month. The club executive group consists of three persons.

Other salaried staff at the Malmö dairy belong to SIF. Fourteen of the eighteen members work at the orders office. Together with their counterparts at three of the places of operation, and at the Head Office, they form their own club. Its executive board consists of five persons and meets once a quarter. The club as a whole normally meets only once a year. Only if a major issue arises is a special meeting held for all members.

In accordance with Section 19 of MBL, information to all union "clubs" is provided to the Central Co-Determination Council, which meets several times a year. Important information is also received via the company board, on which Livs and SALF–SIF each have a representative and alternate. For the purpose of disseminating information at each place of operation, there are local Co-Determination Councils that meet between six and eight times a year.

Cooperation in accordance with the Working Environment Act and Working Environment Agreement takes place in the central or local safety and health committees. Their activities, however, are restricted to the classical workers' protection issues. The planning of the new Malmö dairy, for example, was handled solely as a question of information.

Negotiations within the company take place at three levels, namely with the managing director, a departmental manager, or a local manager. Negotiations on wages and personnel issues are held with the personnel manager, and negotiations on technical changes with the technical manager. Negotiations relating purely to operations are with the local manager concerned.

The issues involved in planning the new Malmö dairy can be classified in three groups: principles and financial frameworks, choice and design of the technology, and the work organization and staffing. The first group has been handled by the managing director, the second by the technical manager, and the third by the personnel manager.

If the questions dealt with affect more than one place of operation, coordination between the various Livs clubs takes place on a joint committee, which includes a dairy worker and a driver from each workplace. This committee meets four times a year and also functions when necessary as a negotiating body.

6. The Process of Change: A Chronology

1972   A new dairy in southwestern Skåne is discussed.

1973   Operations at the Malmö Mjölkcentral are taken over by Skånemejerier.

A project organization with a reference group is set up to select the site.

The study on location is begun.

Study on location, 1974–1976

1974   The question of location is studied and discussed.

1975   Decision made to discontinue Malmö Mjölkcentral.

Study preparatory to modifications at the Kristianstad cheese dairy undertaken.

Revision of priorities in the investment plan—decision to expand the cheese dairy before building the new southwestern dairy.

Site contract signed with Malmö City for the southwestern dairy.

Study of finances and time schedule 1977–1980

1977   A freeze on investments is discussed.

Decision is made regarding new investments in Kristianstad.

Improvements to the Malmö dairy discussed.

Decision in principle to build the southwestern dairy as soon as possible.

1978   Decision to discontinue the dairy in Hässleholm.

Decision regarding certain investments on the new site.

The union discusses collaboration with the research project at the Institute of Technology, Stockholm.

Work on the union program

1979   The union's Working Environment Group starts work on its program, with the assistance of researchers.

The investment costs in Kristianstad worry the Board; it becomes uncertain whether the investment in the southwestern dairy will materialize.

The managing director leaves and the previous vice managing director succeeds.

Election of a new club chairperson of Livs.

Decision to close the plant in Skurup and the cheese-making plant in Eslöv.

Study of programs and sketches 1980–1981

1980   The company's engineers draft a brief program of production volumes for the southwestern dairy.

The company requests "ideas sketches" for the southwestern dairy from various consultants/suppliers.

Time schedules and finance plans are discussed.

Negotiations concerning the project organization are held on the initiative of the union.

Four outline proposals submitted are discussed and evaluated.

Management starts fresh negotiations on the project organization.

Preliminary project planning 1981–1982

1981   The project organization's various groups are appointed, with representatives of management, the unions, and employees from different departments.

The project organization is determined through negotiations.

Preliminary project planning begins.

The Working Environment Group's proposal for a program of action is completed and accepted at club meetings.

Sketches drafted of the layout of the southwestern dairy.

Guiding principles for the project are established.

Study of the materials handling system performed.

Different forms of contracting are discussed.

General sketches are discussed.

The machinery layout in packaging discussed.

Decision to continue the use of gable-top packaging.

Decision to build under own auspices.

Study of layout plan.

Continued discussion of the layout; the cold storage designed with heated zones.

The investment in the southwestern dairy is estimated at MSEK 195 (or U.S. $33 million); with index changes and interest the total investment cost in 1984 would be MSEK 220 (U.S. $37.3 million).

Project planning 1982–1983

1982   Negotiations and a decision on the basis for project planning after certain cutbacks, especially on cold-storage space.

Negotiations and decision on a modified project organization during the project planning phase.

Establishment of a time schedule for the project.

The board decides to make the investment.

Negotiations and a decision on the purchase of packaging machines.

Negotiations and decisions on various contracted works.

Negotiations and design of the cold storage; decision on traditional handling, provided the company collaborates with the research project on the problem of frigid working conditions.

Negotiations and a decision on control equipment.

Work begins on the foundations.

Study of the blanks feed (semimanufactured packages).

Negotiations and a decision on the contract for the shell of the building and certain other remaining contracted works. The cost of the investment is calculated at MSEK 204 (U.S. $34.6 million), which, with index adjustment and interest, means that the budget of MSEK 220 (U.S. $37.3 million) holds good.

Construction

1983   Installation work commences.

Test operation at the end of the year.

Occupation April 1984

1983–   Existing technology and organization were refined. No solu-
1990   tion was found to work in the cold storage, and the old work organization with little operator autonomy persisted.

7. The Postgiro

The Postgiro is one of Sweden's most highly mechanized workplaces. The Postgiro, or postal check account system, has been using office machinery since 1948. Today, some 5,500 persons are employed in the planning, design, and execution of Postgiro operations. Actual execution consists of receiving, recording, and booking incoming and outgoing payments in Postgiro accounts.

In terms of actual numbers, women predominate at the Postgiro, but men predominate in positions of authority. As a workplace, the Postgiro recalls the old films from American insurance companies. The women sit in large open offices, registering or coding in payment orders. The basic service provided has been fairly simple to standardize. A high proportion of the growth in volume has therefore been coped with by an increased degree of mechanization.

Since 1948 the Postgiro has worked with various mechanical equipment for the coding of data on payments. With these machines, it has been possible to convert written information into holes in paper, punched cards or tape, or, as at present, the special optical character recognition (OCR), characters that can be read by machine. The day-to-day work consists of two activities or work processes, namely, the planning of work at the Postgiro so that it can be swiftly and correctly performed, and the registration and booking of incoming payment orders. A customer (A) sends in a payment order (step 1). The Postgiro registers the order. The payment slip and—if the customer has his or her own Postgiro account—a balance statement is then sent to customer (B) who is to receive the money (step 2). An account statement with verification and the new balance is returned to the customer (A) who has originated the payment order (step 3).

This simple routine is complicated by the time limits set by the work, the volume, the competence of staff, the technical equipment, and the rest. Since the very special commodity concerned, money, is highly desirable, the control requirements are stringent. Errors occur for various reasons in the course of the work, and these have to be dealt with. A normal payment order should be expedited within twenty-four hours from the time the Postgiro has received it.

8. Successive Changes in the System

Payments must be handled efficiently, which means that another important activity is reviewing operations and adapting them to changing conditions.

The management's views and assumptions regarding rational and efficient methods of work have been launched and tested, originally on an experimental basis and subsequently on the full scale. When a new system was introduced at specific departments or in certain specific routines, the demand for modifications of other routines increased. Operations today are fairly well integrated. The administrative work has now come to resemble industrial production. Working methods and systems at the Postgiro have developed in a series of "leaps."

The latest major revision of the bookkeeping system started in 1970. The qualitative change was a transition to the optical reading of forms (OCR), text that was easy to read and could also be read by machine. The recoding to OCR is performed by personnel at the Postgiro, unless the forms are precoded on arrival. The coded forms are read onto magnetic tape by special readers and, at the same time, microfilmed. Payment orders are then run off against the computer register of all accounts, and bookkeeping takes place. Results in the form of verifications and statements of account are put into envelopes by the accounting staff and sent to the customers.

This system is called Giro 70, or G 70. By 1976, G 70 was complete. But while the transition had been effected in one sense, systems work was again accelerating at the Organization Department.

What was described as a "final stage" proved in practice to be a transitional stage.

The report on which the further development of G 70 was based is quite logically titled "Development of the Postgiro's New Production System," subsequently known as the PGP project. The modification or system envisaged in both G 70 and the new PGP project relates to the registration and transcription of forms. It was originally intended that this change be introduced by 1980. The timetable has been moved forward, and only minor modifications had been introduced by the time our work on the case study was completed. Soon after, in 1985, a final decision was taken to introduce the new systems. In the same year, the new registration system was introduced at full scale. In 1986, a pilot system for electronic registration and transcription of forms (based on image processing) and automatic inserting of forms in envelopes was tried out and successively introduced during 1987 and the years thereafter.

The present summary describes and analyzes the work of system development during the above-mentioned period, that is, until 1984, with some hints of development until 1990.

The Threat of the "Paperless Office Factory"

The PGP project was initiated in 1977 through a technical study by the Organization Department that looked at how work at the Postgiro would change after the new technology was introduced. The technique used for this is known as image processing. It means that the forms are video-filmed at the Postgiro and that subsequent processing takes place with the electronic image. Sorting, supplementation of data, reconciling, correction, and the rest can take place electronically with the help of video screens. The documents would be available in the form of video pictures of the originals. In the G 70 system, certain of the original documents are sent back to the customers. In a visual handling system, this would be done by a laser printer producing a "new original" from the electronic video copy of the original document. In this way, the coordinated sorting of (the copy of) the original document with extracts from accounts and insertion in envelopes could be performed mechanically.

The initial proposal meant that the bookkeeping staff would:

- lose a great deal of their afternoon work (insertion of documents in envelopes)
- lose their physical overview of the process

- only register certain data, unrelated to any larger whole
- have their jobs reduced to looking at the screen and registering what was apparently ordered up at random
- lose the possibility of making their own judgments regarding the measures to be taken when an account showed a deficit.

The trade union organizations reacted strongly to these proposals. They felt that the employer had not complied with MBA-S (the Co-Determination Agreement for the Central Government Sector), in that this pilot study had been performed without negotiating with the union.

The management's negotiating bid for image processing was thus rejected by the unions when it was formally presented in June 1979. They demanded instead information prior to negotiation under Section 11 of the Co-Determination Act. They demanded that the employer:

- draft a plan for providing information to personnel, indicating the connections between this and other projects
- report on the market premises for the handling of payments
- state whether the Postal Administration or the Postgiro was the party with which to negotiate
- adjourn the meeting until 10 September 1979.

The management accepted that the meeting had been by way of information only and that negotiations should be postponed until September. After this meeting in June 1979 the trade union calculated, with the aid of its employee consultants, the consequences of the solutions proposed to the personnel: Approximately six hundred to eight hundred jobs were threatened, assuming an unchanged volume of work (the documentation provided as a basis for negotiations contained no forecast regarding volume changes).

The trade union kept its members informed regarding the Postgiro's plans through the ST (the Civil Servants' Union) membership's newsletter "Fackblixten" and at major meetings. Preparations were made during the summer for negotiations in the autumn.

The head of the Postgiro commented on the trade union's information in a written statement to all personnel within the Postgiro. He stressed the need to "invest in new technology," to "look after the personnel," and for "consultation and understanding" with the trade union organizations.

Negotiating a Production System Agreement

In September 1979, negotiations began on the development of a new production system. The Postgiro management wanted to negotiate on a preliminary report on image processing from April 1979, which was a continuation of the technical study of 1977. The union organizations were concerned that a local collective agreement for the project be negotiated, that work on the project should return to its starting point, and that the union's demands of June 1979 should be met.

Negotiations were adjourned on several occasions during the autumn. The union's demands regarding the project were organized around the following essential points: improved work, both physically and from the organizational standpoint; an unchanged level of personnel; unchanged customer accounting; and continued high competitiveness on the payments market and labor market. It was further demanded that the connections between this and other projects should be reported and further work on the project be planned carefully.

During the autumn, the Postgiro management met the demands made in June and the above demands regarding the project. Written information was distributed to all employees. The union also informed its membership of the agreement. The objectives of the project, and the measures it was to cover, were incorporated in the "Local Collective Agreement on the Development of a New Production System for the Postgiro" (12 November 1979) (Postgiro 1979).

> The aim of the project is, in connection with the introduction of new machinery, to develop the production system in such a way as to reinforce the Postgiro's status as the country's leading institution for the handling of payments, in competition with the banks. This development shall be implemented with consideration to all justified demands regarding
>
> - an improved working environment
> - an improved content of work
> - the retention of employment
> - the development of new products and an improved level of service, including good customer accounting.

With this, the foundation of the PGP project had been laid. Several factors may have contributed to the fact that management accepted the trade union's demands in the negotiations. All members of the local union board attended the negotiations in June; this was an expression of a strong mobilization. To demand a local co-determination agreement on rationalization just after the central agreement had been reached was something very new: Management was caught by surprise. Also management had made a mistake in not negotiating over the performance of the pilot study, which perhaps made it insecure about violating the rules of co-determination.

Wage-earner consultants and central union support were important in analyzing the consequences of management's proposals on work and employment and for formulating union demands for an alternative solution. Throughout the summer, members were mobilized at major meetings and through the local union newsletter.

A Chronology of Events from 1948 to 1984

1948	The first punched card machines are introduced at the Postgiro.
1970	Proposal for a new OCR-based system, G 70.
1976	G 70 introduced.
1977	Report from a preliminary study by the employer on the future development of the Postgiro's production system.
1978	The union receives information on plans for a new system in the report: "The Future Data Structure of the Postal Administration."
May 1979	Detailed proposals are sent to the union for negotiation prior to negotiations under Section 11 of the Co-Determination Act.
Autumn 1979	Negotiations in which the unions demand better jobs and the retention of employment.
November 1979	Local collective agreement signed for the Postgiro Production System (PGP) project.

Following the agreement, the work of system development got under way. What has happened so far during the project period is described below, in chronological order.

January 1980	The unions withdraw from work on the project, following the management's breach of the Co-Determination Act. Supplementary collective agreements are entered to regulate work on the project.
Summer 1981	The unions study the report of the project group and the supplier, but are dissatisfied because it lacks any market evaluation, organizational discussions, or analysis of the consequences.
August 1981	Management tries to set up technical tests, which have to be discontinued because the unions consider they have not received the statutory information. Central union staff intervene.

	Union study circles are started: twenty groups with ten participants each.
November 1981	The unions having requested resources, according to the co-determination agreement, management accepts that these analyses be made within the framework of the project.
February 1982	The project's working groups are reorganized to provide a more cooperative approach. Further local collective agreements. The market, the organization, and the technology are analyzed. No decisions are to be made on the technology until the market studies and proposals regarding organization are available.
Summer and Autumn 1982	Project work resulting in reports analyzing market assessment, alternative proposals on organization, and plans for implementation. Internal union studies with the assistance of wage-earner consultants.
January 1983	A cross-union seminar. The establishment of union alternatives.
March 1983	Union reports on the history of the project and the alternatives available. Proffers criticisms and proposals regarding organization, implementation, decentralization, the use of video screens, the duties of supervisors, and so forth.
April 1983	The management, in negotiations, presents a final bid on what it intends to allow. The unions enter written reservations on certain points. However, certain union views on the organization have been complied with.
Summer 1983	The management presents specific requirements regarding the technical equipment, together with a basis for bidding that is approved by the unions, and a revised planning document in which management has come closer to the union standpoint.
September 1983	The project plan is approved.
Autumn 1983	Experiments are started with the terminal equipment and organization, and the organizational aspects are studied in detail by management.
December 1983 to Spring 1984	Decision on a new organization for the Postal Administration. The Postgiro is incorporated in a new structure, with new management. Nego-

	tiations on choice of system (organization, technology, supplier) postponed.
July 1985	Negotiations on choice of technology and supplier concluded. New systems for registration and transcription of forms ordered. At the same time a decision is taken on the future organization of the Postgiro. The organization is divided into four "minigiros" with integration of some tasks supplementary to registration, but qualified investigation and contacts with customers are, counter to union demands, kept in a separate department.
1985–1990	Introduction in practice of the PGP system. In 1985 a new project starts to change the central bookkeeping system. So there is, as we have already emphasized, a continuous and gradual development of this complex system. New technologies and control systems are gradually introduced. Still no integration of registration and investigation.

Management's Strategy for Change

The Postgiro management's strategy for change is based on assessments of the competitive position. According to management, the purpose of change is to increase the volume of transactions without increasing the costs of the operation. Management can envisage supplementing this strategy with others, but only on the condition that they are profitable. This strategy is reflected in the Postgiro's organization in three ways: the general approach prevailing, the model used for system development, and the role and duties of the Organization Department.

During the 1960s, the clear starting point for rationalization at the Postgiro was what was technically possible. The volume of operations was growing rapidly, and the Postgiro took its general approach from industry, trying to cope with growth with the help of technology and organizing operations along the same lines as in the manufacturing sector, with, for example, a standardization of its products and range of services. Its organization and workplaces were designed around the technology. This tradition still survives in the Postgiro, parallel with modern managerial theories on operations and the approach to change.

A standardized systems development model—the SIS/RAS— was introduced in the late 1960s, and this was still in use at the Postgiro until the mid 1980s. This method took its starting point in computer technology, a successive structure of decision making (with a consequent constraint upon freedom of action), and a conceptual apparatus for the standardization and formalization of data (with a consequent constraint upon the concept of communications). We can say that this model was a way of steering the work of development toward technical system solutions. The Postgiro management championed the creation of this model and its use in Sweden. SIS/ RAS was the model used by the Postgiro management, and no negotiation took place on the subject: The decision to use it was made prior to the Co-Determination Act.

At an early stage, the Organization Department acquired a role and duties complying with the above policy. It possessed great technical know-how, and one of its major tasks was to follow technological development around the world and initiate applications in the operations of the Postgiro. This often started with a memo in which the systems designers described what technology they wanted, and what they wanted to do with it. At a later stage, a "preliminary study" was presented. This provided a basis for the initiation of work in accordance with the SIS/RAS model. The preliminary phase established various technical alternatives, which were often developed in contact with different suppliers. Only after this preliminary study was a project set up, sometimes with a broad representation of different functions and interested parties. The Organization Department played a decisive role as the unit responsible for technical investments within the Postgiro. Also, it initiated development projects within the Postgiro, and its staff often served as the project managers responsible for implementing the changes. The chairperson of the steering committee was appointed from the same department.

The Market Department also had a pronounced function in the Postgiro's planning for change; it initiated projects for new products and services in collaboration with the Organization Department. For the most part, projects initiated by the Marketing Department involved technical investments and thus were strongly influenced by the Organization Department.

The origins of the current project at the Postgiro lay in the next acquisition of new machinery for bookkeeping. After considerable "teething troubles," the G 70 system had gotten under way. The systems engineers at the Organization Department could be put to work on the acquisition of new machines. The management regarded a continued investment in technical solutions as important. This was due partly to the recruitment problems it had in the early 1970s. A majority of employees regarded their duties as monotonous and stressful and many quit the moment another job was available. At the same time, the volume of payments and transactions, and the Postgiro's share of the market, were increasing. In management's opinion, a reduction in the staffing level was absolutely necessary.

Following union pressure, the project was given a broader framework. The unions maintained that the current problems with job dissatisfaction, injuries from overload, and a high turnover of personnel were due to the one-sided technological thrust of the changes made. They demanded a survey of the customers' needs from the Postgiro system and a radical discussion of the principles of the work organization as a basis for technical renewal. This was accepted by the Postgiro management in a collective agreement. The systems engineers continued work as if nothing had happened. Only in recent years has their work begun to approach the letter and meaning of the agreement.

With time, the PGP project became the forum for a long-term, strategic discussion of development at the Postgiro, with consequent difficulties in bringing the discussion to actual decisions. Late 1983, the situation changed. The Postal Administration as a whole was reorganized on a principle of business sectors, with a stronger management function and other forums for strategic discussion. The PGP project thus reacquired a more limited role from 1984 onward.

9. The Approach of the Unions

At the time of the last reorganization, completed in 1976, the staff took dismal stock of the situation: dismissals, increased control, a heavy workload, increased volume, limited union influence, and poor support from the full-time union officials. Seizing on these conditions, the union was in a position to push its demands before the next step in the rationalization of the Postgiro. When management wanted to change the equipment, the personnel reacted. Full-time union staff and consultants were called in, and after though negotiations an agreement was signed on how the work on upgrading the coding machines should proceed.

The Postgiro and Postal Administration had been experimental organizations for democracy in public administration, part of the Delegation for Democracy in the Public Administration (DEFF) project. The spirit of understanding that this created influenced the initial phase of the PGP project. Earlier union action had also been influenced by the "Postgiro spirit," by which the women, following their traditional role, had rallied round in all circumstances. During previous system changes this "spirit" had been exploited by the

Postgiro management. Prior to negotiations on the PGP project, the Civil Servants Union (ST) changed its executive leadership.

The new executive group put more emphasis on the values held by the labor movement, thus asserting a more active role for women. Following the change in leadership, and with new instruments provided by the labor legislation, a clear improvement has taken place. The turning point was the co-determination agreement in the public sector.

In autumn 1978, ST increased its activity directed toward computer issues and consultants began to give the union support that it was impossible for the regular full-time staff to provide. For reasons of regional policy in the 1960s, the Postgiro had located some computer punchcard work in Kisa, 300 kilometers south of Stockholm. The full introduction of the G 70 technology lead to a concentration of the new production to Stockholm and to dismissal of the hundred or so women employed in Kisa by 1975. The dismissals were a consequence of the technology and organization the Postgiro had ordered. These experiences, which by the beginning of the PGP project in 1979 had almost been forgotten, were reintroduced into the debate by the consultants, and led to the conscious union policy of trying to negotiate the goals of the PGP project beforehand, rather than waiting until afterward to attempt to control the consequences for the employees.

Experience of joint union action prior to and during negotiations on the local collective agreement for the PGP project proved positive. The union organizations institutionalized this collaboration by setting up a special joint union group, subsequently known as the PGP Coordinating Group. All questions relating to the PGP project, as well as certain other projects, have been discussed by this group throughout the project period. The group has also been in charge of the unions' consultants.

The Postgiro unions start from what the laws and agreements actually say. Their approach is clearly legalistic. By exploiting the positive wording of the act and the co-determination agreement for the public sector, they succeeded at an early stage in reaching agreements that set minimum levels of protection under the Working Environment Act (work must not make you ill) and Co-Determination Act (before taking action, you talk things over). The emphasis was also on the systems development model described in the agreement for the public sector, especially Sections 15 to 19. Joint labor–management groups have been complemented by negotiations. The decision-making process is now predominantly a matter of negotiation.

Under the local co-determination agreements, the union has the prior right to interpret the meaning of the text. The old system of "consultation" gave way to negotiations based on the labor legislation. The negotiating approach has been exploited to the full.

The Postgiro constitutes one of TCO–S's (Central Organization of Salaried Employees–State Sector) largest investments in consultancy. Six wage-earner consultants have worked on the Postgiro, on and off, since 1978. Between three and seven full-time union officials have been active. Both the mass media and the unions have devoted a great deal of attention to the Postgiro. These consultants have been available in the context of negotiations. The bulk of the consultancy work has been devoted to participation in the development and organization of work, the analysis of documents and reports, and the drafting of alternatives. All these activities can be seen as preparation for negotiations and as an attempt to abstract the parties' positions and demands. The use of employee consultants at the Postgiro is an example of an interplay between local and central trade union levels. The decision to appoint employee consultants to reinforce trade union resources was made locally and supported by the ST office. The central level of the union, after applications from the local level, decided to use consultancy money at the Postgiro. This had great importance at the local level, and in central union policy work. This is an example of a multilevel strategy within unions.

Employee consultants have played an important role in the PGP program. When consultants were first hired in 1978, personnel found that their own experience and knowledge were given support and that the consultants could acknowledge that conditions were in fact as employees had experienced them. The employee consultants made strict demands on, and had high expectations of, the trade union, which meant that people took responsibility for their work life and made an effort that exceeded anything they had imagined they could produce. The consultants have also contributed to raising expectations by presenting the Postgiro trade union's work in seminars and at conferences. The consultants were one step ahead of the shop stewards, since they could concentrate entirely on certain complete projects. The trade union demands, which were developed with the consultants, have been incorporated in ST's computer policy program, since the Postgiro is now a leader in office technology.

The unions used study circles, or local study groups, to formulate the demands of members, to increase their knowledge, and to step up the pressure on the Postgiro management. Work through the union study circles was started before the 1981 negotiations and went on until 1985; some four-hundred members, most of them women, have taken part. From 1982 and thereafter, a large number of former study group participants became "investigators" in the

PGP project's various bipartite study and working groups. They also participated in a trade union "alternative group" parallel to this, together with the trade union's consultant. The purpose of the alternative group was to develop the demands of the union, and, at the same time, support the delegates who were part of the project's working groups. The alternative group's work resulted in a program of action that was later taken up in the collaboration on PGP, on the trade union board, and at a cross-disciplinary trade union seminar. Using the program as a base, the trade union alternative plan was then developed ahead of negotiations with the Postgiro management in the spring of 1983.

In addition to the purely practical results, work on the program also constituted a widening and consolidation of the trade union base. Members contact their elected representatives spontaneously and ask how things are progressing. An awareness and knowledge that PGP concerns the entire Postgiro is evident among a large number of members. They have learned when and how demands are made. Today it is less common for employers to attempt to drive wedges between the members and the shop stewards by referring to individual conversations with members and suggesting that they should not support trade union demands. The trade union has also appointed a working group among the shop stewards. Together with the trade union's consultants, this group assesses and evaluates the PGP project's upcoming proposals and further develops the demands of the union. The study circles thus constituted an important aspect of independent development of knowledge and mobilization among union members as a basis for participation and negotiation. Proposals were broadly anchored among the members and not just a product of the professional expertise of the consultants.

A further method used by the unions has been trying to obtain information by questioning management. The unions have also utilized internal information sheets to disseminate their views of competing interpretations, thus forcing management to respond.

10. The Outcome

In the autumn of 1979, management and unions signed an initial collective agreement. This was a turning point; a new way of looking at rationalization had been accepted, and an old common law, established in traditional practice, abandoned. The gist of the agreement was that the workplace should be improved and employment maintained, and that the customers should be offered better services. The emphasis on personnel issues has highlighted the difficulties of evaluating workplace conditions and the work organization. This puts to the test the possibilities of lending substance to the model or theory embodied in the Co-Determination and Working Environment Acts, and consequent agreements, in practical union action.

The Postgiro case is a good example of conscious union action. The unions have succeeded in gaining access to management's plans by demanding this in negotiations. They have also helped to uncover information that had previously not been taken into account. With the PGP project, certain categories of staff have acquired entirely new duties. Once a task for specialists, the work of rationalization has become an issue for a high proportion of the work force. The decision-making process that existed before G 70 has been radically changed. Instead of being left to react to management's ready-made proposals, the unions are becoming "decision makers" in the true sense of the term.

This change in the employees' fields of competence has stimulated union ambitions to regain their share of planning and to reduce the division of labor. Unions no longer passively accept management's suggestions and bases for negotiation. They shape present and future work in the course of negotiations, thus approaching the original meaning of "information"—the lending of "form" to an object. By developing their own competence, the unions have disputed management's stance as the sole possessor of know-how.

Local practice differs greatly from other government activities, which means that the Postgiro union has also contributed to the development of competency at the national level. The hoped-for consequences of the PGP project are that the measures of performance laid down in the PGP agreement on improvements for the workers will be introduced in the Postgiro and in other government operations as well.

The work of administrative development at the Postgiro, the planned acquisition of equipment, and the reduced labor requirement have changed with the signing of the co-determination agreement for the public sector. The earlier methods of evaluating results have been abandoned; new aspects (like a broader definition of efficiency) have been added to the old calculations. As yet how the measures of results introduced in the public-sector co-determination agreement, the local rationalization agreement for the Postal Administration, and the project agreement on the PGP are to be applied within the postal system is not clear. The PGP project is still in progress. No decisive conflict over whether or not the project "measures up" has arisen.

The PGP project has helped transform insights and experiences into demands, which have led in their turn to action and negotiation. People's awareness of their rights and local opportunities has grown. One example is that when the report "More Rational Giro Handling" (SOU 1979 No. 35) was published, the unions invited representatives of the Parliamentary parties to a discussion at the Postgiro. Thanks to all the attention attracted by the Postgiro, there is a good chance of implementing the intentions written into the legislation and the PGP agreement. What was previously happening backstage now attracts broad interest and provides free play for further action by the unions. However, the course of events in connection with the reorganization of the Postal Administration has not settled the issues unequivocally.

The DEFF program introduced a harmonized concept of the objectives, measures of success, and working methods of co-determination, but the PGP project has drawn attention to the conflicts between the parties. The unions are no longer hesitant to accept confrontations and conflicts. The agreement signed in the PGP project makes it very difficult indeed for management to dig in its heels on issues relating to the working environment, the work organization, and employment. Thus there is reason to believe that cooperation in the spirit of the public-sector co-determination agreement and a sense of mutual confidence can be established in practice—but it is not a sure thing.

We have already considered the change in work organization that has taken place under the project. We can also note, with regard to work organization, technology, and employment:

- that the Postgiro has decided to integrate the work of book-keeping and investigation and to continue the process of integration with other duties;
- that the Postgiro has acquired fifty new coding machines (out of three hundred), which are not as health-threatening as the previous machines;
- that employment within the Postgiro has increased;
- that present plans point to an adaptation of customer accounting to different categories of customers;
- that several combinations of equipment systems exist, which had not previously been included in the discussion;
- that the Postgiro is contemplating successive changes both in its organization and the equipment;
- that to date over four hundred employees have received training in the Postgiro and the PGP project.

The thrust of all these changes corresponds to union demands, but it is too early to say precisely how work on the handling of payments will be organized as a consequence of the project.

Returning in 1990 to the Postgiro, we find that the positive results achieved by the unions concerning employment, technology, and physical work environment are still in place. The new technology is more flexible than the one originally proposed by management. The number of employees has grown to 5,500. On the division of labor and work organization, the results today are not so successful. The integration between bookkeeping and investigation departments did finally not come about. The pressure for raised productivity in the public sector has been growing, and union demands for work quality from the 1970s have weaker support from management; productivity and new technology are again the dominating perspective in developing Postgiro production. But the issue of job integration is still a burning one among members and for the unions.

Looking at both the "success stories," the Postgiro and the dairy around 1990, we find that it is still fair to say that much was achieved in practical results at the workplace and in developing member and union competence and processes. But we also find clear tendencies of stagnation. In addition to factors mentioned in the case studies, we may add the fact that all unions, like companies, have their ups and downs. We can surely find some success stories today, but probably they would be different ones from those we found during the first half of the 1980s. More generally during the second half of the 1980s, the unions were not so much on the offensive as during the preceding years. Nevertheless, recently we see again tendencies toward a renewal of the strategy behind the "good work."

6

Case Studies
The Engineering Workshop
and the Sugar Mill

Both the Postgiro and the dairy are striking examples of local unions testing out new paths in close interaction with the central unions, that is, multilevel efforts. In contrast, the other two case studies emerge as more everyday examples, in the sense that they have relied on the resources available at the workplace, without the support of researchers or wage-earner consultants. These two cases, a sugar mill and an engineering workshop, took some time to find. One can speculate whether this is due to the paucity of "good examples" of local union work or to the necessity for the central union to focus on "problem cases" rather than "success stories." From the standpoint of this project, we were fortunate to locate two of the success stories, as well as two everyday examples. And, as we have seen, what is and can be a success varies over time. In any event, we learn both from progress and from difficulties.

The third case study, the engineering workshop, covers the purchase and use of several computer-controlled machines and problems in their programming. It also describes how experiences from work on a specific project have led to a general engagement of union members.

The fourth case study comes from the Örtofta sugar mill where the workshop or "club" is an active unit within the national union as a whole, particularly in commercial and industrial issues, but also in computer policy. The mill also has a well-developed information and negotiating system, and cooperation with the management is good. We chose the mill for the case study because of these favorable conditions. In the project we studied in greater detail, however, it still

165

proved difficult for the union to exercise any real influence. This project related to the installation of new equipment and the conversion of the packaging division. Both the favorable conditions and the difficulties are analyzed in the case study. That the difficulties related partly to the fact that the union approach was adapted more to the male workers in the processing division than to the women in the packaging division emerges from the study.

1. The Engineering Workshop

At the beginning of the 1980s, work began at Pullmax Ursviken on the modernization of the workshop by investing in numerically controlled machines. The local plant branch of the Metalworkers' Union has actively supported and participated in this development and has protected and tried to promote the occupational roles of its members. Technological issues have been a very important aspect of union work, and a union Technical Committee has been formed.

Pullmax Ursviken has 170 employees, of whom 120 are workers. Its gross receipts in 1983 were about MSEK 70 (U.S. $11.8 million). As the name indicates, this division is located in Ursviken, outside Skellefteå in northern Sweden. The parent company, Pullmax AB Group, has its registered office in Gothenburg, from which the Group Sales Division also operates. A certain amount of marketing and selling also takes place in Ursviken. The division manufactures heavy power shears and edging presses for the processing and cutting of sheet metal. Production is in short series. Some two hundred machines, of various models, are produced during a year. The turnover of production workers is low, around 5 percent. There are no foreign employees, and only three of the production workers are women. (Further data on the works union and the company are found in section 6.)

In the late 1970s, the company's profits were poor. The production flow was substandard due to inadequate planning and a rundown and largely antiquated workshop. Those working on the floor were extremely disturbed by the situation. They were worried that the company's competitiveness and, in the long run, their employment might be jeopardized. The workshop "club" also felt that the Group Board was too little concerned with Ursviken's interests, as compared with the other divisions. It was afraid of structural rationalizations that would lead to cutbacks. In this respect, the works union and local management had a common interest, but the union felt that management was incapable of solving the problems.

The low turnover of collective employees had no counterpart at the white-collar and managerial level. In its relations with the Group, the local union therefore regarded itself as the party standing for continuity, long-term thinking, and a sense of responsibility. The union also felt that it had the most know-how and the longest production experience.

2. What Did the Union Do?

The local metalworkers' branch considered it important to become involved in the production issues. The works branches of SIF and SALF (the white-collar employees and supervisors) had not involved themselves in questions relating to production and the company's future in the same way as the metalworkers. In the following, therefore, we are describing and analyzing the actions of the metalworkers' plant local, or "club."

When a new production manager was appointed at the company, the union gained a hearing for its demands regarding modernization of the plant. The company established a Production Technology Department and drew up an investment plan with the support of the union. This plan covered the purchase of three Computerized Numerical Control (CNC) machines, which are computer-guided machine tools that can be programmed at the machine itself. They wanted to buy a small CNC multioperating machine, a CNC lathe, and a large CNC multioperating milling machine for the processing of sidepieces for the edging presses and power shears. By Ursviken's standards, this investment plan was on a very large scale. The investment in the last machine alone amounted to around MSEK 5 (U.S. $850,000). (A chronology of the changes made at Pullmax appears in section 7.)

The main purpose of the investment plan was to reduce the throughput time for products at the workshop. The CNC multioperation milling machine was to replace one of the older milling machines, which had insufficient processing capacity. As a result, the company had been obliged to farm out 4,000 to 5,000 hours of work per year on contract.

In this situation, the union was faced with new demands. It had no local experience of handling production issues from the union standpoint. How was it to act vis-à-vis these technical changes? The workshop had no previous experience of numerically controlled machines. Initially, the union did not take the offensive against management regarding the way in which the machines should be introduced. It lacked any well-considered approach. Nor did the central union have any ready-made strategy or other help to offer. Instead, the union in Ursviken concentrated on monitoring the first investments in machinery. The force of union action was based on the workers' professional skill and experience. Management was dependent on the experience and production know-how available on the shop floor.

3. Installation of CNC Machines

When the first machine was to be installed, management decided to assign the task of programming it to the Technology Production Department. Those working at the machine were given some training in programming, so that they could correct and modify programs. Originally, this procedure encountered no opposition from the metalworkers. Only after working for some time at the machines did the operators experience the following shortcomings in the system: First, it took a long time to master the programs sufficiently to be able to correct them. Second, the operators frequently felt that other cutting data, or another processing sequence, would have been more suitable than that chosen by the programmer. Finally, they found it was so much simpler to write programs than they had at first imagined that they felt there would be great advantages in being allowed to write them themselves; but their condition was that they should be given the time to work on these programs in peace and quiet. In the meanwhile, someone else would have to operate the machines.

The union pushed these demands, together with a demand that an entire week's work be distributed to each machine operator, so that they themselves could determine the most suitable sequence for jobs. This demand resulted from complaints by several operators of inadequate planning. It happened on occasion that they got back the same details with a day's interval. They regarded the resulting reprogramming of the machines as unnecessary. They thought it possible to plan so that details of the same type could be processed consecutively.

The result of negotiations with the company was an experimental activity, by which the underlying drawings were given to the operator. The operator would then select a method and sequence of operations and write the program. While the program was being written, a stand-in would be assigned to the machine. Work orders for an entire week would be distributed to the operators so that they themselves could plan the breakdown and sequence of jobs.

This experimental activity started at the CNC lathe, but was not without problems. One of the programmers opposed the experiment. Despite the agreement, a prewritten program could accompany the drawing to the workshop. The Production Technology Department had difficulty in providing information on a whole week's work. Not infrequently, planning was disrupted by unforeseen emergency orders, which meant that the operator's setup for the week's production had to be abandoned. The supervisors also viewed the experiment with disfavor. The planning of work, after all, was one of their most important tasks. They protested when it was taken from them. It therefore also happened, on occasion, that the supervisor retained the drawings for the week's work, and then apportioned the jobs.

Management tried to discuss with SALF (the supervisors' union) what alternate functions the supervisors could assume. The problem was not entirely solved, but an agreement was reached to allow the experiment to continue as planned. Once start-up troubles had been eliminated, the system functioned well enough—apart from disruptions from unforeseen emergency orders, which were difficult to deal with. The operators found it highly advantageous to write their own programs. They could see for themselves the results of programs they had written and in this way continually improve and modify them. When, subsequently, it was planned to invest in a large CNC multioperation milling machine, the union wanted to be in on it from the start. They demanded that a project group be set up that would include the safety and hygiene delegate and two floor workers with experience of the kind of processing to be performed on the machine. The group also included the production manager and two production engineers. The project group studied various alternative machines and finally agreed on one.

Discussions within the group primarily focused on actual performance. In the case of control systems, the workers had little opportunity to compare and evaluate the properties and potential of different systems because the workers in the group had little experience with numerically controlled machines. Nor did the union representatives question the specific investment in a CNC multioperation milling machine. No other alternatives were discussed at all, either in the group or the local union.

The local Metalworkers' Union demanded that all those working with the machine should undergo training in programming. The company's original intention was simply to train a production engineer, who could then train the operators. Management, however, gave way to the union's demands, in order not to jeopardize the smooth introduction of the new equipment. It was decided that the four operators who were to work on it and a production engineer should all undergo the same training with the manufacturer in Italy.

The machine is now run in two shifts, with two operators on each shift. One devotes the shift mainly to monitoring operations, while the other prepares the next job.

The production engineer trained on the machine wrote some programs; the operators wrote the others. For the operators to take over entirely, one would need a stand-in or another operator at the machine. Since processing times are very long, up to two hours for a single detail, the programs were also very extensive. It was therefore important that the operators should be given a place where they could sit undisturbed and write their programs.

At the time of the study (1983), the machine was still new and no fixed procedures for work had yet emerged. Soon after our study, the company was sold to a Danish owner. Further investment in several new CNC machines was made. The union reports that they had good possibilities to influence the investments using the same procedures as during the time of the case study. And their influence was still based on their skills and knowledge as workers.

The production workers and their experience had an important role in the planning of the production of advanced machines ordered by customers. And programming of all the CNC machines is today done by the machine operators themselves. Division of labor has also diminished because transportation of pieces between different work stations and departments is now taken care of by the machine operators and not by special truck drivers. The main problem in the late 1980s was a low volume of orders; the number of employees has gone down drastically.

The lessons learned after the installation of the first two CNC machines hold true for the large multioperation machine: It takes almost as long to master a program written by someone else in order to correct it as it does to write the program oneself. And one has to work at the machine in order to develop and improve programs in the light of experience gained from previous processing.

4. The Lessons Drawn

During its involvement in the installation of the CNC machines, the "club" was faced with problems with which it had had no previous experience on a union basis. It sought the support of the central Metalworkers' Union, but was offered no help. It also contacted the other "clubs" within the same local union branch. A number of these were faced with similar problems. After the members of the Ursviken union executive panel had attended a course in "new technology" arranged by the central union, the local area union branch decided to arrange a joint course. This had a good response, and it was decided to continue along this line, share experiences, and arrange study circles at the companies concerned.

The union executive group in Ursviken was concerned to broaden the discussion on production issues and carry it to the membership, because these questions were decisive for the structuring of future work on the shop floor. A union Technical Committee was set up, the purpose of which was to arrive at a basis for negotiating a technology agreement with the company. The plant union executive group considers it important to establish formal regulations as to how technical changes at the company are to be implemented.

In view of the high turnover of managerial staff, the union executive level is unwilling to base its collaboration exclusively on informal contacts and "tacit agreements." It does not want to risk having to fight for demands already accepted by the present management should a new management appear abruptly. The points it wishes to regulate include the following:

- joint labor–management project groups to be formed prior to technical and organizational changes.
- training to be provided for workers in the context of technical changes.
- the planning of work at individual machines, with the programming, to be assigned to the actual operators.

The strong union influence in Pullmax Ursviken is certainly due in large part to the strong union tradition prevailing in northern Sweden. The company is located in a region that has long struggled against structural rationalization and unemployment. This has promoted solidarity among the membership in a more self-evident way than in other places in Sweden, where there are more job opportunities and thus a greater mobility among employees. The vulnerability of the company is also one of the bases for collaboration between the union and management on the company's future operation.

The extensive studies arranged by unions in the context of the Co-Determination Act and co-determination agreements strengthened the union considerably and raised union awareness in Ursviken. In the discussions between union and management that followed the introduction of the Act and the agreement, the metalworkers felt that they stood on an equal footing with management. This gave the plant union the strength to question the running of the company and to call attention to shortcomings in the planning and maintenance of the workshop. The works union urged a long-term investment plan.

Perhaps the most important explanation, however, of the union's successes is the employees' professional skills in production. These skills were gained at a time when management relied on its being able to handle production, despite inadequate planning and the lack of a Production Technology Department.

With the more systematic approach adopted in recent years and the efforts made to rationalize the workplace, this situation has to some extent changed, but professional skills remain a source of union strength. Thanks to the detailed knowledge it has of production, the union is able to propose changes in the production setup and take a stand on proposals put forward by management. It is this active role, based on professional capability, that the works union in Ursviken is concerned to preserve by ensuring that professional skills are not pared down with the introduction of computer support in production.

5. Results and Experience of Union Work

The main result of the union work done in the period from 1979 to 1983 is the union's beginning to treat production issues as a union concern of the same importance as wages, terms of employment, and access to work. The metalworkers in Ursviken realized that the union has to influence and guide the choice and structure of future technology in order to protect the members' working conditions.

A more practical result is that the workers have retained the greater part of the programming of the CNC machines on the shop floor. The operators have influenced the choice of machines and have been trained on them. On the other hand, the union was not sufficiently prepared to question the actual investment and the way in which it was decided to solve the acute problems of overload on certain machines and farm out work on contract. Could there have been solutions other than investment in a CNC machine? What alternative techniques could have been considered? Such questions underline the importance of having a more general union strategy for the technological development of the company. The union should not only participate in project groups on new investments but also build up the expertise required to be able to set priorities among different investments and to propose reorganizations, modified planning, and training inputs for the collectively employed.

This is another important consequence of the union work from 1979 to 1983.

It is interesting to note the increased activity at central level. The Swedish Metalworkers' Union had for the most part followed and observed technological change without any active attempt to influence the effects on its own members. In the late 1970s and early 1980s, many workshop "clubs" like the one in Ursviken looked for support and involvement from the central executive panel, with a view to a more critical attitude toward technological changes. This they did in a period when the union movement was broadly pursuing a technologically optimistic policy and investments in the "new technology" were seen as a means of improving Sweden's competitiveness in its export markets. Those who had questioned the uses of technology and been concerned to discuss the consequences with regard to working conditions may have been regarded as hostile to technology and hence ignored.

Since 1982, certain changes have taken place in the Metalworkers' Union. It has employed, at the central level, persons of technological competence and has started to arrange studies on the broad effects of technological changes. Also, the union now actively supports works "clubs" that are concerned to draft agreements regulating how technical changes at their companies are to be implemented.

There has thus been a marked shift in the attitude toward technological change—from passive observation to active influence. This change in the attitude of the Metalworkers' Union has come a bit late. The CNC technology is now established in most companies. It has led to a change in the organization of work, especially in the control over the machines. The preparation in detail has in most cases been transferred from the operators to the salaried levels. As a result, the metalworkers as a collective have lost important aspects of their occupational role and acquired no new duties; their professional work has been impoverished.

The trend, however, is not unambiguous. As a rule, the CNC machines have been available for actual processing to a considerably lesser degree than that envisaged by the salespeople and optimistic managements. The managements of several companies have realized that in the hunt for maximal efficient machine time, the operator plays an important role—but the operator must then be given the right training and the qualifications needed to write programs or correct existing programs and to plan the work. Several suppliers of machinery now recommend and offer training in programming for machine operators. The Metalworkers' Union can exploit and influence this development in order to recover, if possible, part of what its members have lost and to support the locals as they encounter impending changes. As we see in Chapter 10, the national Metalworkers' Union developed, during the second half of the 1980s, a program for the "good work" that takes advantage of these new possibilities.

The ambition of the plant union executive board at Pullmax Ursviken is to devise a local union program of action—laying down approaches to the technology, the organization of work, and the actual content of work. This program will then provide a basis for union action at the company on these and other production issues. The Metalworkers' Union there also sees work on such a program of action as a way of raising the level of its members' expertise as well as their interest in technical questions. The executive panel is concerned to maintain and develop the role of skilled labor by exploiting the computer as an aid to workers on the shop floor, rather than as a means of control for production management. One aspect of this work is the recently formed union Technical Committee. The executive panel believes that the work of this committee in producing a basis for agreements on technology must have its roots in a broad discussion among the membership. The union is entitled at present to a twenty-five-minute informative meeting with all members in paid working hours, in connection with meetings of the "management group." It sees these meetings as the most effective means of reaching the membership. It is therefore now trying to have the meetings extended to one hour. It hopes thereby to engage more people actively in the work of the union. The extent to which it succeeds in this attempt at a more general mobilization on the technological issues will be decisive for the influence it can exert over these factors in the future.

6. Basic Facts

The Union Organizations

Apart from the Metalworkers' Union, SIF and SALF are also represented at the company. SIF has forty-two salaried employees who are members. Its executive panel, consisting of a representative from each department: finance, marketing, design, and production, is elected at an annual meeting. Two other regular meetings are held each year. The works branch of SIF has not pursued any particular line on production issues at the company.

SALF has six supervisors as members, one for each production section. SALF, like SIF, has not pursued an aggressive strategy regarding the consequences of technological change at the company. Some supervisors, on the other hand, have opposed changes in the organization of work.

The Metalworkers' Union organizes all those collectively employed in the six production sections. In 1983 its executive panel consisted of a chairperson (a turner), a vice-chairperson (CNC milling machine operator), a treasurer and cultural officer (fitter), a secretary (welder), a studies organizer (welder), a chief safety and hygiene delegate and technical officer (welder), an insurance counsellor (operator of a CNC milling machine), a vice-secretary (stores), and three alternates (an electrician, a milling machine operator, and a fitter). The executive group meets once a month, and otherwise as necessary. The chairperson works half-time in production. Union meetings are held quarterly.

Company Organization and Management

Pullmax Ursviken is one of three divisions in the Pullmax AB Group. The others are the Kumla Division and the Gothenburg Division. The Gothenburg and Ursviken Divisions are of the same size, both in sales and number of employees, while the Kumla Division is one-third their size. All three manufacture machines for the processing of sheet metal, but of different kinds. Cooperation between the three divisions is limited. There is no coordination between the Metalworkers' plant unions at the three divisions.

Pullmax AB Group is a fully owned subsidiary of Statsföretag AB. Statsföretag is an administrative company, in which the owner (central government) makes the same demands regarding yield on capital invested as do private companies of similar type. Central government has also charged Statsföretag AB to promote, within the Group, increased job satisfaction and greater co-determination for employees. The plant union in Ursviken, however, has emphasized that the fact of state ownership has not entailed any real differences or provided any better conditions for union work at the company. (Soon after our study was conducted, as we mentioned earlier, Pullmax was sold to a Danish company.)

The Group's system of financial control means that investment decisions of up to SEK 100,000 (U.S. $16,500) can be made by the divisions themselves. Decisions on larger sums must be discussed by Group management, in which all three divisions are represented. Investments in excess of SEK 500,000 (U.S. $82,750) must be discussed by the Group Board.

The Plant Union and Management

Collaboration between union and management takes place primarily in the "management group." This is mainly a forum for exchanges of opinion regarding the company's use of capital, but issues relating to sales, marketing, and manufacture are also raised there. The management group includes the division manager, the heads of the four departments, and representatives of SIF, SALF, and the Metalworkers' Union. Opinion is to some extent divided over how this group should be used. Management sees it as consultative, while the union organizations maintain that it should have decision-making powers. Apart from contacts with management on wage and personnel issues, collaboration is characterized by frequent informal contacts between the two parties. They both also have something of a common "opponent" in the Group management in Gothenburg. In the case of investments, the union normally supports the division management in its efforts to obtain the necessary funds.

Another forum for cooperation is provided by the "production councils" of each section. On these councils, production issues are discussed among workers, supervisors, and production management. These councils can propose investments in machinery and decide themselves on purchases of tools for up to SEK 10,000 (U.S. $1,700) per year.

7. Chronology

1974   Retirement of a large proportion of the plant union executive panel.
          Pullmax purchased by Statsföretag AB.
1979   Appointment of a new production manager.
          An investment schedule drawn up for 1980 to 1982. The schedule, supported by the union, earmarks funds for three CNC machines.
          The first of these, a CNC multioperation machine, is installed.
1980   The management group discusses the purchase of a CNC multioperation machine for the processing of sidepieces for stands.
          On the initiative of the chief safety and hygiene delegate, a project group is formed to investigate investing in the CNC multioperation milling machine.
          A CNC lathe is installed. The operators undergo training in programming with the supplier, SMT in Västerås, Sweden.
1981   An agreement is reached between union and management to have the operators, on an experimental basis, take over both the programming and the weekly planning of work at the CNC lathe.
          The decision is made to purchase a CNC multioperation milling

machine, Mecof model, as unanimously recommended by the project group.

1982   The four operators who are to work on the Mecof machine and a production engineer undergo a week's training on it with the supplier in Italy.

The machine is installed.

1983   The works union's experience of the installation of the CNC machines leads to the selection of a technically responsible officer on the executive, and the setting up of a Technical Committee.

1990   After sale of Pullmax to a Danish company there are investments in new CNC machines, the workers and the union influence the investments, and in the late 1980s all programming of the machines is handled by the operators. At the same time the number of employees, both white- and blue-collar, is drastically reduced.

8. The Sugar Mill

The workshop union or "club" at the Örtofta sugar mill in southern Sweden is regarded by the national Factory Workers' Union as highly active. It is active alike vis-à-vis management, government, and the union. This is a result of the special situation of the company concerned, Sockerbolaget. It has had a monopoly on the production of sugar in Sweden since 1936, and the price of sugar is determined within the framework of agricultural negotiations (see also section 14). The works union in Örtofta, together with the other "clubs" within Sockerbolaget, has promoted the construction of a well-developed system for information and negotiation. Apart from union representation on the boards of the parent company Cardo and Sockerbolaget, there are industrial councils at the company level and works councils at every plant, which function as informative bodies. Negotiations take place either at the company or plant level. Within each production department, everyone is required to meet regularly for the purposes of planning, information, and discussion. There are also more-or-less ad hoc working groups, on which the union is represented, to study issues of staffing, organization, and the like. Project groups with union representation are set up as a matter of course to deal with technical changes and investments.

In 1982, the local unions have also negotiated an agreement with the company on union time. Apart from the time at the disposal of union officials and members of project groups, every employee is entitled to participate during paid working hours in trade union meetings to a total of five hours per year. The time allocated for different activities is established after negotiations each year. If the need for union time increases, new negotiations are undertaken. The time agreed upon serves as part of the budgetary basis within the plant.

The plant's union's activity vis-à-vis government relates partly to agricultural policy and partly to regional policy. The scale of domestic production and of protectionist measures is regulated in the agricultural negotiations. At the union level, the policy has been to maintain a high degree of self-sufficiency in order to protect employment. From the standpoint of regional policy, union activity has helped to ensure the continued existence of the sugar mills on Öland and Gotland, the two big islands in the Baltic, east of southern Sweden. Operations are subsidized to some extent by the government.

The plant union at Örtofta has played, and still plays, an active role in union coordination within Sockerbolaget. There is a joint working committee that meets once a month for internal discussions, and, also once a month, for negotiations with company management. In addition, conferences are arranged once a month for all the union chairpersons.

Working procedures have also been further developed at the local level. Some years ago, the local union leadership was criticized by some members for a tendency toward "boss rule." In particular, the women in the packaging department complained of the union's lack of interest in their problems. To improve contacts with the membership in different sections of production in the sprawling plant, a system of "club representatives" was introduced. Each department proposes one such representative, who is then elected as a member of the executive panel, which also runs study circles within its own ranks to increase its information and develop joint discussion.

Within the national union, the Örtofta branch has taken the initiative on issues of technological policy, demanding, for example, an increased involvement in questions relating to computerization and its consequences. Against this background, the Factory Workers' Union and SIF, in consultation with the researchers, decided it would be interesting to study how a project activity was run and what it resulted in at the Örtofta sugar mill. It was also known that extensive investments had been made in recent years: The inspection of incoming beets had been automated, the final stage in the extraction of sugar had been streamlined and computerized, and new equipment had been acquired for the packaging department. Of these projects, the "packaging project" was selected since it affected more people and had presented greater problems than the others. We continue this account after further defining the relationship between the union and management.

9. The Relationship between Union and Management

The union's relationship to management is characterized by both collaboration and independent union action. The underlying tradition is that of the mill town or manufacturing estate, with its patriarchal spirit. Before the Co-Determination Act, an industrial council for the exchange of information functioned smoothly. Both parties were concerned to maintain a favorable climate for cooperation, with mutual respect and an emphasis on objective argument in their efforts to reach joint solutions. The independence of the union's work manifests itself in the fact that great efforts are made in its scrutiny of management's arguments for different measures and the acquisition of its own expertise is seen as necessary by both parties.

The production workers' knowledge of production and the technology is unusually sophisticated at the sugar mill, and it is further remarkable for the fact that the production period (known as the "campaign") is limited to three months a year. The rest of the time is devoted to maintenance, adjustments, and modifications to the production equipment. The majority of the workers in the plant perform highly qualified and independent jobs during that period. During the campaign, many also function as instructors for temporary labor. This enhances their self-confidence and provides a basis for union strength. However, conditions are quite different in several ways for the one-tenth of the permanent work force who work in the packaging department. Operations continue through most of the year. Also, more than half the operating personnel here are women.

Technical changes are handled in different stages within the MBL (Co-Determination Act) organization. Negotiations on investment plans for future years are held each year, first at the mill level and later at the company level. An assessment of the investment requirement over a five-year period is also included. Priorities among investments will normally have been discussed by the mill council during the year. To estimate the investment cost, management makes a preliminary study of the price of the equipment in question, then studies the costs of any modifications to buildings, the supply system, and the like. Company management now requires that a pay-off time be calculated for investments motivated on the grounds of profitability.

After an investment schedule has been adopted, a project group is set up for each investment that requires planning before it is implemented. The project group includes managerial staff at one or more levels and workers. In the case of major projects, the project manager is often the mill's development manager. The categories to be represented in the group are determined in consultation between management and the union. The mill union suggests names of suitable persons from its membership. The department's safety and health representatives and "club representative" are normally included. SIF and SALF have no specific union representation, but at least one of their members will be included in his capacity as head of the relevant unit or department.

The task of the project group is to draft proposals on which management can then make a decision. If the project group is unanimous on a proposal, there are normally no negotiations. The plant union, however, has the possibility of demanding negotiations in connection with the information provided prior to a decision. On issues of staffing, however, regular negotiations take place to clarify the situation during and between "campaigns."

The union's attitude to technical changes has so far been positive. Parts of the plant are extremely old and very worn. Experience suggests that investments normally make work easier and eliminate severe environmental hazards. Also, the purpose of investments in new equipment is usually a better use of the raw material, the sugar beets, and thus the investment does not constitute any direct threat to employment.

The union, however, fears that the situation may change in the future, partly because each mill will be an independent profit center directed toward specific targets in the yield on capital and partly through the increased use of computers in production. Apart from the company's general interest in rationalization, a rationalization requirement is included in the agreement between Sockerbolaget and the government. The normal course of events to date, however, has been for the project groups to agree on desirable changes in the production technology and working environment and for discussions to be pursued in an objective way and at a high level of technical expertise, which has been made possible by the technical competence of the employees.

The packaging project, the concrete subject of this study, illustrates certain limitations to such an approach when the premises are different.

10. New Packaging Machines

The packaging of granulated sugar continues almost throughout the year. Unlike the beet, its source, the finished sugar can be stored. Most of the duties in the packaging department are routine and resemble packaging and storage procedures in the industrial sector as a whole. The women, who comprise over half the staff of twenty-six employees, work mainly at the actual packaging machines, while the men handle maintenance and repairs, stocks, and certain other heavy jobs. Conditions in this department differ markedly from those in the mill at large.

The packaging department is located in a separate, four-story building. Adjoining it are the silos in which the finished sugar is kept. The sugar is transported through pipelines and on belts to floor 4, where it is sifted mechanically. It is then conducted to containers on floor 3, which are connected with the bag-packaging machines on floor 2. Here we also find equipment for bundling and palleting of large packs. The sugar to be packaged in sacks (for industrial use) is conducted to floor 1, where there are filling machines for sacks holding from 25 to 1,000 kilos. Here the packaged sugar is also stored on pallets.

In the mid-1970s, the Sockerbolaget central management decided that the existing packaging machines for granulated sugar at the mills should be replaced. The equipment was worn, and it was difficult to obtain spare parts. Management was also aware that the modern machines available on the market had about twice the capacity of the old. At the same time as renewal of the packaging machines was being considered, the future of Sockerbolaget's plant in Arlöv was called into question. That facility was in great need of a radical overhaul, but it was doubtful whether the investments required would pay off. In this situation, the management and union in Arlöv suggested that all packaging of granulated sugar be assigned to the Arlöv plant. This would afford the advantages of a large-scale operation, and would also secure the survival and re-equipping of the plant. This proposal was withdrawn after strong reactions from the other mills.

After an investigation and further discussions, the parties, in confidential negotiations at the central level in the company, concluded a deal whereby the packaging of granulated sugar remained decentralized, and a year-round double shift would be introduced at the packaging departments after the new machines were installed. The Arlöv plant lost its packaging of granulated sugar, but was compensated in other ways and got its overhaul.

The company had concluded that a decentralized solution was the most advantageous from an economic standpoint due to high transport costs. At the same time it wanted shift work in order to exploit the new and expensive packaging machines better. This savings would accrue whether packaging was centralized or not. From the union standpoint, the problem was the halving of the work force that the new equipment, with its higher capacity, would mean. The company's proposal on shift work included an increase in packaging in paper bags, at the expense of sacks and delivery in bulk. Work in two shifts would thus require the same number of workers as before.

An alternative union line would have been to demand more packaging machines, with the same size staff and working hours as previously. That this line was not seriously discussed may have been due to the gambit by Arlöv, when it declared its readiness to work two shifts. The company maintains that it was economically impossible to utilize the capacity of the new machines fully with only one shift, and this would entail the postponement of other urgent investments. However, Sockerbolaget's monopoly status and controlled economy suggest that the economic difference to the company between a single and double shift may be very slight. A comparison can be made with the dairy, which also requires expensive packaging equipment but operates a system of overlapping shifts within normal working hours.

Moreover, the decision for the packaging machines had been made before the project group started its work. When the engineers at Sockerbolaget, at the central level, drew up a list of conceivable makes and models, they did not question the kind of packaging the machines provided, that is, in paper bags. There proved to be five potential manufacturers, of whom only two remained after a rough, preliminary review. At that point the question of choice of machinery was raised in the technical occupational health system and in the central safety and health committee. The occupational health unit drew up a list of important environmental aspects to be considered in selecting the machinery and in the bidding procedure. Management intended that the local safety and health committees at the four mills concerned should then discuss the machinery issue and handle the environmental aspects. The union organizations rejected this plan, since it involved the risk of a fragmented and contradictory assessment, which the company could then exploit to acquire a free hand in the choice of machinery. The union position that the machinery issue should be handled by the central safety and health committee on the company level prevailed.

The two types of machines in question were studied in operation in Denmark by a group including personnel representatives from the central safety and health committee. Shortly afterward, the union organizations involved produced a joint assessment of the two types of machines, recommending the Hesser machine. The central safety and health committee was also persuaded to come out in favor of the machine. The company quickly completed its technical and economic evaluation and also proposed purchase of the Hesser machine. The choice of packaging machine had thus been made.

11. The Packaging Project

The work of the project group started from two pre-established conditions: A double shift was to be introduced and the packaging machine would be a Hesser. The introduction of two shifts was regarded negatively by those employed in packaging. There was another condition, too, that there was no question of enlarging or radically converting the four-story building in which the packaging department was located. The investment framework in the packaging project was around MSEK 15 (U.S. \$2.5 million). The project group consisted of the development manager (head of the project), the production manager, and the head stores clerk (member of SIF) —appointed by management—and a repairperson, a sifter minder, and two union machine operators—members of and appointed by the plant branch of the Factory Workers' Union. One of the machine operators was a safety and health delegate, later also "club representative" for the department. The two machine operators were women; the other members of the group, men.

The project group worked for two years, through 1980 and 1981, and met on thirty-four occasions. It had plenty of time to shape the changes initiated by the introduction of new packaging machines. It has proved difficult to obtain a full account of the processes involved from the minutes of the meetings and talks with the people participating. The group appears, however, to have played an active role in work on the project. Even if the project management and the consultants employed naturally investigated various questions and drafted proposals parallel with the group's meetings, it was precisely this work that was discussed and modified at such meetings. The members of the group also felt that it was easy to make their voices heard and that their various views were taken into account. The group was almost unanimous in its proposals that were later incorporated in the plans.

Some questions were sorted out quite quickly by the project group; others were more difficult and recurred at several meetings. For example, one initial question was the color of the packaging machines. The employees did not want the standard white color; they wanted green. The company ultimately agreed to write to the manufacturers and inquire as to the possibility of getting another color. A second issue arose over the large-pack laying machine. Normally, packets of sugar are bundled and laid on a pallet by automatic equipment. Some packets, however, are sold by the pallet, with the unbundled pallets stacked in a large box of corrugated cardboard, which is known as a "large pack." Stacking was previously performed by hand and was a very strenuous job. Since the sale of large packs was increasing, it was agreed to mechanize this job.

Since no sufficiently reliable equipment of high capacity was available on the market, a great deal of time was spent in discussing and obtaining suggestions for suitable equipment. A manufacturer was also persuaded to develop equipment that was acceptable from the ergonomic standpoint. It is, however, regarded as a prototype, which still needs to be developed to secure reliability of operation.

A third question was the configuration of machinery in the packaging hall. The employees wanted a layout with curved flows, so that the operator of the packaging machines was standing close to the tender of the bundling machine. In this way the two could help each other, and maintain better contact. This request, however, was rejected by the consultant who felt that a layout with straight flows looked better. And that was the final choice.

The "big sacking operation" became the fourth question. With the old equipment, a heavy iron collar on the thousand-kilo bags had to be lifted up high to the level of the filler. This work had long been regarded as unacceptable, and the safety and health committee had requested a change. The engineers in the project group maintained, however, that no technique was available that could make the job easier. The problem was solved with the use of a mechanical lifting arm, thanks to one of the repairers having attended a technical fair where he happened to see just such a device.

The fifth question focused on improvement of the premises. Originally, work on the project related solely to the actual production equipment. The view of the project management appears to have been that the only measures to be taken regarding premises should be those necessitated by the new equipment. In due course, however, the employees pushed through a total overhaul of the packaging hall, including improvements in its acoustics, lighting, and ventilation. It also subsequently proved that the new equipment demanded greater inroads in the joisting than had been envisaged. On the other hand, the employees failed to get the premises for sacking improved in a similar way. The premises, in which at least two people are constantly at work, still resemble a basement storeroom. The technical changes made in the sacking process were also of a very limited nature.

A final question was the organization of work in the actual packaging department. To reduce the division of labor, it was agreed that all those working with the packaging machines and the large-pack layer should be trained on the new packaging machines. In this way it would be possible to rotate among the different duties.

12. Results

If the members of the project group were satisfied on the whole with the actual project work, how did they feel about the results? The employees mentioned a number of things with which they were dissatisfied. Some of them were not covered by work on the project. The configuration of the plant in straight lines created a distance between the packaging machine operator and the bundling machine operator, just as had been feared. Something that would have been an advantage, but was discussed only later, was supplying one of the two packaging machines in a "mirror" or reversed version. The operators would then have stood between their machines, and have had an opportunity for contact and cooperation. Otherwise the machines worked well; the main problem so far has been with the quality of the paper. The machine packages the sugar from reels of paper. Because the quality and strength of the paper vary, the web breaks far too often, interrupting operations and adding to the work load.

The working environment in the sacking department was regarded as unsatisfactory. Those working there felt neglected and there were no signs of the company taking any action. It had also proved difficult to change the cloths in the new sifters. To reduce the sound levels for the sifter tenders, a special area was arranged around the new equipment for monitoring. When a sifter stopped, however, it was necessary to go out. Since the opening of a sifter was unnecessarily complicated, tenders were forced to listen to noise from the other sifters for unnecessarily long periods. Also, a result of the two-shift system was that the tender working during the afternoon was alone for long periods.

The aim of reducing the division of labor in packaging was not achieved. There are several reasons for this. The high capacity of the machines and the problems with the quality of the paper made the work stressful. The tendency was for the most "technically minded" to be left to operate the machines. All those concerned, however, had undergone training and mastered the job so that they could take over as stand-ins. It is perhaps also the case that good cooperation around the overall machinery system was seen as more important by the group than everybody having equally qualified tasks. Nor has the pay grading functioned as the employees expected. The intention was that all workers who had had the same training should belong to the same group. By terms of the agreement, however, this presupposed that operation of the machine is a main duty, not a secondary occupation to, say, tending the bundling machine.

These problems and current shortcomings, however, were overshadowed by the introduction of two shifts, which neither the packaging personnel nor the project group was able to influence and which was supposed to solve the problem of staffing. The more acute problems of individual employees with shift work were solved with some continuing to work only days. Two people, however, left the department to work elsewhere at the mill. But even if a situation has been reached in which people have adapted to shift work, the negative effect on the work force as a community remains. Previously, there was great social solidarity in the department as a whole. Now the morning shift and the evening shift meet each other only when going on and off duty. The conditions for a sense of togetherness in and around the job have already altered drastically.

This problem has been aggravated by the unsatisfactory handling of the staffing issue. In discussions by the project group, and subsequent negotiations, what jobs were required given the new equipment was agreed on. The actual number of reserves was also to remain the same. That number, however, soon proved inadequate. If some workers were out ill, things got very stressful for the others. When everyone had worked the same hours and large quantities were packaged in sacks in the bulk, the effect was not so great. Management maintained that the rate of production could be cut when too few workers were available. This, however, presupposed that the necessary free play had been created in production planning, which was not then the case. Also, the company had not filled the vacancies arising when people left the department.

Since our study of the mill was done, however, the company and union have started to work on these problems, and we have been informed that the situation has improved. During the second half of the 1980s, the work organization was changed. All employed—still mostly women—in the packaging department got training in all tasks, there was rotation among the tasks, and this also resulted in higher wages on the same level as other qualified (male) workers in the plant. So, in contrast to the beginning of the decade, the division of labor has now been diminished. One of the explanations may be that new and younger women have been employed, who in a tougher way demand working and pay conditions equal to those of men.

13. The Lessons Drawn

What did the union learn from the packaging project? The project management took as its task the solving of a technical problem: It was a question of installing new equipment and taking the measures necessary for it to function properly. The perspective of the employees was different: Now that the machines were to be exchanged, it became at last a question of implementing all the improvements they had wanted over the years to create a satisfactory working environment. This conflict of interests was not articulated. As a result, various environmental considerations were introduced piecemeal, and the possibilities of allowing for them were dependent on how the given technical system could be adjusted or supplemented. The employees then found themselves in a difficult situation. Additional demands always stand out as extra costs. The employees' interest in the smooth function of production, in combination with low self-confidence, led them to keep a low profile, so that they would not be accused of complicating the setup and adding to the cost.

The technical thrust also meant that the discussion was conducted in a technical language. This made it more difficult to assert views that could not be justified technically, for example, the desire for a curved flow among the machines. A lack of familiarity with planning also made it difficult for the employees to visualize what was only sketched on paper. Since the machinery layout failed to indicate where different people would be located during production, the advantage of a reversed machine was also not noticed in time. The same applies to the sifting equipment—no one asked how the cloths were to be changed.

The workers' knowledge of what was actually possible to achieve was also limited. They had received no training in, for example, technological development and the organization of work in general. Nor was there any discussion by the union of what sorts of demands might reasonably be met. The predominant experience of those employed in packaging was that they had very little say in the matter. That the color of the packaging machines was so important to the employees illustrates how they experienced the situation: If they could not see any alternatives and bring influence to bear in other matters, it seemed obvious that the machine could at least be of a different color.

Why did the union representatives in the group not get better support from their plant branch? There were several contributory factors. The plant union was used to its members in various project groups managing well on their own. As already mentioned, many of the employees have fairly independent jobs and are technologically well informed and used to solving problems. It is therefore often easy for them to assert themselves in discussions. Most of these production and maintenance workers are men. The union is also male dominated.

Work in packaging is more constrained and machine controlled, but those employed have other qualifications, which are often bound up with the close cooperation required for operations to flow. This competence, however, is not as highly rated at the mill as detailed knowledge of the machinery and its maintenance. Their self-confidence is thus not as great as at other departments. That so many of the packaging employees are women has a bearing on this issue, too. Many women have found that their points of view are less valued both by the company and by the union and that they are expected to have an instrumental view of their work.

That the plant's union executive panel failed to provide better support is, it notes, due to the fact that it is overloaded, as are so many other workplaces, with acute problems and questions. It notes, in retrospect, that it simply did not have the time and the capacity to deal with these issues. It relied on the club representative of the department sounding the alarm when difficult problems arose. But the problems arising in the project group's work at the packaging department were not of an acute nature. Work was on the whole moving well, but help was still needed in developing an independent union position and more direct union support for the demands put forward. Since our case study was finished, the union has further stressed their efforts not only to react negatively to technological change as a threat to their jobs, but also to demand better work organization and influence over the choice of technology. Moreover, the women in the packaging department are now more active.

14. Basic Facts

The Company

The Örtofta sugar mill belongs to Sockerbolaget, or more properly Svenska Sockerfabriks AB, which has enjoyed a monopoly on the production of Swedish sugar since 1936. Sockerbolaget has five other mills for processing granulated sugar, those at Köpingebro, Hasslarp, Karpalund, Mörbylånga, and Roma. Örtofta and Köpingebro are the largest, with a capacity of around six thousand tons of sugar beet per day. Sockerbolaget also has a plant in Jordberga, which produces unrefined sugar, and one in Arlöv, which refines Swedish and imported crude sugar and manufactures and packages various types of special sugars.

The Örtofta sugar mill has some two hundred seventy workers on collective contract and some thirty salaried staff. A further eighty or so persons are employed on a temporary basis during the "campaign" (the three months each year when the beets are harvested and the mill produces sugar). The number of worker-years worked in the sugar company as a whole is around 2,500. Following a peak during the 1940s, the number of employees has successively decreased, and the number employed solely for the "campaigns" has fallen.

Sockerbolaget has been owned since 1968 by AB Cardo. Its share capital is MSEK 415 (U.S. $70.3 million). The largest individual shareholder (as of 1982) is AB Custos with 6.4 percent of the share capital, followed by Skandia (4.4 percent), Trygg-Hansa (3.1 percent), the Handelsbanken Pension Foundation (1.8 percent), the National Pension Insurance Fund (1.6 percent), and Skandinaviska Banken (1.4 percent).

The Cardo Group includes Hilleshög Frö AB, which develops and sells seed products. Hilleshög was formed when Sockerbolaget succeeded in developing a beet seed that produces only one plant, and thus permits rational cultivation. Cardo has also, together with Alfa Laval, started a new company in the field of biotechnology. Research and development is still pursued within Sockerbolaget, but new techniques and products are now frequently passed on to the other companies for further development and sales.

Örtofta is part of Sockerbolaget's Beet Sugar Unit, which includes also the other mills, except Arlöv. Arlöv forms its own profit center. Sales are run at the company level, but the responsibility for marketing rests with the Beet Sugar Unit. By tradition, the mill managers enjoy considerable autonomy regarding operation and maintenance. A manager can make decisions on investments under SEK 40,000 (U.S. $6,800), provided they can be contained within a given investment framework. It is planned that in the future the mills will be steered by set targets relating to yield on capital rather than by directives.

The price of sugar is regulated in the agricultural negotiations. It is determined in three stages: the growers' price, Sockerbolaget's selling price, and the wholesale price. In these negotiations, the area of land devoted to the cultivation of beets is decided on, in relation to the desired degree of self-sufficiency, from 85 to 90 percent. The price of sugar on the world market has long been lower than that of domestically produced sugar. An import levy is exacted on imported sugar, and it is adjusted each month in relation to changes in world sugar prices.

The mills use the beet by-products to produce feed for livestock. Örtofta's annual sugar production, 75,000 metric tonnes, has its counterpart in 20,000 tonnes of molasses, 35,000 tonnes of beet forage, and 100,000 tonnes of wet beet pulp. The growers have the right to take back the beet pulp. Whatever they do not require is bought by Sockerbolaget and processed into forage, which is then sold as feed.

The Unions

All those employed at the Örtofta sugar mill on an annual, collective basis belong to the Swedish Factory Workers' Union. Of those employed for the "campaign," about 50 percent belong to the same union, and about 40 percent to other LO unions. Of the salaried staff, twenty-six belong to SIF (the Union of Clerical and Technical Employees in Industry), three to SALF (the Foremen's and Supervisors' Union), and two to CF (the Graduate Engineers' Association). These three organizations are included in PTK (a joint negotiating cartel).

The plant union normally meets four times a year, and some sixty members usually attend. The executive panel met twelve times in 1982. It consists of nine members and four alternates. Each production section at the mill is represented on the executive board, its members being known as "club representatives." The chief safety and health delegate is also on the executive panel, which constitutes the negotiating committee.

For collaboration between the plant unions at the various mills, there is an annual conference at which members of the Factory Workers' Union working committee, union members of the boards of Cardo and Sockerbolaget, labor representatives on the industrial council, and the central safety and health committee are elected. The working committee meets twice a month, once for internal discussions and once for an exchange of information and negotiations with company management.

The plant branch of SIF normally has three meetings of its membership a year. Its executive group consists of five members, who meet once a month. SIF's branches are normally sovereign, but those within Cardo have obtained a dispensation from the national union to form a joint negotiating body, SIF–Cardo. Locally, it is the PTK that is represented on different bodies. The PTK executive group is elected in connection with SIF's annual meeting; members of SALF and CF are invited to attend for this item on the agenda.

In the following chapters we analyze the case studies and also set them in a comparative context.

7

Implications of the Case Studies

1. Changes in Working Life

All four case studies in the Front project describe changes during the late 1970s and early 1980s. They started during the period when working life was to be democratized, when the unions acquired the right to negotiate on all issues, and when employers were developing their "new factories." It was assumed during this period that a new consultative spirit was beginning to emerge in connection with the Co-Determination Agreements. It emerges, however, that this division into periods was not so clear at the local level, at the actual workplaces.

The case of the Postgiro is the clearest example of co-determination in the sense used in union discussion when the Co-Determination Act (MBL) was introduced. A buildup of union competency and negotiations with the employer were the thrust of union work, with the support of the Co-Determination Agreement (MBA) in the state sector and with further support of wage-earner consultants and full-time union staff. A local rationalization agreement was signed at an early stage. This was followed up by a local project agreement, marking a break with the earlier tradition of consultation developed in the course of joint labor–management experiments in workplace democracy in the public sector. The break was due to union disappointment at its lack of success using consultation on earlier systems development. The process of change at the Postgiro is comprehensive and has dragged on into the late 1980s, with its altered economic and ideological conditions.

191

The case of the dairy has a number of features in common with the Postgiro. Union work prior to the new dairy began shortly after the introduction of MBL, and the cornerstone was a buildup of the union's own competency. As at the Postgiro, outside help was available, in this instance from researchers within the emerging system for working-life research. Supported by MBL and AML (the Working Environment Act), negotiations were held with the employer on the conditions for work on the union program and for participation in work on the project. Within these frameworks, however, a spirit of cooperation and informal contacts predominated.

In the case of the sugar mill we can see, in the 1980s, lingering signs of the consultative line pursued in the 1960s and early 1970s. The years around the advent of MBL were here perhaps more of an interlude that broke off an existing collaboration between the parties at the workplace. This was a collaboration in which union influence on the current project was channeled, as previously, directly through the workers concerned.

At the engineering workshop, the characteristic feature was informal collaboration and influence by the employees based on their professional skill, particularly regarding the acquisition of new machinery. As a result of employee experience with this process, and in interplay with an increased central union effort in technological issues, a new union strategy developed. This strategy emphasized local union work, with a program of action, a technical committee, and so forth. This is an example of how co-determination under the development agreement can be shaped in such a way that the union enjoys greater independence and better expertise at the same time that it cooperates with the employer.

2. Management Strategies

All the Swedish case studies focus on organizations or companies that are either state-owned or incorporated in the state system of controls. Does this mean that their freedom of action is essentially different from that in other Swedish companies and business enterprises? If so, how has this been reflected in management strategies in connection with the projects concerned? Are such differences the main reason that the unions have been so relatively successful in exerting influence? To illustrate this point, let us here discuss the four cases, using our previous description of management strategies (see Chapter 1, section 6). We distinguished there between three groups of strategies aimed at increasing receipts, reducing costs, and increasing control over the free play for future action.

The Engineering Workshop

The engineering workshop most resembles a typical private company. It operates in competition with other companies on the Swedish and foreign markets, with the purpose of rendering a good yield on the capital invested in it. Because it is a member of Stratsföretag AB (a group of state-owned companies), it also, however, has certain complementary objectives. The company is required to strive for long-term security of employment and to promote job satisfaction and increased co-influence. It must also pay special consideration to societal interests in choosing between different production alternatives and locations.

It is difficult to say how far these complementary objectives influenced the present project. It is probably easier, however, for the union in this kind of company to gain a hearing for its demands for insight and participation. Work on the project could also have been influenced by the emphasis on societal interests in locating the company in Norrland, in northern Sweden. Management may have felt a stronger obligation to achieve long-term solutions.

The opportunities to increase *receipts* were limited here, in that this was a small company with scant development resources, thus making it more difficult to meet the customers' sophisticated and often specialized requirements. A modernization of the plant would be necessary if the company was to be able in the future to meet its customers' demands for specially adapted machines, high quality, and rapid deliveries. The union and management agreed that addressing these issues was of central importance.

The possibilities of cutting *costs* were limited by the short series, for varying products, and particularly personnel costs. The handling of this kind of production requires flexibility in the deployment of human labor. Moreover, one goal of the project was an attempt to retrieve the manufacturing of parts that had previously been farmed out to other companies. Hence, the employment of the company's own work force was not at risk. Because most machinery manufactured for particular customers is expensive, the capital costs of goods in process are very important. It is therefore a question of speeding up throughput and reducing vulnerability to disruptions. The company must deliver the machines as soon as possible after an order has been placed. This was another important aspect of the purchase of machinery, and, again, it did not affect the employment levels. On the whole, the union and management had a common interest in the purchase of machinery.

Management's control over the employees was limited by its dependence on the skilled workers' know-how and experience. It had to use their skills. This was also reflected in work on the project. Management did have confidence in the union's choice of people for the project group. At the same time, it had to reckon with greater demands regarding working conditions in the course of the changeover. These demands, however, could be held in check by the employees' roots in the area. This, we can say, was reflected in the union's not having raised the issue of the work organization in the initial phase of the project. However, the level of union aspirations in this respect has been raised following completion of the project.

Regarding the organization of programming work, management was obliged to abandon an established pattern of planning. In the past, this work had been performed in the office. The machine operators, however, could demonstrate that costs could be cut, and the number of disruptions reduced, if they assumed responsibility. These gains could be ascribed to the short series and long processing times. The improvement in job content was also stressed. Management had difficulty in disputing this case. Also, no developed programming function at the office existed before the project was undertaken.

The Sugar Mill

The sugar mill was part of a privately owned company, operating with a view to a good yield on the capital invested. However, its monopoly status—and price controls—entailed certain special opportunities and constraints in reaching its target. It could not simply close down less profitable factories and concentrate its operations at others. This affected the discussion regarding the allocation of packaging work in the initial phase of the project.

The possibilities of increasing *receipts* were limited. Demand was very stable; one way of increasing sales, however, was to edge out the very small proportion of imports. This could be done by increasing production on the area laid down by the state and by an increased extraction of sugar from the beets. Another way was to increase the economic yield on by-products and residual products. A third way was to increase the degree of processing and the range of packaging. One of the starting points of the project was the increased demand for sugar packaged for consumers.

In the case of *costs*, certain demands regarding rationalization were made in the agreement with the state. These were expressed in wage costs for production workers. Naturally, further savings in costs could be made in order to increase profitability. The risk involved was that the societal demands would increase in the next round of negotiations.

In recent years, however, improvement in productivity has been limited. It has occurred at a much lower rate than in other comparable companies. Sockerbolaget has maintained that any radical cut in costs presupposes the concentration of operations to two or three mills (including Örtofta). Even so, the limited improvement in productivity has led to increased pressure from the state in regard to cost cutting. The introduction of shift work in packaging can be seen as a consequence of this pressure. That the company was able to persuade the union to accept these demands was probably and chiefly due to the fact that no one was going to be put out of work.

The company's *control* over development was highly dependent on its relations with the state, which encourages a certain caution regarding long-term investments. It would have been more normal for the owners to invest the sugar operation's surplus in other activities that were not subject to the system of controls. This had been achieved by the incorporation of the sugar industry in a larger group, Cardo, which had several other fields of operation to which the sugar operation's surplus could be diverted (see Chapter 6, section 14). This, however, did not affect the packaging project, which must be seen primarily as a reinvestment.

The company was also dependent on the professional skills of its permanent personnel, because of the special structure of operations, in which the bulk of the work time was devoted to highly qualified maintenance and repairs. The permanent work force also had to function as instructors during the "campaign" as well as take responsibility for discovering and correcting flaws in operations as soon as possible. The management was very concerned to utilize this competency in connection with project work. Conditions in the packaging unit were radically different due to its type of work and continuity of operation. This, however, did not affect the way in which the project was set up. Despite the differences, the changeover project was organized in the same way as projects involving the skilled workers in the production department.

The Dairy

The main purpose of the dairy is to handle all the milk produced by its owners in such a way as to afford them maximum receipts. Profitability, in the usual sense of return on capital, is not the main thrust of the operation. The dairy has a monopoly on sales of its most important products, but this monopoly is only regional. The company's business policy and profitability can be compared with those of other dairies. All these dairy companies, however, are owned by the farmers. It is difficult, on the other hand, to compare their financial results with those of other kinds of companies, since the dairy owners do not receive any direct yield on their capital input, but get their share of earnings in the form of higher prices for the milk they supply.

Receipts were governed by a system of controls exercised by the government. Certain products, however, lie outside the system. These, on the other hand, face competition from other companies. This applies especially to fruit juice and yoghurt, but these were not produced at the new Malmö dairy.

The opportunities to improve earnings by cutting *costs* were greater than at the sugar mill, because the compensation for costs is extended to the dairy industry as a whole. Those dairy companies that can keep their costs below the average level can pay their farmers better. In the short term, favorable results can be achieved by restricting investments, living on "rust and decay." But once the old plant is completely worn out and has to be replaced, there is a heavy financial strain. One of management's most important tasks is to handle investment planning in an optimal manner.

The pressure to cut costs in the context of the new Malmö dairy was not that great for several reasons. One reason was that the modernization of the the cheese factory in Kristianstad had produced considerable rationalization gains. With more or less the same work force, a major increase in production had been achieved, corresponding to the increased demand for cheese. Another reason was the limited opportunity to cut costs in practice. In the packaging and storage departments, where most people are employed, the access to new, labor-saving technology was limited. Personnel costs played a limited role in the project.

In regard to *control* over longer-term development, the state's agricultural policy plays a decisive role. However, the planning of the new Malmö dairy was not influenced by any expected changes in that policy. The dairy companies were also highly dependent on the suppliers of technology. These are few in number and they possess great resources for development. An example is Alfa-Laval. The freedom of choice regarding the construction of technical systems and the level of the technology is thus limited. This was an important factor in the project. Both the technical management and the union felt bound by the solutions that were actually available.

Long-term dependence on the professional skills of the employees is fairly limited. Only a few specific jobs require high qualifications and long experience, and the training period for the majority of employees was quite short. Owing, however, to the short production cycle, and the fact that one day's production cannot be postponed to the next, the demand for reliability in operation is particularly strict. It is very important to utilize the experience of employees and their ability to plan for the timely processing of the milk. This fact characterized the structure of work on the project.

The Postgiro

The expressed objective of the Postgiro was "within the framework of cost coverage, and with due attention to the need of job security and good working conditions, to meet the demands of the market for fast, reliable, and inexpensive payments handling." The Postgiro was also required to try to expand its market by getting involved in other activities. In the pricing of its services, it had to ensure that the capital invested by the state gave a reasonable yield. No profit over and above this was to be planned for.

Receipts consisted mainly of interest on the money while it was being handled. The high level of interest rates and inflation in recent years have produced very good financial results. These, however, were factors over which the Postgiro has no control. It did not, for example, handle the administration of capital. Nor was it certain that it could dispose of its own surplus, which could be absorbed into state revenues by a political decision. The strongest possibilities for increasing receipts lay in an increase in the Postgiro's share of the market compared with the banks. The main means for achieving this would be improved service to the customers. It could also, in accordance with the objectives set, build up a new range of services for which it could charge. These could be services directly connected with the handling of payments or services in which it could use its sophisticated computer equipment.

This, however, was not an important objective in the project under discussion, which was designed rather to save *costs* by introducing new technology relating to the base products. Thanks, however, to union action, the demands of the market acquired a more important role, and this changed the entire thrust of the project. So far as can be judged, this was possible because other forces within management became more dominant. It was some time, however, before the engineers and analysts realized the full consequences of this reorientation.

Some of the original emphasis on costs, however, has persisted throughout the project, for the Postgiro, despite major investments in new technology in recent decades, is highly labor intensive. When work began on the project, it also faced problems with recruitment. The volume of payments was increasing, and the Postgiro was in constant need of new staff. At the same time, staff turnover was high because of the monotonous duties and problems in the working environment.

Control over development in the long term was determined largely by central government policy. Either the Postgiro's status as a social institution would be retained or reinforced, or, alternatively, the emphasis would be on profitability. The choice made would strongly affect the end result of the project. Present management is concerned to operate on a more businesslike footing. Accordingly, the emphasis will be more and more on flexibility, that is, an ability to change course rapidly, to introduce new products, and so forth. This will apply both to choices of technology and to the balance between people and machines. The risk, however, is that the routine tasks will be separated from the more service-oriented and changeable operations and assigned to separate organizational units. The work content of staff in the latter can thus be impoverished. Many routine duties can also be taken over by machines, thus increasing the future threat to employment. The work of the unions has been concerned largely with these issues.

The Postgiro is highly dependent on the suppliers of its technology. For the kind of computer system with which the Postgiro is concerned, there are only a few potential suppliers, whose main market is the banking systems in other countries, and so it is conditions abroad that determine the thrust of their technical development. This restriction to certain specific technical solutions has played a major role in the project (see Chapter 9, section 2).

3. How the Projects Were Steered

The way in which the actual work of change is structured is usually an important part of the company's strategy of control. The idea is to retain the initiative the whole time and ensure that development follows the guidelines that have been established. At the same time, however, it is necessary to utilize the knowledge and experience of both the employees and various suppliers. This can seldom be accomplished without concessions from the standpoint of control. There are various methods of handling this dilemma. Vis-à-vis the employees, management tries in many cases to gloss over the questions of principle that are important to the union, such as the distribution of work between people and machines and the control exercised over the work. All changes are presented as a logical consequence of technological and economic development.

Instead, management tries to concentrate attention on questions of design and detail. The emphasis in collaboration is then, naturally, on the employees directly affected by the change. The demand for an opportunity to coordinate union activities then stands out as an unnecessary bureaucratization of the process. Not infrequently, major changes are also broken down into separate subprojects, making it difficult to discern the main strategy. This approach is sometimes called the "jigsaw" technique. Not until a number of the pieces are in place can one see all the consequences. However, the unions are traditionally attentive to certain questions of principle, especially those relating to employment, wages, and working hours. Management will try to negotiate on them separately.

Why do the unions so seldom protest at this loss of any overall perspective? The most important reason, probably, is that the approach has become so habitual. It also fits in very well with the way the unions work, with their strong emphasis on the mastering and monitoring of distribution issues. In a number of situations, management can probably also claim with justification that it is the union that is preserving old and inadequate procedures.

How, then, was control of the projects exercised in our four case studies? Did it differ from the standard approach? And, if so, is this the reason for the successes achieved by the unions? The sugar mill is a clear example of the distinction made between the traditionally important union issues and questions of design and detail. These were also dealt with at different phases of the project. In the initial phase, which took place centrally within the company, the distribution of packaging work between the mills, that is, the employment aspect and working hours, was raised for discussion. This phase also covered the choice of machinery—and thus also the most important safety issues. Employment and working hours were discussed between company management and the company-level negotiating body set up by the various works unions. Initially these deliberations were informal and confidential, which is to say that the union representatives had only limited opportunity to discuss different alternatives with their member groups. Only when one had already reached an informal agreement did any negotiation take place. The choice of machinery was handled in a different way; discussions were conducted on the central safety and hygiene committee.

The second phase, which took place locally at the individual mills, was of a completely different character. There the project group, made up of engineers and elected union representatives, had an overall responsibility. They actually succeeded in enlarging the established financial framework. This was a traditional procedure. The majority of employees, as a result of their maintenance and repair work between "campaigns," possess important experience and knowledge, which management is concerned to exploit. The fact that this did not apply in similar degree to the packaging staff did not alter the setup.

At the dairy, no such clear division was made between the handling of different questions. The employees took part in the work right from the idea stage. From its experience of earlier projects, the technical management was also concerned to spend time and resources on the initial, creative discussion. This was reflected, for example, in the ideas competition on the design of the dairy (see Chapter 5, section 4). The technical management's motive for this approach was that the technical level of the new plant should not differ essentially from the level at the old plant. It was also important to achieve a high level of reliability very quickly. It was natural to use the professional know-how and experience of the work force right from the start.

This attitude was also reinforced by the union's program of action. It emerged that the unions possessed a strong knowledge base regarding new technical possibilities. And the technical management regarded their views on the design as very similar to its own. This collaboration was successfully maintained, despite the fact that management was concerned to tone down the union influence by an amended project organization. The unions, however, made this move easier for management by accepting a fragmentation of the issues involved in the project. The controversial questions of staffing and organization, which were not handled by the technical department, were postponed until the new facility had been completed and started up.

At the Postgiro, management's control over the process of change was initially limited. It was regarded as the task of the technicians to present proposals. The management would then consider the proposals and negotiate on their choice with the unions. A decision would then be made. This conformed with the SIS/RAS systems development model used by the technicians. When the unions maintained that this working approach was not in line with the Co-Determination Act, management changed its opinion. A new working method was adopted, in which the issues involved in the project were broadened and union representatives were given an opportunity to participate in the process. This was also established in collective agreements. The change in working method was due to other types of analysts coming to dominate the process. Many came from actual operations and had experienced the previous change in system. It became clear that work processes at the Postgiro were difficult to comprehend and modify without support from the people actually doing the work. A number of employees with direct experience of operations were therefore engaged in the work of investigation.

However, no direct control over work on the project was exercised by management even at this point, other than on the few occasions when negotiations were held. The management relied on the investigators. Given, however, the new composition of the management, a change has taken place. The various individuals involved have begun to work more actively, and on a more long-term basis, with the concrete issues. The unions have also taken part in this strategic run-through.

At the engineering workshop strategic discussions between management and union were conducted before any actual work on the project started. Discussion was informal and did not lead to negotiations on any more basic issues. When work on the project subsequently got under way, it assumed the character of traditional bidding procedures for the machinery. Questions relating to the organization arose in earnest only after the employees had acquired practical experience with the new equipment. So far as can be judged, this was not the consequence of any conscious steering by management.

In the previous section we considered the free play available to management in connection with changes and resulting management strategies. Now we can move on to the work of the unions. In at least three of our cases, demands related not only to distribution issues; production issues have also played an important role.

4. Union Perspectives

Our starting point is the discussion of different union perspectives from Chapter 1, section 5. We distinguished there between two fundamental perspectives: the exchange or distribution perspective and the producer perspective. The exchange or distribution perspective had both a positive and a negative side. The positive exchange comprises, for example, security, a fair wage, personal contacts, a good physical environment, freedom of movement, an overview, and a rich and varied job content. The negative exchange comprises, for example, accidents, health hazards, and poor working hours.

The *producer* perspective starts from the interest of the employees in doing a good job. It relates to how the employees view the products, the methods of production, and consequences to the environment; it differs in several respects from the economic perspective of the employers. We distinguished, finally, a future perspective, which may be an aspect of the two fundamental perspectives. This perspective relates to the opportunities of the employees, on the basis of their exchange and producer perspectives, to develop a conscious, effective, and long-term collective policy for action, in other words, the conditions necessary for cohesion and democratic influence.

The clearest example of an expansion in the unions' sphere of interest was the dairy in Malmö. The union program of action contained demands based on all three perspectives. The emphasis, however, was on the producer perspective. Clear views were held on how production should be set up in order to function smoothly, and these views clearly differed from those that have characterized other recently built dairies. In the case of the products, however, and their quality, the unions had the same views as management. They expressed, it is true, a general desire for a more composite production, extended to, for example, cheese and butter. But this did not lead to any concrete demands. They adapted to the planning conditions set up by management.

The future perspective is also well developed. This is reflected in both the work organization and the decision-making system. The emphasis of the work groups is placed on their social role. They bear the responsibility not only for ensuring the flow of production but also for reinforcing cohesion and collaboration among coworkers. The division of labor within the work groups must be constantly reviewed in order to ensure that no one, owing to a lack of self-confidence, ends up with some isolated, routine task. The work groups want to pursue long-term discussions concerning changes in machinery and premises. Collaboration and joint discussion are emphasized at the departmental level. It has been suggested that the breakdown be altered so that the departments provide more kinds of working duties and thus stand on a more even footing. The necessary decisions should be made at departmental meetings, where every employee has a vote. This democratic organization, however, is not intended to replace the work of the union. Instead, the union emphasizes the importance of exploiting the new conditions in a more systematic and independent effort to promote long-term changes. The means for this would be meetings, study visits, and courses given during working hours.

As regards the exchange perspective, the emphasis was on proposals for solutions to difficult working environment problems, including ideas as to how work in frigid temperatures could be eliminated. These were presented in the form of descriptions and simple sketches.

The breadth of discussion at the Postgiro has also been considerable. The starting point has always been that the Postgiro's operation is the production of services, for which the routine handling of payments constitutes only a base. In their producer perspective, the unions have therefore rejected changes that would lend the Postgiro an industrial character with a far-reaching specialization and division of labor—and in the long run more or less complete automation.

Instead, unions have stressed the importance of the organization and working procedures becoming more customer-oriented. Each customer should have one place to which he or she can turn to get his or her questions answered, errors corrected, and various services performed. In this way, the whole core of the operation is the staff, rather than the computer equipment. This presupposes putting together groups of workers who together possess the necessary competence. Experts of different kinds should be available as immediately as possible to these groups. The change in organization should thus result both in an integration of different jobs and in decentralization.

Parallel with demands based on the producer perspective, we find that there were also important demands that can be ascribed to the exchange perspective. These related especially to restrictions in work at video display terminals. The registration of information from pictures on a video screen has been rejected, since the operator's eyes can never leave the screen. Paperless transactions also make it impossible to retain an overview of the actual physical volume of work.

The unions have made demands that limit work at display terminals and similar equipment that puts a strain on the eyes. The solutions suggested were a development of the present technique by which complementary codings of the forms are added in optically legible text and an expansion of working duties by integration with other functions.

The future perspective has also been incorporated, although it is not as readily distinguishable. The most important demand has been for a working approach by which the majority of duties are gathered at as low a level in the organization as possible. This would mean that every employee should regain the overall view of operations that he or she had before the introduction of the big computer systems. Concepts such as the "small-scale giro" have been used in this discussion.

At the engineering workshop, the unions' most important starting point in the project was initially to increase the company's competitiveness. In this, however, it did not differ from management, so that there was no question of any specifically union producer perspective. More of that perspective can be found in the choice of machinery. Union representatives asserted their professional know-how and ensured that the machines would be reliable and turn out a high-quality product. The exchange perspective, in the form of demands regarding protective devices, also played a major role.

Once workers had experience with the new machinery, other aspects of the producer and exchange perspectives entered the picture. The machine operators realized that the proposed division of labor between the shop floor and the office regarding programming was inefficient and impoverished the content of work. The result was a union demand that operators' jobs be "kept whole."

These experiences raised, in their turn, the future perspective. The works union realized that both its knowledge of the new technology and its consequences and the union discussion of objectives had to be developed. It was decided to draft a union program of action. A special technical committee was also commissioned to produce a basis for an agreement on the technology. The dissemination among and anchorage in the membership of these discussions was facilitated by the dissemination of information during working hours, in connection with meetings of the management group, an advantage achieved by union negotiation.

Union work on packaging at the sugar mill was entirely dominated by the exchange perspective. In the initial phase of the project, the object was to guarantee employment at all the mills and reduce the inconveniences of shift work to a minimum level. The union was also concerned that the machines selected would be acceptable from the standpoint of worker safety and protection.

Work in the project group during the second phase of the project required a more integrated discussion. The union representatives, however, never succeeded in developing any cohesive view of how production should be set up and organized. Nor did they obtain any support in this endeavor from the works union executive group. There was no future perspective. Consequently, all these efforts focused on scrutinizing the proposals put forward by the technicians and on trying to reduce the physical and mental strains involved in the work.

5. Union Strategies

In Chapter 4, section 4, we discussed union strategies by distinguishing between two dimensions, namely the internal work of the union and its relations with the employer. Union activities in these two dimensions were combined into a matrix that gave us six abstacted union strategies or "building blocks" for more composite

Figure 4

Local Trade Union Strategies in Project Work

		Internal trade union work		
		Development of simply ex-pressed basic union demands and mobilization	Development of in-depth competence	Weak
	Participation	A	B	C
Relation to the employer				
	Negotiations	D	E	F

Source: Sandberg et al. 1984, 115.

strategies. To make reading of the following section easier, we re-produce this six-field matrix here as Figure 4.

The Four Case Studies

It is impossible to place concrete cases in the squares in any simple manner. Any such allocation we make must be taken with a pinch of salt; it can, however, help in our understanding of the char-acter of different cases, and especially of the above matrix. It will become clear, as has already been suggested, that the squares should be seen primarily as elements that can be used in combina-tion to describe strategies in practical life.

If we consider the cases in terms of the matrix, the Postgiro and the dairy display a number of common features. Early and com-petent trade union intervention fundamentally changed the manage-ment's perspective on the system and the change process itself. The predominant strategy at the Postgiro in the early 1970s was partici-pation, without very much independent preparation (C). Disap-pointment over the results, and the introduction of the state-sector Co-Determination Agreement, contributed to a revision of union strategy in the late 1970s. The emphasis was on a buildup of union competency, partly with the help of experts. Union standpoints were formulated on this basis. These were pushed in negotiations, in the form of both simple demands backed by the membership (D), for example, "no loss of jobs," and in the form of more composite alternative ideas on the form and content of systems development (E). Within the frameworks agreed upon in negotiations, the union took part in work on the project; however, the "negotiating culture" predominated. By developing their own competency the unions have broken the management's exclusive technical authority, and the Postgiro unions by their experience have contributed to the development of competency at the national union level.

Prior to construction of the new dairy, the union made a great effort to develop its competency, which resulted in detailed visions and alternatives and fundamental demands that could often be expressed in a simple manner. On this basis, the union negotiated with management to gain influence in working on the project (D), and subsequently participated with its competency (B), in a dialogue with the company's engineers. In certain phases, it negotiated in order to confirm formally what had been agreed upon (E), but a "cooperative culture" predominated on the whole.

At the sugar mill, the union, in national, industrial, and economic issues, presses quantitative and broadly anchored demands relating, for example, to the proportion of imports and the number of sugar mills (D). Regarding the technology and workplace organization there was no established union line, and little union preparation was made specifically for the participation by members in the project (C). It is usually the members involved, as appointed by the union and by virtue of their knowledge of production and the machinery, who contribute to a dialogue with the employer. The women in the packaging department have a year-round job that is constrained and machine-controlled. This does not give them the same opportunities to develop self-confidence and a knowledge of production. The packaging department is small, and the women working there seem to have a lower status than the men, not only in their work, but also in the union. The union's working approach was not geared to giving the packaging workers the support they would have needed to push through their demands regarding good working conditions.

At the engineering workshop, as at the sugar mill, the union appointed some of the workers concerned to participate in the acquisition and installation of three numerically controlled machines. On the basis of their professional background, they suggested how the machines should be constructed to ensure a smooth flow of production. The union had no policy of its own (C). Issues concerning the work organization and jobs were pursued only as experience was acquired. The metalworkers' club demanded that the operators do their own programming and plan the week's work (D). Thanks to their new experience, the union has now begun to build up its own know-how and policy, which can provide a basis for an influence on future innovative projects. In view of its traditions, this influence can be expected to take the form of participation (B).

An Overall Union View

Union work on production issues, conducted in such a way as to develop the union's own skills and alternatives (B, E), is facilitated if it succeeds in holding together the entire wage-earner collective and if it pursues common demands on the basis of an overall view of how work can best be pursued in the future. This demands a union approach that allows for the varying needs of different groups. As in the case of the packaging workers, it is the weaker groups at the workplace who are hardest hit by the lack of any overall view.

At the engineering workshop we find traces of demarcation disputes between the metalworkers and salaried employees, although these appear to have been bridged. If there are serious demarcation disputes, they can hinder constructive union work on production issues: The dominant strategy can then be the monitoring of distribution issues such as employment and pay levels within the particular group (D).

If, despite demarcation disputes between unions or conflicts among groups within a union, work on production issues is based on a technical-capacity strategy (B, E), there is a danger that this will take place on the terms of the stronger, more highly qualified groups, and that little effort will be devoted to possibly larger, but less qualified groups. Such a strategy developed at the cost of a broad activation of all groups within the membership can present problems for union solidarity and union democracy.

8

Comparative Perspectives

1. European Cases and Swedish Cases

Twenty European Cases

In the European project with twenty case studies, preliminary comparisons between Swedish and other European trade union experiences have been made in reports to the European Commission (Levie and Moore 1984a and 1984b). Since then, in an article in *Economic and Industrial Democracy*, Hugo Levie and Åke Sandberg (1991) reflect on trade union strategies in different national environments. The twenty European cases of technical change are presented in Table 3. This section is directly taken from or based on the article by Levie and Sandberg.

In their analysis of the twenty cases, fourteen issues were singled out: company organization, timing of investment, employment, degree of automation, choice of equipment, health and safety, grading and pay, division of labor, skill requirement, autonomy and cooperation, pace of work, working hours, training, recruitment, and promotion. A pattern seemed to emerge. In seven cases the unions only tried to gain influence in five or fewer of the areas of change. The British insurance and chemicals cases, as well as the Dutch engineering and chemicals cases are good examples. Here, the unions limited themselves to the more traditional issues like employment, recruitment, health and safety, pay. At the other end of the scale we found instances, like the trade unions in the Italian chemicals firm and bank, the Swedish Postgiro and dairy, and the German insur-

208

Table 3

Overview of Twenty Case Studies

Case		*Technical Change*
German	Engineering	CAD equipment
	Chemicals	Automated packing
	Insurance	On-line systems
	Brewing	Automated filling
Dutch	Engineering	Resource planning
	Chemicals	Bulk loading
	Banking	Counter-terminals
	Brewing	Bottling lines
Swedish	Engineering	CNC
	Refinery	Automated packing
	Postgiro	Form reading
	Dairy	New automated site
Italian	Engineering	CNC
	Chemicals	New catalyzers
	Banking	Counter-terminals
	Brewing	Palletizing
British	Engineering	CNC
	Chemicals	Process control
	Insurance	On-line systems
	Brewing	New automated plant

ance company and engineering firm, where an attempt was made to influence nearly all changes. In these case studies it was found that the worker representatives tried to intervene in at least nine issues and not only in the more traditional issues for trade union concern, but also in changes in job content and work organization. The difference between these two clusters of cases seemed significant.

If we tried to classify the twenty cases using our matrix, Figure 3 from Chapter 4, we might have expected the German and Dutch cases to fall in the participation row. This was not valid. The legal right to co-determination of works councils in Germany and Holland did not lead to easy involvement in the design of change. On the contrary, much time was spent negotiating the procedures for actual co-determination, with participation and involvement disappearing over the horizon. This was especially true for the German engineering and chemicals cases. At the two German plants the works councils were reduced to procedural negotiations.

Given the way the twenty cases were selected, it is no surprise to find only two cases characterized by little independent work. It is perhaps more surprising to find only four cases where the union side developed in-depth competence.

We now take a little closer look at six of our case studies from various countries. The two most innovative Swedish cases show some common features. Early and competent trade union intervention fundamentally changed management's perspective on the system and the way it should be developed. The Postgiro and the Dairy cases have been discussed in detail. What follows is a discussion of the German engineering company, the Italian process and engineering companies, and the British brewery.

The German engineering company: The German small-batch engineering company selected was a large subsidiary of a major German steel, pipes, and engineering concern, producing large lifting and conveying equipment. In 1982 the site employed 3,243 workers. The focus of the case was the introduction of computer-aided design (CAD) in the drawing office.

In 1981, the local works council presented an innovative draft agreement on computer-aided design to management. The draft included many substantive points, covering production as well as distribution issues. However, the draft had been made by local works council members in collaboration with experts from their union headquarters, without much information about management's exact plan and without any involvement in management's planning and development process. It is an example of the development of in-depth competence which neither relates to participation in the development of management's plans (A and B in the Matrix in Figure 4 in Chapter 7) nor to basic demands based on a mobilization of the workers involved (D). This externally located development of competence was doomed, since neither the trade union nor the works council was in a position to do much with the detailed demands drawn up. As it happened, not the draft agreement but the right to information and involvement in technical change was the subject of the eventual negotiations (D) between the works council and local management. These negotiations ended in a legal battle, which was won by the works council. Unfortunately, it was granted the right to information in 1982, when the CAD equipment had already been ordered and when the actual process of technical change was already in its fifth year. This case appears to indicate that a development of competence that is not rooted in the local process of change does not further worker representation on production issues. Or perhaps it requires a negotiating power that the worker representatives at the German engineering plant did not have.

The Italian process industry: Two of the Italian case studies describe a mix of participation and negotiation as well as a degree of independent trade union work that led to better results. At the Ferrara plant of Montedison, the process of change was associated with a trade union initiative, with the local works council making the basic demand for new investment to guarantee the future of polypropylene production on site (D). Apart from being a vital research center, the site produced mainly polypropylene and employed 1,276 people in 1982, of whom 60 percent were blue-collar workers. The technological change studied was the introduction of high-output catalyzers, with a loss of 50 percent of the production jobs in the departments concerned and considerable savings in plant, energy, and materials costs. The interesting aspect of this case is that these changes were in fact actively encouraged by the worker representatives, who feared that closure of the production areas was a realistic and far worse alternative.

A year later it transpired that management was considering the investment in new facilities and process with a consequent loss of jobs. The way jobs were lost was negotiated, but the loss of employment itself was accepted, paving the way for some participation in the design of the future work organization (B). The position of the local trade unionists was strengthened by the national agreement on information dissemination, which meant that centrally the unions in formal meetings received information from Montedison management about future plans, including plans for the Ferrara site. This information was coupled with the insight the union representatives received locally through informal contacts with company staff, in particular employees from the Research and Development Department who were involved in designing the new chemical processes. These informal contacts show some similarity to more formal in-depth participation in work organization (B). Finally, formal negotiations took place in which it was agreed that no further redundancies would occur and that the remaining production personnel would be upgraded in view of increased autonomy and flexibility (a combination of D and E). Perhaps the most interesting aspect of this case was that detailed participation in the design of new work organization and subsequent negotiations were possible because of the independent work by the trade unionists in improving their understanding of chemical and technical issues and running courses for the operators and maintenance engineers, so that they could do the same. These courses were set up with the assistance from the company's R&D employees.

The Italian engineering company: The Italian engineering plant investigated was a major location of one of the largest Italian manufacturers of capital equipment for car manufacture and other industries. The study focuses on the introduction of CNC lathes as part of a reorganization of a so-called job shop.

In the job shop there was a traditional basis for trade union involvement in production issues through the high skill levels of the production workers and their representatives. Also, management relied heavily on shopfloor and supervisors' technical know-how. The difference from the chemical site may be noted at this point. The existing technical competence was a useful starting point when the trade unions were faced with major reorganization proposals. For example, the trade union representatives studied questions like subcontracting, capacity utilization, the specifications of different CNC equipment and what types of work could best be done on CNC machines and which work was more suited to conventional machining. This type of knowledge was used both in formal annual information meetings between corporate management and the regional trade unions, and more frequently, at plant-level meetings. As at the chemical works, this was based on the national agreement of 1979. Using these sources of competence the union representatives engaged both in negotiations (E) and participation (B), although they did not participate in any formal project work. Once they had agreed to the basic reorganization of the department with the loss of 40 percent of the jobs, but no redundancies, the trade unions influenced the layout and utilization of the production hall, the exact choice of equipment, the balance between making and buying, skill levels, grading, and training. Perhaps the major success was that the introduction of CNC machinery led to a development instead of an erosion of skills and to a strengthening of the position of the trade unions locally instead of weakening them. One interesting measure of their increased competence was that during the process of change they were for the first time meeting regularly with the production management instead of personnel management, which used to be their main counterpart.

The British brewery: An example of a quite different, but still, in some respects, innovative approach of worker representation was found at the British brewery. Here, no development of in-depth competence leading to advanced negotiations or participation took place. Instead, the originally sophisticated union organization (Batstone et al. 1987) relied on traditional patterns of negotiation and participation.

The focus of the case study was on the construction on site of a small new brewing unit devoted to the production of a new product, lager. The design and construction took place between 1974 and 1979, and involvement of worker representatives was restricted to two sets of issues, decided at different moments during the process of change. First came the decision to invest in the new brewery; the trade unions were consulted on this; and the actual go-ahead was made conditional on their agreement to the building plans. Later, the broad outline of the design and construction plans became a matter for consultation.

The unions based their actual influence on the following simple demands: less division of labor among different grades of operator and less supervision than at the main brewery, considerable training of the operators, and more autonomy. We call these demands simple because no detailed studies were made by the unions to underpin them. They were based on the ideas of the unions' leadership regarding work organization in the whole brewery. The unions did not participate in any development work with management or staff. They just informed management that this was the way they would like to see things moving and relied on management to work out the details. As it happened, management's view of the future was not all that different. However, it seems clear that the unions' traditional strength at this brewery enabled them to direct the design process broadly. One could say that the union acted as a powerful nonexecutive director, drawing some lines and leaving it to the executive management to design changes within those lines. Depending on these traditional patterns (A and D), they still gained influence over some production issues, in particular the division of labor, autonomy and cooperation, grading, and especially the composition of jobs in the new brewery and skill requirements, which varied considerably from the traditional emphasis on seniority, finely defined skill and grade differences, and highly divided work. The union was also successful in that more training was provided to the operators than management had planned; in fact they were trained during the last six months of commissioning the plant, both off and on the job. Despite the three grades of operators at the old brewery, single-grade working was agreed upon, with all operators in the highest grade working under limited supervision. Indeed, without prior intent, a work organization emerged, similar to a semiautonomous group. Originally, management had planned to replicate three grades of operators working under a higher degree of supervision. A combination of technical and production factors, union pressure for single-grade working and more autonomy for these operators, and the success of this new way of working during the first months of the new plant may explain this. The union influence in this case depended on its strong position at the plant. This position was represented by the formal framework of often procedural agreements on work and work organization that had been developed over many years, and the strong informal relations between the senior union representatives on site with both personnel and production management. Influence without any specific in-depth development and a fluid line between participation and negotiation typify this case of best practice.

From the case studies one thing stands out clearly. Whether the main strategy is to achieve the unions' ambitions on production issues via negotiations or via participation, once production issues are involved, a great deal of preparation may be needed.

To gain influence over production issues involved in technical change, worker representatives first of all need clear aims. If these aims differ considerably from management's goals, more will be needed. Yardsticks have been mentioned, as well as knowledge about the present and about the consequences of changes and the support of the membership. Moreover, the aims may have to be made ever more concrete and they may have to be reappraised, as management's or joint development work progresses. All this knowledge and the support of the membership will take careful preparation. What can be achieved by local preparation with some assistance from national trade union staff has been shown in the case studies. However, there obviously will be limits to local influence on technical change.

The Swedish Cases in Perspective

We have reviewed the Swedish case studies and also become acquainted with some other European cases. We may discuss the Swedish cases against this broader background and point to what appears to be one distinguishing feature of the unions' strategy in the Swedish cases, namely, to aim, from the starting point of their own experiences and professional expertise, at an increase and buildup of *knowledge* as a basis for the formulation of both general union ideas and detailed substantial and procedural demands on production issues. (Also, in the successful Italian cases, knowledge, especially the professional knowledge of the employees in combination with the information rights of the unions, is a basic characteristic.) These ideas and demands are put forward, using a broad repertoire of approaches, in order to influence employers' decisions. New procedures are developed and negotiated. Traditional collective bargaining interacts with independent union investigations and studies and with joint project work. Two of the Swedish cases studies, the dairy and the Postgiro, are particularly clear examples of this by comparison with the other Swedish cases and with most of those of other countries. It is these two examples we have foremost in mind in the discussion below.

In relation to the employers, a relatively joint identification of the main current problem seems to exist. In the Swedish cases, stable employment and raised productivity are boundaries, and the main issue to be settled is the choice of the most advanced and reliable equipment acceptable from the standpoint of ergonomics and the work environment. With this definition of the problem, solutions acceptable to both parties could be found. The work organization was also strongly brought up by the unions but full agreement was seldom reached with the employer on this point (see Levie and Moore 1984b, 20).

In the cases from other countries, the union organizations also attack production issues, but seem to choose other strategies—again with Italian exceptions. We have no basis or reason for asserting that any such difference among the cases tells us anything in general about differences among the work of union organizations in the five countries concerned. Our argument is thus suggestive, rather than conclusive. If, however, there are systematic differences between the countries, Swedish labor law may be part of the explanation. The basic conditions of the individual Swedish cases also differ from most of the other European cases, and also from Swedish workplaces in general. In two of the cases, wage-earner consultants and researchers have played an important role. Three of the Swedish companies are relatively small. All of them are in various ways state controlled. The threat to employment was not particularly acute.

The Role of Labor Law and Labor Market Policy

Labor law, including the Co-Determination and Working Environment Acts and Union Officials Acts (the Act Concerning the Status of Shop Stewards), has been of great importance. This legislation was pushed through by an interplay between the unions and the Social Democratic government against the background of growing demands from the workplaces. These acts helped to make technology and work organization issues for the unions; they also provided the time for unions to work on them. They have provided an important background for union attempts to bring influence to bear. They have been followed up by substantial union training and information programs, financially heavily supported by the Work Environment Fund, and national union policies to support local action. With these acts behind them, the unions have negotiated project organization, the free play for continuous influence by the union and employees, and sometimes also the actual objectives of project work. It has sometimes been possible to enter a dialogue in joint work on a given project on acceptable terms. As a basis for their participation, the unions have had good access to information, their own training, the time to perform their own studies—both in-depth investigations and broad study groups among members. Sometimes support from outside has been available. Unions have been in a position to use the information available to them.

The union organizations have therefore not seen themselves forced to restrict their activities to formal post hoc negotiations regarding the consequences of change, resembling wage negotiations in form. And they were not, as in the Dutch and West German case studies, involved in disputes over access to information and the right to participation.

In the cases we have studied, the acts thus appear to have played both an important background role by creating a high level of consensus on union participation and a concrete role in strengthening the unions' resources and influence. Given a strong local union branch, it has not been necessary to seek support in the acts in each individual phase. They are a way of guaranteeing a minimum level of influence. We find, even so, several examples of a direct and express use of provisions in the acts and agreements. This was a dominating feature at the Postgiro. For example, the union used the opportunity provided by the state-sector agreement to exercise a "temporary veto" in a manner that greatly influenced work on the project. In all the cases, the favorable preconditions for union work and studies have been important. There were few problems with access to information, and no conflict arose over the interpretation of laws and agreements, so it is difficult to evaluate the precise influence of the legislation.

In an international study of employee involvement in production issues and identification with the company, Swedish employees ranked high. One hypothetical explanation offered is that labor law and the agreements have laid the ground for positive "invisible contracts" between employees and their companies (Yankelovich et al. 1983; Zetterberg et al. 1983). Employees getting deeply involved in a long-term perspective in a company may need trade union support to dare to take this kind of personal risk. Swedish labor law contributes to the unions' possibilities of developing security of employment and influence at the workplace, so that the employees have a relatively high control of their own work. More generally, cooperation between the unions and the Social Democratic government may lay the fundamental preconditions: An active labor market policy drastically reduces the negative effects for individuals of rationalization and restructuring.

Special Conditions

In two cases, the dairy and the Postgiro, the local union enjoyed the external support of action researchers, wage-earner consultants, and full-time staff from the national union. The national unions have had an express policy on work organization renewal. Additionally, procedures were developed for collaboration with technical experts within the company. The external support provided did not, however, prevent the basic character of the strategy from being a local and independent union one.

The input of resources was large, compared with what is available to most plant unions. At the dairy, the local union was supported by a research project. Moreover, at the dairy, the technical manager also had a special interest in the development of good conditions of work, and made technical expertise and resources available. At the Postgiro, the Civil Servants' Union elected to deploy numerous full-time staff and allocate funds for wage-earner consultants. By comparison with the large number of their own personnel and consultants that managements normally deploy, the support received by the local unions was extremely limited, but this support proved to be of major importance in helping the union to underpin its visions and demands.

Given what must be regarded as reasonable resources, the union appears to have a real chance of playing a constructive role in production issues. At the Postgiro, for example, the union, with the help of experts, acquired sufficient insight to be able to stop, in the initial phase of the project, an investment in machinery that management is today grateful not to have on the premises. At the dairy, union competency, as expressed, for example, in its action program, made a decisive contribution to the shaping of the new facility.

Three of the Swedish workplaces are small compared with those in most of the European case studies, having between one hundred fifty and three hundred employees. This may have facilitated informal contacts and day-to-day cooperation within a project organization. The exception is the Postgiro, where the degree of formalization and actual negotiation was accordingly higher.

One also gains the impression that the Swedish unions have had an easier task, in that the question of employment and redundancy has not predominated over that of the actual content and quality of work. At the Postgiro, however, there had recently been job losses, and there was a threat of further layoffs. The union, on the other hand, succeeded in negotiating an agreement that guaranteed employment and, thus, the peace of mind in which to work on questions relating to the content of work and service.

The Swedish cases can also be said to be in various ways "protected" from an uncontrolled market as a result of state intervention. The Postgiro, as part of a state corporation with no direct profit requirements and a favored status in relation to competitors, affords good conditions for union work on the development of alternatives. The sugar mill is part of a private company that has a monopoly on its product. The price is determined by the state, after negotiations. The dairy is a cooperative, with a regional production monopoly. The market is controlled by an agreement with the state. The engineering workshop is the case that most resembles an ordinary, privately owned company. Pullmax, although it is owned by Statsföretag (that is, the state), is required to operate as a profit-making company, and does so in a tough export market against international competition. However, the Articles of Association drawn up for the Statsföretag group do include trade union representation on the local management board as well as the general development of industrial democracy. (Pullmax was sold in 1986 to a private Danish investment company, but this has not prevented the local union from actively influencing ongoing technological change.)

Conditions in the Swedish cases differ in part from the majority of European cases and also from Swedish companies in general, at least in terms of the support of experts and form of ownership. This does not prevent their constituting interesting examples of local union work in Sweden. However, the fact that our four cases of interesting union work "happen to be" owned or controlled by the state makes it important to investigate whether the local unions in the private industrial sector are faced with other difficulties when they raise production issues.

The cases, even so, are of general interest. Their special feature, from our point of view, is perhaps not so much that they belong to the state and the cooperative sphere, but that the union organizations enjoy particularly favorable conditions in which to develop, with support, their own and their members' knowledge. Also, there seems to be every opportunity to create such favorable conditions in the sectors of industry subject to competition. It is a question of small resources being made available to the unions. These resources, as it has emerged, can be used within new types of consultation and negotiation structures in a manner that is also highly constructive from the standpoint of management.

A national survey of co-determination and strategic decision making in large Swedish companies shows that managing directors

Table 4

Effects of Union Participation on Decision Making. Evaluations by
Managing Directors, in Percentages

	Better	Worse	No Different
From business–economic standpoint, decision was:	21	8	71
For the personnel, decision was:	27	2	71

Source: Berggren 1985. Translated and used with permission.

take a positive view of union influence, not only for the employees
but also from the perspective of business economics. There is even a
tendency, where the union is stronger, for management's evaluation
of union influence to be still more positive (see Table 4; see also
Berggren 1985; 1986). These basically favorable views of co-determination from managers at the company level are interesting if you
compare them with the resistance toward co-determination sometimes put up by national employers' associations. Employer resistance is probably not basically due to economic factors. First, the resources necessary for independent union work and advanced co-
determination are small as compared to the fundamental and strategic changes we are interested in, and second, management thinking
often emphasizes the constructive role of union involvement in company decision making.

So employer resistance to union involvement is probably not
based in a fear of high costs or a lower quality of decision making,
but perhaps it is based on a fear of management losing control of
decision making and its legitimacy as the sole decision maker (see
Cressey 1985, 33). Perhaps this fear is more pronounced in the private than in the public sector. In the public sector, the "manager" is
not the single person with an undisputed right and competence to
interpret the environment, the free market. The manager is subject
to political decisions with a popular influence, even over the goals of
the organization.

This conclusion is supported by data from the survey just referred to by Berggren (1986, 21f.). Management in cooperative companies displays a more favorable attitude toward trade union participation in decision making. In the cooperative companies, 65 percent
of managers believe that such participation brings new resources to
the company, as compared with 48 percent in the private com-

panies; 82 percent as compared to 45 percent are of the opinion that decision making gets slower, but implementation quicker. More cooperatives than private managers, however, believe that union participation claims too much time and too many resources. This may have to do with the fact that unions actually do participate to a higher degree in the strategic decision making of cooperative companies.

As to the effects of trade union participation on the business–economic outcome of decisions and on the conditions for the personnel, we find the same tendency as in the general attitude above. Both unions and management in state and cooperative companies more often say that the effects are positive; private sector responses are more negative. (Berggren 1986, 49ff.). It is also more common in cooperative and state companies for the unions to have wanted to postpone or turn down management's proposals (Berggren 1986, 77).

2. General European Perspectives

Implicitly, we have already pointed to possible differences between Sweden and other countries regarding the preconditions for a trade union influence in production issues. We go back to our introductory presentation of Swedish industrial relations (Chapter 2, section 1) and supplement it with some reflections based on other comparative projects (Cressey 1985; Della Rocca 1986) and on the case studies in four other European countries within our project (Levie and Moore 1984b is the main source for the following sections; Batstone and Gourlay 1986, 278ff. is mainly based on a British survey, but with a cross-national section based on the European case studies).

The Scandinavian countries, and also, for example, West Germany, are characterized by centralized trade unions and regulation by means of central agreements and legislation. This regulation, which is external to the workplace, allows worker representatives the right to information and consultation. In Scandinavia it emphasizes procedures, and in West Germany the more specific, substantive aspects (such as technology agreements on ergonomic and other working conditions on VDTs). In Sweden, worker representation at the local level takes place through the unions. The local union negotiates within a national outline framework, which strengthens the procedures for consultation but at the same time imposes limits regarding local union action (Della Rocca 1986). The Swedish union movement is not only centralized but it also has a high density and active locals (Kjellberg 1983). Local union activity is supported by central regulation at the same time as local experiences are transmitted to higher union levels. The central union can bargain with the state, and there is often a pattern of local regulation with the union as a legitimate partner—all on a wide range of issues (Batstone and Gourlay 1986, 263ff.). The four Swedish cases all fall in the highest quartile among the twenty cases in terms of the number of areas in which the unions played a role (Levie and Moore 1984b, 64f.).

In Italy, as in Scandinavia, our case studies seem to point to an interesting relationship between the national and local levels. In one of our Italian cases this manifests itself in an effective combination of centrally negotiated industry-level information rights and precise workplace-level strategies of worker representation. Individual and collective skills (*professionalitá*) seem to be a key concept in these more proactive strategies, which go beyond ex post facto bargaining. Increasing cooperation among production workers, technicians, and scientists is an interesting approach by which to obtain and be able to use information. The industrial relations system can be characterized as conflict filled and bipolar, with centralized national-level negotiations with a primacy of politics and ideology within three different national confederations. Collective bargaining with little recourse to legislation is the dominating form at the other end of the spectrum—the workplace shop stewards committees elected locally by members of all the confederations. Local negotiations concentrate on immediate shop floor conditions and do not seem to constitute part of any more long-term strategy to influence working life.

A problem in the Dutch, and also the West German cases, is the dual system of worker representation, with local councils handling production issues at the local level. Both these countries have a low union density, as compared to Sweden, and Scandinavia in general, with its local union representation. This leads to problems when trying to influence technological change, where, as we have seen, a close interplay between different levels is a key to successful efforts. With plant councils, the links between levels of representation are more fragile. In the Dutch cases, worker representatives were not able to translate general trade union policy into specific demands for changes at the workplace.

Local-level collective bargaining is a dominant feature in the United Kingdom, but there it is more informal than in Italy. The common tendency in Britain seems to be to treat the introduction of new technology in terms of conventional trade union practice. "Arm's length collective bargaining, reactive and after the event, concentrating upon pay and conditions attaching to jobs, and with its emphasis upon the current interests of members according to sectional union representation, seem to characterize the British trade union approach" (Levie and Moore 1984b, 31). This essentially defensive approach, concentrating on job losses, wages, and working conditions—basically a type of technological inevitabilism—was criticized by Mike Cooley (1980) and others in the Lucas Aerospace shop steward combine committee, in their alternative corporate plan for useful production (Gill 1985).

New technology agreements are common, but most of them restrict themselves, as to procedures, to bargaining rights during implementation, and, as regards content, job security dominates over job design (Della Rocca 1986). A challenge for the British unions seems to be whether they will be able to develop their strong and self-reliant workplace organizations in such a way as to be able to cope with technological change.

The general European picture seems to show continued dominance of local collective bargaining. Among the reasons for this is that it is a long-standing, vested procedure that is flexible enough so that whole sets of related local changes can be treated without specifying areas or substantive demands in advance. General technology agreements tend to be procedural agreements, which can be modified according to local needs (Cressey 1985, 13ff.).

One can perhaps see a tendency toward developing central procedural regulation, including both legislation and agreements. The Scandinavian countries, with regulative systems external to the workplaces, go on developing these systems, reinforcing negotiation and consultation rights at the local level. Like Britain and Italy, other countries are beginning to build up a formal procedural structure (Della Rocca 1986). In countries such as Britain, Canada, and Australia, with strong bargaining traditions, government has recently been active on issues of worker participation and technology (Deutsch 1986b).

A second common aspect is the flexibility of the new technology, which renders the established demarcations among jobs, occupations, and trade unions obsolete. The regulation of such boundaries takes place both in formal negotiations (between management and worker representatives, and among the unions themselves) and in informal processes with new solutions developing locally. It is a fundamental challenge for trade unions to find ways of solving the demarcation problems. With new types of integrated jobs, these problems will become frequent.

A third aspect is that substantial general regulations concern mostly the physical work environment, with ergonomic working conditions at video display terminals as a typical example. This can be handled more or less within the traditional negotiation model.

Work organization and job design, on the other hand, are seldom regulated in substance in that way. This is perfectly understandable against the background of our discussion of what is characteristic of production issues: long processes of change, with information and alternatives developed gradually and locally, making it difficult for workers to formulate clear mandates for their representatives.

The main innovations seem to relate to processes rather than to specific content and substantial aspects. Structures for participation and negotiation are being developed. The handling of context rather than the definition of specific mandates is becoming strategic. Procedural regulations

> not only sanction the right of information, but also determine how negotiation must be phased, on the basis of the time necessary to monitor the introduction of technological and organizational change. Thus as Della Rocca points out, the type of union and employee commitment over organizational change becomes the very subject of bargaining. According to Williams, a new model of industrial relations is now looming in the distance; a model based on more participatory trade union structures, capable of engaging in the formulation of complex policies for shaping the decision-making process over technological change. . . . This does not imply a mere depoliticization of industrial relations. (Berta 1986, 12ff.)

This is shown by Scandinavian experiences. These conclusions by Giuseppe Berta, based on overviews of industrial relations and technological change in a number of European countries are well in line with the findings in our comparative project. Referring to our Swedish case studies, we would emphasize even more the political and long-term strategic dimension. In our "best practice" cases, the local structures developing are "dialectical" ones, offering possibilities of involvement and commitment, as well as of independent union work and conventional negotiations. Additionally, these structures are developing in relation to, and are supported by, policy decisions within central trade union and political bodies.

There are, of course, dangers in this focus upon processes and union and worker participation. One danger is that there are participation processes that seem very advanced, although one has little idea whether working conditions are in fact changing, and if so, for the better or for the worse. As already touched upon, clear-cut negotiations may be a form that helps keep substantial goals and demands alive and helps articulate conflicts of interest. This is a basis for evaluating—although it is intrinsically difficult—the solutions and the degree of influence achieved. It is also a basis for analyzing and developing the preconditions for efficient participation and negotiation. In recent years, Scandinavian unions have developed more substantial ideas about "the good work" (see Chapter 10).

By way of conclusion, we now provide a brief general overview of different types of preconditions for successful co-determination. (The systematization is based on Holm et al. 1986, 76ff., and is their conclusion after analyzing innovative Scandinavian experiences; see also Levie and Moore 1984b, 36f., 62, 72ff., 93ff.; Cressey 1985, 6f., 32f., 68ff.; and Armstrong 1986, 12f.)

Conditions external to the company that contribute to the possibilities of trade union influence are: a sheltered market situation (for example, monopoly or state regulations), the existence of technological alternatives (for example, several producers of custom-made new technology rather than one supplier of a turn-key solution), a situation in which technology is not crucial to the competitiveness of the company, a labor market favorable to the employees, and finally, the existence of laws and agreements supporting and legitimizing such influence.

Favorable conditions relating to management include state ownership, a genuine belief on the part of management in the competence of the workers, decentralized decision making that leaves discretion to the local management, the existence of planned technological change, a limited management knowledge of production, and a dependence on worker skills and experiences.

Examples of preconditions coupled to production are a production technology that is flexible and locally adjustable, a transparent production process with workers with broad qualifications, and, in general, interesting and qualified work.

Essential preconditions relating to the local union itself include earlier experiences of influence, trade union awareness and technical understanding, pressure from members to obtain influence, and, finally, resources (time and money) for trade union work on production issues; this includes investigations, study circles for all members, meetings with members, and access to management and its experts (the latter perhaps in their role as trade union members).

In relation to the wider union, favorable conditions are a general public support for the legitimacy of union influence in technology issues, coordination between different levels and bodies of employee representation, support by a national union policy (including national training activities), development of criteria for "good work" and even of alternative prototypes or finished systems, employee consultants, and, finally, national and regional political support in the form of policy on technology, education, and so forth.

Preconditions of this kind do not in themselves ensure a favorable outcome; the trade union strategies and the activity of its members are crucial. On the subject of strategy, we emphasize two aspects: coordination among levels and involvement in early planning phases. The coordination among levels stresses the importance of coordination at both company and group levels, because technological change is often planned and decided at high levels. This can be a problem, for instance, in the United Kingdom and in the United States, where most bargaining takes place at the local level (Bamber 1986). All this should be part of a national policy, as has been discussed above and will be considered in detail in Chapter 9. This is emphasized in many comparative research reports and also in a trade union evaluation report on a recent study within the European community (in Cressey 1985).

Second, influencing the early planning stages of technological change is crucial in successful processes of co-determination. But the general picture we get seems to indicate that in the planning phase there is (at best) only access to information and that only in the final implementation phase is there any clear shift toward consultation and negotiation as the method of participation. In the planning stage, options are investigated, and the precise nature of the changes to take place is not known. This is often taken as an argument against the possibility of more far-reaching participation (you cannot know what to negotiate until you have a precise proposal); management expresses fears of being disturbed in its planning, while the worker representatives sometimes say they feel unqualified to discuss and negotiate with technical experts (Cressey 1985, 33).

The fact that union information rights are coupled to the timing of the union right to representation and co-determination may actually hinder efficient union and employee influence. With a right to information from the moment management starts its work on the guidelines for future investigations, unions may be in a better position really to participate in the later stages: Members can be informed and mobilized, and special union investigation groups (sometimes with external support) can build up an in-depth knowledge and develop their demands and alternatives. The importance of a right of access to company information, independent of any rights to co-determination, seems to be a key conclusion that we can draw from our European case studies (Levie and Moore 1984a, 10). The unions' inadequate technical knowledge has been discussed at length above, as have the necessary new preconditions relating to the union development of knowledge, which includes planning skills. The planning process itself can be negotiated at the earliest planning stages: Its general goals and stages, points of negotiation and evaluation, the project organization, user and union representation in this organization, trade union resources for independent preparations for participation can all be mandated. And this high level of participation in the planning phase is of course possible without knowing what the precise and detailed outcome of the process will be. It is possible to the extent that management's own planning process is well developed. The Swedish dairy and Postgiro case studies show this fact clearly. In the latter case, the gradually changing process of systems development may be seen as a main outcome of the trade unions' efforts.

3. North American Perspectives

Our final task in this comparative chapter is to relate some of our findings on the role of trade unions in Sweden and Europe to the North American situation. We first comment on a picture drawn of Canadian experiences with changes in the workplace (Mansell 1986; Rankin and Mansell 1986; Rankin 1990).

The typical Canadian situation still seems to be a management trying to organize work according to Tayloristic principles, with detailed control over the way work is performed. The workers and trade unions respond to this by trying to develop a countercontrol, a job control regulating in detail "who is to do what." The procedure for gaining this control is formal collective bargaining. The traditional work organization and formal negotiations are threats neither to most managements nor to most unions. Management has its "residual powers," its prerogative of managing the company; the unions negotiate the consequences of management's decisions affecting wages, working hours, and conditions. On the workplace level, trade unions tend to see negotiation and the specification in detail of worker rights and obligations and detailed job control as the only way they can influence the work. They are thus often opposed to new types of work organization with more integrated and flexible jobs that cannot be regulated in detail in advance. This all occurs in an environment where trade unions often face not only the employers but also an unfriendly labor legislation and labor market policy.

Under economic pressure to use new technology and job design to improve the competitiveness of industry, parallel structures of different kinds have been set up in many companies: quality circles, employee involvement schemes, and systems of joint labor–management committees. The parallel structures, however, leave the basic company and work organization intact and they do not threaten either the management or union structure. Most groups of this kind are not allowed to deal with fundamental changes in policy, management systems, job design, and the like.

Given the rigidity of the traditional structures on both sides, one often seems to try to find a solution by departing from the old structures and ideas, for example, via company and job redesign according to sociotechnical principles. One tries to develop its principles of decentralization and learning in a new kind of joint effort based on mutual trust and shared responsibility among the individuals involved. There is a strong emphasis on the importance of the psychological climate. This is not to deny that in some cases reported, for example, the Shell Sarnia plant, there is a discussion of the relationship between collective bargaining and joint efforts in organizational redesign and of the role of a strong local union. This, however, seems to be the exception rather than the rule.

Within U.S. trade unionism, detailed job control and industrial unions are similar responses to Taylorism and mass production (Howard 1985, 171ff.). American industrial unionism has come to presuppose Taylorism. At the time when a strong union movement was developing in the United States, management had already built up Tayloristic work organizations that laid the foundation for labor relations with large numbers of job classifications and restrictive work rules. To protect their members, and influence management, the unions, given the existing system, insisted on formalizing practices in contractual language. This means:

1. Management could no longer unilaterally decide how to reorganize and assign work.
2. Because of the union's ability to resist reorganization, and to adhere to rules, management was compelled to deal with the union on many issues that were not, strictly speaking, collective bargaining issues.
   In combination with the seniority principle these results gave unions considerable power and allowed them to provide their members with many protections. (Unterweger 1987).

In the U.S. situation, with few bargained or statutory rights to influence or to job security, job classifications and rules offered the workers and their unions some possibility of modifying managements' arbitrary decisions and also a basis for bargaining over working conditions.

There are, however, unions like the Communications Workers of America (CWA), which respond to managements' ideas of corporate cultures and flexible production by trying to supplement the traditional "adversarial" relationship of collective bargaining with a cooperative, problem-solving relationship that tries to address the problems of changes in work and technology. There are many joint quality of working life (QWL) committees; labor–management cooperation in safety and health matters and in technological change is advanced. To the extent that the unions have seen cooperation as the primary strategy there is a risk that they might become hostages to new forms of management without independent alternatives of their own (Howard 1985, 196f.).

One example of this risk is clear when management and the union in a unionized plant cooperate in organizational redesign, with the union knowing it has the means to influence management; management then transfers the new job design, or parts of it, to another plant that is not unionized, and where the consequences for the employees, especially in the long term, may be radically different and negative. This lack of union strength at workplaces may help to explain North American union resistance to organization redesign. (Compare here the Swedish Metalworkers' Union conditions for taking part in a development project at a SKF plant in Gothenburg; see Chapter 3, section 4.)

Steven Deutsch (1986a) sees a lack of coordination on the union side. Deutsch argues for the need for union strategic planning and influence concerning decisions on organizational structure and technology at high levels of management. He gives an interesting example: The Machinist Union (IAM) has proposed a "Technology Workers' Bill of Rights" and is creating a national technology center, thus going beyond job-site contracts.

Several instances are found in U.S. industry (see, for example, Deutsch 1986a) of unions making concessions on wages and work rules and job control, accepting and even preferring a more flexible work organization with multiskilled workers, with a quid pro quo in the form of worker and union influence in decision making and sometimes lifelong employment for current employees. The auto workers (UAW), for example, have cooperated with General Motors in developing classifications and a nontraditional work organization. Fears are expressed, however, that such developments take place only where management lacks any alternatives to raising its competitiveness in cooperation with the unions. The bargaining power of some U.S. unions may already have been eroded so much "that capital no longer depends upon union cooperation, and that it feels no need to offer unions a productivity coalition on acceptable terms" (Wolfgang Streek, according to Luria, undated; see also Luria 1986).

In *The Brave New Workplace,* Robert Howard (1985, 205) asks whether a strong labor movement for the social control of technology would constitute a return to an "adversarial relationship" in American industrial relations. We cannot answer for the American situation, but we believe that this book, and our studies, have shown that, in the Swedish situation at least, strong unions on "production issues" does not mean a return to an earlier type of relationship, but rather an innovative development of union visions and strategies that go beyond both the traditional wage-negotiation model of an adversarial type (as a reaction to Taylorism) and simple participation and cooperation (as a part of soft "new management").

Let us now try to compare the above generalized picture of North American developments with an equally generalized picture of the situation in Sweden. In Sweden, the managements of many companies have for some twenty years, and with a growing intensity, been trying out and propagating ideas of new types of work organization. The "new factories" program (Chapter 3) is an example.

Historically, trade unions in Sweden have formed their policy as a reaction to Taylorism but they do not seem to have become so much a mirror of Taylorism as their North American counterparts. This may be due, all in all, to their strength as part of a broad labor movement in political power pursuing an active labor market policy that results in low unemployment and high job security. The Swedish unions have thus largely been in favor of the changes toward new forms of work organization, provided that they have a say in things. The Co-Determination Act regulates the procedures of decision making and gives the unions a right to information and consultation; the co-determination agreements develop the ideas of direct and representative influence and formulate goals of learning and the development of competence in all jobs; state support is extended to union education and training. The act and agreements legitimize the role of trade unions in such issues as technology and work. In that sense the "residual powers" of management are reduced. After information and consultation, however, management has the right to make the final decision.

The differences between the North American and the Scandinavian situations help explain, for example, the UAW's view of new kinds of work organization. If the union agrees to take part in such renewal it wants management to change as well. The union demands a reduction in "overblown office and supervisor structures" and "unnecessary layers of management" and "if management really wants workers to invest their human resources in the production process they must provide a real measure of job security." A UAW spokesman concludes:

> The unions cannot yield influence based on classifications, work rules, and seniority without a quid pro quo. We will not

give up the hard won gains on which the rights and powers of our Union rests without success in negotiating rights similar to those that many European unions have by law. This means a sharing of information and decision-making power on the shop floor and at all higher corporate levels. (Unterweger 1987)

When the Co-Determination Act was introduced in Sweden in 1976, unions first tried procedures of co-determination that were very formalistic and close to the traditional wage-negotiation model. The unions had few ideas regarding changes in the basic work organization. Today the situation is different. We are beginning to find new innovative procedures for internal trade union work, as well as for relations to the employer, combining negotiations, joint labor—management committees, and changes in the work organization itself. Although certain parallel structures (like certain quality circles) may be circumscribed and not allowed to raise any wider issues, many joint committees, in an interplay with formal negotiations, are set up explicitly to deal with fundamental changes in technology and organization. Changes in work organization, qualifications, and the like are seen as closely related to traditional distribution issues like wage levels and systems. Thus, the new procedures do not attempt to move away from the old procedures but rather to build on them. In the historical and political Swedish and Scandinavian situation, this means that a concrete and new role for the trade unions is part of the innovative solutions.

However, the growing integration of production and administration and the integration of manual and mental labor that characterizes the new kinds of work organization sometimes entail conflicts of demarcation between blue-collar and white-collar unions. As this division, between LO and TCO, is fundamental in the Swedish union structure, we may very well be facing a period with a growing number of conflicts among unions. Also, the "good examples" of innovative union practice we have given are not the general rule. Many unions have not gone that far. But many are struggling to achieve ways of developing the old structures and procedures, so that they will be able to represent their members efficiently in the "production issues." We must also remember that a basic precondition for a new and comparatively strong role for the unions in Sweden seems, in short, to be labor movement cooperation between unions and Social Democrats in political power, creating favorable labor law, supporting union training, and setting a priority for low rates of unemployment.

9

Multilevel Technology Strategies

1. Long-Term Managerial and Union Perspectives

From the managerial perspective, co-determination is sometimes seen as a bureaucratic restriction on decision making. It has, however, also been seen as a way of developing the trade unions into "efficient sparring partners of the management" (*Dagens Nyheter*, 17 January 1979). Arguing along the same lines and emphasizing especially strategies that combine a development of trade union competence with negotiations, management consultants have talked about the trade unions as a "challenger," asking themselves whether "it would not be possible to use an increased co-determination . . . to create better possibilities for learning and renewal in companies" (Skärvad and Lundahl 1979). These tensions, then are to be exploited: Competent managements have the ability to "handle competition between ideas" by "supporting or struggling against different frames of interpretation" (Rhenman and Skärvad 1977, 38ff.).

From a trade union point of view, co-determination can be seen as an instrument exclusively designed to better conditions, and competitiveness, at the individual workplace. Trade union independence would not then be the fundamental condition we have assumed above. Co-determination, however, can also be seen in a producer and future-oriented perspective as part of a long-term trade union strategy for the democratization of working life as a whole. An independent trade union build-up of competence then emerges as an important part of the strategy: Gradually, via participation and negotiation, the position of the unions and the workers

231

will be moved forward. The fifteen-year history of the Co-Determination Act makes it fairly clear that trade union resources are too small for any buildup of in-depth competence and concrete alternatives in all areas of management; there are even fewer chances that such alternatives will be adopted by the employers. What we find, instead, are examples of trade unions that, at least for some period of time, have succeeded in exercising a major influence in one area, for example, the work organization. Our case studies illustrate this fact. Concrete, if limited, steps forward are, however, important examples of what can be achieved. They are also necessary in order to build up self-confidence and a belief in the individual's and the collective's abilities and opportunities to exert influence.

Strategies based on a trade union development of competence and on the formulation of fundamental demands are an essential basis for any real influence on current changes at the workplaces. This has been demonstrated by our examples and analysis in this book. A well-founded and clear trade union line is perhaps even more necessary in order to clarify the limits of local union influence and develop demands as part of a more long-term process of democratization. To encounter, reflect upon, and try to eliminate obstacles constitutes, we can say, a sort of strategic or political learning in the field of working life, a complement to the frequently discussed local or sociotechnical learning in and about local development processes (see Abrahamsson 1977, on sociotechnical and political participation).

This complementarity, however, may become problematic, as sociotechnical learning can be developed in joint labor–management schemes and by union participation in managerial activities, while political learning may perhaps best be developed in a relation of negotiation, in which the limits and contradictions can be made clear. In a long-term perspective, the union relationship to the employer would seem more important than the internal work of the unions. Political learning may even sometimes best take place in independent trade union investigations and education, without any short-term relationship to ongoing managerial projects (neither participation nor negotiation).

To find ways of combining sociotechnical and political learning is a challenge to any union movement concerned to develop its involvement, and the involvement of its membership, in production issues. Participation and local learning alone can teach the "spontaneous" political lesson that the union is unnecessary in matters of production. This may be true as regards actual day-to-day work. A necessary condition, however, is that there is, for example, a work organization that offers opportunities for participation and a dialogue on acceptable terms. In creating such a work organization, the union, as we have seen, may play an absolutely central role. Problems of this type cannot be solved, nor influence exerted, at the individual level.

There are, however, limits to trade unions' ability to create good work for their members. These limits point to the need for multilevel strategies both within companies and at the societal level. We consider here two aspects of the need for multilevel strategies. The first aspect has to do with close links—in a situation of increasing automation—between company-level work organization and use of technology, on the one hand, and the national and international development of new technology, on the other. The second aspect has to do with the development of "new managerial strategies," with a close link between changes in technology and work and managerial efforts to control employees and production at the company level.

This chapter focuses on examples of trade union policy and experiments in the field of technological development. We are not developing a representative picture, but we do illustrate new tendencies that have a growing importance. In Chapter 10, we discuss new managerial strategies and what they may mean in terms of challenges for trade union strategies. We see that there are links between these two aspects of the need for multilevel strategies. The use of technology and development of the work organization and management at the company level are all related to the development of ideologies and new technologies on the societal level.

2. The Use and Development of Technology

How can influence on the use of technology at workplaces interact with influences on the development of new technology and the preconditions for its use? Such an interaction is becoming even more crucial to the extent that new technology is developed in special research and development companies, separate from the production organizations in which they will be used.

The Utopia project at the Swedish Center for Working Life has influenced discussions about multilevel trade union strategies and a "new Swedish model" or "new Scandinavian model" for the development of technology. The Utopia project was an effort to develop alternative systems for text and picture processing in newspaper production. (It is described in section 4.) It is important to underline that our discussions of a long-term trade union policy on technology are based on limited research experiences. There are not, as yet, many concrete developments in this direction.

Technology Choices and a Policy of Consequences

Given the various limitations, what is it then possible to influence at the local level? At some workplaces, there are some opportunities to select a technical solution among those available on the market. Alternatively, local unions involve themselves in developing an *active* policy of consequences (Hingel 1983a), in other words, an attempt to influence the consequences of the technological developments and solutions at the workplace. One of the items that can be selected is the work organization; this is known in the sociotechnical tradition as "organizational choice."

The following items are open to influence at the local level: choice of technology (hardware), the introduction and implementation of the solution chosen, theoretical and practical training, wages, terms of employment (working hours, etc.), the working environment, and the work organization (duties, formal positions, job rotation, planning, and control). These are important places for local influence. There are, however, limits to local influence, and some of these are determined by the available technology: At any given time, there are a limited number of technical solutions for sale. While it may be possible to buy any of these, the choice of technical solutions is still limited. Also, the technology choice provides the free play for certain organizational choices but it also excludes certain organizational possibilities.

The existing, available, and selected technical solutions set certain (not necessarily purely technical) limits and offer certain opportunities; what technologies exist and are selected is, of course, socially determined. The decisive power lies with the companies developing the new technical solutions and with the managements deciding on the selection and purchase of a given solution. The criteria of business economics steer, if not each individual decision, at least what changes are retained.

Local unions can decide how satisfactory their choices on technical solutions are and whether the final decision is acceptable only if they have fairly well-developed union objectives and concrete criteria and models. It is obviously not good enough simply to say, "After all, there are plenty of systems on the market, and even given a specific system there remains an organizational choice." The question is what choices are available, and, ultimately, what alternatives are realized. If the available systems are found to be satisfactory, it is reasonable to go ahead with a local union strategy to influence the choice among systems and, in a policy of consequences, to try to influence the work organization, the training provided, and so forth. If developed demands are lacking, the role of the union can easily be reduced to a *passive* policy of consequences, that is, the administration and distribution of social consequences that it has not influenced (Hingel 1983b, 15).

We are critical of both technological determinism and of what might be called technological voluntarism. Critical social theory (Habermas and others) addresses this distinction between determinism and voluntarism. Critical social theory emphasizes that empirical regularities are often "ideologically frozen" and presented as laws of nature that are impossible to change, and it indicates alternative possibilities of development. But there are also what we may call "ideologically thawed" possible actions, which do not exist in practice under given conditions. The semblance of possible alternatives may lead people to accept conditions that limit their possibilities. It is just as important to determine when the possibilities of action are exaggerated as when they are concealed. Otherwise, failure to reach a desired alternative is blamed on the individual who does not succeed, and the possibility of collective action to create real alternatives and action remains hidden. A good understanding of the social and organizational structure and the possibilities for and restrictions to action it creates is a good basis for both individual and collective action in a fruitful interplay (Sandberg 1976, 29ff.).

A Central Policy of Technology and Work

If the available technology is not satisfactory, an alternative probably cannot be realized by applying union pressure to a single local company. The question thus arises: Could the unions influence future technological development by formulating specific demands regarding industrial research and development? Unions with a radical view of technology (Chapter 1, section 4) may tend to develop such a more aggressive strategy. We believe this to be reasonable as part of a broader union policy on technology, which we could perhaps term a "work and technology policy" (as a supplement to the union's labor market policy). Such a broad, global, and long-term strategy is necessary because of the character of technological change: It is an ongoing process (not the installation of a single machine), changing whole systems or networks of production (not only individual jobs or firms) and encompassing such spheres of activity as material production, administration, construction, banking, the households, and leisure time (cf. Fricke 1986 on West Germany and Deutsch 1986a on the United States).

As we have seen, detailed demands regarding technical solutions are needed as a basis even for a local and active policy of consequences. They are apparently indispensable in any policy on technology. To develop demands and models, major, central investments in specific projects may be necessary. Such central projects can take different forms. Broad study circles (local self-study groups) may be a way of collecting employee experiences and formulating basic demands and action programs. Study circles were used, for example, by the Food Workers' Union and at the Postgiro and, in a different way, in the Swedish public insurance system (see later in this section).

Another way of developing ideas and formulating more technical specifications is a "laboratory environment" that allows experiments to be made in peace and quiet, so that union objectives, the experiences of the employees, and the know-how of technical and social researchers can interact in the search for good technical solutions. This latter is probably one of the most essential tasks of any central union operation in the field of technological change, and it is discussed in more detail in section 4, with the "Utopia" project as an example.

Central union organizations can influence technological development and support local union strategies. These tactics, some of which are already being used, are listed below. (A basic task, not raised as a separate point, is the further development of co-determination rights at the workplace.)

1. The development of instruments and methods for the evaluation of technological and organizational changes and for the development of alternative models for the technology and work organization. Such development work demands large-scale and long-term input in research, design, and laboratory environments. Checklists and case studies of the type performed in the Front project also make a contribution in this respect, particularly when it comes to instruments for the evaluation of changes.

2. Influence on concrete research and development projects, through co-determination in R&D companies and R&D projects in other companies, through state or local government procurement of new technology, and other means.

3. Development of a trade union policy and action program for the organization and management of companies. This would include ideas about work and company organization, about different forms of democratic bodies, about the employees' self-management in certain areas, and about trade union access to and use of the resources of management.

4. The development of a policy and action program on education and training relating to the sort of knowledge the worker needs.

Is it sufficient to have the knowledge to press the right buttons without understanding the underlying process? Or should workers understand the technology and be able to use it as a tool? Or as an instrument of collective control over a sophisticated production process? How—and this question is bound up with the work organization—are the different levels of knowledge to be distributed among the employees? Are they all to know everything, or are only some of them to possess in-depth understanding?

5. A policy for the development of the union organization itself would include:

- a combination of a local activity and a central activity that supports the local activity by means of educational material, consultation, and the development of offensive alternatives;
- the development of the union's organizational structure so that it is not locked in by the demarcations between occupations and tasks that were the result of a division of labor linked to an earlier technology; and
- the development of a union strategy that permits involvement in the company's productive operation (in the organization of work and the thrust and quality of production, not only in traditional wage and distribution issues) without a simultaneous integration into management, as well as a broad activation of all member groups.

6. A general influence on the thrust of long-term, applied technical research and research in the social sciences, insofar as these relate to the development and consequences of the work organization and technology. Part of this long-term research involves the development of criteria and demands regarding the "good work organization" (point 1 above).

Within the Swedish labor movement, study circles are sometimes used not only for learning at the local level but also for the local formulation of demands that are used in the development of national policies and programs. This type of activity has also been used when trade unions develop their programs on technological change.

A most interesting example is the study circle and action program on electronic data processing (EDP) that was developed by the Swedish Union of Insurance Employees (FF) (Försäkringsanställdas Förbund 1981). The study material was developed in close cooperation between the national union and researchers at the Swedish Center for Working Life. The main purpose of the material was to assist union members to understand the effects of earlier EDP systems and to formulate their own demands on future systems.

About 9,000 FF members (out of 12,000) participated in the study circles. Participants in about 700 study circles provided written answers to a number of questions which were collated by the FF branch offices. This material provided the foundation for drawing up the action program. An FF committee at the request of the FF Board produced a draft program of action using the material described above. (Göranzon et al. 1982, 72ff.; quotation from p. 78)

The study circles, after their discussions, wrote down their comments and demands from a qualitative standpoint. To support the trade union's development of the program, researchers helped systematize the answers from the study circles. Some quantitative calculations were possible, for example, all study circles rejected the computerization of more advanced tasks. More than half of the replies on skills emphasized the need for a large amount of training. But equally important were the qualitative aspects. Here is a quotation from the chapter on training and skills:

A comment by a study circle concerns the degree of computerization of various jobs: "The kinds of routine jobs that should not be computerized are those involving direct contact with the public, such as payments over the counter. It is important that personal service should be retained. The more skilled jobs should not be computerized. If that were to happen, our present stock of professional knowledge would disappear."

FF demands:

- that skilled jobs in social insurance shall not be computerized;
- that the computerization of routine jobs shall be tried out on a case-to-case basis with regard to the repercussions on service and the working conditions of the personnel;
- that the professional knowledge of the personnel must be maintained on a level that satisfies the requirements of the insured for service and security before law, and that the personnel must have opportunities for development through their work;
- that training for the personnel must provide them with an overall view of the various sectors of social insurance;
- that more thorough research must be done to clarify the connection between computerization and deterioration in

professional knowledge. (Försäkringsanställdas Förburd 1981, 25)

A Multilevel Strategy for Technology

When the union organization has found that the existing technology restricts the solutions possible at the local level, several possible alternative actions are available. One possible step is to move in and try to influence industrial development projects directly. This is also a rational move in the current situation in Sweden, where companies and their employees are already cooperating in combining new technology and productivity. Efforts of this kind, if they prove successful, provide important and inspiring demonstration models that point to the possibility of influencing technological development itself and broaden the limits of what is seen to be technically possible. In this way it is possible to demonstrate the political character of the technology that already exists, and technological research and development can become a political issue and an issue for the trade union movement.

What happens when the new technology is to be used? An essential basis of the design of technological alternatives is the use and development of the workers' best skills and efforts. Technological choices are marketed, purchased by firms, and then used in concrete work organizations (that is, in specific training contexts with specific union structures). Will they then be used in a manner harmonizing with the union objectives that influenced the design of the technology (hardware) itself? In favorable circumstances, such a use can accord with the desires of several parties (for both profits and "good jobs") and may therefore be realized in a relatively unproblematical way. In other contexts, a broad realization would be possible only as part of major trade union efforts in the various fields indicated above: research policy, training policy, organizational structure of the union, and so forth. In a long-term union policy on technology, successful efforts in these and other areas will be essential conditions for attempts to influence specific R&D projects leading, for example, to the desired work organization at the workplace. However, the necessity of such long-term and radical efforts in no way impairs the demonstrational effect of successful attempts to shape R&D projects.

There is thus a need for a multilevel interaction between a local union policy of consequences and a central policy on technology. Sometimes, however, one can sense tendencies toward a separation between the two levels. The policy of consequences then tends to become an issue subordinate to the development of productivity at the workplace with the help of new technology. The policy on technology tends to become part of an industrial policy to achieve increased competitiveness (where the demands of the users can lead to marginal changes in the technology).

The current division of work between the local and central union levels has evolved in the course of work on distribution issues. On such questions as wages and terms of employment, it is possible to formulate simple guidelines and principles (for example, in the form of laws and agreements) that can be applied in the same fashion at numerous workplaces. The central organizations are also in a position to study local problems and offer suggestions for solutions. In production issues relating to the company's operation, it is difficult to conclude any detailed central agreements, and the central level cannot study all local problems and find solutions. The new assignment of roles, created by a producer perspective, can be found in the direction indicated by the slogan "central support for local union action" (cf. Nygaard and Bergo 1974).

Both the work organization and the use of technology must and can be influenced at the local level. Decentralization and development of local activities and local resources within the union organizations are necessary. But it is unrealistic to say, as people sometimes say in Sweden, "Co-determination laws and agreements exist, so now it is up to you people at the workplaces." There are, as we have seen, limits to local union influence, and there is therefore a need for central union support of local action.

A strategic interplay between the levels might look something like this: Technological choice and use are influenced at the local level; experience is gathered and demands for alternative developments formulated. At the central level, these demands are developed in laboratory and experimental environments, and prototypes may be developed for alternative technologies and alternative organizational models. The new solutions are tested out at the workplaces, and new local experiences and demands are developed. A special aspect of this interplay is education. Local experiences and central studies make possible the development of trade union educational materials that form part of the "central support to local action."

This sketch of a coherent strategy over several levels underlines the fact that, even if the long-term development of technology and some influence on this development occupy center stage, it is the local union operation that finally determines the real possibilities of a successful policy on technology. The knowledge and self-confidence necessary can be developed only in relation to efforts and successes at the workplaces. The experience, knowledge, activity, and involvement in technological questions of the membership is the linchpin of the union movement.

3. A "New Scandinavian Model"

In various contexts, one hears mention of a "Swedish model for technological development and computerization." There is not really any such a developed model but rather only the vision of the possibility of combining union goals with industrial and technological development. This idea is found in various forms in various quarters, both union and political. We find it, for example, in a government bill put forward by the nonsocialist government in 1981, in communications from the Metalworkers' Union, Food Workers' Union, LO and TCO, and in the Union of Civil Servants. It can be seen as one of several elements in a policy on technology and work. (See, for example, Livsmedelsarbetareförbundets Kongress 1981; Metallarbetareförbundet 1981; Boivie and Östberg 1982; *Samordnad datapolitik* 1982; Statstjänstemannaförbundet 1982a; Arbetsmarknadsdepartementet 1984; LO 1986.)

The Idea

The basic idea seems to be roughly as follows: The task is to develop new technology that serves simultaneously the objectives of industrial policy and objectives that are central to a policy on working life. The objectives in question can be competitiveness, employment, a good work content, qualifications, product quality, or social usefulness. Such a combination of objectives in different fields is conceived of as possible through government and union involvement in the development of technology. It is assumed that the union organizations are able to capture and formulate clearly the demands of employees and that they can also capture and draw upon the employees' expertise and experience of work and the working environment. Smoothly functioning and strong union organizations would give Scandinavian industry a competitive advantage. Technology that satisfies the demands of employees and draws upon their unique knowledge and experience could be developed rapidly and efficiently. This is of growing importance as the competence of employees is seen as the most important resource for productivity and prospering business operations, given today's flexible, customer-oriented production. Scandinavia's traditionally calm labor market also affords different sectors of industry the opportunity to experiment and test out new technical and organizational solutions.

It also might provide the stability needed to acquire, perhaps with union support, a domestic market of sufficient size to achieve a greater economy in the production of an initial series. Together these policies would enable Scandinavian industry to develop its international competitiveness, while job content and competence would be developed among the employees. This idea is discussed in Chapter 10 in the context of the "new managerial philosophies." There we ask whether this possible consonance of goals from industrial policy and work policy is true for all employees and "forever."

Project Proposals

LO and TCO have both tried to put into concrete form their ideas on technological development work, on the basis of demands for a good working environment and work organization. The Swedish Board for Technical Development (STU) has financed these studies. In the introduction to its report, LO writes,

> Development along these lines would increase the work content, and the opportunities of broad groups of employees to take responsibility in their jobs. This would have a bearing on the work environment in its broad sense. It is also important to retain and develop Sweden's position regarding industrial policy, which has been achieved, among other things, by competency alike on the part of workers, salaried employees, and management. (LO 1983a, 3f.)

One of LO's project ideas relates to the development of operator programming at numerically controlled machine tools. Other project ideas concern future CAD/CAM systems. One of these projects looks at how to exploit and develop the competency of the machine operator in manufacturing tools by developing new computer-assisted aids. The procedure is envisaged in outline as follows:

> The machine operator receives the design from the Design Department on his own display terminal, and with the help of existing software he can produce a program for its manufacture. By exploiting his professional skill, the toolmaker can successively—for example by applying the technique of models—refine the control program for manufacture of the tool. Apart from the production of specifications covering the workplace and aids, this phase requires also development work and experimentation to evolve a work station that will meet these specifications. (LO 1983a, 69)

TCO emphasizes that the employees and their unions made demands regarding physical and system ergonomics and that good ergonomics has become a successful selling point for Swedish companies in their export markets (TCO 1983b, 8ff.). In its report, TCO proposes two large-scale studies relating to the development of hardware and software for wage and personnel administrative systems and for CAD/CAM systems in engineering. The CAD/CAM study, for example (TCO 1983b, 17ff.), is designed as a bid to develop and supply a new technology, with the specifications phase followed by a prototype phase. It is intended to develop and test union demands, for example, by testing the flexibility of systems against demands regarding the work organization.

Given our previous discussion of union strategies, it is reasonable that both LO and TCO are, to some extent, considering the same parts of the labor process. Questions relating to occupational demarcation, union delimitations, and union collaboration to achieve new and constructive solutions will be central aspects of any "work-oriented development of technology."

Both LO and TCO are proposing projects in line with the "new model for technological development." This is a new, but still weak, trend that may grow in significance. One initiative in this direction has recently been taken in Sweden. The Work Environment Fund and STU have decided jointly to finance an interdisciplinary research program that focuses on the behavioral work environment and computer technology development. It is called People and Information Technology in Working Life (MDA). Examples of research areas are people–computer interaction, technology and work organization, learning/competence in computerized systems and effects on work content, the development of resources, and well-being and health. The emphasis is on research of practical value. Both research-related development projects such as demonstration examples and basic knowledge generation as a basis for more applied projects are planned. It remains to be seen whether only joint labor–management projects will be promoted or also autonomous union-oriented research like the Utopia project. The program has SEK 60 million (U.S. $10.2 million) at its disposal for the period from July 1987 to June 1992.

4. The Utopia Project

The Utopia project may serve as an example of the research efforts we have described, although, starting in 1982, it predated the "new Scandinavian model." Its purpose was to develop alternatives for the processing of text and pictures in the printing sector. These alternatives could apply both to the actual technology and to the organization of work and training. The alternatives were to promote a high quality of product, strong professional skills, and democracy and equality in work. They were to be "utopian" in the sense that the project's best conceptions of work and products would be realized: "Quality of Work and Product" was the slogan. The alternatives put forward entailed major advantages for the printing and other workers concerned; powerful skill-enhancing tools were developed. All proposals were to be technically feasible. Whether these alternatives would be accepted by the market was not, in the initial stage, a central question (see Ehn 1988).

The dual value of "quality of work and product" was inspired by the notion of "meaningful production" within the movement for alternative production during the 1970s: Production was intended to enhance the competence of workers producing socially useful products. Such ideas among, for instance, British shop stewards developed in connection with efforts to convert the arms industry. Mike Cooley, a designer and trade union leader at the British Lucas Aerospace Industry, was the chairman of a shop stewards' combine committee that developed an alternative corporate plan for that industry and proposed useful products that could be manufactured by workers using and developing their skills (Cooley 1981). He pursued some of these ideas as one of the directors on the Greater London Enterprise Board (GLEB) that tried to develop industry in the London area. Similarly, at the University of Manchester Institute of Science and Technology (UMIST), a group led by Howard Rosenbrock (1982) worked on "human-centered design"; a lathe that allows workers to use their skills has been developed, and the team is now working on the development of a flexible manufacturing system (FMS), with the same goal of enhancing user competence.

Background

The Utopia project was carried out at Arbetslivscentrum, at the Royal Institute of Technology in Stockholm, and at Aarhus University. The total cost was about $400,000, with Arbetslivscentrum the main source of funds. Skilled workers participated in the project at these various institutions; their union organizations followed and supported the project through a reference group with representatives from Finland, Norway, Denmark, and Sweden, which had been set up by the Nordic Graphic Union. The researchers in the group at Arbetslivscentrum were specialists in research into working life and ergonomics. The researchers at the Royal Institute of Technology and at Aarhus University were computer scientists. Pelle Ehn at Arbetslivscentrum led the project.

From the standpoint of Arbetslivscentrum, the Utopia project can be seen partly as a follow-up of previous projects that supported and tracked the attempts of local union organizations to influence the use of technology at workplaces. One of the workplaces in the Demos project was in the printing sector, at a daily newspaper (see Chapter 4, section 1). These local attempts to exert influence suggested that a number of obstacles to realizing union demands lay in the existing technology itself. First of all, job design with the use of existing technology often cannot meet union demands. Second, and more specifically, the increasing preponderance of utterly inflexible turnkey systems with a standard work organization makes local influence difficult (Brytningstid 1983). The Due project at Aarhus University had similar experiences (Kyng and Mathiasen 1982).

The development of technical and organizational alternatives is a prolonged and resource-demanding process. Ideas and demands, and sometimes alternatives, emerge locally. In such a situation, it becomes an important task for the central organizations to support local efforts by, for example, trying to find solutions to the problems that cannot be solved locally. In the Utopia project, the development of an alternative technology was seen as an example of such an input. It was intended that development work at the central level would be followed by experiments with prototypes at the workplace level, where alternative work organizations could be tested.

Apart from this background in previous cooperation between researchers and local printing union organizations, there are other reasons for the thrust of the Utopia project's work. The project was limited to the development of "software," that is, systems and programs, and training for those who were to work with the system. These aspects were assumed to demand considerably fewer resources than the machines themselves, or the hardware. The hardware, of course, sets clear limitations on which demands can be realized, but these limitations are less narrow when the item processed is information, as it is in the printing sector and in offices. The printing sector was chosen, beyond the reasons above, because of the awareness, on the part of the graphic workers' union, of the role that technology plays. The union possessed technical skills, had experience of technical change, and was ideologically sophisticated.

Graphic workers had long persisted as true craftspeople, proud of their history and competence. They were thus well suited for a project like Utopia. As Robert Blauner writes, the combination of "craft technology, favorable economic conditions, and powerful work organization and traditions result in the highest levels of freedom and control in the work process among industrial workers" (1964, 56). During the preceding decade, however, graphic workers had seen some of their metal-type–based tools and skills disappear, to be replaced by phototypesetting and the pasteup of columns on page boards, and, finally, interactive page makeup on the computer. The Utopia project was developed when the introduction of early computer systems made the work extremely abstract. At that time, typesetters talked about codes and formulas instead of typography and layout. Only more recent developments in technology have allowed them to create the typography of a text or the layout of a page in small steps, seeing the continuous changes in the layout on the screen; technology may once more be a real tool for graphics workers. It was with these new possibilities on the horizon that the Utopia project was conceived.

The Utopia project was to be an independent union exercise in technical development with an analytical and charting phase, a development and design phase, and a phase involving experimentation and the construction and introduction of alternative systems, which would be followed by experimental activities at a workplace. The investment in independent technological development on the part of the union was motivated by the superior status of management, both by its clearly formulated objectives and its long-term experience of technological development.

The Phases of the Project

In accordance with a schedule, a charting phase was performed in which trends in newspaper technology and economy were outlined and various scenarios written. This led to the choice of two "production situations," namely, the prepress production of a daily newspaper and a "graphic workshop" for the small-scale production of fairly simple printed matter. (On the development of this project, see *Graffiti*, the newsletter of the project; and Bödker et al. 1987.) Visits were made to newspapers, technical exhibitions, suppliers, and research laboratories in Scandinavia and the United States. A study of the technology and work organization at United States newspapers played an important role in illustrating a "Dystopia," or a future not to be desired. We saw examples of deterioration of the quality of both work and product and of trade unions being steamrollered by technological change and management strategies. In this phase, a mutual learning took place between workers and researchers, although difficulties were encountered due to the abstract and long-term character of the study, something unfamiliar to the graphic workers.

After a year and a half in the charting phase, the Utopia project was contacted in the spring of 1982 by the management of the Liber printing group, which is a member of Statsföretag (a group of state-owned companies) (Ehn 1983, *Graffiti*). The managers wanted to investigate the possibility of cooperating on their development project Tips (Text and Image Processing System), an integrated computer system for text and picture processing and the electronic makeup of whole pages, mainly for newspaper production. Liber's subsidiary, Liber System AB, was responsible for project management, marketing, and training; two other companies were responsible for the development of picture processing (hardware and software) and the software for text processing and page makeup.

An agreement was reached on cooperation: The Tips project would draw upon the competency available in the Utopia project (work organization, interaction, graphic skills, training) in its development work and the Utopia project would have an opportunity to try out some of its ideas by offering suggestions on the design of the system and on training. In addition to potential influence on the Tips system, the Utopia project would acquire expertise in this type of large-scale industrial system-development work (approximately $10 million U.S.) and in this particular approach to achieving union influence over technological development. However, Tips was not obliged in any way to comply with the requirements of the Utopia project—although they were to be considered, and arguments against using them presented—and the Utopia project was free to circulate information concerning all of its viewpoints and requirements.

Work within the Utopia project became entirely concentrated on the case of production at a daily newspaper, with the emphasis on sophisticated technologies for the makeup of whole pages and for picture processing. Just talking and writing was not a useful form for researcher–worker cooperation. A "technology laboratory" was therefore set up with the potential to simulate workstations, page makeup, and work organization (see below, "Tools for Design").

As a supplement to and follow-up of the short-term collaboration on development with one supplier, the specifications of requirements provided on a continuous basis for the Tips project were developed and generalized, so that they could be used as a basis for the formulation of union demands in the installation of computerized text and picture processing systems, regardless of supplier. Specifications included a section on functional demands regarding recomposition and picture processing and general demands relating to the work organization, work environment, interaction, and training. A condensed summary of the detailed specifications in the form of a checklist can be seen in Figure 5. Instructional material

Figure 5

Utopia's Requirement Specification: Some Key Words

PAGE MAKE-UP

- *Work procedures:* In principle these are the same as in paper paste-up. The page is shown as "natural" as possible on the display. Work consists of allocating and modifying text, images, and graphics until the required result is obtained.
- *The display screen:* The page is shown in scales which allow a detailed inspection (legible body text), natural size, as well as a comprehensive view of the whole page. There must also be room for a work area, menu, list of material, and status information. Material must appear in black on a light background.
- *Man-machine interaction devices:* Keyboard and at least one pointing device with which to move the cursor about on the display.
  Operations: The basic principle is that first the material is chosen and then it is decided what to do with it (operand before operation).
  — General tools: gravity/free pointing, aligning, reference pointing, haircross, ruler, magnifying glass.
  — Overall display layout: activate/move lenses, scaling, spreads, several pages.
  — Choice of page/spread/advertisement including page ground.
  — Placing material: make columns, extra leading, centering, indention.
  — Graphic material: lines, corners, frames, geometrical figures, freehand drawing.
  — Text: column width, font, size, letter spacing, hyphenation and justification.
  — Images: cropping, enlarging/ reducing size, mirroring, insert and rotate text in picture.
  — Paper copies: proof printing (on printers), phototypesetting.
  — Administration: display, select from material list, search and save material, production and material status information.

IMAGE PROCESSING

- *Work Procedures:* Selected image(s) are shown in a life-like manner on the display, as are successive results of the operations.
- *The display screen:* Must have a gray scale of at least 50 levels. Windows containing the images, menu (operations), list of material, status information. Large enough to contain natural size images.
  Man-Machine Interaction Devices: As in page make-up.
- *Scanner:* Electronic adjustment of corrections concerning size, tone, and mirroring must be possible during scanning. Resolution for magnifying slide-originals must be at minimum 10 fold.
- *Operations:* Basic principles as in page make-up.
  — General tools: box, haircross, ruler, magnifying glass, reference pointing, histogram, densitometer.
  — Geometrical alternations: cropping, rotating, mirroring, scaling the same/different scale horizontally as well as vertically.

Figure 5 (continued)

— Changes in tone: darker/lighter, gray tones, contrast, accentuating contours, softening, negative, drop out.
— Retouch: "brushes" with "ink".
— Allocation: move, move under, align with.
— Composition: combine, add, copy.
— Graphic material: as in page make-up.
— Paper copies: as in page make-up.
— Administration: get, list, save, finish.

WORK ORGANIZATION

The basic principles are: improve rather than depreciate skills and quality of product; integrated planning and execution; cooperation between the professional groups involved, work rotation; and decentralized decision-making.

The technology does not determine, but rather places limits on the content and work organization. That is why the following should be considered when evaluating a system:

• *Influence:* on production volume, quality of product, work procedures, work load.
• *Control:* possibility for contact between colleagues, autonomous working groups, influence on working hours.
• *Changes:* in content, division and organization of page make-up, editing, advertisement layout, reproduction, service and maintenance, etc.

WORK ENVIRONMENT

• Workstations, keyboards, pointing device, workchair, and worktable should be flexible and ergonomically designed.
• Visual strain at the display: text is only displayed with at least 18 pixels between base lines, otherwise with gray lines corresponding to the words, sufficient contrast, sharp and square pixels, no flicker, reflection, aberrations, or "ghost shadows."

MAN-MACHINE INTERACTION

The skilled graphic worker's control of the computer system based on:

• A natural and well-planned conceptual model of the system (a user model).
• Command issuing via menus, forms, questions-answers, and with direct feedback.
• Careful choice of cursors and colours.
• Help and status information, including "logging" (history).
• Possibility to undo or correct mistakes by erasing characters, undo (last instruction, further back).
• Updating and restarting without loss of information.
• Possibility to create new tools (operations).

TRAINING

• Plans concerning the introduction of new technology must include training.
• Training in the tools' functions must include "graphic datology," and supplier-related topics.

Figure 5 (continued)

- Must be based on a good user model which relates the new technology to the traditional skills.
- Must include development and maintenance of system, work organization, work environment.
- Teaching and material must be presented in the users' terminology and native language.

Source: Utopia Project 1985, 25.

---

on the graphic handling of text and pictures has been produced. One of the implications of the Utopia project is that a "specification of requirements" not only influenced the design of the Tips system but also served as a basis for local negotiations. The technology laboratory provided the techniques used in local development and adaptations of specifications in printing and other types of production as well as in vocational training. The project as a whole is at least a "demonstration example" of the possibility of developing a technology with aims like competence and quality in direct union–researcher cooperation.

The final stage of the Utopia project would be the development of an experimental work organization around one of the first pilot installations of the system for trying out some of the ideas of quality in work and products. This stage was to take place at *Aftonbladet*, a Stockholm evening paper owned by LO. The Graphic Workers' Union wanted an experiment, but it proved impossible to reach an agreement with the journalists' union (within the TCO) as to how it was to be carried out. *Aftonbladet's* management was able to continue, as it preferred, without any experiment in research participation. The resistance of the journalists can be understood as reflecting their dissatisfaction at not having participated in the first part of the Utopia project; this, in its turn, was due to the inability of the researchers to bridge the demarcation gap between the two unions that existed long before the project started; the researchers had to choose one union or the other as their primary partner.

The Utopia project's study at *Aftonbladet* was thus confined to observation and documentation of what happened when Tips was tried out at the newspaper. Bartholdy and others (1987) from this limited evaluation reported that the new electronic possibilities of processing pictures, their form as well as content (a new picture can be constructed, for example, by combining elements from several other pictures), placed a new responsibility on those working with the pictures. The pilot installation at *Aftonbladet* includes two Image

500 workstations, one scanner, and one photocompositor. Functionally, Image 500 fulfils most of the requirements specified in the Utopia project. Unsatisfactory elements include the impossibility of obtaining pictures in natural size and the degree of dissolution of the text and graphics (such as line art) in pictures.

This was the last stage in the Utopia project complex feedback loop, moving from local participation (in the Demos project ten years earlier), to the formulation of demands for technological and organizational alternatives, to the development of prototypes and specification of requirements, and then, finally, local testing and the input for a new round of development and use of technology. Our experiences show the importance of strong unions in vitalizing this feedback loop (see also Sirianni 1987, 13).

The very close cooperation with an actual producer meant a change in the original plans for the project. The original plan called for continuing with independent union work in specifying requirements and then approaching a supplier. When the offer came from Liber–Tips at an early stage of the project, it was nonetheless welcome: The project needed opportunities to work concretely, and the time pressure introduced by a commercial project helped speed up creative thinking on approaches to the new problems. As the research group decided to enter this cooperative situation, the plan changed so that after the "commercial" phase, the research group would return to its original work independent of the need to adapt to short-term technological and commercial constraints. This final phase of the project was not realized. Experiences from the Utopia project, however, and earlier local-level projects, emphasized the need for independent union work, in a long-term multilevel interaction, in order to bring the experiences of workers to bear on the development and use of technology.

Tools for Design

Project results of general interest included methods or tools for the development of alternative specifications and ideas. The development and testing of alternative methods of formulating alternative demands in the development of technology and the work organization have become the entire core of the project. (This perhaps says more about the emphasis of the project than the designation "union technological development.")

If the experiences and ideas of the skilled workers are to be incorporated in the development of alternative solutions, the sort of abstract, written models that researchers use are not adequate. The

collaboration between researchers and printing workers in the project group proved to be much more fruitful when attempts were
made in practical terms to build simple "mock-ups" for trying out
possible future work processes. In such "designing by doing,"
workers can use their experience and tacit knowledge (Cooley 1986).
This forms a basis for a mutual learning between workers and researchers, the latter contributing concrete examples of the possibilities and limitations of new technology. The practical competence
of both researchers and workers comes into play. To make such a
dialogue possible there is a need for long-term cooperation so that
they understand each others' "tacit knowledge." This puts restrictions on the work of the designer. He or she cannot just "computer-
ize" certain abstract work functions, but rather has to set about
learning a great deal, getting acquainted over the course of several
years with the concrete reality, material, tools, and language of the
employees in the area of application (Ehn and Kyng 1987, 52f.).

Using very simple means like height-adjustable stands and
chipboard, it is possible to simulate different workstations and test
their ergonomic properties and their functioning in the course of
work. A computerized graphic workstation may have a whole range
of tools for interaction with the computer: a picture screen (similar to
a television screen), a screen for text, a keyboard, and a joystick or
mouse to move the cursor on the screen—all of which are simulated. Work on, for example, the makeup of a page and the bleeding
of a picture can be drawn in stages on a paper, showing what is
envisaged as happening on the display terminal, and, with nota-
tions as to which operations the operator wants to be able to carry
out, what aids are needed for interaction with the computer, and
what problems seem likely to arise. This simulation on paper was
followed by a more realistic mock-up using back-screen projection.
The drawings are photographed and displayed on a projector screen
resembling a terminal. At the same time, the graphic workers perform various operations with the help of simulated interaction tools.
With simulated terminal work of this kind, it is possible to test suitable forms for the dialogue between the graphics worker and the
computer.

A more advanced aid to simulation is a modern graphic workstation: a computer with a graphic display terminal and interactive
tools. By means of a succession of simplified "experimental systems," it is possible in practice to investigate the varying properties
of different systems, for example, the coordination between the
movements of interaction tools and screen image changes. In this
way, ideas on the work process can be translated into requirements
regarding the software. The program can then be evaluated and new
ideas incorporated.

A "work organization building-box" or "construction box" with cards symbolizing various work functions, machines, and working material makes it possible to "lay out" different production flows and organizational solutions on a table. This is an aid to researchers and workers in trying to create and give shape to possible forms of work organization. It is easy for a group of people to work with, it is cheap, and it provides both details and an overall picture of a work organization (see Dilschmann and Ehn 1984; Ehn and Sjögren 1986). On the basis of experiences at a Norwegian daily newspaper, a model for the work organization was developed that allowed journalists and graphic workers to work together on computer-based page makeup.

The simulation equipment developed is used on the recently established studies program in graphics at the College of Occupational Technology, Stockholm. This institution is also using the Utopia project's reports on recomposition, picture processing, and work organization as study material.

Research Perspective: The Computer as a Tool

Apart from design methods, Utopia project results include influence on hardware and also development of a research perspective, regarding the computer as a tool. Let us first give two examples of influence on the hardware. The scanner, which electronically "reads" and stores pictures in a computer, is built to allow for some picture processing. This furthers the trade union goal that all jobs in the new system should require an acceptable level of skills. Without union influence, the Tips project scanner would probably have allowed only for straight "reading" of the picture, and thus downgraded the job. It would probably also have been less economically efficient. By doing some basic image processing at an early stage of production, the picture can at a later stage, in which time pressure is a key factor, quickly be introduced on a page almost "ready to use."

A further example is from the workstation requirements for the keying in of text. They specify that the stations use no terminals at which only the "rough entry" of basic text is possible. Instead, each workstation must include not only the capability for typing in text but also for performing a certain amount of typographic work, preparatory to the final typography and page makeup. This presupposes a workstation with a graphic screen of a certain minimum size on which one can see the typography selected. The typing in of text has largely been a "woman's job." Women were employed at an earlier stage of typesetting when the text was "written in" on perforators (producing a punched tape that steered the traditional lead composing machines, "hot metal"). Women's jobs have subsequently moved to keyboarding text via computer terminals, text that is then phototypeset. In her exciting study called *Brothers* (1983), Cynthia Cockburn has investigated the division of labor between the sexes in the traditionally male-dominated craft of printing. Her results encourage us to think very carefully about the development of "computers as tools" not only for the fraction of the work force that, according to the traditional criteria and values of the craft, is most skilled, but also for other groups, especially women. The development of workstations that combine typographical work with the input of text is thus essential from the perspective of the Utopia project, which emphasizes quality of work for all (see Williams 1987).

An example of results from the discussion in the project reveals how certain important principles of design for full-page–makeup computer systems support the graphic worker's use of his or her qualifications and typographical skills to turn out good quality products with a good job content. The project discussion concerned the general qualitative choice in the design of software for page makeup systems. The first such system was introduced in a pilot installation some years ago, and followed a model of work in which a page is composed in two stages: Initially, a box layout for the whole page is designed in detail; later, the boxes are filled with "material" (text, images, logotypes, or drawings). It is a small step from this system to a high degree of automatic layout. When similar systems were introduced in pilot newspapers in the United States, poor typography was one result.

A better model, which has been made possible by recent developments in computer technology, enables the graphic worker to move the material around on the screen until it meets a good typographical standard, using powerful human–machine interaction tools for pointing and placing on the screen. This development has created work and products of very high quality (Sundblad 1983).

The basic goal of the Utopia project was to develop computers as tools for skilled workers. First the functions to be performed by the technology were specified, using some of the methods discussed above. Then it was gradually determined how those functions could be performed: What would the worker like to be able to do? How could this be done using advanced computer technology (with its limits and potentialities)? Could "new" functions be performed that were not possible with the old technology? To stick to our example of page makeup, essential graphic competence was defined as the understanding (partially "tacit knowledge") that enables the worker to give typographical form to the model the journalists have of the page (including the text and pictures and a rough idea of how the items could be presented). Ideally, the system should be "transparent," so that it allows the graphic worker to concentrate fully on what to create, rather than how to get the machine or system to do it; then it is a good tool. An expert car driver is a common, and relevant, example of this condition (Bödker et al. 1987).

In the mutual learning process between researchers and printers, what printers first asked for was a high-quality screen big enough to show the whole page with a resolution that allowed for effortless reading of the body text. No such screens existed. To work out ways of meeting some of these requirements, to keep in mind that one is working with an electronic representation of a page and not the page itself, and to demonstrate the advantages as well as disadvantages of computer technology in this work situation, a "user model" was devised. Andrew Martin sums it up well:

> The model postulated a "table" on which a page ground, menus, material lists, status information, and a work area were placed. Given the limited screen size, a capability for viewing the whole page and any portions of it at various levels of re- duction or magnification, along with the other items on the table, was conceived as a set "lenses" at the worker's disposal. To look at the same portion with different magnifications at the same time, different lenses could be used simultaneously (e.g., to look at one portion in its position within the whole page through one lens and to look at it in higher magnification in the work space through another, which apparently might be on an adjacent screen). All operations could be implemented on the material, regardless of the lenses through which it was viewed. (1987, 130)

In the study of the pilot installation of part of the Tips system at the newspaper *Aftonbladet*, some changes are suggested in the original specification; one of them relates to the "user model." The printers find it confusing to work with "lenses," and they do not find them immediately useful. The concept of a lens in the user model is very general and one could conceive of less general concepts with very concrete areas of application, like a "table overview" showing a re- duced picture of the whole table, a "hole" covering the whole screen through which you can see part of the table with the pictures shown in natural size, and a "magnifying glass" with a preset standard as to size and place (Bartholdy et al. 1987). Based on this user model, further requirements were specified including interaction tools and work environment. The project group tried to design a system that was as good as possible given the technological limitations (Bödker et al. 1987, 262):

Even the best current technology has its limitations where graphic display screens are concerned:

- they present new work environment problems;
- they are too small to reproduce a whole page in natural size;
- their resolution is too poor to make the body text legible in its natural size.

The question is whether these drawbacks can be counterbalanced by new possibilities, such as:

- changes in typography and graphic material can perhaps be executed more easily later in the process, and performed more quickly;
- the relative ease of changing the typography and the graphic design makes it possible to try out several alternatives in a short space of time;
- the ease of changing the material makes it feasible to start making up the pages at a much earlier stage of production, before all the material is available, and then to successively complete and correct them;
- the positioning can be made more precise—all the text can be set exactly horizontally; it is possible to get exactly the same leading between all sections in the article; the material in the surrounding columns can be exactly aligned, etc.

Although a starting point for the Utopia project was that local influence on the work organization (which was the focus of the Demos project) is not enough, because existing technology severely limits the possibilities for creating good jobs, it is probably true to say that the project's ideas on work organization are as essential—although less spectacular—as its ideas on software and hardware design. It turns out that there is an organizational choice, and that given the new technology that was developed at the same time as the Utopia project ran—and of which the Utopia project was a part—this choice is very wide. New computer-based technology in the printing industry, as in many other types of production, is very flexible and facilitates, and sometimes even presupposes, an integration of tasks and a development of competence if it is to be put to productive use. Figure 6 summarizes three models of work organization from the project's summary report.

Figure 6
Models of Work Organization

THE "AMERICAN WAY" OF ORGANIZING WORK

Star News is published in the Los Angeles suburb of Pasadena. The management of this paper has consciously introduced new technology to get rid of graphic workers. The graphic workstations are placed in the news room where they are operated by editorial staff. The organization does not allow any room for make-up staff, but the journalistic model is still transformed into a graphically designed page.

The problem is that the people who perform the work do not have the necessary graphic competence which results in a deteriorating product quality. Furthermore, the news staff is not organized in trade unions, they receive lower wages, and have usually not received a journalistic education.

THE "TRADITIONAL WAY" OF ORGANIZING WORK

With the introduction of graphic workstations it may seem apt to try to maintain the traditional way of organizing work. The make-up staff in the composition room get powerful computer based tools. The assistant-editors may get expensive electronic sketch pads. Both professional groups and their respective competences are intact, and may even be developed. But the technical possibilities for a more flexible production with a later "deadline" for manuscripts are not exploited.

The instructions from the editorial staff to the composition room are written instructions, primarily rough lay-out sketches even in situations where oral instructions would have been sufficient. If the assistant-editors have electronic sketch pads, the instructions are communicated electronically in the form of boxes on a display.

These instructions are formal and static. The intentions behind the instructions are not expressed. Assistant-editors and make-up staff do not cooperate closely, even though they work with the same pages. The division between the news room and the composition room obstruct the necessary dialogue in connection with questions, suggestions, changes, follow-up, and exchange of ideas.

THE "SCANDINAVIAN WAY" OF ORGANIZING WORK?

There are, however, work organization alternatives. The newspaper *Østlændingen* is published in Elverum. It is the Norwegian answer to the American challenge. The first steps on the path towards what hopefully may be called the "Scandinavian way" of organizing integrated production have been taken.

Assistant-editors and make-up staff work in the same room—the borderland. The graphic workers have powerful computer-based tools for make-up. The journalists have suitable computer-based facilities for editorial planning and text editing.

Assistant-editors and make-up staff become acquainted with each other's working conditions and prerequisites. Together they can plan and coordinate the work. Instructions are given orally, or as a list of priorities.

Figure 6 (continued)

Oral communication of journalistic intentions also increases the make-up person's understanding of the assitant-editor's idea for the page. Should the make-up person become uncertain or get ideas for improvements when he makes up the page on the computer based make-up table, he may easily and quickly discuss it with the assistant-editor. There is also a simple laser printer which makes it easy to take out proof-prints of the page for closer study and correction.

Because the assistant-editor spends less time on making detailed drafts, there is more time for things like working on the language and "image thinking", areas which are often neglected today. This way of organizing the work makes it possible to exploit the technology so that both editing and making-up can start much earlier than is the case today, and the "deadline" can be prolonged. Both make-up staff and assistent-editors can maintain and develop their respective professional competence and together contribute to improving the quality of the product.

Source: Utopia Project 1985, 29–31.

This type of integrated work organization, however, presupposes cooperation between the journalists' and printers' unions that was impossible to create within the Utopia project. During the second half of the 1980s, however, we have seen examples at several newspapers of efforts to build this type of organization, and we also see a better understanding between the two union organizations at the national level.

5. The Carpentry Shop Project

Like the Utopia project, the Carpentry Shop project at the Swedish Center for Working Life and the Ergonomics Design Group is a contribution to the development of participative, skill-based design methods and a more skill-based production layout and work organization. The quality of products and work had been deteriorating, having been determined not by consumer needs but by the demands of machine systems. (This brief presentation is based on newsletters from the project edited by Dan Sjögren and on Ehn and Sjögren 1986.) Hence, one of the goals of the project was to develop methods for the do-it-yourself design of workstations and shop layout and to create instruments of control over the organization and the economy to promote good quality in both the work and the products. The main result so far has been design methods that have been developed into an educational program for carpentry shop workers. The design was carried out *by* the producers themselves not *for* them (in designing *for* producers, their professional and tacit knowledge is ignored, and the jobs created tend to become un-skilled).

> Design by producers is supported mainly by the following two arguments: it is more democratic than design with (or for) producers; and it can avoid the use of professional designers, who are a costly and scarce resource. Both arguments are valid, and the Carpentry Shop project intentionally developed design methods that can be used by carpenters on the shop floor, after education in basic design methods. The project emphasized the need for methods to improve the workstations through a series of steps that do not require large investments. The prime factor in reducing the level of investment was the development of skills so that the work force is capable of making the improvements themselves. However, in many cases, the technical, design-oriented knowledge necessary exceeds that of the producers. The Utopian digital picture-processing and make-up tools could not have been designed without access to specialized technical skills. (Ehn and Sjögren 1986, 3)

The Utopia project is thus by necessity an example of a strategy of design *with* the producers, in contrast to the Carpentry Shop project.

One argument against design both with and by producers is that the producers, with their existing practices, have become too conservative to participate in the design of new solutions. This is why *mutual* learning is an essential aspect of the work of a design group. The workers not only contribute their experiences but they also learn basic design principles and, in the case of fundamental technological change, advanced technology.

In the Carpentry Shop project, with its tangible machine functions and work material, learning took place through studies of good and bad examples. The design team worked in a laboratory that offered opportunities to design and construct models and prototypes of workstations. At first, several examples of production systems were visualized by means of a layout building box (similar to, and forerunner of the Utopia project's work organization building box). Three-dimensional 1:10 scale models and in some cases prototypes were built. Team members moved directly from the idea to the "physical gestalt." Six carpenters and six researchers–industrial designers worked together using this think-and-build method. Training materials were developed for use in local carpentry shops. The layout building box and other methods developed by the team were used to analyze and formulate demands regarding the employees' workplace. During the course of the project, a newsletter was produced to keep communication going between the design group and a reference group with twenty-five local shop stewards and safety delegates.

At the Laboratory for Industrial Ergonomics at the Royal Institute of Technology in Stockholm, similar methods have been used and developed in the design of workstations for the steel and food industries (Broms 1988). Their experiences of successful human-centered design include the following points:

- A wide definition of the problem, with an overall perspective on production. A wide definition of the problem gives room for a large number of new solutions, in which human needs can be combined with high productivity.
- The production process should be studied from the human point of view. A good working environment and stimulating work are priorities. This can result in new, creative solutions that might never have been imagined in conventional design processes.
- The personnel engaged should be involved in both problem definition and problem solving. An important tool by which to facilitate communication and stimulate the employees is afforded by physical models, which are more concrete than drawings. The models should be simple and easy to modify. A start is made with rough models of the workplace as a whole, looking at possible changes at that level. One moves on to more detailed models of the department, and finally the workstation. In this way, the new solutions are "tried out" in the models, without costly disruptions to production. The personnel engaged are trained and aware of the new equipment from an early stage.

Gunnar Broms (1988) emphasizes the possibilities of combining human with business considerations, especially if a wide definition of the problems is permitted. He does not discuss situations in which employee solutions might run contrary to managerial interests. Nor does he touch on the independent role of the trade unions. This is perhaps due to his focus on physical layout, rather than work organization, and, still less, on influence and power in planning and control issues at the higher levels.

6. The TCO Screen Checker

A different example of interaction between union levels in the field of use and development of technology is the screen checker from TCO, the Central Organization of Salaried Employees (on

TCO, see Chapter 2, section 1). The screen checker is an instrument enabling the individual user to test his or her VDT for image quality and ergonomic qualities of the screen and keyboard. The results are summarized in a checklist. A special report is sent to the supplier who is asked to submit technical information about the equipment; at the same time, the supplier receives input and information from the user.

The individual user learns more about his or her equipment and work environment. Discussions with colleagues may start. The local unions may gather experiences among their members and use them to influence their employer's decisions, for example, when employers procure new equipment. National unions may use results for their policy development, for national negotiations, and for influence on governments and suppliers.

The screen checker has been translated into several languages. It is well adapted to new developments in company organization and management, that is, to the simultaneous trends to decentralization and centralization. Like "modern management," the screen checker puts the individual in focus; the individual can use the tool to analyze and demand changes concerning his or her own workplace. At the same time, the screen checker lays a good basis for international union cooperation in evaluating technical solutions and in putting pressure on suppliers.

7. Some Reflections

Experiences of the kind of development work we are discussing have shown, among other things, that the initial restriction to deal solely with software was unsuitable. In practical work on the Utopia project, questions and demands relating, for example, to the quality of screens, processor speeds, and similar issues, have proved decisive. Also, the original emphasis on technology, rather than giving it equal weight with the work organization, proved less than fruitful. The collaboration with the Tips project stepped up the tempo of work, since it was steered by the Tips project's time schedule; ideas on alternatives and the wording of specifications had to be ready by a specific date if they were going to influence system development. This experience confirms the project's original idea as to the necessity of independent and long-term union development work.

The Utopia project and other, similar experiences can provide a basis for further important discussions on union strategy with regard to technological development. The following questions are raised:

On researcher–union cooperation: What are the possibilities of collaboration between skilled workers, computer scientists, and work life researchers? Within the union organization, how are efforts to influence technological development working in relation to the central level and in relation to the employees out in the companies and local unions?

On union organization: How does the close cooperation with a commercial supplier function? How can an "alternative design" project be better organized in order to overcome demarcation conflicts between, in our case, graphic workers and journalists? With ongoing automation and integration of functions, this will be an aspect of growing importance in the whole of industry and administration.

On the relationship between technology and organization: To what extent does the alternative technology make alternative organizations possible, and to what extent does it prevent unwanted organizational solutions? With today's technology, which is much more flexible and tool-like than the technologies on the market when the Utopia project started; how crucial is technological development in relation to development of competence and the work organization? The planned study of an installation at an actual workplace could have provided important empirical material to illustrate these last questions.

On qualifications and work organization: With the focus on tools for skilled workers, is there a risk that the skilled workers, on whom management is dependent, will acquire better tools and an even stronger position in the company, while the less skilled employees (often women) fall outside the unions' and the researchers' interest in advanced technology and competence? It is of course a task for the unions, but also for work life researchers, to avoid this risk of contributing to a continued polarization of skills.

A project like Utopia can exercise a direct influence on one supplier. But at the same time it may have a much broader influence. Specifications of requirements may be, and are, used by local unions when negotiating with their employers; they influence the demand side of the market for production technology. Such specifications can also directly influence the producers, that is, the supply side of the market. (TCO's screen checker may result in similar effects.) The entire market for a production technology may thus be influenced—provided only that a strategy of this type is generalized in international trade union cooperation.

The project shows that a market-driven model of participatory work organization development such as that offered by Michael Piore and Charles Sabel (1984) is not the only possibility. Organized trade union demands and constructive action can directly influence the supply of organizational and technological solutions, if only the unions are given the resources to organize their own researcher co-operation. Today's technology is flexible, and creative alternatives can be the result only if the starting point is alternative; for example, quality of work is the goal rather than mere productivity, which does not preclude an efficient use of the technology. The factors in national and international markets favoring and hindering flexible participatory systems require further specification. Carmen Sirianni argues that local participation is difficult to achieve. "Of course, the international dominance of multinationals from countries with weak labor movements unable to shape the design process significantly (e.g., IBM), the increasing availability of 'package systems,' and the funding of technology and work organization development by the military place severe constraints on local participation in the design process" (Sirianni 1987, 14f.; on the U.S. Air Force's $100-billion project for a factory of the future, see Howard 1985, 210ff.).

Union research policy, and the resources available for union-oriented industrial R&D, like the development of new production technology, are key preconditions for the development of technology for the "good work." Our experiences show that where extra resources are available the unions can play a very dynamic role in the development of technology related to shop-floor know-how. A 1981 report by LO's research policy group underlined the importance of technical development in raising society's material and cultural levels and acknowledged the importance of industry–university cooperation. This cooperation, however, was seen as one-sided, and it was argued that the trade union movement had to define research problems and bring research resources to bear on these.

During the early 1980s, the Utopia project met with problems in financing the computer science components of the project that were not financed by the Arbetslivscentrum. Researchers applied for money to the Board for Technical Development (STU), which normally finances engineering research and development work. According to Andrew Martin (1987), who made a study of STU, the board had great difficulties in handling this application: It was not regarded, by the section responsible for computer technology research, as "knowledge development"; technological research with goals like the "quality of work" apparently could not be taken seriously. With the backing of LO, a new proposal was approved by STU's technology procurement section, although the project did not automatically fit in there either. It was necessary to present not only an association with a supplier (Liber–Tips) but also a specific customer whose procurement was to be supported; the newspaper *Aftonbladet* became part of the project. Eventually, STU's final decision provided Utopia with some resources: "But the terms on which it was made did not resolve the underlying policy issue of public support for autonomous trade union development of alternative technologies" (Martin 1987, 126).

Trade unions do not possess the large resources that companies have for industrial R&D. They thus have to rely on their ability to influence the R&D of other institutions. This can take the form of participation in industrial development projects or in joint projects. But, as Martin notes,

> All of these forms of influence are contingent on at least a sufficient command of technical resources to be able to autonomously operationalize union objectives as specific technical problems and to evaluate the solutions that result from R&D efforts. In the last analysis, as LO argued, unions cannot have that minimal command over R&D resources without public funding, and this will not be available except insofar as the unions' work-quality objectives become incorporated into public policy, as have the other kinds of objectives that have been incorporated into policy guiding public funding of R&D, such as industrial competitiveness, defense, health, and education. Since the extent to which this happens ultimately depends on the political strength of the unions, this might at least have been expected to happen in Sweden. (1987, 135)

As long as a shift in research policy enabling unions to play an autonomous role has not occurred, "Utopia is likely to remain an isolated demonstration of what could be a 'new Scandinavian model' of technological development, rather than an important step in the realization of that potential" (1987, 136).

In a similar vein, Loet Leydesdorff and Peter van den Besselaar studied grassroot experiences (workers' alternative plans) and surveyed experts and researchers in the field of sociology of labor and technology. They argue that, in contrast to the increase in the ability of management in knowledge-intensive industries to direct technological development, "The workers' point of view does not seem to penetrate to the level of longer-term scientific and technological development, even when resources are made available and R&D personnel in the public service are willing to do research on labor-oriented questions" (1987, 348f.). Despite the fact that they see the Demos and Utopia projects as possible exceptions, we view their pessimistic conclusions as partially wrong. With decent public funding and good relations with several organizational levels within a strong union movement, it might be possible to bring research on the quality of work to bear on the development of technology. But Leydesdorff and Besselaar are right in the sense that to get beyond the demonstration example, a general and long-term public research policy and organization must be established to further such goals as employee competence, and not focus exclusively on such goals as productivity:

> Only if the political subsystem is capable of developing new functions . . . on the interface between science and technology and public demands which are not automatically fulfilled by the market, can a perspective be developed in which technological innovation and social renewal are not contradictory but mutually reinforcing. This requires the intervention of a state—or even interstate organization—which aims specifically at the social guidance of technological developments. (1987, 349)

One historical reflection may be helpful at this point. The Utopia project took place in an intellectual, economic, political, and technological situation that differed from the situation almost ten years previously, when we were working with local unions on the offensive, after an economic boom, to establish an influence over a technological development that had degraded many jobs in the way articulated by Harry Braverman (1974) and others. As the economy stagnated and the winds of conservatism blew over Sweden, the unions began to look not primarily for power, but for secure jobs in a competitive industry.

In current thinking about industrial management, the possibility of combining good jobs with competent workers with resulting high productivity and competitiveness is paramount. Such a work organization is seen as necessary due to fluctuating markets with customer demand for quality. We return to this issue in Chapter 10. For the moment, we emphasize one precondition for this convergence of quality of work and productivity, namely recent developments in technology. We consider computer technology in particular because this technology seems to make possible highly qualified jobs that are also productive (see Sten Henriksson 1988). In the 1960s, the huge computers of that era were an expensive resource to be used efficiently; they were automata created by human beings, but once in operation, they delivered their results without human interaction. Time-sharing techniques were introduced in the early 1970s; computer workstations were developed in the latter part of that decade, initially for use in graphic work (e.g., computer-aided design, or CAD systems). The pioneering work was done at the Xerox Park laboratory in Palo Alto, California. Workstations then meant a dramatically raised capacity for an individual user.

One important development in computer science is the "user model" that enables the user to understand the functions of the system as an integrated whole. The designer develops a metaphor, preferably taken from a physical reality, and operations are named and function in a way that corresponds to that physical reality. One such a metaphor was used and developed in the Utopia project: A "table" was set up for the handling of documents, and "scissors" were used for cutting. The second important idea evolved during the 1980s as computers came to be recognized as tools (rather than as automatic systems). "With higher speed, good graphics, a well-designed user interface on the screen based on a 'user model,' and with good possibilities for interaction, it was now possible to let the computer system appear as a qualified tool" (Henriksson 1988, 13). The tool perspective is to some extent a consequence of the user model. If a metaphor builds on someone's reality, there is reason to imitate also the tools he or she is accustomed to using. A further step is direct manipulation. One example comes from the Macintosh program where the user "takes" a physical representation of the "document" on the "table," and "moves" it to the symbol for a "wastepaper basket" to delete it. Users work in small steps, internalizing the way in which they control the process. We have seen how some of these new concepts work in the Utopia project.

Sten Henriksson (1988, 13ff.) sees the user model and the tool perspective as a new humility on the part of computer science in relation to work and human beings. You can see the steps of changes in perspective: from the computer as an automatic system to the computer as a partner in a dialogue, similar to human communication. A further step back is the tool perspective, where the computer is an instrument for display, with tools by means of which someone competent in the area of work and application, rather than in the computer field, does the job. It is interesting to note that the steps "backward" in perspectives on the use of computers have become possible thanks to important technological steps forward. These steps would not have been possible ten years ago. The new possibilities of today present a challenge to researchers, employees, and unions to design good jobs in cooperation with those managements that are striving for high-quality production as a way of coping with international competition.

8. Conclusions

Among the companies' rationalization strategies, those aimed at capital, at the instruments and objects of work, appear to be becoming ever more central. With the breakthrough of computers and microelectronics, the issue relates not only to the use of a given technology but especially to the development of new technology. There are signs of union and political involvement in such questions. The union organizations, for example, have received money from the Board for Technical Development (STU) to enable them to formulate their demands on technological development projects. Another sign pointing in the same direction is the idea of a "new Scandinavian model" for computerization and the development of technology, which would at the same time promote the objectives of industrial policy and objectives relating to work content and co-determination.

If the union organizations enter into major cooperative projects on the use of technology at the workplaces and technological development in the R&D context, they are entering the old domains of management. In that case, it is necessary that they should be very clear about what they want. They should know what type of work and work organization they wish to achieve and what demands they want to make in local development and negotiation. There is a need for union strategies and action programs that incorporate the employees' experience, union objectives, and a knowledge of development trends.

To be able to formulate its own alternative models and specific demands on development processes, work, and technology, the union may also need to be able to perform its own development work. In experimental environments, the skills of experienced workers, union representatives, and researchers (both technicians and sociologists) can benefit each other. If the capabilities and demands of the skilled workers are to assert themselves, precisely this sort of environment is required, where the course of work and possible technological and organizational futures can be simulated.

All this demands research resources for the central union organizations. Union organizations should receive a share of what the Swedish government grants to support industrial research and development work in new technology. Resources will also be necessary for the research performed in cooperation with the union organizations. This necessitates, for example, a redefinition of STU's mission, so that union goals such as quality of work become part of public R&D policy, along with traditional goals such as industrial competitiveness. Then the unions, like industry, may be able to obtain public funds for their independent R&D projects. In addition, the situation demands that employees and local unions should have access to company information. This can be achieved in part by participating in management projects of different kinds and in part by a statutory right to early information on the part of the union. But mere access to information, a passive role as a recipient of information, is not enough. Unions can be drowned in masses of paper and meetings (a tendency in the public sector) or have difficulty in getting access to these (a tendency in the private sector). The union must be able to "create meaningful information," in the sense that it can demand certain information, get studies performed, and, finally, use the knowledge it has obtained as a basis for action. This creation of information presupposes, and also creates the conditions for, an overall knowledge on the part of the unions.

Independent union work of this kind constitutes, in its turn, a necessary condition for the union playing any constructive role in the development and use of new technology, in joint projects with the employer. Otherwise, it seems probable that the emphasis on joint projects, as happened around 1970, will end in disappointment, resulting in locked positions on both sides. The vital issue for the democratization of working life is not the forms for union relations with the employer. Early access to information, opportunities for negotiation, and participation are all basic and necessary conditions for a continuing democratization. But they are not enough. In the Swedish situation today, the decisive question is the content of the actual union activity. The Swedish cases studied in the Front project concerned processes of change, in which the union and the employees emphasized their roles as producers, as skilled workers who were concerned to produce something useful and of high quality. Influence in qualitative production issues was based largely on the employees' expertise in production, the operation as such.

To be able to develop this new, constructive, and knowledge-based strategy, the union needs resources over and above these mentioned above. Here are some suggestions: The union and its members need time (paid working hours) for their own studies and investigatory activities. The union needs access to the company's technical and economic expertise. It needs a share of the company's resources for investigation, as well as employer-paid wage-earner consultants. Finally, the unions, like industry, need state support for their own R&D efforts. This may sound like a lot, but this work of creating knowledge and alternatives requires far greater resources than the unions normally have at their disposal.

But such resources will still be meager as compared with those of management. Also, our case studies and analyses show that these are well used resources from the managerial perspective. The unions and their members have demonstrated their ability to contribute constructively in production issues, provided that they acquire a few extra opportunities.

One result of co-determination is that unions and their members are taking on some of the traditional management concerns. For example, management and unions together formulate the important problems arising in a company and seek constructive solutions on which agreement can be reached. As we have seen, the classical union approach, with clear demands followed by negotiations, does not function very well in such unstructured situations. It may be possible, of course, for unions simply to participate in the activities of management as a further partner to discussions, but the price is that the union organization's identity and legitimacy may then be threatened. However, the future of the trade union movement will also be threatened should it decide not to concern itself with the future's decisive technological and organizational questions.

These and other difficulties inherent in developing a union strategy in production issues and in harmony with the producer perspective perhaps invite the question whether such efforts really are union issues. One can be tempted to revert to the traditional union policy that operates parallel with or perhaps in opposition to production. However, the development of a union approach and working method in harmony with the producer perspective is a necessary condition for the forms of co-determination being filled with a content that makes the content of work and quality of product such important issues for the future.

The challenge and the opportunities lie in devising a content and forms for union activities that will permit a contribution to constructive problem solving at companies and administrations, while retaining a union independence that allows democratic responsibility on the part of active members.

10

"New Management" and Good Jobs

1. The Problem

There are several reasons for recent development within management being of interest here. The development of new forms of company organization can be understood in the light of technological change and new forms of work organization. Some of these ideas, such as the integration of tasks in direct production, are similar to ideas that we have seen the unions striving to achieve. But the unions have sometimes viewed the changes in technology and in work in isolation, not as they relate to changes in systems of managerial control and company organization. This is contrary to various declarations of union policy, but it is understandable. The unions have had enough to do trying to influence the work organization. Also, the new forms of management have only recently been applied on any broad basis, and thus become more visible.

One of the characteristics of the "new management" is the effort on management's part to involve the workers in the ideas and business activities of the company. In combination with other methods of control, this can prevent potentially good, integrated jobs from being fully realized because job intensity might be driven up to a very high level. This can also create a conflict with growing trade union efforts to participate in and influence production issues. In this way, the new tendencies within management are reinforcing the need for new union strategies, a theme that runs through this book. The changes lead to an emphasis on the need for a multilevel strategy both within companies—encompassing an influence on direct production and the work organization as well as on managerial issues—and in society at large—where there is a possible relationship between the development of corporate cultures and ideologies and ideological contradictions at the political level. And all these changes relate to the issue of the use and development of new technology.

Today, the concept of "leadership" gleams brightly in the mass media, in the bookshops, and on the magazine shelves. Exciting, charismatic leaders of industry provide the main characters for some heroic tales. Companies and working life are being transformed, and a whole succession of new phenomena are appearing at the workplaces. Slogans of the day are "market orientation" and "flexibility" in the production systems and forms of employment. The production of services is growing rapidly. The process of automation in actual production continues. New working duties for workers and salaried staff with all-round skills and teamwork are being developed. At the same time, we see tendencies toward workers being "burned out" and becoming "market rejects" and growing unemployment. Company managements are trying to create flat organizations, with a broad base, few people at the intermediate level, and a strong management. Their war cry is "Tear down the pyramids!"

Through modern, computer-supported information and control systems, central management maintains a grip on conditions and target-achievement with more or less independent production groups and profit centers at different levels, from the company level, down through divisions or departments, to the work teams.

"Tough" control systems of this kind are supplemented by more "tender" methods, such as quality circles and consciously developed company "cultures" or "philosophies." By the attachment of pay to company profits, profit sharing, and advantageous offers to buy shares, management is linking the interests of employees to the company's goals regarding profit. In aggregate, management is trying to take the entire person, soul included, into its service.

The vast quantity of management literature defining modern principles of company management is often inspired by the concepts of "Japanese management." Many such books have their origin in the experience of consultants in successful major corporations, often in America. On closer inspection, their empirical foundation proves weak in many cases, or at least incompletely reported. (This is true, for example of Peters and Waterman's *In Search of Excellence* [1982].) Theoretically based studies and critical reviews from perspectives other than those of management are hard to come by.

Union organizations and the trade union press report fears over this new development, critical views are being put forward, and attention is being drawn to the need for new knowledge and a new approach. Here, by way of introduction, let us hint at certain challenges to the union organization:

- If the free play for pay negotiations is becoming steadily less, as a result of low growth rate and perhaps also state interventions in the formation of wages, and if the small piece of the cake that remains is divided up locally (outside any regular pay negotiations), by profit sharing, advantageous offers of shares, or pay-by-results, then what is left for the traditional wage movements to accomplish?
- Can the union organizations cope without Taylor? In other words, if more and more members are acquiring interesting and personally developmental working tasks, what is the union to fight for in the field of co-determination?
- If the employer, to an increasing extent, addresses the individual with offers of both a material and incorporeal nature and with a "corporate culture" that demonstrates the meaningfulness of the individual's contribution to the corporate operation as a whole, what has the union movement, and the union ideology, to set against this?

To put it briefly, are the unions necessary? Sven Rydenfelt wrote in *SAF–tidningen* (the journal of the Swedish Employers' Confederation) in 1986: "And, indeed, the union is quite right that the efforts of employers to eliminate the causes of conflict, and instead build up feelings of togetherness and trust, are a threat to the union. . . . Our own business leaders have for far too long been wasting their energy on vain attempts to prevail over the union. Now they are trying instead to win over their employees" (1986, 23).

Abroad, a political campaign is being waged in some countries to "tame the unions" by means of legislation. In the United States, some corporate managements are trying to weaken unions by hiring special consultants for the purpose of "union busting." The AFL–CIO has called some of the elements incorporated in the new managerial techniques "soft union busting," and these measures may indeed have been consciously used for this purpose in the United States. In Sweden, so far we have found no legislation that union organizations regard as hostile in this way. At the company level, however, the new individual-oriented forms of control can lead to the union being "left out of things" and, in the long term, weakened. There is little ground for contending that the "new managerial philosophies" constitute a conscious attempt by employers to weaken unions. The aggregate result of a number of firms individually, but simultaneously and aggressively, introducing new managerial methods, however, *can* be the weakening of unions.

There is another side to the present trends and challenges. Management is increasingly dependent on their skilled blue-collar and white-collar workers. This is why managers are referring more and more frequently to their employees as "the corporation's greatest resource." It is, of course, flattering to be regarded as the greatest resource. But a resource for *whom?* It is by no means impertinent to ask the question: Who is to husband this resource? Is this something for which management is to be responsible in the classical manner, just as it stewards such material resources as machinery, buildings, and stocks? Or is it not the case that human resources differ from machinery and that employees should be permitted to assist in, or perhaps assume the entire responsibility for, husbanding themselves? It is difficult to maintain any other claim than that employees and their organizations are best fitted themselves to formulate their interests and demands regarding qualifications and on-the-job development.

The increased dependence on the knowledge of the employees constitutes a foundation for their direct influence on the day-to-day work of the company and on changes in that work. For many, it also offers a basis for involvement in the work of the union to promote a long-term development of competency and the work organization and thereby a foundation for stronger union influence.

Here, obviously, workers can find themselves involved in conflicts between, on the one hand, a commitment to the day-to-day work and production by the company for which they work and on which they depend for their livelihood, and, on the other, their commitment to the union and its objectives. Such a conflict can emerge with particular clarity in cases where managements, with their "new managerial methods" are claiming to try to involve the individual worker as a whole in the service of the company, and where there exists at the same time a union organization that is renewing its approach and raising issues of production and of the need of individual members for support and development in their work. The two perspectives and two types of "meaningfulness" are in competition. The white-collar unions have long felt the tensions existing between a career in the company and involvement in the union; in the "new" companies, this is also a problem for the unions affiliated with LO.

Several elements in the "new management" have been promoted or supported by union organizations. Unions have supported the integration of working tasks and the organization of work on a group basis. These new phenomena did not simply "hit" the employees from out of nowhere. They were developing in what is both an interplay and a conflict between different actors. Their significance in the long-term development of working life is ambiguous. In a new situation, new managerial ideas develop. Hence union organizations may also have to reconsider, and are indeed now revising, their organization and working approach.

We see the changes enacted by companies as potential areas of conflict. Where they lead in terms of efficiency, job content, and influence are to some extent open questions. They may lead to strengthened managerial control over employees whose short-term interests coincide with those of management. They may, on the other hand, lead to a growing freedom and self-determination for the employees. This will be determined, within the existing economic and technological restrictions, by the resources and strategies of the actors in the field.

We give an account below of the dominant managerial perspectives and glimpses of incipient union perspectives on the transformation of companies.

2. Elements of the New Managerial Strategies

In this section we discuss a number of elements of the new managerial ideas, as they are found in the popular literature. This is not a description of what companies actually look like nor how they are run—but rather an account of the ideas that have a major impact on the debate as to how companies are steered—and we look at actual phenomena that appear to be emerging but whose spread is little known. They are here summed up under six points. (A wealth of literature is available in this field, and reference is made only to a number of general texts: Bergman 1986; Eriksson 1986; *Metallarbetaren* 1986a; Ramström 1986. See also *Ledning för alla?* 1987.) Not all of this is new. One can recognize ideas from the field of "human relations," where the emphasis is on informal group relationships; sociotechnical design, with its emphasis on the simultaneous optimization of the technology *and* the social organization; and Management-by-Objectives (MBO). What is new is the breadth and the force with which these ideas are being disseminated.

Performing empirical studies emerges as an urgent matter, since the whole basis of the picture offered in the popular literature, and described below, is unclear. Is general validity being ascribed to isolated examples? Or, are the ideas of consultants and ambitions of managements as to how affairs *should* be coloring the views of what actually is happening? Or, are these changes making a broad actual impact? Are these different elements connected, or do they occur individually? Research into these questions can provide the basis for a discussion of the desirability of different phenomena and their consequences with regard to work content and influence.

1. It is intended that the company organization shall have fewer hierarchical levels, *a flatter organization*. (The extent to which it really becomes flat will depend not only on the number of levels but also on the size of the "stairs" [Eriksson 1986, 22].) Both the base and the top management will be reinforced, while the intermediate levels are thinned out. This entails a simultaneous centralization and decentralization. Central control over the achievement of production targets in quality, time, and results will be needed, as will a centralization of factors determining performance and current productivity planning. Metaphors are used in an attempt to break with the hierarchic way of thinking, of which SAS Chief Executive Jan Carlzon's slogan was an example. "Tear down the pyramids," he said, or, more carefully, "Flatten the pyramids," as it appears in the English translation of his book (Carlzon 1987). What is termed, in the hierarchical image, the "base of the pyramid" is called in today's martial linguistic usage the market "front," where soldier-workers battle. Behind the front are the staffs and the leader. One of the duties of management is to provide a rallying idea that will promote the struggle on the market, and give the "frontline soldiers" (the sales representatives who meet the customers, the workers in direct production) good working opportunities and see to it that they are served by the ranks behind. The martial emphasis is marked by the title of Jan Carlzon's little book for the personnel at SAS, "Let's Start Fighting"; there was talk of the "Little Red Book" and of a "cultural revolution" (Björkman 1986).

2. Production is divided into more or less *independent units* at different levels: companies, product workshops, production teams. This applies both to the company organization as a whole and to the organization of work. Not only whole companies but also production units and groups are subject to frequent checks of their contributions to the profits of the parent company or group (profit centers).

3. The various units are coordinated and controlled with the help of computer-supported information systems, primarily in the form of *economic control*. The result (that is, profit) achieved is compared with the budgeted profit. Top management can also directly examine the effects of a unit's behavior on the market, and influence, in the following phase, the market conditions under which it operates. At lower levels, it controls in a similar manner, for example, the production teams through their budgets, profits or losses,

and various conditions under which they operate. In other words, we are now getting a "new technology" not only in actual production, but also new computer-supported information systems for the control and follow-up of each individual's or group's contribution to the company's profit. In a decentralized organization, this is how management controls the work and pushes up the pace as forcefully as it did before with the foremen and the installation of the moving belt system.

4. The individual feels the new economic control most particularly in the *pay and reward systems* that are directly linked to the profit of the company or to an individual profit center. These include pay-by-results, profit sharing, "convertibles" and shares at favorable prices, gratuities and bonuses, and various benefits connected with employment. Rates of pay are set more individually and are performance-oriented. This latter creates a means of control for the employer, but it also creates problems: Local wage increases cause a wage drift (over and beyond the central agreements) and the subsequent consequential demands can start an uncontrolled pay and inflation spiral.

"Convertibles," or convertible bonds, are perhaps the new system of payment that has attracted most attention. A succession of major corporations have offered their employees convertibles. A convertible is a certificate of loan of a specific sum of money to the company, corresponding to a certain number of shares. The company pays interest on this sum. Anyone offered the opportunity to buy convertibles can borrow money from a bank to subscribe. The convertible functions as security, and the company often stands guarantor. The interest payable in the bank is higher than the interest received from the company. If the market price of the share has fallen by the time the convertible can be redeemed, one will always get back the sum one has paid: One will not have lost more than the difference between the rate paid to the bank and that received from the company. If the rate paid for the share is higher, one converts the convertibles against shares and makes a profit corresponding to the rise in share prices. The risk is that, if the company goes bankrupt, the convertible could become totally worthless.

5. *Ideological control* means an effort to exercise control by "soft" methods: clear, inspiring, and charismatic leaders, quality circles and development groups, a system for taking up proposals, and direct channels between manager and employee. By "internal marketing," attempts are made to shape the employees' image of the firm, with the use, for example, of publicity, campaigns, and courses and conferences. The more substantial company training provided and internal labor markets can function this way. In aggregate, an effort is made to build up a team spirit, a common corporate culture, and

thus win the hearts and minds of the work force. This sort of "soft control," when successful, makes it look as if people were being guided from within. New, sophisticated methods of business management can draw upon our current knowledge of people's sometimes very deep need to lead and to be led.

One reason for taking an interest in the psychoanalytical perspectives is the role played by Michael Maccoby in Swedish management research. Maccoby collaborated with Erich Fromm who, with a background in psychoanalysis and critical theory, studied social character in a Mexican village. Social character was used as an instrument by which to understand the underlying causes for a politically promoted land reform in Mexico leading to alcoholism and irresponsibility among the villagers rather than to positive development. In Maccoby's later studies of leadership, this critical perspective has been watered down, and the concept of "social character" has become a description of patterns of adjustment to an "inevitable development." The earlier insight that members of a group may renounce their capacity for critical thought can be used, following Freud, to reveal uncritical postures vis-à-vis authorities, but it can also be used to seek out leaders who will activate people's unsatisfied needs of dependence.

The new trends in the managerial literature also assign greater importance to social competency and the "rationality of caring," which it is customary to claim are distinctive of the "female stereotype." The perspective here hinted at is an intrapsychic one that seeks explanations at the level of the individual. In a structural perspective, the emphasis is rather on the need for changes in the company and work organization that would create more free play for social competency. The result of the new language and new symbols ("emphasis on the individual" and "social competency") may be to provide new instruments of control within the framework of an unchanged power structure in the organization.

6. A breaking up of the *employer–employee relationship* and new forms of activity both tend to reduce the importance of the wage-earner role. The employer–employee relationship is being broken up by short-term, part-time, and seasonal employment. Corporate fragmentation, labor hired from outside, and the farming out of production to other companies restrict security of employment to a smaller unit. Self-employment and franchising involve a sort of small-scale entrepreneurship in extreme dependence on the companies that buy the services or on whose account the goods or services are sold in controlled forms.

The Swedish Metalworkers' Union has studied how common some of the phenomena listed under points 4 and 5 are (*Metallarbetaren* 1986a). The study was addressed to all the locals within the union with more than 150 members; this represented 337 locals comprising 185,000 members, which is to say roughly half of all the actively employed members. Within two weeks, 95 percent of the locals had answered, which is an extremely high response rate. The members clearly regard these questions as extremely urgent and the changes as having an important bearing on the work of unions—and very much on the increase. For example, pay-by-result methods and convertible bonds are spreading rapidly, while profit sharing is stagnating. Almost 100,000 members work with firms that run quality circles, as compared with 20,000 in 1980. The study fails to show how many members are in fact members of such circles.

The locals are unclear as to whether these phenomena should be interpreted as offering opportunities or whether they mainly create difficulties; the latter view tends to prevail. This lack of clarity may reflect the dual or contradictory nature of the new development. This is especially evident in point 5, where such elements as proposals "from the floor," quality circles, and certain training may be in line with, and in part the result of, union demands, while "cultural manipulation" is a more outright expression of the art of ideological control.

By way of illustration, let us look more closely at the development of convertibles. The tendency is for considerably more salaried employees than workers to subscribe to convertibles. In 1986, convertibles were signed by employees to a value of SEK 2.4 billion (U.S. $396 million) (*SIF-tidningen* 1987a). In 1980 convertibles were offered to 15,000 members of Metall, the Metalworkers' Union. By 1986, 100,000 of Metall's members had received such offers. With the sharply rising share prices noted in the 1980s, the press contained reports about workers who had made very large *nominal* profits (these were often compared with the small increases in actual rates of salary/wages). By December 1987, a number of employees were in a position to redeem their convertibles. In Metall's sector, offers of convertibles have been made in twelve major corporations, including SKF, ASEA, PLM, Atlas Copco, Volvo, and Ericson. At Volvo, for example, all employees were reinvited to subscribe to a maximum of SEK 182,500 (U.S. $30,200). The interest was so high that the allocation was reduced to a maximum of SEK 55,285 (U.S. $9,150). In this way Volvo was able to borrow over SEK 1 billion (U.S. $165 million) from its employees; 21,000 employees signed up, 9,000 of whom were metalworkers (which is to say 25 percent of the metalworkers at Volvo). At ASEA, the employees were able to subscribe in 1985 for a maximum of SEK 48,000 (U.S. $7,950), and when they were able to convert in 1987 the value was twice that. Volvo and PLM were among the companies where all employees, including the chief executive officers, were able to subscribe to the same amount. At ASEA, for example, both the CEO and president were permitted to subscribe convertibles to a value of over SEK 2 million each (U.S. $345,000) (Metallarbetaren 1987a; for the ASEA management's subscription of convertibles, see *SIF-tidningen* 1987b).

3. Changes in the Work Organization

How are we to understand the emergence of these new managerial strategies? One possibility is to enter the "secret workshop" of production. Work in the most sophisticated industrial production has long been chopped up in ever small parts. The worker becomes an appendage to the machine and is steered by the speed of the moving belt, the cogent arguments of a piece rate, or the supervision and reports of a supervisor. This "scientific management," the Taylor system, has long been regarded as best for the company's finances and the only right way to organize production. Even within the trade union movement, the detailed division of labor was regarded as a necessary aspect of industrialization, the raising of standards, and general progress.

Some division of labor is obviously necessary: Not everyone can do everything or be good at everything. Specialization makes production more efficient, goods cheaper, and material standards high. But when the division of labor is driven to such an extreme that the car workers, for example, are only allowed to learn manual operations that must be repeated every few minutes, it is a detailed division of labor that impoverishes the job. To call it "specialization" is pure euphemism.

Voices critical of Taylorism have been raised not only from among those directly affected, the workers, and from within the trade union movement, but also from among writers and researchers. These people have spoken not of specialization and progress, but of impoverishment and preying upon others. Some twenty years ago, these voices found particularly clear expression in the strike movements in Europe. In Sweden, the strike in the ore fields in Kiruna is a most important example. There, the strikes were mainly directed at the poor working environment, the carving up of the work, and MTM systems. The union organizations, as we have seen in Chapter 3, began to push demands for a better working environment, a richer work content, and influence at the workplace. Gradually Sweden acquired a Working Environment Act, a Co-Determination Act, and a reinforcement of the status of union officials as well as some progress toward job enlargement.

Figure 7

Ill Health as a Function of Work Load and Self-Determination

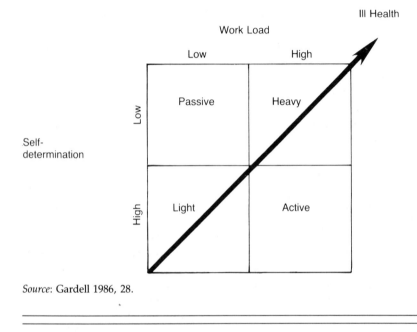

Source: Gardell 1986, 28.

As we have seen above, Harry Braverman (1974) painted a picture of the continuing degradation of work. A similar thrust was evident, in the German-speaking world, in Horst Kern and Michael Schumann's study of 1970. These publications can be said to have pointed to a tendency toward a polarization within companies between a few highly qualified employees and numerous poorly qualified ones.

Research pointing to a one-sided tendency toward polarization has subsequently been criticized and modified. Braverman, for example, has been criticized for not having seen signs that management, for example, uses the group organization of work as a complement to Taylorism. He also failed to observe that management is not all-powerful and that the employees and union organizations have sometimes successfully resisted the Taylorization of work. In

Sweden, research into working life has illustrated the impoverishment of labor but has also investigated possible constructive alternatives, especially in collaboration with the union (Dahlström 1980, 116ff.). One example is provided by the studies of Bertil Gardell and Bob Karasek et al. (summarized in Gardell 1986) of the correlation between high working demands, a low degree of self-determination, and ill health at work (see Figure 7). To be able to exercise control over one's own work and having opportunities to cooperate are ways of avoiding stress and ill health. They also provide a basis for continuous learning and the development of a collective control over the labor process.

Today management and the employers admit that industrial work under Taylorism is impoverished—and even inefficient. But, they say in the same breath, that today fresh opportunities exist to combine richness of working duties with productivity. We summarize below the bright, uncomplicated picture of changes in production and work that one encounters so frequently at conferences and in the popular literature on production and personnel (see Giertz 1986 on production organization; Södergren 1987 on company organization).

In the engineering industry, planning and production are combined, in that the programming of computer-controlled machines is largely being taken over by the workers who operate them. In the process industry, the monitoring of the automated process is often combined with an in-depth knowledge of it and with maintenance work. In the service industries, employees have a sound knowledge of the company's products and the needs of its customers and are extremely capable when it comes to communicating with each other and with the customer, so that a sense of high quality is created precisely in this interplay.

Working duties are becoming more composite, and anyone who must handle these new duties has to have many competencies. It must be possible for both workers and salaried staff to alternate between different duties, and work in teams, in which every member rallies round to achieve a rapid flow of production. The basic theme is: "So maybe it used to be pretty terrible working on the production line, but today the possibilities are there, and in the future everyone will have good jobs."

"Good" jobs can be achieved despite management's efforts to rationalize. In fact, such efforts often further the cause. There are great opportunities for both workers and salaried employees to be offered better jobs without any union struggle. There are also great opportunities for employees and their representatives to be invited to participate in the development of production, to become members of product groups, and so forth. Union commitment to the change, and the new order, is thus ensured.

We are entering a new era, in which the survival and productivity of the company, the quality of its products and services, the work content of its employees' jobs, and the development of their competency go hand in hand. After almost half a century of dominance, Taylorism is being replaced by a new theory of organization and control that claims to be of general application. The conflicts between employers and the unions and between employees and management, we are told, will be eliminated, at least as far as production and its organization are concerned. Wage questions may still remain. We argue that the development is in fact more composite and ambiguous than this.

4. Motive Forces: Productivity

What is causing these changes in technology, work, and management? In the literature on production technology and industrial organization, the essential background is taken to be productivity under altered conditions. The picture given is roughly as follows: The changes are being generated by the great production capacity that follows in the wake of computerization, the threat of overproduction, and the consequently ever-sharper competition among companies and among countries. Companies must be able to adapt production rapidly to the oscillations of the market and to numerous and varied submarkets. *Market adaptation* and *flexibility* are the bywords. The demands of customers, marketing, and merchandising are moving into the production line. The quality of the products, fast deliveries to the customers' specifications, and a high level of service are becoming vital competitive instruments. A further motive force is insight into the high warehousing costs involved in the storage of raw materials, goods in process, and finished products. That means paring down the amount of capital tied up in in-process inventories by maintaining a rapid flow and "suction" from the market, that is, capital rationalization.

Rapid technological development and reduced prices for computer-supported production techniques are creating conditions for many changes. Today's automation offers more personally rewarding working duties than did the mechanization of the 1960s or the computers of the earlier generations, which were poor "tools" for skilled workers. Development projects in industry during the 1980s reveal, however, that in several cases where new technology provided the starting point for a reorganization that worked toward an integration of fragmented workings tasks, new technology has proved subsequently not to be any sort of *necessary* condition. There are instances where the technology envisaged has proved inadequate, while the new work organization has provided rationalization gains, despite retention of a conventional production technology. The highly specialized, mechanized production of long series of parts and products is too cumbersome and intractable a system. Workers schooled in detail and learning only isolated skills, are too "rigid" a "production factor." Such a production system cannot cope with market adaption, capital rationalization, or the demands of the unions.

The alternatives that are being promoted, and are becoming possible, are product workshops, production groups, and automation. Multiskilled workers in teams, who also have an insight into the demands of the market, help create a rapid flow in production and promote the success of the company in an ever tougher market (see Chapter 3).

The specific elements in the growing production of services, in which quality is created in interplay with the customer, make demands of the employee's motivation and involvement in such "moments of truth." Many service companies are knowledge-intensive and have a high proportion of extremely well qualified personnel. A great deal of the new managerial thinking has been developed in the form of "service management" and has established a whole school of thought, just as Taylorism did previously in the production of goods (Eriksson 1986 discusses corporate cultures and "service management" from the standpoint of organizational theory and the perspective of the unions).

5. Motive Forces: Control

Another explanation of what causes the current changes in work life reflects the protests of ever-more-educated employees against impoverished jobs and the demands of union organizations. Management literature often assumes a harmony between the development of good jobs and productivity. If such a harmony is not taken for granted, a further explanation of the development of new managerial strategies may be the need to exercise control. We know from several studies that the local union organizations frequently encounter limits in their efforts to bring together fragmented work operations into single jobs, particularly when it comes to entire groups or collectives of workers. Examples include the Front project's case studies of the dairy and the Postgiro (Chapter 5) and the

Demos project's action research at the Swedish State Rail engineering shop in Örebro (Chapter 4). The resistance of the employers can, we have suggested, be due to their not having realized that multiskilled and independent workers constitute a potential for rationalization and also to their viewing competent and independent groups of workers as a possible threat to control by management.

The study at the Swedish State Rail (SJ) workshop was performed within the Demos project around 1976. Now, almost fifteen years later, the SJ management is implementing decentralization, competence development, and group organization very much in line with the old union demands. New ideas about profit-oriented control and management by objectives of partially independent units are also being included. These new management techniques had not been developed at SJ fifteen years ago. Using them now, management can decentralize and exploit the creativity of the employees without the loss of overall control. A background to these changes was a renewal of staff in the SJ management that paralleled continued union pressure.

Composite work duties performed by multiskilled workers and teams and a growing production of services tend to promote a decentralization of decisions regarding the performance of work and a certain degree of on-the-job freedom. This entails less detailed control by management and, at the same time, a more flexible and efficient organization, which can ensure large profits. This conflict between efficiency and detailed control is very prominent today. For management, it is a matter of combining control with a certain degree of freedom for the workers. In the new managerial strategies, detailed control of how the work is performed has been replaced by worker motivation and the control of target fulfillment and contributions to profit.

It is often necessary for managements to invest in the development of human resources as a means of protecting their investments in advanced technology. The investment in new economic and ideological systems of control that, in many companies, takes place simultaneously with this is related not only to the efficient production of products that are in demand but also to power and influence in the production system. This is an aspect that is seldom considered when dealing with production technology or with business economics and management. The explanation is rather like that once given by John Kenneth Galbraith for why "power" is a factor that is often absent from the traditional economic analyses: A discipline that serves essentially as an instrument for the exercise of power, and of control, is disinclined to treat power and control as an object of study.

We have kept thus far to the company level, trying to create a picture of changes in production and the extent to which they can explain the new managerial strategies. One can speculate as to how far this outpouring of management literature, and its ideas, can also be seen as a social phenomenon at the ideological and political level, a way of escaping from the economic decline by inculcating in people an image of the terms of successful enterprise. The picture includes decentralization, a breaking up of organizational structures, and an atomization into smaller, allegedly market-steered units that bear the responsibility for results. Market relationships, it is alleged, are thus spreading at the expense of the organization. The simultaneous reinforcement of central coordination and control becomes—and in the multinationals to an ever-increasing extent—overshadowed.

6. For Everyone? Forever?

That good jobs and higher qualifications go hand in hand with increased productivity is thus a dominant line of thought in the contemporary debate and managerial philosophy. An essential contribution to our understanding of this development has been made by Horst Kern's and Michael Schumann's book *Das Ende der Arbeitsteilung?* (1985). In 1970, these two tone-setting West German industrial sociologists published a study of industrial work that pointed to an ongoing polarization between skilled and unskilled jobs. It was the jobs of the many that became impoverished, while a few jobs became increasingly sophisticated. This created an A team and a B team within the company. In their 1985 study, Kern and Schumann revise their thesis on polarization. In the more sophisticated parts of industry that they have studied, they see a tendency for the unqualified jobs quite simply to disappear, while a small number of skilled jobs remains. A research group at the Free University in Berlin has pursued, in a succession of books, a similar thesis (PAQ 1987). Kern and Schumann write about "new production concepts" that put the specific qualities of human labor in the center; it is not a question, as it is in Taylorism, of making production independent of professional skill; skill is instead really regarded as a productive force.

What Kern and Schumann see, however, is not a kingdom of heaven, with highly skilled, proud workers, but a society characterized by a new polarization between the few who have interesting jobs and those who are unemployed. They also emphasize that skilled work, with the opportunities it offers for development and personal initiative, has another side to it. A job that is organized and controlled in a way that erases the pauses for rest becomes "more dense" and intensified, with a heavy burden of stress. In West Germany, a critical discussion of these issues has begun (see Broady and Helgesson 1985). Similar views have also emerged in the Swedish discussion of the new work organization and the new management.

The "new polarization" between the winners and the losers, between the people with jobs and those without (i.e., the process of rejection), is an initial serious complication and objection to the bright, uncomplicated view of the future promulgated in management literature in section 3. Within the OECD, there were in 1989 almost 25 millions persons unemployed (OECD 1990), including a rapidly growing proportion of long-term unemployed (this proportion, however, varies, depending on the labor market and educational policies applied). Sweden is coping relatively well. Another complication is the tendency toward a breaking up of the employer–employee relationship, reducing its importance by a process of marginalization from the labor market: part-time jobs, work at home, small enterprises and subsuppliers who are dependent on a major company without responsibility for short-term employees, seasonal workers, and the like. Within companies, the importance of the employer–employee relationship is being undermined by various forms of divisionalization and corporate fragmentation, which mean that each production unit has to be viable and provide sufficient profit. If a unit does not live up to group management's expectations, it may be eliminated with no responsibility taken for its employees.

Franchising is a system, by which a hamburger joint or car rental firm, for example, is operated under a well-entrenched brand name and by methods, working procedures, and marketing that make the business appear to be a branch of a major corporation. In fact, the holder of the franchise is running the operation as a small business and is taking major risks at the same time that he or she is tied by a tough contract to the franchiser. The employees' job security lies entirely with the small firm, and not, as it might appear with the big corporation. Another form of job structure, and one of growing importance, is self-employment. The formerly employed hairdresser, for example, rents a chair and equipment and runs his or her own firm; forest workers are offered loans by their former employers to buy the felling equipment, and then as a small business— economically dependent, on the whole, on their former employers—survive on work farmed out by the latter.

A third complication is that the consequences of industry's ongoing rationalization of the workers, and the content of their work, can vary over time. The story does not necessarily end with today's possibilities of an upgrading of qualifications. In the previous history of labor, we have seen periods in which the trends have been both upgrading and downgrading. Even in a shorter-term perspective, studies of automation show an initial phase involving the integration of duties into composite jobs for skilled versatile workers. In a subsequent stage, the all-round jobs have been fragmented into a new division of labor, between top and routine all-rounders (Dorewaard 1986).

Fourth, the idea of good jobs for all seems to be based on the experiences of certain advanced key industries, such as automobile production, mechanical engineering, and the chemical industry and the production of sophisticated services. It is far from clear how far similar tendencies can be expected to assert themselves in more traditional types of production and in such growth industries as computer manufacture. Even in major areas within the production of services, we may see a continued polarization of professional skills (even if all the employees learn to say "Have a nice day"). The detailed control characteristic of Taylorism can often persist in companies where the employees are easily replaceable, where no great involvement is required, and where quality problems do not entail such costs that management would consider it feasible to invest in some development of the employees' competence.

A continued impoverishment of professional skills can also be concealed by management's borrowing a bit of "cultural glamour" ("Here we work proudly, toward a common goal!") from other activities where it may have more justification. There is a tendency for today's theses regarding the benevolent effects of technology from the workers' standpoint to be as linear and single-dimensional as the earlier analyses that were criticized for being linear models of impoverishment. There is reason to underline the range in technological level and work content of the different companies that congratulate themselves on their positive corporate culture and personality-developing operations. In activities where the jobs continue to be relatively unskilled, the role of the new management philosophies as an instrument of control becomes particularly clear.

A fifth complication relates to the perspective of control. Despite increased play for action in the day-to-day work, the "hard" and "soft" methods of control we have described exert pressure on the individual: "There is an obvious risk of the employees becoming mentally fatigued, economically exploited, socially indoctrinated, and politically manipulated. The refined control and steering system applied is an obstacle to union mobilization, and the process of making the members aware" (von Otter 1983a, 93).

The five objections put forward above against the picture of "good jobs for everyone" relate to the empirical validity of such a generalization. They give us reason to formulate questions that can be tested empirically, but complications, such as the ambiguous driving forces involved (productivity, control, good jobs, democratization), make it difficult to point to any reliably established trend.

7. Challenges to the Unions

The conflict-free image of the future promoted by organized capital envisages highly qualified employees who are deeply involved in the company by which they are employed. Their teams will be working to the same ends as the company as a whole. The dominant threat to each company's success is overproduction, or, as it has usually been put, international competition. These threats from the market demand quality of production, and adaptation to the customer. The main labor issue of the late 1980s is the threat of a labor shortage paralleled with demands for highly qualified jobs from steadily better trained employees. Additionally, organized labor demands, with varying degrees of force, co-determination at the workplaces and various types of "economic democracy" in business and industry as a whole. The new management philosophies can be seen, in part, as the companies' response to these challenges. The employees and their organizations are a step behind. The theme of this section is the challenge to organized labor presented by the new management philosophies.

The new forms of work organization and the elements of the new managerial strategies, as they were briefly presented above, can entail advantages for the employees at various workplaces. The competency of the employees and their commitment to their work can raise productivity and offer the company competitive advantages vis-à-vis companies that may have the same technology, but have a work organization that fails to permit a full use of that technology and of the resources constituted by the personnel. Increased competitiveness can be in harmony to some extent with good jobs and, indeed, with co-determination. This view finds support in Christian Berggren's (1986) study of the views of managing directors of major Swedish corporations as to the role of the union in strategic decision making. Managing directors have a generally positive view of how the union influences the quality of decisions from the standpoint of business economics.

The new forms of work and management, however, contain certain problems and disadvantages for the employees. Such changes, as they present themselves to both workers and salaried employees, entail new challenges for the union organizations. These relate to the unions' working procedures, structure, and ideology. The scale of these upheavals will depend, among other things, on how widespread the various elements are and will become. We now consider what these changes can entail in the form of challenges to the union organizations, challenges that for the unions, as with individuals, involve both threats and opportunities. The opportunities are connected with such new phenomena as increases in competency, cooperation in work groups, and the decentralization of certain decisions. They can provide freedom and influence over the day-to-day work that afford, in their turn, a basis for activation and influence through the union organization. The threats and problems are connected with the fact that union demands are sometimes met in a particular way, namely reinterpreted and incorporated in an overall strategy that also involves new forms of management and control. One example of this is how wage increases are being replaced by advantages distributed by the employer, including convertibles or bonuses if the worker has not been sicklisted or the like.

Within the field of "small group research," such concepts as "group think" and "minority influence" point to the risks of unexamined agreements in the decision-making process. Research findings in this area provide interesting perspectives on the efforts made to exploit group processes as a tool in the creation of joint approval and a general backing for a common corporate idea. The needs of members to have their expertise taken seriously can be countered, for example, by their being allowed to engage in the joint discussion of a quality circle. This takes place, however, in an unchanged work organization and within the framework of a corporate culture. This kind of control actually hinders any follow-up of member demands via the union. Quality circles can be regarded as a sort of company-controlled study circle during paid working hours. Study circles are normally conducted in people's free time, independent of the company's hierarchy, and aim at popular education, and not primarily problem solving. Union study circles, however, not infrequently aim at an inventory of problems and a formulation of demands at the workplace, demands that can be asserted via union channels.

The first challenge to the unions lies in the fact that many employees in certain sectors are offered more personality-developing, exciting, and often well-paid jobs, with a direct influence over production (Geijerstam and Reitberger 1986). Paradoxically, one can claim, with von Otter (1983a, 86), that "Taylorism has been a great help in the unions' efforts to organize labor, in that many wage-earners have been constantly reminded of their subordinate status in the company. How will the unions cope without Taylor?"

The offers made by the employer directly to the individual can be set in contrast to the collective influence of the union. The union would apparently then be needed only in local wage issues and to defend the weaker members, those who cannot "keep up" with development. On the issues relating to production, and operations in general, the union would have no independent role to play and no perspective of its own, but would be concerned rather with supporting management and the corporate culture, acting as a sort of "sparring partner" (see the views of chief executives in af Geijerstam and Reitberger 1986). What is questioned in this context is not least the role of the central union organization. The conflict between individual and collective influence is a problem with which the organizations of salaried employees have been confronted previously (see Nilsson and Gehlin 1986 on the subject of professional careers and work within a union). Today it is more pronounced and it also affects the lower grades of salaried employees and major groups of workers.

Companies that buy labor power today are interested to an increasing extent not only in workers' physical capacities but also in their mental involvement. "Labor power as a commodity" is being used in an increasingly diversified way. The unions, as the representatives of the common interests of those who work, thus acquire expanded functions. They have to ensure that the involvement of those employed in production does not degenerate into manipulation, exploitation, and rejection. They must also try to establish conditions for their members' autonomy and their involvement in objectives and in forms that they have themselves been able to influence. One aspect of this can be the development of independent union perspectives and activities. These break up and create cracks in management's control over more and more facets of the employees' lives.

The need of union renewal is emphasized in firms that supplement their new work organization with a decentralized company organization, which is centrally steered by new methods toward the profit targets set by management. Centrally planned adjustment to the market, with profit as the target, will naturally not always coincide with such union concerns as meaningful production to meet people's actual needs, and a good life environment. The informal control exercised through corporate "cultures" is difficult to see through and difficult to influence. The breakdown of groups of companies into individual corporations means that group management, even if it exercises great influence over the group's companies in reality, may refer to the fact that they are steered by the market. This sort of corporate organization and control hinder any collective union influence on managerial and group-level issues. Shortcomings of Co-Determination Act procedures regarding influence on the group as a whole are prevalent in "modern" companies of this kind.

The new forms of employment and business operation (franchising, self-employed persons commissioned by former employers, and the like) tend to erode the "employer–employee relationship." The wage-earner role becomes diffuse, and union membership is called into question (Bergman 1986, chap. 2).

Convertible bonds, profit sharing, and sales of stock to the employees at a favorable rate, together with a local and more "flexible" setting of wages and salaries, serve to tie the individual employee closer to the company and its objectives and thus reinforce the tendencies we have just considered. Convertibles and the like are also a way of acquiring an increment of capital at low cost. In some firms, it is a way of rewarding the employees outside the regular wage movements. Conflicts can arise between the local and central level of the unions. A local union might have difficulty in motivating a refusal of the management's offer to members, which can result in difficulties with central union coordination. Other conflicts can arise between union organizations in corporations and sectors whose capacity for offering additional rewards differ (companies with different levels of profit and private companies as compared with the public sector).

Some of the employees at Garphyttan, in the metal industry, who bought convertible bonds say laughingly: "What's bad for the Metall people is good for us!" And the chairman of the local says: "It's an investment in the employees' loyalty and feeling for the company. . . . This company is going tremendously well just now. . . . At the same time it's practically impossible to get out any decent pay increases. . . . And who would dare, in a conflict situation, go on strike and put the company's profitability at risk, if it's going to have an impact on the stock market, and thus on the value of your own convertibles" (Metallarbetaren 1987a). At the SIF (Union of Clerical and Technical Employees in Industry) office they say in effect: "It seems fair enough in a way that the employees should be getting some of the benefits that were previously reserved for the few. On the other hand, this broadening of ownership can make it legitimate for the top executives to make large fortunes. Still, our most important objection is that we are getting more fringe benefits outside actual pay. This money is paid without the unions being able to exercise control to ensure a fair distribution."

These local and profit-oriented pay schemes constitute a challenge to LO's policy of wage solidarity and to the concept of equality. They can also entail a breakdown of the employee's identity as a wage earner and union member in favor of his or her identity as a member of the company's work force. His or her solidarity with the wage-earner collective is weakened (Bergman 1986; Meidner in *Metallarbetaren* 1986b). A weakening of union influence on the formation of pay rates can in its turn undermine the co-determination process (Edlund 1987).

A final challenge relates directly to the organizational structure of the unions. The prevailing structure was determined largely by earlier technologies and work organizations and the jobs and occupations connected with them. The trend toward composite working duties means that some of the boundaries among different occupations, and thus also among the unions, are becoming obsolete. Multiskilled employees are highly capable of coping with both planning and execution and administration and production. This fusion of working duties at different levels of the company, or "vertical integration," is erasing the boundary between the traditional white-collar and blue-collar jobs, between, for example, engineers and metalworkers, between journalists and printers, and between their respective union organizations.

The integration of working duties can lead to conflicts among union organizations. Potential disputes can start from these questions: What are the jobs and the work organization going to look like? And who is going to organize the employees holding the different jobs? The latter question can affect the former, so that a union, instead of concerning itself with the creation of good jobs, tries to shape jobs that fall within its own organizational sphere. It is not certain that the two types of effort will coincide. The unions can emerge as bureaucratic nitpickers, or in the worst case, in open conflict with one another, while the employer can appear to be the only party seeking creative solutions to the organization of work. Contributing to such conflicts is the fact that the forms of payment, the pay scales, and terms of employment can differ among different sectors of collective agreement (with different union organizations). Often blue-collar workers have worse conditions of employment than white-collar workers; it is also common for collective pay arrangements to be negotiated for the former while individually scaled salaries and career opportunities are the norm for the latter. The differences in terms of employment (such as vacation and sickness benefits) are slowly being leveled out; in its 1988 agreement Metall negotiated successfully for workers enjoying the same sick pay as salaried employees (*Dagens Nyheter*, 14 February 1988). In the case of pay levels, Metall, for example, is now discussing elements of individual salary setting and opportunities to move up the salary scale, while developing on the job and acquiring greater competency. According to Metall, one doesn't have to become a white-collar worker simply because one has acquired greater competency and is drawing more pay. Similar discussions are taking place in other sectors.

An example is provided by a woman worker in the food industry, at the Findus canning factory in Bjuv. She had previously worked on the line, supervising the transport of cans on the belt and their packaging. She now, using computer-supported equipment, secures the supply of materials for her line. She calculates the consumption of raw materials, cooperates with the buyers, and takes part in planning sessions. But she is also responsible for ensuring that the raw materials are available on the line, so that, for example, she drives goods out from the depot by truck. She has undergone training for her new job. Her job is both blue-collar and white-collar. The manager of the plant says: "It's not important to us whether the job is done by a worker or a salaried staff member. We are happy to see that the demarcation lines can be a bit fluid." The chairman of the branch of the Food Workers' Union (Livs) says that the union has no clear strategy in cases like this. LO says that the job still constitutes work in production, and is thus within LO's and Livs' province (*LO-tidningen*, 1987c).

One aspect of the wage policy of "solidarity" is to raise the wages of low-wage categories. Another aspect is equal pay for equal work. But the new type of integrated job could perfectly well be organized within a TCO union such as SIF, and the salary would then probably be on a higher level than the highest salaries earned by LO members. The LO and TCO unions have no common wage policy or system for determining wages. Employers sometimes use this situation to offer selected individuals within an LO union opportunities to make a career, acquire further education, and transform themselves into white-collar employees within a TCO union, with higher wages, and still further career opportunities. The LO unions see the development of competency and salaries for their members as crucial and strategic issues at the same time that they are trying to find ways of applying both aspects of their "wage policy of solidarity" in this new situation.

As a result of such integration, one of the very foundations of union organization is being called into question, namely, the distinction between workers and salaried employees. This is especially the case in Sweden, with its two separate federations, LO for workers and TCO for salaried employees. A further complication is the close relationship that exists between LO and the Social Democratic party (the TCO has no formal ties with any party). A successful union effort will be facilitated by a collaboration between the different unions, in which every attempt is made to design a work organization with "good jobs for all," not only for the members of one specific union; this may be called a "solidaristic policy of work" (Nilsson and Sandberg 1988). An initial step might be a continued harmonization of terms of employment, and agreements in general, including standardization of pay systems.

In aggregate, all these challenges constitute a threat to the Swedish trade union movement as a strong and cohesive organization. They thus constitute a threat to the "Swedish model" in working life and in the labor market. The Swedish model is based on a national, independent organization of working people, which will make it possible to develop a policy of equal pay for equal work. This is a basis for solidarity and cooperation among the trade unions. A weakening of the union organization is, of course, also a matter of concern from the standpoint of democracy. It will reduce the chances for employees to develop alternative perspectives and solutions that can challenge those of management in an open dialogue.

The challenges presented, however, also offer possibilities. In those cases where management's new methods of control can be understood in the light of an increased dependence on the professional skills and involvement of the employees, there is a further opportunity. The involvement and influence of members in their own work can be developed in a movement concerned with "good jobs" and influence over the long term. This is the aspect to which forward-looking union organizations relate when they survey the needs and wants of their members and show that the union has effective ways of pushing these demands. If company managements are growing, to an increasing extent, to believe that they don't need the union and can appeal directly to the employees, the members' continued need of the union is the basis on which union renewal can build. The union has the advantage of having as its overriding aim the promotion of the employees' long-term interests. It is in a position to stand very clearly for high ambitions as regards its members' professional skills and influence in their daily work.

8. Production Issues and Quality

These changes and challenges confront the union organizations with a need to develop their working approach, structure, and ideology so that they will still have an essential contribution to make as to the way companies and public authorities operate—that is, their organization, production, and the daily work of union members. This need exists when the union concerns itself with production issues, regardless of how the work is organized and regardless of the management's strategy. The new challenges, however, make this need particularly acute.

Historical studies, like studies of current development, show that technology, the organization of work, and production are issues for the unions, and thus are a field in which the outcome is determined by the actions of management and labor. One historical example is the struggle of the printing workers over the organization of work and their demands for training, during the latter half of the nineteenth century (Ekdahl 1983). From the postwar period until the 1970s and 1980s, these questions lay dormant.

We have referred to questions relating to technology and work organization, namely, what is produced and how it is produced, or "production issues." These differ from the issues of distribution, which relate to how the results of production are divided (pay and general terms of employment). The conception of production issues is thus a wide one. We see signs of a development of union perspectives on such issues in the context of ideas relating to the roles played by union members outside a particular company. The aims and interests of the employees in these questions are very much concerned with quality. We can distinguish quality of work, which relates to the raw materials, the technology, and organization; the quality of the products, which relates to the thrust of production and its use value to the consumer; and quality of the life environment as experienced by the employee as citizen. The quality of the work is an aspect with a status all its own; it has to do with autonomy, professional skill, and influence over the daily work of members. Union strivings in production issues can therefore be described as an integrated work policy.

A distinction can be made, in the production issues, between short-term and long-term perspectives. The short-term perspectives include those relating to more or less given raw materials, machinery, and production results. The long-term perspectives include those relating to the development and change of the production technology, the materials, and the products. We found that in those cases where the union had proved successful in influencing the work organization and the technology, they had developed new union work procedures that differed from the wage-negotiation model. This was a result of internal union work to develop visions of "good jobs" and concrete proposals for solutions as well as work to develop new paths for their achievement through local negotiations and participation. We also found changes in the relationship among levels within the unions. Rather than the local application of centrally established rules, it is a matter of local solutions being developed with support from the central union level; the latter can consist of models for concrete solutions to problems *and* a developed perspective on the production issues.

The relationship among the levels can be problematic. Rather than an interplay, it can become a collision: A structural process, say radical automation, encroaches on the everyday life of the work-place, and a defensive war commences. What we have discussed is the unions' defensive reactions and the opportunities to develop these over the long term. But we then run into the problem that the structure (of the union) can remove itself from the daily reality at the workplace.

The concept of the "paradox of everyday reality" can help us to understand the problem: "First, the everyday reality is made up of a large quantity of things, over whose genesis the individual exercises no power. In that sense, the individual is 'alienated' and powerless. On the other hand, everyday life is defined and described as the world in which the individual exercises power and control over his surroundings" (Ahrne 1981, 44).

When one speaks, in the context of the Co-Determination Act, of people's opportunities to influence the circumstances that affect them daily, and at the same time talks of the Co-Determination Act and other contemporary reforms in labor law as parts of the greatest democratic breakthrough of the century, one has landed straight into the "paradox of everyday reality." Conditions at a workplace are often only marginally subject to influence on the part of the em-ployees and the local union organization. Given, for instance, any radical technical change, the local range of options is not usually very great. The "new technology" descends upon, or, rather, in-vades the workplace; what one can influence to some extent is the organization relating to the technology. If one is concerned, on the other hand, to influence in any decisive way the circumstances de-termining how the "daily and immediate" situation appears to those working there, what has to be influenced is conditions at the societal level, perhaps the international level. Technological development must be influenced; the specific targets are the major companies and research institutes where the new technology and new forms of or-ganization are developed. And how can this happen without the organizations starting to live a life of their own, now that the task is on such a global scale? The activities of members, and the interac-tion among levels, must be continuous.

Casten von Otter maintains that "it is becoming an ever more important task to achieve an identification and solidarity with a broader collective than that of the companies" (1983a, 93). The defi-nition of a narrow wage-earner interest, as von Otter observes, would imply that the role of the company in society, and its use to society, is the employer's own business. It would also mean abandoning to the employers the possibility of creating meaning in work with the help of their new corporate cultures. Von Otter wants to see the development of a "production interest" based in unselfishness, or in a self-interest derived from the members' roles as consumers and citizens outside the workplace (1983a, 95).

This, however, need not reduce the importance of union activities, nor the importance of raising demands concerning the production issues at the company level. As we have already hinted, fruitful efforts can be devoted to independent union work on the development of its own many-faceted perspective on production issues, all the way from the content of work and control at the individual workshop to the quality of the products and the consequences to the life environment. A union organization that takes an interest, say, in the quality of food production and its environmental effects and in the content of work has a great deal to win by linking up an analysis at the societal level with experiences and demands at the individual workplace. The union's objectives, however, can be ambiguous, with, say, environmental demands versus wage demands, and both of these versus competitiveness and employment. The decisive aspect is that union deliberations can provide a different picture from that of management. The differences can consist of promulgating alternative approaches locally as well as developing a way of looking at the company in society from a national union perspective that includes such aspects as regional policy and the life environment. Even if company managements are now taking an interest in the employees' knowledge, minds, and social competence, their perspective differs from that of the union, for which such qualities are not simply a competitive instrument, but aims per se. The chains of means and ends are different.

It can thus be fruitful to keep apart a couple of dimensions. One relates to the type of issue: production issues versus the issues of distribution. The other dimension relates to whether the perspectives of the two parties coincide or differ. A union perspective on production questions can be quite different from management's perspective on the same issues. In wage issues, and other distribution issues, it is generally accepted that the parties have different goals and interests: Such issues as the level of pay, the length of the vacation, and so forth pose questions about how to distribute available resources. The parties can have a common interest in keeping cost increases within certain frameworks in order to ensure competitiveness; however, the parties may not always agree on the frameworks. In Sweden, the view of those representing management is often that, because of a policy of free negotiations between parties, one occasionally has to pay the price of a strike, but that a community of interests always exists regarding production. This latter is often asserted in connection with the "new management" thinking on corporate cultures. In Chapter 3 we asserted that such a view dominated the agreements on joint industrial councils in the 1950s and 1960s. A distinction was made between questions of differing interests (the "interest issues"), which is to say wages and the like, and the rest, which were "issues of collaboration" (such as the organization of work and its rationalization). The Co-Determination Act, however, takes for granted that production issues can be divisive matters, which are subject to negotiation. As we have seen from numerous examples, and also argued, it is reasonable to assume that the parties have divergent perspectives and interests in production issues. Good jobs and democratic influence are ends so far as the union organizations are concerned; for employers, as a rule, they are only a means of raising productivity and cutting costs. (This naturally does not exclude the possibility of the parties having identical aims in some concrete issues and conflicting aims in others.) It is thus far from certain that management's business idea will coincide with the employees'' "production idea," or that the corporate culture or ideology will harmonize with the "work culture" that has developed in the company. Additionally, the management's ideas regarding individual careers and the development of competency can differ from the employees' and the union's ideas concerning a broad development of competency, particularly among the least-favored employees.

Examples here and earlier of union perspectives, or "counter-cultures," in production matters pose problems both to the company and the union. A lot of management literature appears to assume an identity of views. The precondition for offering individuals a certain amount of independence in their day-to-day work would be one all-permeating culture. Where a union view lies close to the "management culture," the unions, in an interplay with management, can try to bring influence to bear. Where its culture does not coincide with that of management, the two cultures compete at the workplace. Historically, the union organizations have been of great importance as a movement providing people with a content, a meaning, and a togetherness in their working lives, and in their lives as a whole, in a situation in which the companies were mainly interested in exploiting the physical strength of the workers. If business firms are now making every effort to develop company cultures and to win people's hearts and minds, the unions, with their lesser resources, can easily find themselves in a position of inferiority. This would render the development of well-anchored "union cultures" in production questions particularly important.

New forms of company management and organization, with uniform, "totalized" cultures, can further restrict the public nature of company decision making. In combination with group processes that can superficially produce an identicality of view ("groupthink"), a "monolithic exercise of power" could well be the result. An independent union organization, and independent union perspectives on the production issues, can make an essential contribution to openness, a fruitful encounter between perspectives, and a sharing of powers in companies, and in working life as a whole. The basis for this is provided by activity and knowledge in local union work.

9. Achieving Good Jobs and Democracy

Faced with the investment of the employers in individual development, a certain degree of decentralization, and a progressive image, the union, compared with an "employer on the move" can emerge as boring, negative, defensive, and bureaucratic. The future unions are in jeopardy unless a new movement arises within the union movement: a movement with its base in the workplaces and supported by central union resources of knowledge, opinion-forming capacity, and influence at the political level. Such a movement could perhaps gather strength from incipient frustration in the workplaces over inadequate opportunities to exercise influence, despite all the talk of a "common culture."

Some Swedish union organizations are in the process of accepting the challenges and seeking—and sometimes finding—new paths and new working procedures. It is a matter of developing new approaches within firms at the local level, new procedures for central union support for local union work, and new union perspectives on the production issues. As with the new forms of corporate organization, the interplay between the local and the central level is decisive. The explanation for such union efforts in Sweden lies partly in the particularly favorable conditions that exist here.

The Swedish labor law is a necessary condition in many ways. It appears to provide such security for many employees that they dare to tackle responsible and demanding tasks, both as employees and as representatives of the union. The good "invisible contract" (Zetterberg et al. 1983) between the employees and the company is based in "visible contracts," in laws and agreements that offer opportunities to exert influence and make clear the limits to these. In direct attempts to influence decision making, a particularly important fact is the good and relatively early access to information; this access could be improved if employers were subject to a primary obligation to provide information when drawing up guidelines for future studies and planning processes. The Union Representatives Act gives union officials a strong position and an opportunity to develop new working approaches. Wage-earner consultants appear in many cases to be providing an essential contribution to the unions' own opportunities to develop knowledge.

It is sometimes said that the Swedish Co-Determination Act is based on a view of the company as a machine for rational decision making. In today's modern management, "decisions" are often regarded as a legitimatization of ongoing processes of change. The conclusion drawn is that a new approach to co-determination is required. We believe this to be true. But what, in fact, is needed if the unions will now have to deal with a continuous flow of problems, alternatives, and solutions, which from time to time fit together and result in a change or action, legitimatized through consciously developed corporate cultures, improved group processes, and the rest? We think that part of this renewal must involve strengthening the traditional means of co-determination: resources for the independent union development of competence by means of study circles, investigations, and meetings of the membership. This would enable the workers, through their unions, to develop their own flow of ideas, alternatives, and perspectives. And since the flow of problems and solutions arising in the companies is continuous, unions need a *continuous* development of competency, founded on rights and resources, which is not related to the union's ability to point to any specific management decision with consequences for its members. The assumption should be that important changes are taking place all the time and that the union and its members, therefore, need to be working constantly on these issues.

The processes of change are experienced locally, but they are similar at different workplaces, and they are often part of the same macropolitical processes. The central unions have a role to play in supporting the local unions that find themselves involved in development processes. Just as the "new management" combines decentralization with centralization, so perhaps the "new unions" should try a similar combination.

The organizational structure of the Swedish union movement is distinguished by strong central federations, which is something we know and hear frequently. But Sweden also has uniquely strong local union organizations, without any competition from "workers' councils" (Kjellberg 1983). The new areas of union work demand the development of a strong understanding of production and organization from union perspectives. Here both the tradition of "study circles" for the purpose of broad schooling and activation and the specialized training of union officers and expert resources at the central level help to create unique opportunities for a multilevel, knowledge-based union strategy.

The strong Swedish trade union movement, with its very high level of membership, collaborates with a Social Democratic party that has enjoyed long periods of political tenure. This has resulted, among other things, in an economic policy and a labor market policy that have secured an exceptionally high level of employment (unemployment at less than 2 percent in 1990). This strengthens the status of the workers and the unions. In his comparative study of technology and work, Colin Gill (1985, 142, 159) emphasizes that the social aspects have been accorded most attention in countries with a "social consensus" between the labor movement and government. The trade unions could rely on favorable legislation to open up management decision making and to support trade union–oriented education and research.

The low level of unemployment in Sweden is now starting to entail an actual shortage of workers, especially of skilled workers. This is because the number of young people moving into the labor market will be decreasing in the next fifteen years. (Unemployment in the European Community is expected to fall for the same sort of reason, although not until the turn of the century.) Nor, in Sweden, do women, owing to their present high rate of gainful employment, constitute any labor reserve. Industry is now demanding that increased immigration be permitted. This could be a partial solution, but considering the number that would be required, it cannot be regarded as a realistic total response. Other possible ways out of the problem include moving production abroad, automation, and a renewal of the work organization so that jobs become more attractive in the competition for labor (*Administration*, 1988).

The development toward new forms of work organization, involving teamwork and the development of competency, is not, however, specifically Swedish. It is, in fact, more of an international trend. People speak of a "Japanese model," where conflicts of interest are minimal and where employees become involved in solving the company's problems. It is often said, however, that the tendency to a renewal of work organizations has had an early and very strong impact in Sweden. Why is this? Perhaps the most common explanation emphasizes the vulnerability of Swedish industry to competition and the farsightedness of Swedish management.

One explanation, which does not contradict the above, but has a different emphasis and sees other causal relationships at the national level, has been reported in a number of comparative studies. Robert Cole (1987) suggests that the leading place occupied by Sweden may be due to a broad macroprocess, in which Swedish managements saw a renewal of the work organization as a way of solving problems relating to the labor market (for example, turnover of personnel), while the union organizations, to some extent under pressure to secure Sweden's international competitiveness, had no objections to make. Wolfgang Streek (1987) criticizes the view, common around 1980, that the importance of industrial relations for industrial development has been exaggerated. Different strategies for industrial development, and changes in the work organization, can be due to the relationships between the parties, that is, industrial relations.

> High-wage industries and countries can compete with individualized, high-quality products. There seems to be a strong "elective affinity" between upmarket strategies of industrial adjustment—requiring as they do high and long-term investment in market and product development, a flexible sociotechnical production system, a motivated workforce, and an abundant supply of broad qualifications—and a "cluster" of industrial relations characteristics comprising stable employment, co-determination, shared responsibility for the management of a well-developed internal labor market, a flexible work organization, and a market-independent training system.
>
> Strong trade unions with an institutionalized presence in the polity at large and in the enterprise . . . may leave management no alternative but to embark on the demanding path of upmarket restructuring. At the same time, institutionalized strength, in giving trade unions the confidence that the future benefits of cooperation with management will not be kept from their members, makes it possible for them to adopt the same long-term perspective on economic rewards that an upmarket restructuring strategy requires of management and capital giver. (Streek 1987, 455–56)

Expressed in words used in recent metalworkers' and LO discussions, there is, and should be, a strong relation between work organization (jobs), possibilities for competence development, and wages. All these aspects should be continuously developed. With the strivings toward the "good work" as a focus in union policy, training and education policy will be an important instrument and possibilities for high and solidaristic wages will grow if all members get "good jobs." A labor market policy will create both employment and employee strength.

With new management strategies and decentralization of wage negotiations one of the elements in the "classical Swedish model," the solidaristic wage policy is weakened. But at the same time a new element is introduced, that is, a "solidaristic policy for the good work." This new element is a union goal in its own right but it may also, like the traditional solidaristic wage policy, be a dynamic instrument for industrial restructuring: Bad workplaces in old industries may be forced to change or be forced out of the market. The "good work" thus becomes a new element in the model, both as a goal and as an instrument. Our empirical comparisons (Chapter 8) indicate that full employment probably is a key precondition for the development of a solidaristic policy of the good work. An active labor market policy is thus absolutely fundamental, as in the classical model, but it now creates the preconditions for demands for good work, and also guides employees toward companies with good work, and takes care of any loss of employment as a result of this policy. New concrete instruments in labor market and work policy need to be developed to supplement solidaristic wage policy with solidaristic work policy as a key element in a renewed Swedish model—a key element which, if successful, will contribute also to solidaristic wages. (Communications from Rudolf Meidner influenced this section.)

The configuration of favorable preconditions that Streek finds in Sweden, and elsewhere, has not, in his opinion, been consciously created to meet the challenges of the world market during the 1980s; it was hardly more than a fortunate coincidence. From the perspective of traditional Swedish social engineering, it may seem that the development of an active labor market policy, training, and a labor law was not quite as random as Streek suggests.

In this book, we have given examples of new tendencies in Sweden regarding technology, the organization of work, management strategies, and trade union activities—all on the workplace level. We have also tried to show how the local experiences constitute part of a macrosociological and macroeconomic situation and process of change. Thus, the experiences reported cannot be mechanically transferred and introduced in other national contexts. But they may, we hope, inspire efforts to develop work force competency, freedom at the workplace, and creative efforts on the part of the unions to achieve the same end. Advanced production technology and an advanced work organization open up such possibilities. The trade union movements have a crucial role in creating such relations of production as will help ensure the realization of the opportunities thus offered for "good jobs" in practice.

Appendix
Some Labor Laws
and Agreements

1. The Co-Determination Act of 1976

Negotiation

The nucleus of the Co-Determination Act (MBL) is the obligation of employers to negotiate in accordance with Sections 10 and 11, and especially their obligation, in the context of any major changes, to enter primary negotiations as envisaged in Section 11. Around this kernel are certain further rules governing labor's opportunities to demand negotiations and its right to information. (This discussion of MBL is based on Edlund and Gustavsson 1976; Schmidt 1979; Kjellén 1982; and the report of the New Labor Law Committee/SOU [Swedish Official Reports Series] 1982, No. 60.)

According to the terms of Section 10, negotiations can be initiated on anything that either social partner has an interest in negotiating within the framework of the labor–management relationship. Negotiations can relate both to arrival at agreements and to the interpretation of agreements. The field of negotiation covers both the terms of employment of individual persons, and such management issues as the thrust and management of operations. (See also the discussion on Section 32 below.)

Section 11 stipulates that the employer must negotiate with the unions before deciding on any major changes in the business operation or in the working conditions or terms of employment of individual union members (primary negotiations). In other cases, the union can demand negotiations prior to a decision (Section 12). The purpose of the employer's obligation to enter primary negotiations is to ensure that the views of employees are included in the decision-making process at an early stage and are not simply post hoc complaints about decisions already made.

If, however, the parties cannot agree in such negotiations, employers makes what they consider to be the right decision. The local union organization, however, acting through its national federation, can demand central negotiations with the employer, in which case the employer has to defer the decision until the negotiations have been completed.

The intensified right of negotiation provided for under Sections 11 and 12 is conditional on the employer being currently or normally bound by a collective agreement. Even unions with no agreement, however, enjoy negotiating powers of this kind where the working conditions of individual employees are concerned. Important changes in individual conditions of employment include, for example, the transfer of individual employees or groups of employees to other duties.

"Major changes" in the business operation are considered to be, for example, long-term decisions concerning work organization, the choice of working duties and methods, the planning and setting up of work premises, and such personnel issues as the principles of recruitment and training. According to decisions by the Labor Court, appointments of personnel at the middle management level are regarded as major changes (AD [Labor Court] judgment 1979, No. 188), as are decisions on the budget (AD 1979, No. 149). In the latter case there is also, according to the Labor Court, an obligation for the employer to negotiate before implementing the plans contained in the budget.

The legislator's preliminary material regarding the Co-determination Act repeatedly state that negotiations shall, in the context of any large-scale changes, be incorporated as a natural aspect of employers' efforts to obtain a good basis for their decision. A decision, however, cannot be reduced to an isolated "point." As a rule, a prolonged planning and decision-making process is involved. So at what point does the obligation to negotiate enter the picture? According to the practice of the Labor Court, the obligation to negotiate arises only when the employers have reached—for example, as the result of investigations—a point at which they can indicate the alternative courses of action under consideration. In such a situation, the pressure of time and de facto commitments in the decision-making process can limit the free play for union influence. The employer can maintain that there is no time for further negotiation. On the other hand, the Labor Court has ruled that a primary duty of negotiation can arise without the decision contemplated having immediate implications for the employees. The employer immediately incurs an obligation to negotiate if there is an appreciable risk of major changes at the time of the decision. In one case, the Labor Court thus ruled that a reorganization of production methods could be regarded as a major change in the business operation if, in the longer term, it could conceivably involve substantial changes from the standpoint of the employees (AD 1978, No. 56). In another case, the opposite ruling was made (AD 1981, No. 99). This latter case concerned the introduction of new technology at a print shop. The employer had made certain technical modifications for the reception of copy from word-processing machines via the telephone network. The Court found that the decisions made in this connection related more to technical development. Even if they might conceivably lead to major changes in the business operation, no development process could be readily attributed to these specific decisions.

The employer is excused from primary negotiations when "very cogent" cause exists (Section 11), for example, "a risk to safety at the workplace, to important civic functions, or to comparable interests" (quotations from the preliminary material).

If the reason for the employer having omitted to negotiate is disinclination or faulty planning, the union can claim damages. However, violation of the union's right to negotiate does not render the decision invalid. The right of decision, as we have said, rests with the employer alone. When negotiations have been requested by the union (Section 12), the employer is obliged (as when the employer has called for negotiation) to delay a decision until negotiations have been held, but the employer's freedom of action is in this context greater (as soon as any "special cause" exists) than in negotiations under Section 11.

Information

The primary obligation to negotiate also entails a duty to provide information by stating a position, and the grounds for that position. The essential and specific rules on the obligation to provide/right to receive information are contained in Sections 18 and 19. Section 18 covers the obligation to divulge, and runs as follows: "A party who, in the course of negotiation, quotes a written document shall make this document available to the other party, if the latter so requests." The rule is mutual, that is, it applies to documents quoted by both the employer and the union, and it applies regardless of whether the workplace is or is not covered by a collective agreement.

Of great importance are the rules in Section 19 concerning the obligation of the employer to provide continuous information "on how his operation is developing from the standpoint of production, and financially, and on the guidelines applied in personnel policy." Also, the union is given the opportunity to study the documents needed to protect the interests of its members. It also receives copies of documents and assistance with investigation, "if this can be done without unreasonable cost or inconvenience." Excepted from this obligation to provide information are contingency plans in the event of industrial disputes, certain business secrets, and certain research and development work.

The obligation to provide information is designed to give employees insight into the development of the company. It does not, however, aim at covering individual decisions to the extent that the employer is required to provide information before deciding. There is no "primary obligation to provide information." The idea is that, when major changes are envisaged, negotiations shall be entered at an early stage and the employees supplied with the information they need during the negotiating process. As we have seen, however, the employer is in a position to perform various studies and investigations before primary negotiations are requested. Section 19 may give the employees the right to get information during this initial phase, but, to quote a judgment by the Labor Court (AD 1978, No. 166), only "in more complicated courses of events," when "the issue concerns plans or initiatives on a major scale."

According to the terms of Section 21, the employer (and unions) can negotiate concerning the confidentiality of information that is provided. If agreement cannot be reached, the employer can take the matter to the Labor Court. The court declares confidentiality if it finds that there is otherwise a risk of "considerable damage" to the enterprise in question. Regardless of confidentiality, labor representatives who receive information are always permitted to pass it on to the excecutive committees of their organization, in which case the latter are also bound by confidentiality.

Priority of Interpretation

One innovation in the new Swedish labor legislation is that in various situations the employees have been given a form of preliminary priority of interpretation regarding statutory provisions and collective agreements in the event that their interpretation differs from that of the employer.

The Co-determination Act gives the trade unions priority of interpretation in three kinds of cases. The union interpretation applies until the parties have agreed on a different solution or, an action having been filed by the employer, the Labor Court has overridden the union interpretation.

Section 33 gives the union an initial priority of interpretation in all disputes concerning the proper implementation of provisions concerning co-determination contained in a collective agreement or concerning decisions made with reference to such provisions. Section 34 gives the employees priority of interpretation in disputes concerning duties at work, for example, the nature of duties, the place where work is to be performed, transfers to other duties, and working hours. In certain exceptional cases, however, employers can insist on work being done in accordance with their views concerning the nature of the duties involved.

Section 35 makes it the employers' duty to request negotiations as soon as a dispute has arisen concerning pay or other negotiated benefits for a trade union member. If the dispute cannot be settled by local negotiations, employers have a short respite in which to refer the dispute to national federation level and, ultimately, to the Labor Court. If the dispute cannot be settled by negotiation or legal proceedings, employers have to meet the pay demand, unless it is manifestly "oppressive."

2. Co-Determination Agreements

Central Government Authorities

The first agreement concluded was with the central government authorities (Co-Determination Agreement for the Central Government Labor Sector, MBA–S, 1978). It emphasizes that flexible forms for co-determination are of major importance to the efficiency of central government operations and it presents a broadened definition of the term efficiency:

> By efficiency is meant that an authority will achieve its objectives
>
>   • while stewarding its resources well;
>   • with due attention to requirements as regards service, openness to the public, and the legal integrity of the individual;
>   • and with due attention to the needs of personnel regarding job satisfaction, a good working environment, security of employment, and opportunities for co-determination and personnel development.

The agreement deals with six different areas. It indicates what is valid as a direct result of the central agreement and what matters should be the subject of local collective agreements. These six areas are rationalization and administrative development, planning, mobility of personnel, personnel development, work supervision, and staff and union information. We discuss rationalization below; planning is treated briefly.

On the subject of rationalization and administrative development, Section 15 states:

- that every attempt should be made to utilize the knowledge and experience of staff;
- that the work of rationalization should be carefully planned;
- that the work of planning, investigation, and realization should be performed in an open manner;
- that the employees affected should be informed concerning planning, investigative work, its implementation and results;
- that union representatives shall have the right to participate in different groups.

These provisions involve a more extensive obligation to provide information than those of MBL. All employees are to receive information, and the union has the right to continuous information and the right to join different groups.

On the subject of rationalization, the employer and the local union may reach local collective agreements on a number of given questions, among them methods of rationalization, information, and personnel and union participation (Article 16). Several such local agreements exist, including at the Postgiro, one of the case studies of the Front project (Chapter 5). If no local agreement is reached, questions may be raised for central negotiation. If there is still no agreement, the employer decides.

When a public authority has reached the stage of a concrete proposal, it is obliged in certain cases to postpone the decision (Section 17). If a local collective agreement is in force covering, for example, working procedures in rationalization, the union organizations are entitled to demand reasonable time in which to draft an alternative proposal. Even where there is no local agreement, the union must be offered reasonable time to inform its members and obtain their views. This regulation is customarily termed the "temporary right of veto." It was used, for example, by the union at the Postgiro in Stockholm; union representatives said they needed a seven-month postponement to work out their own alternative. Faced with this prospect, the Postgiro management chose to comply with union wishes in the subsequent work of investigation.

On the subject of the local union's right to inform the employees, the agreement (Article 37) states that this may take place during paid working hours. There is still, as yet, no formal agreement as to the scale of this right; its application varies from authority to authority.

On the subject of planning, the general guidelines (Section 20) state:

> In planning its operation, the authority shall take into account the need for delegation and decentralization. The professional know-how and experience, ambitions, and involvement of both individuals and groups of employees should be drawn upon even at the planning stage. The planning process should be such that the employees at different levels are given an opportunity to participate in the work of preparation.

Similar provisions concerning the right of the union, and of all employees, to information and their right to participate in various project groups exist in other fields of co-determination. In this situation, if an independent union activity and line is lacking, there is naturally a major risk of the union being "drowned" in information and integrated in the employer's decision-making processes. This risk, however, is offset by the fact that the agreement emphasizes fairly strongly the union's opportunities to make its own investigations and the need for actual negotiations. In a few areas, it is possible to reach local agreements on a union right of veto (e.g., on the use of psychological suitability tests and the introduction of new employees) and a union right of self-determination (e.g., information to the employees on rationalization). The more recently concluded agreements, which cover state and cooperative enterprises and private companies, assign still more emphasis to various procedures for joint work.

State and Cooperative Enterprises

The agreements covering the state and consumer-cooperative enterprises (1979) state that the local parties can agree that certain questions of co-determination should in general be raised in "integrated negotiation," by their being dealt with in joint bodies. A party, however, may request that any individual issue be made the subject of regular negotiations. Areas for co-determination are planning, organization, and personnel work; work organization and the new technology are not emphasized. The local unions can demand negotiations. After local, and if necessary central, negotiations the employer has the right of final decision making. The minimum level of co-determination is that stated in the central agreement. Personnel issues may be submitted to a central Co-determination Council to help the parties reach an agreement.

The agreement with the municipal and county authorities will not be considered here.

Private Companies (LO/PTK/SAF)

The Development Agreement on efficiency and participation, which is the co-determination agreement between LO/PTK and SAF, covers most private companies. It was concluded during the spring of 1982. This agreement dealt in particular with the issues of development of the work organization, technological development, and the company's economic situation.

By way of introduction, the agreement gives an account of certain common and agreed upon values "as regards improving the efficiency of the firm, its profitability and competitiveness, and as regards creating the conditions for employment, security, and development at work." The improvement of efficiency and the safeguarding of employment are seen as matters of common interest.

In developing the work organization, the aim shall be to enable individual employees to increase their knowledge and experience and their influence over their work. To enable them to take part in planning their own work, the "employees shall, individually or in groups, be given proper information—principally from an immediate superior—about conditions at the workplace" (Section 3).

> In the event of technical change the goal shall be a sound job content; skills, responsibility, and ability to co-operate with colleagues are emphasized. The trade unions shall participate in the planning of major technical changes, in the forms presented below. The employer shall describe the considerations underlying the new technology, and the technical, financial/ economic, work environment, and employment consequences that can be foreseen and shall also describe any proposals for appointing project groups. (Section 4)

The need for information and education is emphasized in questions concerning the financial situation of the company. "The management's estimation of future prospects should be reported, so that the unions in the company have the possibility, together with management, of discussing and considering the company's market prospects, purchasing activity, competitive position, product development, production equipment, and the security of employment and development at work for the employees" (Section 5).

Regarding the forms or procedures for co-determination, the Development Agreement (Sections 6–8) emphasizes local adaptation and delegation to the individuals actuallly concerned. Regarding union influence, the agreement provides an opening for local agreements by which information and negotiation in accordance with MBL are replaced in certain fields by "trade union representatives at various levels participating in the company's ordinary line organization (line negotiations and line information)" or by "co-determination through bipartite bodies for participation and information." In the case, for example, of investments or organizational changes, "It can be agreed locally that matters that are limited in time . . . shall be considered and implemented in the form of projects with the participation of the local union organization" (Section 8).

"When participating in line negotiations, bipartite bodies and project work, the trade union representatives shall be given reasonable time to enable them to evaluate matters arising." They are also "entitled to refer certain co-determination issues to negotiation in accordance with MBL" (Section 8).

All trade union members are entitled to participate during paid working hours (normally outside hours with overtime pay) for a maximum of five hours per year in trade union meetings and activities at the company (Section 10).

The agreement further considers co-determination in Groups and in companies with several workplaces. On the subject of information, it states: "In Groups, this Agreement applies to each company individually. First of all, matters shall be dealt with that relate to the company itself. However, as regards information, general information about the Group—including operations abroad—shall be provided at the companies within the Group" (Section 11, subsection 1). On the subject of negotiation, it states:

> Matters referred to in Section 11 of MBL that are of importance to several units in a Group can be dealt with under special arrangements. Group management and the local trade union organizations concerned should reach agreement about the way co-determination is to be exercised in such cases. The local trade union organizations should appoint a group of representatives with responsibility to discuss and negotiate with the group management.
>
> In cases where overriding decisions involve major changes at the local level, negotiations concerning implementation of the decision shall be held in accordance with Section 11 of MBL, except where otherwise decided under an agreement.

The Agreement can incorporate provisions that negotiations in accordance with Section 12 of MBL can be dealt with in accordance with this item. (Section 11, subsection 2)

The agreement also contains provisions concerning working life research. The parties declared themselves in agreement that workplaces should be kept as open as possible for research concerning working life and its effects on people and their employment. If the employer or the local union organization wishes outside researchers to be given access to the workplace for purposes of working life research, local negotiations shall be opened. If agreement cannot be reached, the question shall be made the subject of central negotiations (Section 13).

SAF, LO, and PTK have set up a permanent joint Development Council to monitor and encourage the implementation and further development of the Agreement and to make recommendations to the parties in matters referred to the Council (Sections 14–15).

An arbitration committee has also been set up to deal with certain aspects of the application of the agreements that are excluded from the jurisdiction of the Labor Court.

3. Certain Other Laws

Labor Representatives on Company Boards

This act (LSA) gives the employees in companies with at least twenty-five employees the right to be represented on the company board, normally with two representatives (and alternates). The same right applies to holding companies, if the total number of employees in the company group is twenty-five. (This and the two following subsections are directly based on Kjellén 1982.)

Employee representatives under this act have the same rights to information that company law gives to any board member. However, the Limited Companies Act (ABL) contains provisions to the effect that board members shall not only have real opportunities to participate in board decisions but also that the background material for the decision must be "satisfactory." This latter provision was added in connection with LSA. What is considered "satisfactory" is that the material and its presentation should be provided in Swedish or in translation, be comprehensible, and cover all essential aspects of the issue.

The Limited Companies Act contains no specific provisions on confidentiality. However, board members have an obligation to protect the interests of the company and this extends to the labor representatives. The labor representative receives information in his or her capacity as a board member, and is subject to the same obligation to keep that information confidential. If information relates to matters that the board wishes to keep secret, it shall not be divulged.

The Limited Companies Act

The Limited Companies Act (ABL) contains detailed regulations on the financial statements, annual reports, and other information that companies are required to provide. Even if these requirements are not primarily designed for the use of employees and trade unions, they still can provide a useful source of information.

In connection with the 1975 Accounting Act, a special board (the Swedish Accounting Standards Board) was set up to supervise the development of "good accounting practices." The members of this board include trade union representatives, and there is an obligation for the board to consider how far the information requirements of employees are met by present accounting standards.

Act Concerning the Status of Shop Stewards

This act was passed to improve the conditions of work and security of employment of shop stewards. In cases of redundancy or layoffs, a shop steward is to have the first chance of retaining his or her job, if it is important to trade union activities on the shop floor. The employer is also required by law to provide the shop steward with the premises necessary for him or her to conduct union work. One of the most important clauses of the act states that a shop steward has the right to any leave of absence necessary in order to be able to fulfil his or her union obligations. This right to leave applies both to trade union activities at the place of work and to other trade union activities. An employer cannot, for instance, refuse a person leave to participate in union activities at either the branch or the central level. When union activities at the place of work are concerned with relations with the employer there, the employer is also required to pay the shop steward the full wage for the duration of his or her absence from work.

The Act Concerning the Status of Shop Stewards has played a very important part in the work aimed at improving working life. The trade unions' experience of the act is positive. This does not, however, mean that the unions are satisfied with all the stipulations, and they have in fact asked for it to be given broader scope. The problems emerge most sharply when trying to ensure that trade union affairs are conducted at smaller workplaces.

The Working Environment Act

The Working Environment Act (AML) states that conditions of work should be adapted to the mental and physical capabilities of the worker and that every attempt should be made to arrange work in such a way that employees can influence their own work situations. Regarding the formal procedures for influence, the act stipulates that in companies with five or more employees a main safety delegate shall be appointed from among the employees. This delegate has the right to information and participation in planning. This delegate also has the right to stop work if there is a risk of serious injury. Of particular importance in the case of technical changes is the provision in the act that the unions shall participate and provide views on the work environment even in the introductory stages of planning and designing premises, plant, working methods, and work processes. At workplaces with more than fifty employees, a safety and health committee shall be set up. Union representatives, including a safety delegate, shall serve on this committee. The safety and health committee deals with all questions relating to safety and the working environment. The act does not, however, lay down in more detail the formal procedures for the union's participation in planning.

By the terms of, for example, the work environment agreement covering the bulk of the private sector, the union representatives on the safety and health committee shall together outnumber the company's representatives. If the union representatives agree, they will always have a simple majority for their proposals. This does not mean that a majority decision by the safety and health committee is binding on the company. Decisions concerning measures involving economic undertakings by the company are binding on the company only if there is agreement within the committee, the agreement states. In practice, this means that if the union's proposals cost money, the company management has a right of veto. In delimited questions, however, for which the parties have agreed that the committee should have its own budget, decisions are made by the committee on the majority principle.

By the terms of the agreement, it is part of the committee's task to establish the objectives of the company's activities in regard to the working environment an to draw up guidelines with a view to incorporating these objectives in the day-to-day work.

The act's radical provision that working conditions should be adapted to human beings and the agreement's assignment to the safety and health committee the task of establishing objectives and guidelines for the company's working environment activity can hardly be said to have led to any union effort to specify the demands and test out in practice how far the article on objectives will bear weight.

The Working Environment Act covers, as we have seen, not only the physical work environment in a narrow sense, but also the work organization and other issues covered by the Co-Determination Act. This means that the unions will have to coordinate their use of different laws when handling concrete issues. One aspect is the formal procedures: The Co-Determination Act emphasizes negotiations and the roles of the two parties at the workplace, while the Working Environment Act emphasizes the "technical aspects" and cooperation on the safety and health committee. In addition to the intentions of the law, and the new institutions created, an intensive training program has been established and financed to a sum of (U.S.) $10 million a year by the Work Environment Fund.

The Equality Act and Equality Agreements

The Equality Act forbids the employer to discriminate against an employee or job applicant on the grounds of his or her sex. It further requires the employer to work actively to improve equality in the workplace. A special equality ombudsman or -woman ensures compliance with the act. The act opens an opportunity for the establishment, in collective agreements, of supplementary or alternative rules for the active work of achieving equality. It is the union organizations that monitor compliance with such agreements.

In the agreement covering most of the private sector (between SAF and LO–PTK), reference is made to Section 2.1 of the Development Agreement, which states that, "The organization of the work, and the jobs of individual employees shall be designed so that the employees are given as engaging and stimulating a job situation as possible. Equal opportunity for men and women is also an important objective." The Equality Agreement indicates as objectives for the planned work of achieving equality "that workplaces, working methods, work organizations, and working conditions in general shall be so organized that they are suitable for both women and men" (Section 1). "This can be achieved, among other things, by . . . technical aids being made available when required to make the work easier" (Section 5). LO (1983c) comments: "It is often said that certain working duties are too heavy for women to perform, but in such cases, these working duties are also too heavy for men. Ultimately, it can be a question of a pure work environment issue, on which action must be taken." Apart from the design of workplaces, Section 1 stresses that working hours shall be such that both men and women can combine gainful employment with parental responsibility.

The Protection of Employment Act

The 1974 Protection of Employment Act (LAS) (amended 1982) put an end to the employers' "right to fire at will." Only dismissals for "just cause" are permitted, and the requirements are often difficult to meet. (This section is based mainly on Fahlbeck 1980; and on the 1982 Act; see Henning 1984;127ff.) The act is fairly exhaustive; and not just a general framework, like the Co-Determination Act. There are two major causes for dismissal, namely shortage of work and misconduct on the part of the employee (the latter will not be treated here). "Shortage of work" covers not only a real lack of work at the workplace; considerations of size, technology, and efficiency with regard to the proper running of the company also constitute "just cause" (Fahlbeck 1980;43).

The act defines the persons affected in such a way as to include the employees of a specific category (by area of agreeement or by qualifications) in all departments of the workplace. A second idea is that the burden of redundancy should be borne by those employees likely to suffer least from it, which by the terms of the act means "last in, first out," that is, according to a principle of seniority. This act is very important from the point of view of the individuals, and it puts severe restraints upon the employer.

The act has been criticized in public debate: It may, it is claimed, have become more difficult than before for those who do not have a job to obtain one. This is true particularly of young people. It has also been criticized by employers: A sharper demand for just cause for dismissals, in combination with the demand for employment "until further notice," is said to have a detrimental effect on the possibilities of recruiting labor. The ban against employment on a trial basis has come in for particular criticism. The 1982 Act permits trial employment for a period of at most six months; it also permits employment by reason of a temporary extra workload for at most six months over a two-year period.

Two expected effects, the difficulties with recruitment and the favoring of elderly labor by the seniority rule, have been illustrated in a study of twenty-five companies (Hellberg and Vrethem 1982). This study provides no confirmation that the act hinders recruitment. The act's priority rule of "last in, first out" is applied when a shutdown is already a fact. At earlier stages, when the survival of the company is under severe threat, local agreements are usually reached concerning the order of layoffs, by which the most "efficient" and usable employees are retained: The union does try to promote the survival of the company. "When the rule governing the order of layoffs is put out of play, the union organizations have been able to negotiate better terms, for example, better pension offers and extra severance pay for those redundant, compared with what was possible before the Act came into force" (Hellberg and Vrethem 1982, 67).

In the case of major rationalization projects, the rule concerning order often hinders outright dismissals; the solutions adopted instead are usually a freeze on recruitment, training, reassignment, and early retirement. The Act provides an uncertain protection for the individual against dismissal by reason of a lack of work. But in major rationalization processes, when there is no immediate threat of a shutdown, the act appears to provide good protection, at least in major companies where there are opportunities for reassignment.

Strong criticism has been voiced by the trade unions, especially against Section 39, which says that an employer can pay an indemnity instead of reemploying someone who has been dismissed without "just cause" (as decided by the Labor Court). This indemnity is between six and forty-eight months' pay to a dismissed person. All verdicts of the Labor Court that have invalidated dismissals between January 1984 and June 1987 have been investigated by the labor law journal *Lag & Avtal* (Snis and Sigtryggsson 1988). Forty-four of sixty-four persons got their jobs back, but almost one-third were "bought out" by the employer. Thirty-one persons had been dismissed due to lack of work in the company, and they all got their jobs back. Among those who had been dismissed for what the employers called "personal reasons," thirteen got their jobs back, but in June 1987, only four of them were still in their old workplace. Twenty of them were bought out by the employer. According to LO, it is usually persons who are active trade unionists and regarded as troublemakers that management tries to get rid of in this way (*LO-tidningen* 1987b).

References

Abrahamsson, Bengt. 1977. *Bureaucracy or Participation?* Sage, Beverly Hills, Calif.

———. 1980. "Sweden: Industrial Democracy in the 1970s." Report to the Commission of the European Communities. Arbetslivscentrum. Stockholm. Mimeo.

Administration. 1988. "Editorial," no. 1–2.

af Geijerstam, Elmire, and Göran Reitberger. 1986. *Nya företag! Nytt fack?* Arbetslivscentrum, Stockholm.

Agreement on Efficiency and Participation. 1982. Development Agreement (Utvecklingsavtal). SAF/LO/PTK, Stockholm.

Agurén, Stefan, et al. 1984. *Volvo Kalmar Revisited: Ten Years of Experience.* Development Council, SAF/LO/PTK, Stockholm.

Agurén, Stefan, and Jan Edgren. 1980. *New Factories: Job Design through Factory Planning in Sweden.* SAF, Stockholm.

Ahrne, Göran. 1981. *Vardagsverklighet och struktur.* Korpen, Gothenburg.

Alvesson, Mats. 1987. "Kultur och symbolism i organisationer." In *Ledning för alla? Om perspektivbrytningar i företagsledning*, edited by Åke Sandberg. Arbetslivscentrum, Stockholm.

Arbetsmarknadsdepartementat. 1977a. *Fackliga förtroendemän, möten på betald arbetstid och arbetslivsforskning.* DsA, no. 4. Stockholm.

———. 1977b. *Förhållandet mellan medbestämmandelagen och viss annan lagstiftning*, no. 20. Department of Labor, Stockholm.

———. 1984. *Computers and Changes in Working Life.* Department of Labor, Stockholm.

Arbetsmiljö. 1987. "Volvos nya fabrik i Uddevalla," no. 15.

Arbetsmiljöfonden. 1987a. *Rewarding Work.* Stockholm.

———. 1987b. *New Technology, Working Life and Management in Sweden.* Stockholm.

———. 1988a. *En ny arbetsvärld.* Stockholm. (Tra. as *A New World of Work*).

———. 1988b. *Nytt arbetsinnehåll ger bra resultat.* Stockholm

Armstrong, Peter. 1986. "Labour and Monopoly Capital: The Degradation of

Debate." Paper presented at a conference on Trade Unions, New Technology, and Industrial Democracy, Warwick, England, June.

Avotie, Leena. 1987. "Kvinnoperspektiv på ledare." In *Ledning för alla? Om perspektivbrytningar i företagsledning*, edited by Åke Sandberg. Arbetslivscentrum, Stockholm.

Bamber, Greg. 1986. "Technological Change and Unions." Paper presented at a conference on Trade Unions, New Technology, and Industrial Democracy, Warwick, England, June.

Bartholdy, Merete, et al. 1987. *Datorstödd bildbehandling på Aftonbladet*. Arbetslivscentrum, Stockholm.

Batstone, Eric, and Stephen Gourlay, with Hugo Levie and Roy Moore. 1986. *Unions, Unemployment and Innovation*. Basil Blackwell, Oxford.

Batstone, Eric, Stephen Gourlay, Hugo Levie, and Roy Moore. 1987. *New Technology and the Process of Labour Regulation*. Clarendon Press, Oxford.

Bengtson, Gunilla, and Åke Sandberg. 1987. "Om kvalitetscirklar." In *Ledning för alla? Om perspektivbrytningar i företagsledning*, edited by Åke Sandberg. Arbetslivscentrum, Stockholm.

Berggren, Christian. 1982. "Viktigt med starkt fack när arbetet organiseras om i grupper." *LO-tidningen*, no. 44.

———. 1985. "Ju mer inflytande, desto bättre beslut." *Dagens Nyheter*, 4 August.

———. 1986. *Fack, företagsledning och besluten om företagens framtid*. Arkiv förlag, Lund.

Berggren, Christian, and Paavo Bergman. 1984. "Farväl till vadå i Södertälje?" *Arbetsmiljö*, no. 9.

Berggren, Christian, and Anna Holmgren. 1985. "Volvo Kalmarverken och monteringsarbetets utveckling." *Arbete, människa, miljö*, no. 3.

Berggren, Christian, and Sven-Åke Kjellström. 1981. *Verkstadsrationalisering och arbetsorganisation*. Liber Läromedel, Stockholm.

Bergman, Åke. 1986. *Den nya given*. Tiden, Stockholm.

Bergström, P. O. 1990. "Team Concept vs. Swedish Group Work." Metallarbetareförbundet, Stockholm. Mimeo.

Berta, Giuseppe, ed. 1986. *Industrial Relations in Information Society*, Olivetti Foundation, Rome.

Björkman, Torsten. 1986. *I vems stjänst?* TCO-S. Stockholm.

Björkman, Torsten, and Karin Lundqvist. 1981. *Från Max till Pia. Reformstratgier inom arbetsmiljöområdet*. Arkiv, Malmö.

Bjökman, Torsten, and Åke Sandberg. 1988. "Lönearbetets villkor." In *Sverige—vardag och struktur*, edited by Ulf Himmelstrand and Göran Svensson. Norstedts, Stockholm.

Blauner, Robert. 1964. *Alienation and Freedom*. University of Chicago Press, Chicago.

Bödker, Susanne et al. 1987. "A Utopian Experience." In *Computers and Democracy*, edited by G. Bjerknes et al. Gower, London.

Boivie, Per-Erik, and Olov Östberg. 1982. "Program of Data Policy for the Central Organization of Salaried Employees in Sweden (TCO)." TCO, Stockholm. Mimeo.

Bostrom, Robert P., and J. Stephen Heinen. 1977. "MIS Problems and Failures: A Socio-technical Perspective. Part II: The Application of Sociotechnical Theory." *MIS Quarterly* (December).

Braverman, Harry. 1974. *Labor and Monopoly Capital*. Monthly Review Press, New York.

Brevskolan. 1980. *The Study Circle: A Brief Introduction.* Brevskolan, Os-karshamn.
Broady, Donald, and Bo Helgeson. 1985. "Farväl till arbetsdelningen?" In *Professionaliseringsfällan,* edited by Donald Broady. Carlssons, Stockholm.
Broms, Gunnar. 1988. "Better Working Conditions—For the Benefit of Workers As Well As Management." Paper prepared for the International Conference on Ergonomics, Occupational Safety and Health, and the Environment. Peking, October.
Broms, Gunnar, and Karin Gehlin. 1985. *The Machine Tool Factory in Ursviken.* Arbetslivscentrum/Brevskolan, Stockholm.
Broström, Anders. 1982. *MBLs gränser. Den privata äganderätten.* Arbetslivscentrum, Stockholm.
———. ed. 1983. *Arbetsrättens utveckling,* Arbetslivscentrum, Stockholm.
Brulin, Göran. 1987. "Motsägelsefull ledning och styrning." In *Ledning för alla? Om perspektivbrytningar i företagsledning,* edited by Åke Sandberg. Arbetslivscentrum, Stockholm.
Brulin, Göran, and Åke Sandberg. 1987. "Sociology of Organization in Sweden." In *The Multiparadigmatic Trend in Sociology,* edited by Ulf Himmelstrand. Acta Universitatis Upsaliensis, Uppsala.
Carlsson, Jan, et al. 1978. "Planning and Control from the Perspective of Labour." *Accounting, Organizations and Society,* 3, no. 3–4.
Carlzon, Jan. 1987. *Moments of Truth.* Ballinger, Cambridge, Mass.
Cockburn, Cynthia. 1983. *Brothers: Male Dominance and Technological Change.* Pluto, London.
Co-Determination Agreement for the State Sector. 1978. TCO–S. Stockholm.
Cole, Robert. 1987. "The Macropolitics of Organizational Change: A Comparative Analysis of the Spread of Small-group Activities." In *Worker Participation and the Politics of Reform,* edited by Carmen Sirianni, Temple University Press, Philadelphia.
Cooley, Mike. 1981. *Architect or Bee?* Langley Technical Services, Slough, Berks, U.K.
———. 1986. "Socially Useful Design: A Form of Anticipatory Democracy." *Economic and Industrial Democracy* 7, no. 4.
Cressey, Peter. 1985. *The Role of the Parties Concerned in the Introduction of New Technology. Consolidated Report.* European Foundation, Dublin.
Dagens Nyheter. Stockholm daily newspaper.
Dahlström, Edmund. 1978. "The Role of Social Science in Working Life Policy." In *Sociology of Work in the Nordic Countries.* Scandinavian Sociological Association, Oslo.
———. 1980. *Samhällsvetenskap och praktik.* Publica/Liber, Stockholm.
———. 1982. "Handlingsorienterad forskning på olika nivåer." *Sociologisk Forskning* 19, no. 2–3.
Deal, Terence, and Allen Kennedy. 1982. *Corporate Cultures.* Addison-Wesley, Reading, Mass.
Della Rocca, Giuseppe. 1986. "Improving Participation: The Negotiation of New Technology in Italy and Europe. A Cross National Analysis." Paper presented at a conference on Trade Unions, New Technology, and Industrial Democracy. Warwick, England, June.
Deutsch, Steven. 1986a. "New Technology, Union Strategies and Worker Participation." *Economic and Industrial Democracy* 7, no. 4.
———. 1986b. "International Experiences with Technological Change." *Monthly Labor Review.* 19, no. 3.

322   *References*

Development Agreement. 1982. *Agreement on Efficiency and Participation SAF-LO-PTK.* SAF, Stockholm.
Dilschmann, Angelika. 1981. "Arbetstagarkonsult som stöd vid utvecklingen av en alternativ facklig strategi för teknikpåverkan." Sociologiska instituionen/ATO-konsult, Stockholm. Mimeo.
———. 1983. *Konflikten mellan grafiker och journalister. Datateknikens inverkan på gränsen mellan grafiskt och journalistiskt arbete inom tidningsbranschen.* Arbetslivscentrum, Stockholm.
Dilschmann, Angelika, and Pelle Ehn. 1984. *Gränslandet.* Arbetslivscentrum, Stockholm.
Docherty, Peter, and Lars Loman. 1983. *Personalinflytande och datorisering.* EFI/PTK, Stockholm.
Dorewaard, Hans. 1986. "How to Control Reorganization." Department of Sociology, University of Nijmegen, Nijmegen. Mimeo.
Edgren, Jan. 1977. *Kriterier på bra produktionssystem.* SAF, Stockholm.
Edlund, Sten, ed. 1986. *Labour Law Research in 12 Countries.* Arbetslivscentrum/Arbetarskyddsfonden/Almqvist & Wiksell International, Stockholm.
———. 1987. "Parterna bör ge mer stöd åt lokalt utvecklingsarbete." *Arbetslivet i centrum,* no. 60. Arbetslivscentrum, Stockholm.
Edlund, Sten, and Stig Gustafsson. 1976. *Medbestämmanderätten.* Tiden, Borås.
Ehn, Pelle. 1983. *Utopia-projektet—lägesrapport och arbetsplan.* Arbetslivscentrum, Stockholm.
———. 1988. *Work-Oriented Design of Computer Artifacts.* Arbetslivscentrum, Stockholm.
Ehn, Pelle, and Morten Kyng. 1987. "The Collective Resources Approach." In *Computers and Democracy: A Scandinavian Challenge,* edited by Gro Bjerknes et al. Gower, Aldershot, U.K.
Ehn, Pelle, Maja-Lisa Perby, and Åke Sandberg. 1983. *Brytningstid. Teknik, arbete och facklig kamp i grafiska branschen.* Rapport från samarbbetet mellan Svenska Dagbladets Kamratklubb och Demos-projektet. Arbetslivscentrum, Stockholm.
Ehn, Pelle, and Åke Sandberg. 1983. "Local Union Influence on Technology and Work Organization." *System Design For, With and By the Users.* North Holland/IFIP, Amsterdam.
Ehn, Pelle, and Dan Sjögren. 1986. "Typographers and Carpenters as Designers—Lessons from Two Projects Designing Skill Based Technology." In *Skill Based Automated Manufacturing,* edited by P. Brödner. Pergamon, Oxford.
Ekdahl, Lars. 1983. *Arbete mot kapital.* Arikiv, Lund.
Elden, Max. 1979. "Three Generations of Work Democracy in Norway." In *The Quality of Working Life in Eastern and Western Europe,* edited by Cary L. Cooper and Enid Mumford. Ass Business Press, London.
Ellegård, Kajsa. 1989. *Metalls medverkan i projekteringen av Volvos Uddevallafabrik.* Metallarbetarförbundet/Handelshoögskolan i Göteborg, Stockholm.
Ellegård, Kajsa, Tomas Engström, and Lennart Nilsson. 1989. *Principer och realiteter. Projekteringen av Volvos bilfabrik i Uddevalla.* Arbetsmiljöfonden, Stockholm.
Emery, Fred, and Einar Thorsrud. 1976. *Democracy at Work.* Nijhoff, Leiden.
Emery, Fred, and Eric Trist. 1973. *Towards a Social Ecology.* Plenum Press, New York.
Enqvist, Jan. 1983. "Arbetet vid Saab-Scanias nya bensinmotorlinje. Mindre förslitande men tråkigare." *Arbetsmiljö,* no. 15:11–15.

Eriksson, Arne H. 1986. *Service Kultur Förändring: Ny organisationslära i facklig belysning.* TCO, Stockholm.

Fahlbeck, Reinhold. 1980. *Labour Law in Sweden.* Juridiska Föreningen i Lund, Studentlitteratur, Lund.

Försäkringsanställdas Förbund (FF). 1981. *Electronic Data Processing in the Social Insurance Offices.* Programme of action. FF, Stockholm.

Forsberg, Gunnel, et al. 1981. *Näringspolitik. Livsmedelsindustrin i fackligt perspektiv.* Arbetslivscentrum, Stockholm.

Frejhagen, Birgitta. 1987. "Nya tekniken river stängsel." LO-tidningen, no. 49.

Fricke, Werner. 1986. "New Technologies and German Co-Determination." *Economic and Industrial Democracy* 7, no. 4. (November).

Fricke, Werner, and Wilgart Schuchardt, eds. 1984. *Beteilgung als Element gewerkschaftlicher Arbeitspolitik.* Verlag Neue Gesellschaft, Bonn.

Friedman, Andrew L. 1977. *Industry and Labour.* Macmillan, London.

Gardell, Bertil. 1983. "Worker Participation and Autonomy: A Multi-Level Approach to Democracy at the Work Place." *International Yearbook of Organizational Democracy,* vol. 1. John Wiley, London.

————. 1986. *Arbetets organisation och människans natur.* Arbetsmiljöfonden, Stockholm.

Giertz, Eric. 1986. *Det framtida verkstadsarbetet.* Arbetarskyddsfonden, Stockholm.

Gill, Colin. 1985. *Work, Unemployment and the New Technology.* Polity Press, Oxford.

Goldmann, Robert B. 1976. *A Work Experiment. Six Americans in a Swedish Plant.* Ford Foundation, New York.

Göransson, Bengt, ed. 1978. *Produktionslivets förnyelse.* Arbetarskyddsfonden, Stockholm.

Göransson, Ingemar. 1987. "Montörer blir yrkesarbetare." *Metallarbetaren.* no. 47.

Göranzon, Bo, et al. 1982. *Job Design and Automation in Sweden.* Arbetslivscentrum, Stockholm.

Graffiti. Newsletter of the Utopia Project. 1981–1985. Arbetslivscentrum, Stockholm. (No. 7, 1985, is a summary report, also available in an English edition.)

Grafiska Fackförbundets Kongress. 1982. *Förslag till fackligt handlingsprogram.* Stockholm.

Greenbaum, Joan M. 1979. *In the Name of Efficiency.* Temple University Press, Philadelphia.

Grenninger, Carl Magnus. 1983. *Vetorätt och självbestämmande.* TCO, Stockholm.

Grip, Arne, and Lars Sundström. 1985. *The Postgiro.* Arbetslivscentrum/Brevskolan, Stockholm.

Gunnarsson, Ewa, and Evy Lodin. 1984. *Perforatörernas arbetssituation.* Arbetslivscentrum, Stockholm.

Gustavsen, Bjørn. 1976. "Design of Jobs and Work Organizations in a Changing Political Context." Paper presented at the conference Participation on the Shop Floor, in Dubrovnik, February. Work Research Institutes, Oslo.

————. 1985. "Workplace Reform and Democratic Dialogue." *Economic and Industrial Democracy* 6.

Hadenius, Axel. 1983. *Medbestämmandereformen.* Almqvist & Wiksell, Stockholm.

Hallerby, Per. 1983. "Medbestämmande-/utvecklingsavtalens betydelse för arbetstagarkonsultrollen." Arbetstagarkonsult, Stockholm. Mimeo.

Hallinder, Hans-Olof, et al. 1985. "SAF T's medverkan vid försök med ny arbetsorganisation." In *Förändringsprogram i arbetslivet*, edited by B. Gustavsen and Å. Sandberg. Arbetslivscentrum, Stockholm.

Hammarström, Olle. 1987. "Swedish Industrial Relations." In *International and Comparative Industrial Relations*, edited by Greg J. Bamber and Russel D. Lansbury. Allen & Unwin, London.

Hammarström, Olle, et al. 1980. *Förhandling eller partssammansatta grupper*. Arbetslivscentrum, Stockholm.

———. 1982. *MBL-förhandlingar i praktiken*, Forskningsrapport no. 35. Arbetslivscentrum, Stockholm.

Hammarström, Rut. 1983. "Trade Union Consultation." Arbetslivscentrum, Stockholm. Mimeo.

Hart, Horst. 1984. *Former för medbestämmande*. Forskningsrapport no. 74, Sociologiska institutionen. Göteborgs universitet, Gothenburg.

Hart, Horst, and Sven-Åke Hörte. 1982. *Medbestämmandets utveckling*. Forskiningsrapport no. 72, Sociologiska institutionen. Göteborgs universitet, Gothenburg.

———. 1989. *Medbestämmandets stagnation. Medbestämmandets utveckling 1978–1985*. Arbetsvetenskapliga kollegiet, Gothenburg.

Haug, Frigga. 1985. "Automatization as a Field of Contradictions." In *Work in the 1980s*, edited by Bengt-Ove Gustavsson et al. Gower, Aldershot, U.K.

Hedberg, Bo. 1978. "Using Computerized Information Systems to Design Better Organizations and Jobs." Working Papers, Swedish Center for Working Life, Stockholm.

Hedberg, Bo, and Enid Mumford. 1975. "The Design of Computer Systems: Man's Vision of Man as an Integral Part of the System Design Process." In *Human Choice and Computers*, edited by Enid Mumford and Harold Sackman. North Holland, Amsterdam.

Hellberg, Inga, and Mats Vrethem. 1982. "Lagen om anställningsskydd och dess effekter." *1970-talets reformer i arbetslivet*. Tiden, Stockholm.

Henning, Ann. 1984. *Tidsbegränsad anställning*. Juridiska Föreningen i Lund, Lund.

Henrikssson, Sten. 1988. *Människor och datorer—mot en ny realism?* MDA-projektet. Arbetsmiljöfondens rapporter, Stockholm.

Herbst, P. G. 1971. "Utviklingen av sosio-teknisk analyse." *Demokratiseringsprocessen i arbeidslivet*, edited by P. G. Herbst. Sosio-tekniske studier. Universitetsforlaget, Oslo.

Himmelstrand, Ulf. 1982. "Innovative Processes in Social Change." In *Sociology: The State of the Art*, edited by T. Bottomore, S. Nowak, and M. Sokolowska. Sage, London & Beverly Hills.

Himmelstrand, Ulf, Göran Ahrne, Lars Lundberg, and Leif Lundberg. 1981. *Beyond Welfare Capitalism*. Heinemann, London.

Hingel, Anders. 1983a. *Ny teknologis sociale funktioner og konsekvenser*. Nyt Nordisk Forlag, Copenhagen.

———. 1983b. "80' ernes faglige teknologipolitik—et oplaeg til en debat." Handelshøjskolen i København, Copenhagen. Mimeo.

Hirschman, Albert O. 1974. *Exit, Voice and Loyalty*. Harvard University Press, Cambridge, Mass.

Hoel, Marit, and Björn Hvinden. 1979. "Investigation Groups in the Trade Union and Informal Workers Solidarity." In *Computers Dividing Man and Work*, edited by Åke Sandberg. Arbetslivscentrum, Stockholm.

Holm, Jesper, et al. 1986. *Fagbevaegelsen og Alternativ Teknolgi*. Teknisk landsforbund, Copenhagen.

Hörte, Sven-Åke. 1980. *Kontakter mellan arbetsgivare och fackliga organisationer på det lokala planet.* Arbetsrapport, Sociologiska institutionen, Göteborgs universitet, Gothenburg.

Howard, Robert. 1985. *Brave New Workplace.* Viking, New York.

Hydén, Håkan. 1984. *Arbetslivets reglering—Mellan vardagsverklighet och samhällsstruktur.* LiberFörlag, Stockholm.

Janérus, Inge. 1983. "Lagstiftningsarbetet på 70-talet." In *Arbetsrättens utveckling,* edited by Å. Broström. Arbetslivscentrum, Stockholm.

Johansson, Anders. 1989. *Tillväxt och klassamarbete. En studie av den svenska modellens uppkomst.* Tiden, Stockholm.

Karlsson, Ulf. 1979. Alternativa produktionssystem till lineproduktion. Ph. D. diss., Sociologiska institutionen, Göteborgs universitet.

Kern, Horst, and Michael Schumann. 1970. *Industriearbeit und Arbeiterbewusstsein I, II.* EVA, Frankfurt am Main.

———. 1984. "Work and Social Character: Old and New Contours." *Economic and Industrial Democracy* 5, no. 1.

———. 1985. *Das Ende der Arbeitsteilung?* C. H. Beck, Munich.

Kjellberg, Anders. 1983. *Facklig organisering i tolv länder.* Arkiv Förlag, Lund.

Kjellén, Bengt. 1980. "Employee Consultants and Information Disclosure." Discussion paper no. 21. TURU, Oxford. Mimeo.

———. 1982. "Provisions and Problems of Disclosure and Use of Company Information: Sweden," Seminar paper. TURU, Oxford. Mimeo.

———. 1983. "Löntagarkonsulten idag—underlag till arbetslivscentrums temadag om löntagarkonsultation." Arbetstagarkonsult, Stockholm. Mimeo.

Kjellqvist, Else-Britt. 1987. "Psykologiska perspektiv på ledaren." In *Ledning för alla? Om perspektivbrytningar i företagsledning,* edited by Åke Sandberg. Arbetslivscentrum, Stockholm.

Korpi, Walter. 1978. *The Working Class in Welfare Capitalism.* Routledge and Kegan Paul, London.

———. 1981. "Sweden: Conflict, Power and Politics in Industrial Relations." In *Industrial Relations in International Perspective,* edited by P. B. Doeringer. Macmillan, London.

Korpi, Walter, and MIchael Shalev. 1979. "Strikes, Industrial Relations and Class Conflict in Capitalist Societies." *British Journal of Sociology* 30, no. 2.

Kronlund, Jan. 1978. Contribution in the section "Produktionsuppläggning och produktionsenheter." In *Produktionslivets förnyelse,* edited by Bengt Göransson. Arbetarskyddsfonden, Stockholm.

Kuttner, Robert. 1984. "Can Labor Lead?" *New Republic,* 12 March.

———. 1985. "Sharing Power at Eastern Air Lines." *Harvard Business Review* (November–December).

Kyng, Morten, and Lars Mathiasen. 1982. "Systems Development and Trade Union Activities." In *Information Society—for Richer, for Poorer,* edited by Niels Bjørn-Andersen et al. North Holland, Amsterdam.

Leffler, Jonas. 1983. *Fackliga informationssystem.* Forskningsrapport, no. 42, BAS, Göteborg/Arbetslivscentrum, Stockholm.

Leion, Anders. 1985. "Sverige." *Västeuropa inför 1990.* SAF, Stockholm.

Levie, Hugo, and Roy Moore. 1984a. *Workers and New Technology; Disclosure and Use of Company Information, Summary Report.* Ruskin College, Oxford.

———. 1984b. *Workers and New Technology; Disclosure and Use of Company Information, Final Report.* Ruskin College, Oxford.

Levie, Hugo, and Åke Sandberg. 1991. "Trade Unions and Workplace Technical Change in Europe." In *Economic and Industrial Democracy*, 12, no. 2.

Levinson, Klas, and Jan Holzhausen. 1987. "Medbestämmande och förhandlingar." Arbetslivscentrum, Stockholm. Mimeo.

Leydesdorff, Loet, and Peter van den Besselaar. 1987. "Squeezed between Capital and Technology: On the Participation of Labour in the Knowledge Society." *Acta Sociologica* 30, no. 3/4.

Lindkvist, Kent. 1981. "Teknik och ideologi." Research Policy Institute, Lund. Mimeo.

Livsmedelsarbetareförbundets Kongress. 1981. *Handlingsprogram näringspolitik*. Stockholm.

Ljunggren, Olof. 1983. "Samverkan för effektivitet, lönsamhet och tillväxt." SAF, Stockholm. Mimeo.

LO. 1970. Letter to SAF, 23 February, demanding negotiations.

———. 1971. *Demokrati i företagen*, Stockholm.

———. 1971. *Arbetsorganisation*. Stockholm.

———. 1977. *Co-Determination on the Foundation of Solidarity*. Stockholm.

———. 1981. *Fackföreningsrörelsen och forskningen*. Tiden, Stockholm.

———. 1983a. "Tekniken som en hävstång för att nå fackliga mål? LOs krav på datateknisk forskning vid STU." Stockholm. Mimeo.

———. 1983b. *Handbok för utvecklingsavtalet LO-PTK-SAF*. Stockholm.

———. 1983c. Jämställdhetsavtalet SAF, LO, PTK med kommentarer. Stockholm.

———. 1986d. *Swedish Trade Union Confederation*. Stockholm.

———. 1986. *Utmaningen*. Stockholm.

———. 1990. "Det utvecklande arbetet." Stockholm. Draft. Mimeo.

LO and PTK. 1977. *Förslag till medkestämmandeavtal*. Stockholm.

LO-tidningen. 1986. "Livs vill ha kunniga medlemmar," no. 18/20.

———. 1987a. "Bojkott-seger som stärkte kampandan." Interview with Arne Dahlberg, no. 7.

———. 1987b. "Höj skadestånd kraftigt för brott mot LAS." Interview with Göran Karlsson, no. 41.

———. 1987c. "Ny teknik ger bättre jobb," no. 47.

———. 1990. "Vi är fruktansvärt beroende av varandra," no. 12.

LO:s Dataråd. 1981. *Facklig datapolitk*. Stockholm.

Luria, Daniel D. 1986. "New Labor-Management Models from Detroit?" *Business Review* 64, no. 5.

Luria, Daniel, D. Undated. "Toward Constructive Deal-Making in the U.S. Auto Industry?" Mimeo.

Lysgaard, Sverre. 1961. *Arbeiderkollektivet*. Universitetsförlaget, Oslo.

Mansell, Jacquie. 1986. "Workplace Innovation in Canada." Economic Council of Canada, Ottawa. Mimeo.

Martin, Andrew. 1987. "Unions, the Quality of Work and Technological Change in Sweden." In *Worker Participation and the Politics of Reform*, edited by Carmen Sirianni. Temple University Press, Philadelphia.

Medbestämmandeavtal för det statliga arbetstagarområdet (MBA–S). 1978. Statens avtalsverk, cirkulär 1, 30 March. Stockholm.

Medbestämmandeavtal KFO–LO/PTK. 7 April 1979. Stockholm.

Medbestämmandeavtal SFO–LO/PTK. 3 March 1979. Stockholm.

Meidner, Rudolf. 1986. "Labour Market Policy in the Welfare State." In *Towards a Democratic Rationality*, edited by John Fry. Gower, Aldershot, U.K.

Metallarbetareföbundet. 1981. *Metallarbetsplats i förändring*. Stockholm.

References   327

————. 1984. "Utvecklingsavtalet." Cirkulär no. 54, March. Stockholm. Mimeo.

————. 1985. *Det goda arbetet*. Stockholm.

————. 1989. *Solidarisk arbetspolitik*. Stockholm.

Metallarbetaren. 1986a. Articles and interviews concerning "Arbetsgivarnas nya grepp," no. 18.

————. 1986b. "Nu knakar facket i fogarna," Interview with Rudolf Meidner by Tommy Öberg, no. 46

————. 1987a. Articles on convertibles, nos. 42 and 43.

————. 1987b. "Slaget om Uddevalla," no. 47.

Mohlin, Roger. 1982. "Att göra områden till frågor." In *Det lokala fackets arbete*, edited by M. Sterner. Tiden, Falun.

Mumford, Enid. 1983. *Designing Human Systems*. Manchester Business School, Manchester, U.K.

————. 1987. "Sociotechnical Systems Design. Evolving Theory and Practice." In *Computers and Democracy. A Scandinavian Challenge*, edited by G. Berknes et al. Gower, Aldershot, U.K.

Nilsson, Tommy, and Jan Gehlin. 1986. *Tjänstemän, facket och yrkesrollen*. Arbetslivscentrum, Stockholm.

Nilsson, Tommy, and Åke Sandberg. 1988. *Teknisk förändring och facklig organisering*. Arkiv Förlag, Lund.

Noble, David. 1978. "Social choice in machine design." *Politics and Society* 8, no. 3/4.

Nygaard, Kristen. 1979. "The Iron and Metal Project." In *Computers Dividing Man and Work*, edited by Åke Sandberg. Arbetslivscentrum, Stockholm.

Nygaard, Kristen, and Olav Terje Bergo. 1974. *Planlegging, styring og databehandling*. Tiden, Oslo.

Ny teknik. 1984. Interview with P G. Gyllenhammar, no. 7.

Ødegaard, Lars A. 1981. *Tilbake til det typografiske fag*. API Publikasjon, Arbeidpsykologisk Institutt/Arbeidsforskningsinstituttene, Oslo.

Odhnoff, Jan, and Casten von Otter. 1987. "Att forma framtiden." *Arbetets rationaliteter*. Arbetslivscentrum, Stockholm.

OECD. 1990. *Employment Outlook*. Paris.

PAQ. 1983. *Zerreissproben. Automation im Arbeiterleben*. Argument Verlag, West Berlin.

————. 1987. *Widersprüche der Automationsarbeit*. Argument Verlag, West Berlin.

Peters, Thomas J., and Robert H. Waterman, Jr. 1982. *In Search of Excellence*. Harper & Row, New York.

Pettersson, Leif. 1987. "Ta steget bort från skoputsarsamhället." *LO-tidningen*, no. 49.

Piore, Michael, and Charles Sabel. 1984. *The Second Industrial Divide*. Basic Books, New York.

Postgirot. 1979. "Förhandling om lokalt kollektivavtal avseende inriktningen av Postgirots produktionssystem, 1979-11-12." Stockholm. Unpublished minutes.

PTK. 1984. *Handbok, Fackligt arbete med lokalt utvecklings—och medbestämmandeavtal*. PTK, Borås.

Ramström, Dick. 1986. *Det moderna företaget*. TCO, Stockholm.

Rankin, Tom. 1990. *New Forms of Work Organization—The Challenge for North American Unions*. University of Toronto Press, Toronto.

Rankin, Tom, and Jacquie Mansell. 1986. "Integrating Collective Bargaining and New Forms of Work Organization," *National Productivity Review* (Autumn).

Rhenman, Eric, and Per-Hugo Skärvad. 1977. "Svåra beslut, makt och medbestämmande." *Besluten i företagen.* Rapport till Svenska Arbetsgivareföreningens Kongress 1977. Stockholm.

Rosenbrock, Howard H. 1982. "Social and Engineering Design of an FMS." Paper presented at the conference CAPE 1983. UMIST, Manchester, U.K.

Rydenfelt, Sven. 1986. "Det svenska fackets ödesväg." *SAF-tidningen,* no. 34.

SAF. 1971. *Om samarbetet i företagen.* Stockholm.

———. 1974. *Nya arbetsformer.* Stockholm.

———. 1976. *Förslag till medbestämmandeavtal.* Stockholm.

———. 1977. *Den individuella arbetsplatsen och arbetsrollen.* Nya fabrikerprojektet, Stockholm.

SAF-tidingen. 1988. "Hos Volvo Uddevalla går det *inte* som på löpande band," no. 5.

Samko/TCO. 1984. *Som vi ser det.* Stockholm.

Samordnad datapolitik. 1981. Rapport från Datadelegationen, DsB 1981: No. 20. Stockholm.

———. 1982. Regeringens proposition 1981/82:No. 123. Stockholm.

Sandberg, Åke. 1976. *The Limits to Democratic Planning: Knowledge, Power and Methods in the Struggle for the Future.* LiberFörlag, Stockholm.

———, ed. 1979. *Computers Dividing Man and Work.* Arbetslivscentrum, Stockholm.

———. 1980. *Varken offer eller herre.* LiberFörlag, Stockholm.

———, ed. 1981. *Forskning för förändring.* Arbetslivscentrum, Stockholm.

———. 1982. "From Satisfaction to Democratization." Arbetslivscentrum, Stockholm. Mimeo.

———. 1983. "Trade Union-Oriented Research for Democratization of Planning in Work Life." *Journal of Occupational Behaviour* 4:59–71.

———, ed. 1984. *Framtidsfrågor på arbetsplatsen.* Arbetslivscentrum, Stockholm.

———. 1985. "Socio-Technical Design, Trade Union Strategies and Action Research." In *Research Methods in Information Systems,* edited by E. Mumford et al. North Holland, Amsterdam.

———, ed. 1987. *Ledning för alla? Om perspektivbrytningar i företagsledning.* Arbetslivscentrum, Stockholm.

Sandberg, Thomas. 1982. *Work Organization and Autonomous Groups.* LiberFörlag, Stockholm.

Schiller, Bernt. 1983. "Tiden fram till 1970." In *Arbetsrättens utveckling,* edited by A. Broström. Arbetslivscentrum, Stockholm.

Schmid, Herman. 1973. "On the Conditions of Applied Social Science." *Social Science Information* 12, no. 5.

Schmidt, Folke. 1979. *Facklig arbetsrätt.* Norstedts, Stockholm.

SIF-tidningen. 1987a. "Modell Japan," no. 18.

———. 1987b. "När fotfolket handlade för tusenlappar bollade ledningen med miljarder," no. 8.

Simonsen, Tommy. 1986. "Lärttare att stå ut med jobbet." *Arbetsmiljö,* no. 8.

Sirianni, Carmen. 1987. "Worker Participation in the Late 20th Century: Some Critical Issues." In his *Worker Participation and the Politics of Reform.* Temple University Press, Philadelphia.

Skärvad, Per-Hugo, and Ulf Lundahl. 1979. "Facket, företagsledningen och de svåra besluten." In *Från företagskriser till industripolitik,* edited by Bo Hedberg and Sven-Erik Sjöstrand. Liber Läromedel, Stockholm.

Sköldebrand, Barbro. 1989. *Anställd och ägare—konvertibler.* Arbetslivscentrum, Stockholm.

Snis, Anita, and Jón Sigtryggsson. 1988. "Var tredje blev utköpt efter segern i AD." *Lag & Avtal*, no. 1.

Sociologisk Forskning. 1982. Special issue "Aktionsforskning," nos. 2–3. Contributions by Herman Schmid, Bjørn Gustavsen, Edmund Dahlström, Ulf Himmelstrand, Harald Swedner, Ingalill Eriksson, and Sverre Lysgaard.

Södergren, Birgitta. 1987. *När pyramiderna rivits.* Timbro, Stockholm.

Söderholm, Gunnar. 1987. "Rätten att anlita arbetstagarkonsult." In *Metallinfo*. Metallarbetareförbundet, Stockholm.

SOU. 1979. (Statens offentliga utredningar). *Rationellare girohantering*, no. 35. Stockholm.

———. 1982. *MBL i utveckling.* Betänkande av nya arbetsrättskommittén, no. 60. Stockholm.

Stange, Jan. 1983. *Franchising—omfattning och utvecklingstendenser.* Arbetslivscentrum, Stockholm.

Statstjänstemannaförbundet. 1982a. *Action Programme on Computer Policy for the Union of Civil Servants in Sweden.* Stockholm.

———. 1982b. *Some Examples of Local Collective Agreements on the Introduction and Use of Computer Technology in Sweden.* Stockholm.

Steen, Jesper, and Peter Ullmark. 1982. *En egen väg—att göra fackliga handlingsprogram.* Arkitektursektionen, Tekniska Högskolan, Stockholm.

———. 1985a. *The Dairy in Malmö.* Arbetslivscentrum/Brevskolan, Stockholm.

———. 1985b. *The Sugar Refinery in Örtofta.* Arbetslivscentrum/Brevskolan, Stockholm.

Streek, Wolfgang. 1987. "Industrial Relations and Industrial Change," *Economic and Industrial Democracy* 6, no. 4.

Sundblad, Yngve. 1983. "The Utopia Project." Paper presented at HdA (Humanisierung der Arbeit) and ASF (Arbetarskyddsfonden) conference Technischen Wandel und Arbeitsstrukturierung in der Industrie. Stuttgart, 10–11 October.

Sundström, Lars. 1983. "Arbetstagarkonsult som partsgemensam konsult— är det önskvärt/möjligt?" Arbetstagarkonsult AB, Stockholm. Mimeo.

Swedish Institute. 1983. *Labour Relations in Sweden.* Fact Sheet on Sweden, Stockholm.

Széll, György. 1988. "Participation, Workers' Control and Self-Management," *Current Sociology* 36, no. 3.

TCO. 1975. *Villkor i arbetet.* Stockholm.

———. 1983a. *Förstärk medbestämmanderätten.* Stockholm.

———. 1983b. *Utveckla datatekniken! Rapport från en förstudie till STU.* Stockholm.

———. 1988. *TCO—The Swedish Confederation of Professional Employees.* Stockholm.

Therborn, Göran. 1976. "Vad gör den härskande klassen när den härskar?" *Häften för kritiska studier*, 6, no. 4.

———. 1980. *What Does the Ruling Class Do When It Rules?* Verso, London.

———. 1987. "Den svenska välfärdsstatens särart och framtid." *Lycksalighetens halvö.* FRN-Framtidsstudier, Stockholm.

Thorsrud, Einar, and Fred Emery. 1969. *Medinflytande och engagemang i arbetet.* Utvecklingsrådet, Stockholm.

Ullmark, Peter, Jesper Steen, and Anna Holmgren. 1986. *Det matnyttiga arbetet.* Tiden, Stockholm.

Unterweger, Peter. 1987. "A Union View of Job Classifications." UAW presentation at the University of Notre Dame Annual Union–Management Conference, 12 June.

Utopia Project. 1982. *On Training, Technology and Products Viewed from the Quality of Work Perspective*. Arbetslivscentrum, Stockholm.

———. 1985. "An Alternative in Text and Images," *Graffiti* no. 7. Arbetslivscentrum, Stockholm. (Summary report in English.)

Utopia-projektet. 1983. *Kravspecifikation: Datorstödd bildbehandling och ombrytning*. Arbetslivscentrum, Stockholm.

Victorin, Anders. 1982. "Medbestämmande i framtiden," *Facklig företagsledning?* SAF, Stockholm.

von Otter, Casten. 1980. "Löntagarstyre inom den offentliga sektorn?" *Tre år med MBL*. Arbetslivscentrum, LiberFörlag/Publica, Helsingborg.

———. 1983a. "Facket och det post-industriella företaget." *Vägval: Uppsatser om några demokratiproblem*. Brevskolan, Stockholm.

———. 1983b. *Worker Participation in the Public Sector*. Arbetslivscentrum/Almqvist & Wiksell International, Stockholm.

Wessman, Jan, and Andreas de Klerk. 1987. "Psykologiska aspekter på grupprocesser." In *Ledning för alla? Om perspektivbrytningar i företagsledning*, edited by Åke Sandberg. Arbetslivscentrum, Stockholm.

Williams, Robin. 1987. "Democratizing Systems Development." In *Computers and Democracy*, edited by G. Bjerknes et al. Gower, Aldershot, U.K.

Wisén, Leif. 1983. "Demokratisk arbetsorganisation och ny teknik—en facklig ansats." Statstjänstemannaförbundet, Stockholm. Mimeo.

Wood, Stephen. 1986. "The Cooperative Labour Strategy in the U.S. Auto Industry." *Economic and Industrial Democracy* 7, no. 4 (November).

WSI Informationsdienst zur Humanisierung der Arbeit. 1982. Extra no. 3 (August). "IG Metall, Entwurf eines Lohnrahmentarifvertrages für Südwürtemberg/Hohenzollern and Südbaden." DGB, Bonn.

Yankelovich, Daniel, et al. 1983. *Work and Human Values: An International Report on Jobs in the 1980s and 1990s*. Aspen Institute for Humanistic Studies, New York.

Zetterberg, Hans, et al. 1983. *Det osynliga kontraktet*. Sifo, Stockholm.

Index

About the Authors

Åke Sandberg is research director at the Swedish Center for Working Life (*Arbetslivscentrum*) and professor in the Department of Industrial Economics and Management at the Royal Institute of Technology, Stockholm.

Gunnar Broms is project manager and member of the board of IFA (Institute for the Development of Production and Workplaces) and Master of Science, the Royal Institute of Technology.

Arne Grip is senior lecturer in Industrial Organization at the University of Linköping and coauthor (with Lars Sundström) of *The Postgiro* (1984).

Lars Sundström is a trade union consultant and coauthor (with Arne Grip) of *The Postgiro* (1984).

Jesper Steen and **Peter Ullmark** are both architects and associate professors of architecture at the Royal Institute of Technology. They have written books and articles on union participation in work environment planning and industrial architecture.